MODERN ECONOMICS

AN INTRODUCTION FOR BUSINESS AND PROFESSIONAL STUDENTS

MODERN ECONOMICS

*An Introduction for Business and
Professional Students*

J. HARVEY, B.SC.(ECON.)

Lecturer in Economics, University of Reading

SECOND EDITION

M

First edition 1969
Reprinted 1970 (twice), 1971 (twice), 1972, 1973 (twice), 1974
Second edition 1974
Reprinted 1975, 1976

Published by
THE MACMILLAN PRESS LTD
London and Basingstoke
Associated companies in New York Dublin
Melbourne Johannesburg and Madras

SBN 333 16778 3 (hard cover)
333 16779 1 (paper cover)

Made and printed in Great Britain by
R J ACFORD LTD
Industrial Estate, Chichester, Sussex

CONTENTS

I. INTRODUCTION

II. WHAT TO PRODUCE

IV. FOR WHOM? HOW THE FACTORS OF PRODUCTION ARE REWARDED— THE THEORY OF DISTRIBUTION

V. MONEY AND FINANCIAL INSTITUTIONS

VIII. SOME CURRENT ECONOMIC PROBLEMS OF THE UNITED KINGDOM

FIGURES

TABLES

PREFACE TO THE FIRST EDITION

THE primary aim of this textbook is to meet the needs of students taking economics as part of their professional examinations in banking, company-secretaryship, accountancy, insurance, surveying, transport, hospital administration, business studies and commerce. It provides, too, a useful groundwork in economics for G.C.E. 'A' Level and degree and C.N.A.A. courses.

But its starting-point is not economics as an examination subject. The author's experience as an examiner has convinced him that the standard of attainment will improve only if the student's approach is on the right lines. Unfortunately, many students still seem to think that their Examining Board includes economics as a part of the course only out of sheer cussedness. Hence preparation consists mostly of a dull memorisation of facts in the hope that this will scrape the necessary pass.

This book can claim to deal with 'modern economics' in two senses. First, it presents economics as a method of thought, not a mere body of knowledge. It explains simple economic analysis and shows how it can be applied both to the problems of everyday life and to the particular decisions of the professional man. Instead of being merely a dull grind, economics is shown to be as relevant vocationally as other course subjects. In this way it is hoped to change the motivation of the student, for only by such an approach will he gain any value from his study.

Secondly, the book recognises that modern economics is increasingly concerned with the difficulties of maintaining full employment, a stable level of prices, a steady rate of growth, balance of payments equilibrium, etc. It is therefore divided almost equally between a study of the determination of prices in individual markets and of the factors which govern the level of activity as a whole.

In deciding what to include, the author has had two basic considerations—the requirements of the examination syllabus and the level of difficulty with which a student, often studying part-time and without the help of a tutor, can be expected to cope. The first presents few problems, for the syllabuses of the various Examining Boards are fairly similar in their requirements. Thus elementary analysis is supplemented by some description of the economy and its institutions. The second lies far more within the discretion of the author. Here the basis of selection has been 'when in doubt, leave out'. The dominant aim is that the student should understand, and be able to apply competently, simple basic concepts rather than be confused with half-digested advanced refinements.

Numerous diagrams have been included. Not only do these aid learning by the impact of the visual impression, but they are a neat form of expressing relationships. Moreover, in order to assist reading and note-taking, the text is, wherever possible, enumerated under headings and sub-headings.

Although the book is complete in itself, there is a Study Guide and Workbook to accompany it. This consists of notes on the salient points of the text, simple exercises in the use of diagrams and in the application of principles, and quiz and multiple-choice questions to concentrate the student's attention on the essential groundwork. There is also a selection of questions taken from past examination papers of the various examining bodies.

Some apology may be due to students who are already familiar with my *Elementary Economics* or *Intermediate Economics*. This book tends to come half-way between, but borrows from each where it is felt that little improvement in exposition could be achieved by rewriting.

I would like to place on record my indebtedness to Mr M. K. Johnson, Lecturer in Economics, Hatfield Polytechnic. Not only has he suggested many of the diagrams, but he has also been kind enough to read the typescript and to make many valuable comments.

PREFACE TO THE SECOND EDITION

The opportunity has been taken with this new edition to bring facts up to date and to introduce decimal currency.

Two new chapters have been added: The Distribution of Goods to the Consumer and The European Economic Community. Chapters 16, 23, 27, 29, 31, 33 and 36 have been largely re-written.

I would like to express my thanks to Mr M. Oxley, University of Reading, for his help in preparing this new edition.

GUIDANCE TO THE STUDENT

THE saying that 'a little practice is worth a lot of theory' is a dangerous half-truth. There is nothing so practical as sound theory. That is why this book is concerned mainly with simple economic theory. By applying it, the professional man can find the answer to many of the problems with which he is continually being confronted. 'Would it be wise to lend so large a sum to Farmer Giles in view of current government policy as regards subsidies to agriculture?' asks the bank manager. 'What effect will the construction of a motorway have on the value of different types of property in the vicinity?' ask the surveyor, valuer and estate agent. 'Is the government likely to increase the rate of income tax or capital gains tax in the next budget?' asks the accountant. 'How best can the liquid assets of the company be invested?' asks the company secretary. And so on.

You are urged to study economics, therefore, not merely to pass an examination, but because it will make you a better professional man. Indeed, if you approach it in this way, the examination will take care of itself.

But you must study systematically and thoroughly. To this end, you are advised to proceed as follows:

(1) Read through the whole book quickly.
(2) Read the Study Guide to the particular chapter.
(3) Study each chapter carefully in the textbook. Underline important points, and try to find illustrations of these points from your own particular professional experience. Be sure that you *understand* each stage in the argument before proceeding to the next. At times progress may appear slow, but there are no short cuts. Theory cannot be memorised.
(4) Write notes covering the chapter material, tabulating points and linking them in diagrams wherever possible. Such notes will give precision to your ideas, consolidate

your understanding, and prove invaluable for examination revision.

(5) Answer the questions in the Workbook. Check your answers with those given. Add to your notes where necessary.

(6) Obtain practice in answering the type of question set by the appropriate examining body. Remember that even the simplest-looking question usually requires the statement and application of a fundamental principle.

PART I

INTRODUCTION

CHAPTER 1

WHAT ECONOMICS IS ABOUT

I. THE ECONOMIC PROBLEM

Wants and limited means

'You must cut your coat according to your cloth.' 'You can't get a quart out of a pint pot.' 'You can't make a silk purse out of a sow's ear.' How many of our everyday sayings draw attention to the fact that, in comparison with all the things we want, our means of satisfying those wants are quite inadequate! Just think of the extra things we could buy if our incomes were larger—new clothes, new furniture, a better car, a tape-recorder, a ciné-camera. The list has no end, for, even if these wants were satisfied, new wants would arise.

This then is the 'economic problem'—unlimited wants, very limited means. And we can never completely overcome the difficulty. But what we can do is to make the most of what we have. In other words, we *economise*.

In order to see more clearly what is meant by 'economising', we can study the spending decisions of a housewife. Indeed, this illustration is more appropriate than it may seem at first sight, for 'economics' is derived from a Greek word meaning 'the management of a household'.

Our housewife's task is to make her fixed housekeeping allowance 'go as far as possible'; in other words, from her limited resources she seeks to obtain the maximum satisfaction for the family. Certain goods—those she regards as necessities, such as bread, milk, tea and butter—are purchased in regular quantities almost by habit; but this does not mean that she would not vary her spending on them were there to be any significant change in their prices. Nevertheless, what really lies behind her spending decisions can best be seen if we concentrate on those goods to which she gives frequent consideration. As our housewife walks past the shop windows in the High Street, a hundred and one different goods compete for the limited amount of money in her purse. Should she buy beef or chicken for the Sunday dinner? Peas would be nice—but they are still so dear that cabbage will have to do for one more week. But how everybody would love new potatoes! And they've gone down twopence a pound since last week! Yes, she will buy new potatoes instead of old. And so our capable housewife goes on, comparing the prices of different goods and asking herself whether the pleasure her family will obtain from them will be worth their cost—the inroads they make on her limited housekeeping allowance.

But it is not only the housewife who has to economise. How the schoolboy schemes to get the most out of his pocket-money! And the businessman faces the same problems in running his factory. Should he produce this good or that, or some of both? How many of each good? Should he employ extra labourers or would it be better to install a machine to do the work? Would it be more profitable to hire transport or to buy his own lorry? And so on.

Turn to the newspaper any morning, and it soon becomes obvious how often the government, too, is forced to choose as it plans the broad lines upon which the economy shall develop. More houses, new roads, and better hospitals—all are competing for the materials and labour used by the building industry. Extra playing-fields, new factory sites, and farmland—all are claiming a share of the limited land available. In these and many other instances, the government has the task of making the most of the nation's resources.

Opportunity cost

Thus we see that economics is really concerned with the problem of choice—the decisions forced upon us by the smallness of our resources compared with our wants. And, as we choose, so we have to sacrifice. If the newspaper boy spends his Christmas tips on a bicycle, then it is likely that he will have to go without the air-rifle that he also wanted. If the housewife buys a new cooker for the kitchen, she will have to make do for a time with the old armchair in the sitting-room. In deciding to work overtime on a Saturday afternoon, a worker forgoes leisure time and the football match he would otherwise have watched. When the farmer sows his land with wheat, he accepts that there will be less barley at harvest time. And so with the nation. If extra men and materials are required to accelerate the building of houses, roads and hospitals, then there will be fewer left for producing other goods—offices, power stations, sports centres, and so on. In all walks of life, having 'this' means going without 'that'. We therefore speak of 'opportunity cost'—the cost of something in terms of alternatives forgone (more accurately, in terms of the *best* alternative forgone).

In practice, economising is not so much a complete rejection of one good in favour of another, but rather deciding whether to have a little bit more of one and not quite so much of another. It is principally, as we shall see in Chapter 5, an adjustment at the margin.

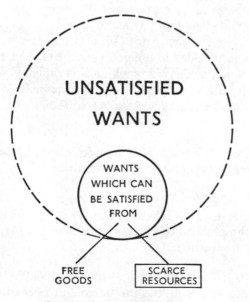

FIG. I.—The economic problem.

'Free' and 'scarce' goods

Few goods are so abundant that nobody will give anything for them. Air, perhaps, is one of the few exceptions. Occasionally, too, there is such an excellent apple harvest that a farmer says 'help yourself'. Such goods are termed 'free' goods. Usually, goods are 'scarce'—they can be obtained only by going without something else. With such goods we have to economise, and so they are often referred to as 'economic goods'. It is worth noting, however, that over time there is no hard-and-fast dividing line between economic and non-economic goods. Desert wastes can be transformed into rich agricultural land by irrigation; coal-mines are left to go derelict as new fuels are developed. Scarcity is relative to demand.

In future when we speak of 'goods' we shall be referring to economic goods, including, without further distinction, both commodities and services.

II. THE SCOPE OF ECONOMICS

Definition of economics

Scarcity forces us to economise. We weigh up the various alternatives and select that particular assortment of goods which yields the highest return from our limited resources. Modern economists use this idea to define the scope of their studies. But since there is no one definition which is completely satisfactory, we will keep ours as simple as possible. *Economics is the study of how men allocate their limited resources to provide for their wants.*

Amplification

The field which a study of economics covers becomes clearer if we examine certain points of this definition.

(1) *Economics is a social science*

This follows from the fact that economics studies how *men act.* (Compare the physical sciences, which examine various aspects of man's environment.)

(2) *Economics is closely concerned with the findings of other sciences*

Because economics studies the behaviour of men, it must, in reaching conclusions, refer to other branches of study. The alternative, advocated by some economists, of restricting economics to pure scientific analysis, curtails its usefulness. Thus most people would consider that the economist should have something to say on the question 'Should the income tax be made more progressive?' But his reply would have to be along the following lines: 'The tax yield would almost certainly increase; but higher-income groups might not work so hard. While I can suggest theoretical reasons for this, you should also see what the psychologist has to say. Furthermore, the pattern of consumption may change as the rich have less income to spend. For possible social effects, consult the sociologist. Finally, it will also help in making incomes more equal. That concerns me in that it may increase the proportion of total income spent—but ethics and politics have most weight in deciding whether greater equality of incomes is desirable.'

(3) *Economics selects a particular aspect of human behaviour*

But, although economics is closely connected with such social sciences as ethics, politics, sociology, psychology and anthropology, it is distinguished from them by its concentration on one particular aspect of human behaviour—choosing between alternatives in order to obtain the maximum satisfaction from limited resources. This modern, narrower approach is an improvement on Professor Alfred Marshall's definition—'a study of mankind in the ordinary business of life'—because this, as it stands, would embrace all forms of human activity.

In effect, the economist limits his study by selecting four fundamental characteristics of human existence and investigating what happens when they are all found together, as they usually are. First, the ends of human beings are without limit. Second, those ends are of varying importance. Third, the means available for achieving those ends—human time and energy and material resources—are limited. Fourth, the means can be used in many different ways; that is, they can produce many different goods.

But no one characteristic *by itself* is necessarily of interest to the economist. If, for instance, you have two wants and you cannot choose between them, you are between the devil and the deep blue sea, and you will never get as far as the problem of allocating resources between them. Similarly, 'free' goods are of no interest to the economist if resources do not have to be allocated to obtain them. Nor is the mere scarcity of means necessarily of significance to him. Where resources can be used only in one way, e.g. lichen-bearing volcanic land in Iceland for rearing sheep, they do not, although scarce, have to be 'economised'. Using such land for sheep does not mean that the owner has less of other things. Its use, therefore, gives rise to no problems, and the economist is interested only in the relatively minor point of determining the earnings of such land. Only when all four characteristics are found together does an economic problem arise.

(4) *Economics accepts ends as given*

The economist is not concerned with the ends as such—why, for instance, people prefer milk to wine or beef to lamb. Nor must he pass judgement on those ends on *moral* grounds. That is the task of ethics rather than of economics. Ends must be accepted as they are.

But although wants are given, the economist must point out the full cost of achieving them. Individual ends have economic implications for the ends of society as a whole. A man, for instance, may decide that he wants to get drunk every day. Here the economist must point out the full cost of this end—the cost to the man of getting drunk, plus the cost to society if he cannot work the next morning or eventually becomes a charge on the National Health Service as an alcoholic.

(5) *Economics concentrates in practice on market phenomena*

The scope of economics covers all circumstances in which man is forced to choose because of limited means. It includes, therefore, both the decisions made by Robinson Crusoe on his desert island and those of consumers and producers in a modern society where choice involves exchange.

In practice, however, the economist prefers to limit his investigations to those goods and services which are exchanged against money. Since all these have a 'price', he is able to make use of exact measurement and total dissimilar goods in terms of the common standard.

Nevertheless, as pointed out above, he must be careful to include any social costs or social benefits which are not allowed for by an individual in making a decision. Or, if the project is so large that it is likely to have external effects elsewhere, for example the proposed third London airport, a cost–benefit analysis may have to be used to cover these full effects. Moreover, since the economist can only quantify in terms of money, some costs and benefits which are not exchanged directly in a market, e.g. environmental, have to be given 'shadow prices'.

(6) *Economics covers the distribution of goods as well as their consumption and production.*

Since the economist is concerned with how people provide for their wants, his investigation of the production of goods must be followed by an examination of how those goods are distributed among the various members of society. The economic effects of any redistribution of goods by the government, e.g. on incentives to produce, must also be studied.

To sum up, the economist is not interested in ends. Nor is he concerned directly about the physical aspects of the limited means—the mechanical principles of the plough, the chemical properties of the soil or the biological characteristics of the seed. Both ends and resources he accepts as given. The subject of his study is how men mobilise these resources to achieve their ends and how efficient are the methods which they choose.

III. THE METHODS OF THE ECONOMIST

The object of his study

It is possible to study economics for the pleasure it yields as an intellectual discipline; people solve mathematical problems for this reason. But the great economists have pursued their study chiefly because it can benefit mankind. The investigation of an economic system is necessary to see how and where it can be improved—how more wants can be satisfied with the given resources. Hence the economist endeavours to solve problems as scientifically as possible and then applies the results to secure increased welfare in the real world. For example, by studying how the price system works in theoretical conditions, it is possible to suggest how it can be made to work better in real life.

His difficulties

But, in pursuing his studies, the economist faces three major difficulties.

(1) *He cannot experiment*

The task of a science is to formulate laws describing what will happen when there is a change in a given set of circumstances. The physicist and chemist can conduct their investigations by experimenting under controlled conditions in a laboratory. But because he is dealing with human behaviour rather than with physical properties, these means are denied the economist. (*a*) He will never be quite sure of the initial position, for facts concerning people are difficult to ascertain. (*b*) It is impossible to isolate a group of consumers or businessmen in a test-tube to see how they would react to a given change. The most the economist can usually do as regards consumers' behaviour, for instance, is to take a sample survey. (*c*) The economy is subject to continuous change, and so conditions cannot be held constant while the effect of one particular measure is observed. (*d*) Because the economy is so complex, no body of economists could follow through all the results of any given change. (*e*) Any measurements are only approximate, and even so take time to collect.

Because of these difficulties, the economist can only be approximate in his investigations in real life. Nevertheless, the information available is increasing and becoming more precise, e.g. through market research and government statistical enquiries. Thus economists' predictions are likely to gain in accuracy.

(2) *His studies are rarely distinct from those of other sciences*

Even though the economist may derive propositions which could have a bearing on policy, their usefulness may be restricted until they are combined with the findings of other sciences (see p. 26). Moreover, as state planning of the economy increases, so the area over which economics overlaps with politics increases.

(3) *He cannot directly measure welfare*

The economist who is concerned with social welfare must

recognise that in the last resort people do not want the goods themselves, but simply the satisfaction they obtain when consuming those goods. But while goods can be measured either in quantity or money value, it is quite impossible to measure satisfaction. It is probable, for instance, that a working man derives more enjoyment from £10 spent on a holiday at Brighton than a millionaire does from £10 spent on a dinner. But we can never be sure—simply because satisfaction, like pain, is a personal feeling which cannot be measured objectively.

So the economist, using the best approximation, works on the principle that, because two loaves are better than one, an increase in goods represents an increase in welfare. Even so, he cannot measure all goods. If he gives a value to the vegetables a man grows in his garden or the repairs he does to his car, should he not logically include also in the same calculations something for the wife's services in cleaning the house and cooking the meals, etc.? Because it is impossible to know where to draw the line, the economist simplifies matters by confining his attention to those goods which are exchanged against money (see p. 340).

The scientific approach

In spite of the above difficulties, economics can still claim to be a science. It is not the facts of a subject but how it is studied that makes a science. Economics, although it studies a particular aspect of human behaviour, adopts scientific methods.

In the first place, it does not attempt to set out criteria for determining what is good or bad, what ought or what ought not to be—any more than physics attempts to say that liquids are 'better' than solids. It is concerned only with objective or positive statements—those which can be tested by an appeal to facts, even though those facts have not yet been collected—and with the consequences of certain actions. As soon as the economist says what ought or ought not to be, he introduces subjective views or, as they are more usually described, 'normative statements' or 'value judgements'. That is why, for instance, he must accept ends as given, expressing no opinion as to whether those ends are 'good' or 'bad'.

Secondly, the study of economics has a particular object in view—the establishment of principles, propositions, theories or generalisations expressing fundamental relationships within the subject matter. In this it goes beyond *descriptive economics* which concentrates on a mere description of an economy—its institutions (firms, banks, government organisations, etc.), its population, its system of taxation, and so on. For, if its studies ended there, they could hardly be termed 'scientific'. While descriptive economics is desirable, indeed necessary, it merely describes the mechanism. What we really want to know is how the mechanism operates.

That is the task of *analytical economics*, which sets out to establish general principles about the way in which an economic system works. In discovering these principles, economics makes use of the methods of other sciences. These methods are: (1) induction, (2) deduction.

(1) Induction

In the inductive approach, the economist observes facts, classifies those facts, and then tries to observe any causal relationship between them. For instance, he may discover that the price of eggs falls in the spring. He would connect this with the increase in the supply of eggs at that time of the year, and from this establish a generalisation that an increase in supply, other things being equal, leads to a fall in price.

The weakness of the inductive approach is that the scientist can never be sure that the principles he has established are a hundred per cent foolproof. Hence, whenever possible, he will endeavour to substantiate by deduction what he has discovered by induction.

(2) Deduction

With deduction, the scientist starts from hypothetical assumptions (frequently referred to as postulates). Then, by a process of logical reasoning, he derives propositions from these assumptions. This is often termed 'model-building'. The sequence is as follows:

(a) The economic phenomenon to be explained is selected. Of course, if the analysis is to be useful, the problem must be of practical significance.

(b) The initial assumptions are made. These should be as close to reality as possible, and this is where descriptive economics can be very helpful. But, although we are concerned with human behaviour, realistic assumptions are not impossible. In the main we are interested in market, not individual, reactions. Dealing in large numbers means that patterns of behaviour emerge, and we can thus think in terms of an 'average economic man'. Thus it is quite reasonable to assume that, in disposing of his income, this average consumer will act rationally, seeking to obtain maximum satisfaction from it.

Of course, we have to simplify initially, confining ourselves to broad assumptions, from which we can obtain only broad generalisations. Later the assumptions can be changed according to particular circumstances, and the conclusions modified accordingly.

(c) Logical reasoning establishes what follows from the assumptions. Let us take a simple example. We wish to discover what price will prevail in a market. We make three assumptions:

(i) a high degree of competition, on the basis of price, among buyers and among sellers, and between buyers and sellers; (ii) more will be demanded the lower the price; (iii) more will be supplied the higher the price.

Demand and supply thus move in opposite directions for a given change in price. The conclusion we come to is that the price of the good will settle where the amount supplied equals the amount demanded. Any other price will not be a settled price. If it is above, there will be more offered for sale than is demanded. Stocks will pile up, and some suppliers will lower their prices. As the price falls, so more will be demanded, and this will go on until demand equals supply. Similarly, when the price is below that where demand equals supply, shortages lead buyers to offer higher prices. As the price rises, so more will be supplied, and this goes on until demand equals supply (see p. 65). We have thus built up a model showing how price is determined in a market—a very useful piece of economic theory.

By modifying the assumptions we can make the model closer to real life or show how changes in the economic system work. For instance, let us make the assumption that, as a result of an advertising campaign, people's tastes change, so that they want more of the good at the market price than formerly. The economist describes this by saying that the conditions of demand have changed, and that demand has increased (*see* p. 59). At the original price, demand now exceeds supply. As before, this will cause the price to rise and supply to expand until a new price is arrived at where once more demand and supply are equal.

(*d*) Propositions derived by deduction are tested by observed data. If conclusions and facts are inconsistent, the theory has to be modified or even rejected. The process of deduction may have been wrong, or the wrong assumptions may have been made.

If the principles established are not disproved by such testing, they can be used to predict what will happen in particular instances, for they show how the different parts of a system are related to one another. It should be noted, however, that such forecasts are not unconditional statements of what *will* occur. The nature of an economic proposition is simply of the form '*if* this occurs, *then* such and such will result'. For example, *if* demand increases, *then*, other things being equal, price will rise (*see* p. 66). When we apply general principles to particular cases, we are in the realm of what is often called *applied economics*.

It is this power to predict which enables firms (including the professional man) and governments to plan with a reasonable degree of accuracy. The theory of price, for instance, would enable a building firm to make some forecast of the effect of an increase in the demand for houses on bricklayers' wages. Or, if there was widespread unemployment in the economy, a knowledge of the principles determining the level of activity could suggest appropriate measures to reduce it.

IV. ECONOMIC THEORY AND POLICY

But why, it might be asked, if propositions have been arrived at scientifically, should economists appear to disagree so often?

Take the statement, 'Britain must remain in the Common Market because it will lead to a faster rate of economic growth.' Why might economists disagree on this?

(1) *They may not agree on the facts*

How can we ascertain that membership of the Common Market *will* increase the rate of economic growth? Facts are deficient. Even if we look at the growth rates of the original six members, there are differences in calculating Gross National Product which make comparisons ambiguous.

(2) *They disagree on the causal connection*

Even if the faster rate of economic growth of the six founder countries is substantiated, is membership the cause of this increase? There may be more than one explanation, e.g. the impetus given by Marshall Aid, the switch from an agricultural economy (where diminishing returns result in a higher cost per unit as output increases) to an industrial economy (where increasing returns may occur, resulting in lower costs per unit as output increases). It may be difficult to decide which explanation fits the facts best.

(3) *The statement really rests on a value judgement*—that economic growth is a good thing. But some economists might consider that other objectives—more leisure, less worry, the avoidance of friction through competition, and so on—are in a fairly affluent society more desirable.

(4) *They may unconsciously let individual bias creep into their analysis and interpretation of the facts*

While, as scientists, economists try to be as objective as possible, they are often examining subjects upon which they have strong personal feelings. Thus an economist who is an ardent supporter of Anglo-American relationships may unconsciously fail to give full weight to evidence suggesting an increase in the European growth rate.

But this does not mean that the economist is without value. If, for instance, he is employed in a business enterprise, the scope of his work is fairly well defined—to promote the success of the business in terms of profits.

As regards government policy, however, the advice the economist can give may be less definite. In any case, the final decision will usually rest on the judgement of the politician. For one thing, a government is seldom faced with a simple choice, since ends are usually a compromise between alternatives. The first task of the economist is to point out any inconsistency between aims. For instance, in certain circumstances, the aim of economic expansion may conflict with the aim of balance of payments equilibrium.

Secondly, the economist can show the full implications of a particular policy. For instance, if a very high level of employment is the aim, then he should point out that this will probably make it more difficult to maintain a steady price level.

Thirdly, he may be able to recommend more economic ways of achieving a given end. This is possible because, although ends may be given, there are economic and non-economic means of achieving those ends. Is it better, for instance, to obtain food supplies by importing from abroad or by home production?

CHAPTER 2

METHODS OF ALLOCATING RESOURCES

I. THE QUESTIONS THAT HAVE TO BE ANSWERED

How we 'economise'

As we have seen, we respond to the economic problem by 'economising'.

(*a*) Wants are placed in some order of importance, and the more important are satisfied first. Of course, some wants can be satisfied more easily than others because some goods take less of the scarce means of production than other goods. Allowance must be made for this. For example, if a person wants a car only twice as much as he wants a motorcycle, but its real cost (that is, in terms of the factors of production used) is eight times as much, then probably he will have to be content with the motorcycle and his want for the car must go unsatisfied.

(*b*) Factors of production are used as effectively as possible, without waste.

Waste occurs when factors stand idle. If, for instance, workers are unemployed, we are not making full use of scarce labour. The same applies when land and machinery stand idle, unless the cost of using them is greater than the value of what they can produce.

Secondly, waste occurs if factors are employed to make things which are not really wanted. Relating production to wants has become more difficult in the modern complex economic organisation. The peasant farmer of the middle ages produced to satisfy the wants of his family, and he could allocate his resources between wheat, rye, barley, meat, etc., according to their needs. But today people specialise in the work they do. Each day, the bank manager, the office boy, the bus conductor,

37

the tinker, the tailor, the soldier and sailor all go about their respective tasks. Other people are baking bread, growing potatoes, bringing milk to town. Thus our system must now provide answers to a multitude of questions. How many suits shall the tailor make? Have we got the right number of bank managers? How much bread shall the baker bake? How much milk shall the farmer send to town? If too much bread is baked, it will go stale; if too much milk is sent to town, the surplus will go sour, and it would have been better if the farmer had turned it into cheese. Over-production involves waste, and waste means that the factors could have been used to satisfy some of our other 'wants'. Clearly then, any organisation of production requires a method of estimating the size of wants.

Thirdly, waste occurs if the organisation of production is faulty. This takes place, for instance, when many small firms are producing goods which could be made by a few large firms using fewer factors of production. It happens, too, when the layout of the factory is such that men have to spend unnecessary time in passing from one particular machine to another. Likewise the organisation may be defective because processes are not fully integrated—as occurs when steel ingots are allowed to cool before being rolled into steel sheets. Or it may be that the centre of production was badly chosen. If a blast furnace, for instance, were situated without regard to its accessibility to supplies of iron ore, coke and limestone, waste would result, because extra factors of production are needed to transport those materials. Finally, for full efficiency, the organisation of production must be continually revised to allow for new techniques, new processes and new power supplies.

It follows, therefore, that any system which is adopted for solving the economic problem must answer the following questions:

(1) What assortment of goods will yield the greatest possible satisfaction?

(2) How, out of the various alternatives, do we employ our limited resources to produce this assortment as efficiently as possible?

(3) Who are to enjoy the goods which are produced?

In short, the questions are: What? How? For whom? These are

the divisions of consumption, production and distribution of
the old classical economists.

Alternative economic systems

Broadly speaking, there are two distinct methods by which
these questions are answered. Either the decisions can be made
by an over-riding authority, such as the state, or they can
follow automatically from the free operation of the price system
motivated by private enterprise. Communist countries lean
towards the first, and the Western world towards the second.
But neither method by itself is completely satisfactory, and so
all economies contain a mixture of both.

II. A CENTRAL PLANNING AUTHORITY

Where there is an all-powerful planning authority, it estimates the assortment of goods which it considers people want
and directs the means of production accordingly. It decides,
too, the basis upon which the goods produced are distributed.
Economic efficiency depends largely, therefore, on how accurately
wants are estimated and resources allocated. Here we may
mention four criticisms of the system.

First, ascertaining the satisfaction which individuals derive
from consuming different goods is impossible. But a modified
price system can be introduced to help, changes in prices
signalling possible changes in wants.

Secondly, many officials are required to estimate wants and
to direct factors of production. Inasmuch as such officials are
avoidable in a private enterprise economy, they represent wasted
factors of production, for they could be employed to satisfy more
wants. Moreover, the use of officials may give rise to bureau-
cracy—excessive form-filling, an addiction to 'red tape', slow-
ness in coming to a decision and an impersonal approach to
consumers. At times, too, officialdom has been accompanied by
corruption.

Thirdly, even when wants have been decided upon, difficulties of co-ordination arise. On the one hand, wants have to
be dovetailed and awarded priorities. On the other, factors have
to be combined in the best proportions. Usually plans are co-
ordinated through numerous committees, directed at the top by

a central planning committee. Yet members of this committee would be primarily politicians with little experience of administration. And, even if they were able, they would still have to face the difficulties of managing a large organisation (*see* p. 135).

Fourthly, it is argued that state ownership of the factors of production, by lessening incentives, diminishes effort and initiative. Direction of labour may mean that persons are dissatisfied with their allotted jobs. Officials may follow cautious policies because they find it easier to earn 'brickbats' than 'bouquets' (*see* p. 118). Thus it is possible that production is less than under private enterprise.

III. PRIVATE ENTERPRISE

Under private enterprise, the emphasis is laid on the freedom of the individual, both as a consumer and as the owner of a factor of production (usually labour).

As a consumer, he expresses his wants through the price system. As the owner of a factor of production, he seeks to obtain as large a reward as possible. Where a good is relatively scarce, consumers 'bid' up its price. This increases the earnings of factors and the profits of firms producing that good. As a result, factors are attracted into the industry, and supply increases in accordance with consumers' wishes. On the other hand, if consumers do not want a particular good, its price falls, producers make a loss, and factors leave the industry.

The price system, therefore, indicates the wishes of consumers (subject to the existing distribution of income) and allocates the community's productive resources accordingly (Fig. 2). There is no direction of labour; people are free to work wherever they choose. Efficiency is achieved simply through its effect on the size of private 'profit'. Furthermore, the rewards which the factors earn decide who shall obtain the goods produced, for such earnings are spent by their owners in the market.

In this way, the price system acts, as it were, like a marvellous computer, registering people's preferences for different goods, transmitting these preferences to those responsible for producing the goods, and moving the factors to produce them. What is more, all this occurs without employing a host of officials.

FIG. 2.—The price mechanism under private enterprise.

Unfortunately, in practice the price system does not produce entirely satisfactory results, nor does it work quite so smoothly as indicated above.

First, it is those consumers with the most money who exercise the greatest weight in spending. Thus the means of production may be devoted to producing luxuries for the rich to the exclusion of necessities for the poor. While this results from the unequal distribution of wealth rather than from the private enterprise system, it must be remembered that the latter tends to produce, and even to increase, such inequality.

Secondly, some vital services which are not marketable, e.g. defence, police and justice, would not be produced adequately by private enterprise. Indeed, in most advanced countries, the state now provides for what are considered to be basic needs—education, medical care, insurance against sickness, industrial accident, unemployment, etc.

Thirdly, competition itself may sometimes lead to inefficiency. Small units may persist when co-ordination is vital to securing the advantages of large-scale production. Competitive advertising may waste resources. Uncertainty as to rivals' plans may hold back investment.

All the above defects can be avoided where the state decides what to produce. More working-class flats and fewer large mansions are built, bombers are produced as well as bowling alleys, the wastes of competition do not arise.

Fourthly, in practice, the competition upon which the efficiency of the capitalist system depends, is liable to break down. An employer may be the *only* buyer of a certain type of labour in a locality. If so, he is in a strong position when fixing wage-rates with a number of independent and unorganised workers. The state must, therefore, often protect the individual worker. Similarly, on the selling side, there may be only one seller because competitors can be excluded. This weakens the consumer's position because he cannot take his custom elsewhere. Later we shall discuss monopolies in more detail. Here we need only note that where they result in inefficiency and the restriction of supplies, as for instance when fish are dumped back into the sea, they are harmful to the community. Of course, under a central planning system, the state represents one big monopoly, but the supposition is that it would not act contrary to the interests of the people.

Fifthly, in practice the mechanism of the price system may not work smoothly because there are obstacles to the movement of factors of production in response to price changes (*see* Chapter 16). As a result, supply is not adjusted easily and quickly to changes in demand.

Sixthly, the private profit motive does not always ensure that *public* wealth (as distinct from the sum total of *private* wealth) will be maximised. A manufacturer building a factory does not consider the soot which falls from his factory chimney on the nearby washing-lines. It is not a cost to him, but it is a cost to the community who live in the neighbourhood. On the other hand, there may exist certain 'social benefits' which are not allowed for by the individual producer when calculating the return to his outlay. Thus, when considering whether to build a civil airbus, he merely estimates whether the receipts from fares will cover the costs. The fact that in the process he gains 'know-how' for the development of military aircraft does not enter his calculations. Under central planning, the state can allow for such social costs and social benefits when planning production.

Lastly, and most important of all, under private enterprise, where individuals decide what to produce, there occur periods when factors of production are allowed to stand idle because producers as a whole consider that the prospects of making a profit are poor. Under central planning, on the other hand, the people who decide which wants shall be satisfied are also the people who direct factors into the production of the necessary goods and services. All factors, therefore, are fully employed.

The advantages of the private enterprise system correspond closely to the defects of the central planning system, and vice versa. But one big defect of the central planning system has remained unstated. Once individuals have given power to the state to prescribe what is good for them, to own all the factors of production and to direct labour, it may not be long before the state has usurped absolute political power in addition to its economic power and the people are at the mercy of a dictatorship. Individuals then exist for the state, and not the state for the individual. In short, we are in George Orwell's *1984*. Thus the ultimate decision as to whether a capitalist economy is to be preferred to a central planning economy (in their extreme forms) really hinges on the question whether you are prepared to run the risk of being ruled by a dictator or whether you would rather be left free to choose your own job accepting such defects of the private enterprise system as unemployment, inadequate provision for future production, and the existence of wide variations in wealth.

IV. BRITAIN'S MIXED ECONOMY

Second thoughts over the desirability of private enterprise have arisen largely because serious unemployment resulted from defects in its mechanism. Fortunately today we know a lot more about why these defects occur and how they can be put right (*see* Chapter 26).

Thus we are not faced with a straight choice between complete private enterprise and full central planning. Instead we can use the state, not so much as a dictator, but rather as a wise father who allows his children a large measure of personal freedom, but looks ahead and lays plans in order to avoid many of the dangers into which they might stumble.

Britain, therefore, has a mixed economy, her economic system making use of both methods in an attempt, as it were, to get the best of both worlds. In the main, however, production is still carried on under private enterprise, for the public sector (central and local government and the nationalised industries) accounts for only about a quarter of total production. Nevertheless, even in the other three-quarters, there is regulation to varying degrees.

Thus the economic activities of the government of the United Kingdom can be said to have one or more of the following objects:

(1) To produce those goods and services which would either not be provided by private enterprise, or might be provided very indifferently (*see* Chapter 29).

(2) To take over the production of certain goods and services because they can be produced more efficiently by the resources of the state than by the resources of private enterprise. Under this heading we are thinking principally of the nationalised industries, but it also applies to roads, libraries, and other goods provided by local authorities.

(3) To overcome great inequalities in the distribution of wealth and to ensure:
   (*a*) a minimum standard of life for all;
   (*b*) equality of opportunity for all.

(4) To protect the individual, both as a consumer and a worker, from the operations of powerful interests, such as monopolies.

(5) To overcome frictions, e.g. to the movement of labour, which hamper the efficient operation of the price system.

(6) To modify the price mechanism when shortages, e.g. in housing, would entail hardship.

(7) To control the entrepreneur in order to allow for the public costs or public benefits of his own plans.

(8) To regulate the economy in order to secure full employment.

  (9) To obtain a balanced regional development.

 (10) To maintain a stable level of prices.

 (11) To improve the balance of payments in order that:

      (a) foreign currency reserves may be strengthened;

      (b) aid may be given to underdeveloped countries.

 (12) To ensure a steady growth of the national product.

Some of these objectives may be complementary. Thus a strengthening of the foreign currency reserves may be a prerequisite for steady growth, for they provide the cushion against balance of payments deficits which are liable to occur from time to time when the level of activity is high. On the other hand some objectives may be competitive. Thus the nearer the economy moves to full employment, the greater is the danger of inflation.

Politically some persons would like more government control and others less. This book tries to avoid taking sides. It simply explains how the price mechanism operates, where the defects occur, and what the government can do to avoid or to mitigate the results of such defects. Often, as we go along, we shall direct attention to government action in the particular sphere under discussion. At other times, we shall discuss government policy specifically and in more detail, as with interference in the price system, nationalisation, the localisation of industry, the control of monopoly, the regulation of international trade, the promotion of employment and the maintenance of a stable currency.

V. MICRO- AND MACRO-ECONOMICS

An economic system

Broadly speaking, any economic system consists of two parts:

  (1) Firms—business units from the sole proprietor to the government, deciding what to produce and employing the productive resources (Fig. 3).

  (2) Households—the consumers of the goods and services produced and the suppliers of the productive resources.

Micro-economics

A study of the price system, therefore, is largely concerned with:

(1) how the supply of a particular good or service is related to the demand for it;

(2) how the demand for a particular factor of production is related to its supply.

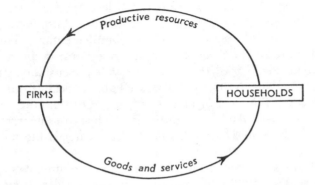

FIG. 3.—The flow of goods and productive resources in an economic system.

As we shall see, this relationship of demand to supply is based upon prices established in the different product and factor markets. Furthermore, all prices are relative to one another. A change in any one price in the economic system establishes a

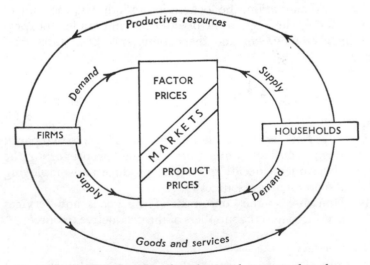

FIG. 4.—The allocation of products and resources through prices in the market.

ripple which touches all markets, both product and factor, sometimes directly (as in the case of substitutes) but usually indirectly and even remotely.

This allocation of the different goods and factors through markets is shown in Fig. 4, which is an extension of Fig. 3. A development of Fig. 4, through demand and supply analysis, is the concern of the first part of this book. Since it is largely a study of individual markets—small parts of the economy—it is usually referred to as *micro-economics*.

Macro-economics

So far, so good. And, if we had been studying economics sixty years ago, this would have been the scope of our investigations— the allocation of goods and services between different uses through the mechanism of the price system. But is it possible that the price system could give rise to another problem—that some productive resources might remain unemployed?

The classical economists thought not. They held that, if there were unemployed factors of production, competition between them would lead to a fall in their price, and this would make it profitable to employ them.

Experience of unemployment towards the end of the nineteenth century, and particularly in the twentieth century, however, convinced economists that this need not happen. Even when the level of activity was at its peak, as in 1937, there could still be nearly $1\frac{1}{2}$ million workers (11.3 per cent) out of a job.

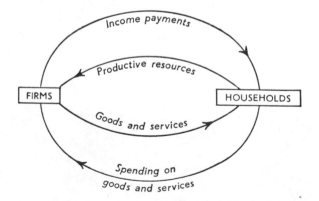

Fig. 5.—Real and money flows in an economic system.

It was left to Lord Keynes to highlight the cause: a break-down in the flow of money income. To analyse the level of activity, we need a diagram showing the money payments in total which result from the exchange of goods and resources (Fig. 5).

Since we are now looking at the flow of goods and services in total, we speak of *macro-economics* (from the Greek word *macro,* meaning large). Fig. 5 outlines the model which is developed for most of the second part of the book. The only reason why micro-economics is taken before macro-economics is that it is felt it is the easier for beginners to understand.

PART II

WHAT TO PRODUCE

CHAPTER 3

HOW PRICE IS FORMED IN
THE FREE MARKET

I. VALUE AND PRICE

As soon as we wish to know what to produce, there immediately arises the question: 'How can people indicate what they want?' A mere statement of want is meaningless for, as we showed in Chapter 1, people always *want* something. A want is significant in economics only when a person is prepared to give up something in order to satisfy it. As the strength of the different wants varies, so will the amounts which people are willing to give up. In other words, different goods have a different *value* to them. Value is measured in terms of 'opportunity cost'. For example, if Miss 'A' is willing to work 5 hours for the money which will buy a hat, we say that the value of the hat to her is greater than the value of the 5 hours' leisure forgone. Value therefore means the rate at which a particular good or service will exchange for other goods. It is important to note, however, that, while a good to have value must be capable of satisfying a want, a good which satisfies a want need not necessarily have value. For example, air satisfies a want; but, in normal circumstances, the supply of it is so great that nobody will give anything in exchange for it. Because it has no power to command other goods in exchange, it has, in economics, no value.

In modern economic systems we rarely exchange goods directly against other goods. We make use of a 'go-between', or, as it is usually said, a medium of exchange. This medium of exchange is money and the values of goods are expressed in terms of money. In other words, we *price* the goods and

49

services. Price can be defined, therefore, as the value of a commodity or service measured in terms of the standard monetary unit. By comparing prices, we can compare the *rates* at which different goods can be exchanged.

Changes in *relative* prices, if supply conditions have not changed, indicate a relative shift in the importance of those goods. Thus price changes can signal a change in what people want. We must, therefore, examine the mechanism by which these signals are flashed up. We begin by looking at the 'market' —where values are established by exchange.

II. MARKETS

Definition

'I'm offered £150 for this heifer. Surely, gentlemen, you're going to offer more than that for such a fine animal. No more offers? Going at £150. For the last time of asking, any advance on £150? Going at £150, going, gone.' Down comes the hammer. 'Sold at £150 to Mr Giles on my right.'

This is the local cattle market. On his stand above the auction ring is the auctioneer. Inside the ring, a black-and-white heifer paces round and round. Appraising the animal are the farmers from the neighbouring countryside. Some are buyers, some sellers. The market fixes the price at which those who want a good can obtain it from those who have it to sell.

Note that to the economist only exchange value is of significance. The farmer selling the heifer may have considered that it ought to have made more than £150. Or, as it was the first calf reared by his son, it may have had great 'sentimental value' to him. Such niceties, however, mean little to the economist.

Of course, prices are not always fixed by auction as in the local cattle market. Auction is the method usually employed where there are many potential buyers but the seller only comes to the market infrequently or wishes to dispose of his goods quickly. If there are few buyers and sellers, e.g. in the purchase of a house or a second-hand car, the final price may be arrived at by 'higgling', the seller meeting the prospective buyer personally and bargaining with him.

But where goods are in frequent and regular demand, to dispose of them by auction or higgling would take far too long.

Hence goods such as foodstuffs, clothing, household utensils, and new cars are given a definite price by the shopkeeper. However, this does not mean that buyers have not influenced this price. If it is too high, the good will not be sold. If it is too low, the shopkeeper will be left without stocks. His final price will have taken account of this.

Nor should it be assumed that a market must be held in a particular place. Second-hand cars are often bought and sold through newspaper advertisements. Second-hand furniture may be disposed of by a card in a local shop window. Above all, developments in transport, communications, and methods of selling (e.g. by grade or sample) may mean that the area of the market is extended.

Therefore, we can no longer speak of a market as being that particular place where the goods are bought and sold, for the whole business might be conducted by telephone. The organisation by which buyers and sellers are brought together may be formal or informal. Moreover the economist is chiefly interested in the market from the point of view of its function—the fixing of the price of the particular commodity—and the actual organisation is studied chiefly from this aspect. Thus we can define a market simply as *all those buyers and sellers of a good who influence its price.* The result is that there is a tendency for the same price, allowing for costs of transport, to be established for the same commodity within the market.

World markets

Today modern transport is so extensive and so rapid that many commodities have a 'world' market; that is, a change in the price of the commodity in one part of the world affects the price in the rest of the world. Such commodities are wheat, frozen meat, oils, fats and the basic raw materials such as wool, cotton, mineral oil, rubber, tin, lead, zinc and uranium. What are the necessary requirements for a commodity to have such a wide market?

In the first place, there must be a wide demand. The basic necessities of life (e.g. wheat, frozen meat, wool, cotton) answer this requirement. Goods, however, which have only a local demand, such as national costumes, books translated into little-used languages, souvenirs, post-cards of local views and foods which satisfy local tastes, do not have a wide demand.

Secondly, commodities must be physically capable of being transported. Land and buildings are almost impossible to transport. A customer may require a personal service from the producer, but the distance he can travel is usually limited. Labour, too, is particularly immobile, workers being loath, in spite of the attraction of a higher wage, to move to a different country or even to a different locality (*see* Chapter 16). Closely connected with this is the action of governments who, by a tariff policy or import quotas, may effectively prevent certain commodities from entering the country. Today, the movement of capital out of the United Kingdom is restricted by the government.

Thirdly, the costs of transport must not be prohibitive—they must be small in relation to the value of the commodity. Thus the market for bricks is small, whilst that for diamonds is world-wide. Similarly, wheat and oil are cheap to transport compared with coal because they are more easily handled, though as sea transport is the cheapest form of transport, coal mined near the coast of Northumberland, Durham and South Wales can be sent long distances.

Lastly, the commodity must be durable. Goods which perish quickly, such as milk, bread, fresh cream and strawberries, cannot be sent long distances. Nevertheless, modern developments, such as refrigeration and canning and the development of air freight transport, are extending the area of the market.

Perfect and imperfect markets

In any market, the price of a commodity ruling in one part of it affects the price paid for the same commodity in another part. Hence the same price tends to be established. Where any price differences are eliminated quickly, we say the market is a 'perfect' market. *Note:* This is not quite the same as 'perfect competition' (*see* Chapter 11).

For a market to be perfect, certain conditions have to be fulfilled. First, buyers and sellers must have exact knowledge of the prices which are being paid elsewhere in the market. The development of communications, particularly the telephone, has facilitated this. Secondly, both buyers and sellers must base their actions solely on price. Neither buyers nor sellers have a preference to purchase from or to sell to one particular person because of loyalty or mere unreasonableness. If, for instance, one seller suddenly puts up the price of his good, then his customers immediately go to one of the other sellers in the market who are cheaper. Similarly, if he were to lower his price, customers would so flock to him that he would sell out quickly unless he raised his price to that asked elsewhere.

Examples of perfect markets are the precious stones market of Hatton Garden and, above all, the organised produce markets and the Stock Exchange, both of which will be described later. In these markets the two essential conditions are fulfilled. The buyers and sellers are usually professional dealers who make their income by watching prices carefully and buying accordingly. It is essential, therefore, for them to be acquainted with any fluctuations in price in any part of the market and the result of their operations is that variations in price are quickly eliminated.

But these conditions are not usually satisfied in other markets. Buyers and sellers neither have perfect knowledge nor act solely on the basis of price. The ordinary housewife, for instance cannot always afford the time to go from one shop to another in order to compare the prices of her everyday purchases, though it is noticeable that she is usually much more careful when spending on the more expensive goods bought at infrequent intervals. In the same way, shopkeepers do not always have the means to know what other shopkeepers are charging for similar goods. Moreover, purchasers are influenced by considerations other than price when deciding from whom to buy. Thus they may continue to deal with one particular trader even though he is charging a slightly higher price simply because they are loyal to someone who has given them good service in the past. It is this personal relationship which is the basis of the 'goodwill' built up by a business. Moreover, although two goods may be virtually the same physically, in the mind of the purchaser they may be entirely different. This process of making the good slightly different from other producers is known as 'product differentiation', and over one-half of present-day advertising is directed to convincing people of the superiority of these individual brands of goods. Such advertising, therefore, renders the market less perfect and should be contrasted with the other type of advertising where the aim is to inform the public. This latter type tends to widen the market and to render it more perfect.

The result is that only where the market is composed of many professional dealers is it likely to be fully perfect. In other markets, price differences persist and such markets are said to be 'imperfect'. As we have already hinted, imperfect markets are often found in retailing.

Organised produce markets

As we have shown above, the market for certain commodities is a very wide one, largely because they have a high value relative to their cost of transport and are non-perishable over a fairly long period. Moreover, many of these commodities are in general and constant demand, either because they form a basic raw material for a widely-used finished good or because they constitute one of the main foodstuffs or beverages for a large section of the world's people. Such commodities, therefore, figure prominently in international trade and it is these with which we are concerned in the following discussion.

England's foreign trade commenced with the export of raw wool in the thirteenth century, and it was extended by the subsequent development of the Chartered Companies. These were based on London, and it was here that merchants gathered to buy and sell the produce which the Companies' ships brought from abroad. This commerce conducted by London not only grew larger as trade extended but became more continuous as supplies of commodities came forward at different times of the year from different parts of the world. It was natural, therefore, that in London the same buyers and sellers would meet regularly to conduct business and to exchange information.

The big change, however, came about with the expansion of international trade following the Industrial Revolution. The United Kingdom became the greatest importing and exporting nation of the world. London, her chief port and commercial city, not only imported the goods which were required for the people of her own country but, assisted by the fact that British ships were the great carriers of the world's trade, built up an important entrepôt business, acting as a 'go-between' in the distribution of such commodities as tea, sugar, hides, skins and wool, to many other countries, particularly those of Western Europe.

Hence formal 'organised markets' developed. These markets

are distinguished from other sorts of market in that buying and selling takes place in a recognised building, business is governed by agreed rules and conventions, and often only special persons are allowed to engage in transactions. Generally the public are excluded, even from watching. They are thus a highly developed form of market, and today London has exchanges or auction centres for buying and selling such commodities as rubber, wool tea, coffee, furs, metals (tin, copper, lead and zinc), grain and shipping freights (the Baltic Exchange). It must not be thought, however, that such organised produce markets exist only in London. Liverpool has exchanges for cotton and grain which are as important as London's exchanges, while most of the large trading countries such as the United States (wheat, maize, and cotton) and Australia and New Zealand (wool) have their own exchanges. In fact, with the development of shipping services by other countries, the tendency has been for trade which formerly passed through London to be sent direct from the producing countries to markets nearer the consuming populations. Even so, a considerable amount of buying and selling in certain commodities such as sugar, metals and grain is still conducted in London although the goods go directly to other countries. Payment to merchants for the business they transact forms a part of Britain's 'invisible exports' (see p. 465).

Broadly speaking, organised markets fulfil three main functions. First, they enable manufacturers and wholesalers to obtain supplies of the commodities they require easily, quickly and at the competitive market price. This is achieved by the fact that the markets provide a centre where expert buyers and sellers, each having very complete knowledge of the particular commodity, can meet for the purpose of dealing. In them, price is very sensitive to any change in demand and supply; thus they are 'perfect markets'.

Secondly, for those commodities which can be graded very accurately, these markets provide a means whereby persons who would be adversely affected by a change in their prices can protect themselves from heavy loss. Thus producers of rubber or tin prefer to know what price they will receive for their output before it is actually delivered to the market. On the other hand, a cotton spinner has to protect himself from a rise in the price of raw materials between the time of quoting a price for his yarn and the time of manufacture. This is achieved, through what is known as 'hedging' on the 'futures' market.

Where a good is bought today for delivery today, the deal is known as a 'spot' transaction and the price agreed upon is the 'spot price'. With many goods, however, it is possible to buy today for delivery sometime in the future. The good may not actually be in stock, but the seller contracts to obtain and deliver the good at the agreed time. Such a deal is known as a 'futures' transaction, and the price agreed upon as the 'future' or 'forward' price. For a commodity to be dealt in on a 'futures' market, certain conditions must be fulfilled. These are: (a) that the commodity is durable, thereby enabling stocks to be carried; (b) that the commodity can be easily graded and its quality determined by tests which yield almost identical results without the aid of samples when applied by different experts; (c) that dealings are sufficiently frequent to occupy professional dealers; (d) that the commodity is one which is subject to price fluctuations.

Where future dealings take place the market is usually divided between brokers and dealers. The broker merely carries out the wishes of his client, whereas the dealer is the person who uses his expert knowledge to make a profit on what he considers will be the future price of the commodity. If he thinks that the price is likely to rise, he is known as a 'bull', and he will buy and accumulate stocks now in order to sell at a profit iater. On the other hand, if he thinks the price is going to fall, he is known as a 'bear' and he will sell stocks, even if he does not have them, hoping to buy at a lower price when delivery is due. At any time, a dealer will quote a price (according to the view he takes of the future movement of prices) at which he is prepared to buy or sell at some future date. Thus a cotton grower can cover himself against the risk of a fall in price by selling his produce forward at a price which will cover his cost of production and yield a reasonable profit, while a cotton spinner can quote a weaver a price for yarn and guard himself against loss by buying the raw cotton forward. Both are covered against adverse price changes, the risk being accepted by the dealer.

In doing this, the dealer usually performs the third main function of organised markets—the evening-out of price fluctuations due to changes in demand and supply. At a time when an increase in supply would cause the price to fall considerably, he adds his demand to the normal demand in order to build up his stocks, and thereby keeps the price up. On the other hand, when the good is in short supply, he releases stocks, and so prevents a violent rise in price. In this respect the dealer performs a parallel function to the wholesaler (*see* Chapter 8). The difficulty is that speculation on the future price may dominate the real forces which influence it, and then prices are subject to violent fluctuations in response to changes in optimism and pessimism.

III. FORCES DETERMINING PRICE

Demand and supply

'That animal was cheap', remarks Dan Archer as the auctioneer's hammer falls. 'And no wonder', replies Fred Barrett. 'This has been a long winter. We're now in the middle of April, and the grass is hardly growing. Hay is getting pretty short, I can tell you. It's mostly breeders who are bringing their cattle into the market today—they're being forced to sell quicker than they expected. Old Giles is about the only farmer who will take the risk of buying extra cattle to feed. When you come to think about it, Dan, it's many a year since you saw so many fine-looking animals knocked down at around £150.'

What can we learn from Fred Barrett's observations? Simply that the £150 at which the heifer was sold was not really determined by the final bid. The real factors producing the relatively low price were the reluctance of farmers to buy and the number of young animals being offered for sale. In short, the price was determined by the interaction of the forces of demand and supply. We shall examine each in turn.

Preliminary assumptions

Our first task must be to analyse how these forces work in an imaginary market—for eggs. To simplify our investigation, we shall assume:

(*a*) a single grade of eggs—all eggs are exactly the same in size and quality;

(*b*) no transport costs within the market;

(c) the market consists of so many relatively small buyers and sellers that there is keen competition;

(d) a *perfect market* in the sense that price differences are quickly eliminated, because buyers and sellers (i) have complete knowledge of prices and conditions in other parts of the market, and (ii) act solely on the basis of price;

(e) no interference by the government in the free operation of market forces, e.g. by price control, regulating supply, etc.

IV. DEMAND

Demand in economics is the desire to possess something and the willingness and the ability to pay a certain price in order to possess it. In other words, it is not merely a wish or a desire but an effective demand, that is, desire backed by money. It refers specifically to how much of a good persons would actually be willing to buy at a given price over a period of time.

For the purposes of exposition, it is helpful if we separate the factors affecting demand into: (1) price; (2) the conditions of demand.

(1) *Price, the conditions of demand remaining unchanged*

Normally a person will demand more of a good the lower its price. Why this is so will be shown later (Chapter 5). For the present it can be accepted because it conforms to our everyday observation. 'Winter sale, prices slashed' announce the shops when they wish to clear their stocks of winter clothing—and women scramble to secure cheap fur coats and woollen jumpers!

If we take a single commodity, say eggs, we can draw up a table showing how many eggs a person would be willing to buy at different prices. If they are very expensive, other foodstuffs will, as far as possible, be substituted; if they are cheap, persons may even pickle them. By adding up the demand of all buyers of eggs in the market at different prices for a given period of time it is possible to obtain a table for the whole market which we call a *market-demand schedule*. Let us assume that this is as follows:

DEMAND SCHEDULE FOR NONSUCH MARKET
FOR THE WEEK ENDING 26 JANUARY 1974

Price (pence per egg)	Eggs demanded (thousands)*
6	3
5	9
4	15
3	20
2	25
1	35

* What buyers would take at each price.

Note that this schedule does not tell us anything about the actual market price or how much is in fact sold. All it says is: '*If* the price is so much, then this quantity will be demanded.' It is an 'if' schedule.

This schedule can be plotted on a graph (Fig. 6). If we assume that demand can be plotted for all intermediary prices we obtain a demand curve *D*. It is now conventional for price to be measured up the *y*-axis and the quantity along the *x*-axis.

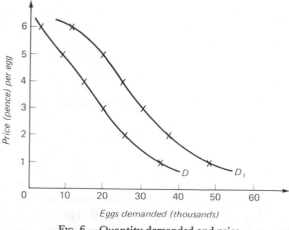

FIG. 6.—Quantity demanded and price.

(2) *The conditions of demand*

It may well happen that something occurs to cause house-wives to demand more or less eggs at each given price. In other words, the demand schedule is revised. Suppose, for instance, that farmers join together to run an advertising campaign describing new egg dishes. More eggs are now likely to be demanded at all prices. This gives us a revised demand schedule as follows:

Price (pence per egg)	Eggs demanded (thousands)
6	12
5	20
4	25
3	30
2	37
1	49

When we plot this revised demand schedule, we have a new curve, D_1, to the right of the old one. Had conditions so changed that demand decreased at all prices, the new demand curve would have been to the left of the old one.

The influence of both (a) price, and (b) the conditions of demand on the quantity demanded is thus shown on the graph. The former determines the shape of the demand curve—its slope downwards from left to right; the latter determines its position within the axes—an increase in demand shifting the curve to the right, a decrease to the left. To assist clarity of exposition, a change in demand resulting from a change in price of the commodity will in future be referred to as an *extension or contraction* of demand; a change in demand due to new conditions of demand will be described as an *increase or decrease* in demand.

Conditions of demand may change in a short period of time through:

(a) *A change in the price of other goods.* Because our incomes are limited nearly all goods, in that they compete for our limited income, are to some extent substitutes for one another. When the prices of other goods fall, the particular good under discussion becomes *relatively dearer*, and therefore less of it is demanded. When the prices of other goods rise, the particular good under discussion becomes relatively cheaper, and therefore more of it is demanded.

But the effect on the demand for the particular good is likely to be more pronounced where the good whose price has changed is a close substitute. Suppose that fried tomatoes are an alternative to eggs for breakfast. If now the price of tomatoes falls, housewives will tend to buy them rather than eggs. Thus although there has been no initial increase in the price of eggs, the demand for them has decreased. Similarly, where goods are complementary, a change in the price of one good has a pronounced effect on the demand for the other. For example, a fall in the price of cars results in more cars being purchased, and eventually this leads to an increase in the demand for tyres and petrol.

(b) *A change in tastes and fashion.* An advertising campaign on behalf of eggs would increase demand; a scare that eggs were the source of an infection would decrease it.

(c) *Expectations of future price changes or shortages.* The fear that the price of eggs may rise considerably the following week will induce people to increase their demand now in order to have eggs in stock.

(d) *Government policy.* A selective tax on eggs paid by the consumer, by increasing the price, would decrease demand; a rebate paid to the consumer would increase it (*see* Chapter 29).

In the longer period, a change in the conditions of demand can result from:

(e) *A change in real income.* If there was an all-round increase in income, people could afford more eggs, and demand would probably increase. On the other hand, it might now be possible to afford mushrooms for breakfast, and these would take the place of eggs (*see* p. 83).

(f) *Greater equality in the distribution of wealth.* The wealth of a country may be so distributed that there are a few exceptionally rich persons whereas the remainder are exceedingly poor. If many poor persons felt they could not afford eggs, greater equality of wealth would be likely to increase the demand for eggs.

(g) *A change in the size or composition of the population.* Additional people coming into the market increase demand, especially if eggs figure prominently in their diet.

V. SUPPLY

Supply in economics refers to how much of a good will be offered for sale at a given price over a given period of time. As with demand, this quantity depends on (1) the price of the good, and (2) the conditions of supply.

(1) *Price, the conditions of supply remaining unchanged*

Normally more of a good will be supplied the higher its price. The real reason for this is explained in Chapter 12. But even a brief consideration of how the individual farmer reacts to a change in price will show that it is likely to be true. If the price of eggs is high, he will probably consume fewer himself in order to send as many as possible to market. Moreover, the higher price would allow him to give his chickens more food so that they would lay a few extra eggs. When we extend our analysis to the market supply, it is obvious that a higher price for eggs would enable other farmers—the less efficient—to go in for egg production.

Hence we are able to draw up a *market-supply schedule* for eggs. This consists of the total amounts supplied at different prices by all the sellers in the market for a given period of time. Let us assume that this is as follows:

SUPPLY SCHEDULE FOR NONSUCH MARKET
FOR THE WEEK ENDING 26 JANUARY 1974

Price (pence per egg)	Eggs supplied (thousands)*
6	40
5	32
4	25
3	20
2	13
1	7

* What sellers would offer at each price.

Once again it must be noted that this is an 'if' schedule, for all it says is: '*If* the price is so much, then this quantity will be offered for sale.'

We can plot this schedule (Fig. 7), and, assuming supply can be obtained for all intermediate prices, obtain a supply curve *S*.

There is a fundamental difference between demand and supply. Whereas demand can respond almost immediately to a change in price, a period of time must usually elapse before supply can be fully adjusted. For the first day or two the only way in which the farmer can send more eggs to market because their price has risen is by eating fewer himself. By the end of the week, he may have increased output by giving the hens more

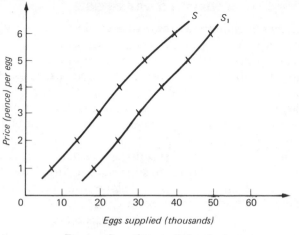

FIG. 7.—Quantity supplied and price.

food or by leaving the light on in the hen-house all night; the higher price covers the extra cost. But, to obtain any sizeable increase, the farmer must add to his hens; if all farmers are following the same policy, this will take about five months, the period required to rear laying hens from chicks.

These different periods of time are dealt with more fully in Chapter 11. Put simply, each period of time produces a supply curve of a different slope.

(2) *The conditions of supply*

The number of eggs supplied may change although there has been no alteration in the price. In the spring, for instance, chickens lay more eggs, and in the autumn less. Thus more eggs will be supplied at all prices in the spring, and fewer in the autumn. In other words, the supply schedule changes from time to time. A new supply schedule for the spring could read as follows:

Price (pence per egg)	Eggs supplied (thousands)
6	50
5	43
4	36
3	30
2	25
1	19

This new schedule shows that, whereas in winter only 25,000 eggs were supplied at 4p each, during the spring 36,000 could be supplied at that price. Or, looked at in another way, 25,000 eggs can be supplied in the spring at 2p each compared with 4p each in the winter. When plotted, the revised supply schedule gives a new supply curve, S_1, to the right of the old one. Had supply decreased, the new supply curve would have been to the left.

Like demand, therefore, supply is influenced by both (1) price, and (2) the conditions of supply. The former determines the shape of the curve—its upward slope from left to right. The latter determines its position within the axes—an increase in supply shifts the curve to the right, a decrease to the left. To distinguish between the two, we shall refer to a change in supply resulting from a change in price of the commodity as an *extension* or *contraction* of supply; a change in supply due to new conditions of supply will be described as an *increase* or *decrease* in supply.

In general, conditions of supply may change fairly quickly through:

(a) *A change in the prices of other goods, especially when it is easy to shift resources into producing those goods.* Suppose there is a considerable increase in the price of chicken meat, including boiling fowls. It may now pay the farmer to kill some of his laying pullets. Thus fewer eggs are supplied at the old price.

(b) *A change in the prices of factors of production.* A fall in the cost of pullets or of their feeding-stuffs would reduce the cost of egg production. As a result, more eggs could be supplied at the old price, or, looked at in another way, the original quantity could be produced at a lower price per egg. A rise in the wages of workers on chicken farms would have the opposite effect.

(c) *Changes resulting from nature,* e.g. the weather, floods, drought, pest, or from *abnormal circumstances,* e.g. war, fire political events.

(d) *Government policy.* A tax on the output of eggs or an increase in the employer's contribution to the farm workers' National Insurance would result in fewer eggs being offered for sale at the old price. That is, the supply curve moves to the left. A subsidy, on the other hand, by decreasing costs, would move the supply curve to the right (*see* Chapter 29).

Other changes in supply take a longer period of time. Such changes can occur through:

(*e*) *Improved techniques.* Technical improvements reduce costs of production, shifting the supply curve to the right. Thus automatic feeding appliances might be developed, or selective breeding produce hens which would lay more eggs over a given period.

(*f*) *The discovery of new or the exhaustion of old supplies of raw materials.*

(*g*) *The entry of new firms into the industry.*

VI. THE DETERMINATION OF PRICE

The demand and supply curves can be combined in a single diagram (Fig. 8):

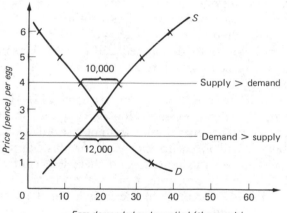

FIG. 8.—The determination of equilibrium price.

Now let us show the economist at work as he establishes principles. Remember our original assumptions were:

(1) many relatively small buyers and sellers;

(2) keen competition between buyers, between sellers, and between buyers and sellers.

We must add to these our two assumptions (we shall put them on a firmer footing later) regarding demand and supply:

(3) more will be demanded at a lower price than at a higher price;

(4) less will be supplied at a lower price than at a higher price. These two assumptions are illustrated by the slope of the demand and supply curves in Fig. 8.

Given assumptions (3) and (4), the two curves slope in opposite directions. Thus they cut at a single point—in our example where the price is 3p. The economist predicts that in Nonsuch market, where these conditions of demand and supply exist, the price of eggs will move towards and eventually settle at 3p. He calls this price *the equilibrium or market price*.

This proposition can be proved as follows. Suppose that initially the price of eggs is fixed at 4p. Here 15,000 will be demanded but 25,000 supplied. There is thus an excess supply of 10,000. This means that sellers are left with surplus supplies. Competition between sellers means that some are willing to sell their supplies at less than 4p. Thus the price falls. As this happens, some supplies are withdrawn from the market, and there is an extension of demand. This continues until a price of 3p is reached, when there is no excess of supply over demand, 20,000 eggs being both demanded and offered for sale. Thus 3p is the only price at which there is harmony between buyers and sellers.

Similarly, if the initial price is 2p, 25,000 will be demanded but only 13,000 offered for sale. Housewives queue to buy eggs, and sellers see that their supplies will not last out. Competition among buyers will force up the price. As this happens more supplies are put on the market, and there is a contraction of demand. This continues until a price of 3p is reached. Then there is no impulse for price to rise further, for demand equals supply at 20,000 eggs.

VII. CHANGES IN THE CONDITIONS OF DEMAND AND SUPPLY

The equilibrium price will persist until there is a change in the conditions of either demand or supply. Let us commence with our market price of 3p.

Suppose tastes alter, and people eat more eggs. The conditions of demand have now changed, and the demand curve shifts to the right from D to D_1 (Fig. 9).

At the original price of 3p we now have an excess of demand over supply—30,000 eggs are demanded, but only 20,000

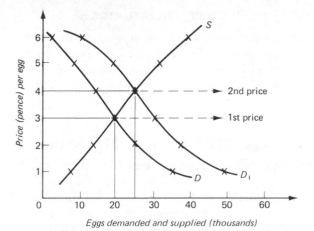

FIG. 9.—The effect on price of a change in the conditions of demand.

supplied. As explained in the previous section, competition amongst buyers will now force the price up—to 4p—where 25,000 eggs are both demanded and supplied.

Similarly a decrease in demand, resulting, for instance, from a significant fall in the price of tomatoes, would cause the curve to shift to the left and the price of eggs to fall (*see* pp. 60–1).

Likewise, a change may occur in the conditions of supply. At any given price, more eggs can be produced during the spring than at other periods of the year, and so the supply curve shifts to the right from S to S_1 (Fig. 10).

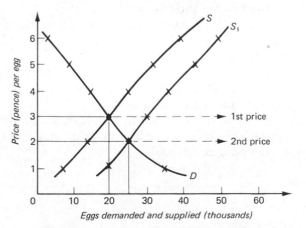

FIG. 10.—The effect on price of a change in the conditions of supply.

At the original price of 3p we now have an excess supply over demand—30,000 eggs are supplied, but only 20,000 are demanded. Here competition amongst sellers will mean that the price falls to 2p, where 25,000 eggs are both demanded and supplied.

VIII. THE 'LAWS' OF PRICE

Our analysis above has been based on three main assumptions:

(1) the demand curve slopes downwards from left to right;

(2) the supply curve slopes upwards from left to right;

(3) market conditions are such that an excess of demand over supply causes price to rise; an excess of supply over demand causes price to fall.

The conclusions which we can derive are of such general application that they can be termed 'laws'. They can be stated as follows:

(1) Price tends to make equal the amount which buyers wish to buy and the amount which sellers are prepared to offer for sale.

(2) Price will settle at one point—where the quantity offered for sale equals the quantity demanded.

(3) An increase in demand (that is, a shift of the demand curve to the right) will lead to a rise in price and in the quantity bought and sold.

(4) A decrease in demand (that is, a shift of the demand curve to the left) will lead to a fall in price and in the quantity bought and sold.

(5) An increase in supply (that is, a shift in the supply curve to the right) will lead to a fall in price and a rise in the quantity bought and sold.

(6) A decrease in supply (that is, a shift in the supply curve to the left) will lead to a rise in price and a fall in the quantity bought and sold.

CHAPTER 4

APPLICATIONS OF DEMAND AND SUPPLY ANALYSIS

WE have shown how price is determined in the free market, illustrating the explanation with demand and supply curves. Our task now is to show how this analysis can be applied to practical problems, especially those relating to government policy. First, we consider questions concerned with the role of price in the free enterprise economy; second, we look at other problems and examine how demand and supply analysis can help.

I. THE FUNCTIONS OF PRICE IN THE FREE MARKET

In a free market, price both indicates and motivates.

(1) It 'rations out' scarce goods

At any one time the supply of a good is relatively fixed. It therefore has to be apportioned among the many people wanting it. This is done by adjusting price. As price rises, demand contracts; as it falls, demand expands. At the equilibrium price, demand just equals the supply. Should supply increase, the total quantity can still be disposed of by lowering the price; should supply decrease, price would have to be raised.

We can illustrate how price works by considering two current problems:

(a) *Who shall be allowed to park his car in a congested area?* There is traffic congestion in the centre of Barthem City because of the many cars parked at the kerbside. The City Council decide that this is because parking is a free good—it costs motorists nothing to park their cars. It is decided to limit car-parking to one side of the road and to 800 places, each with a parking meter. The demand schedule for 2-hour parking is estimated to be as follows:

Price (pence)	Demand
30	450
20	800
10	1,200
0	1,800

The Council therefore fixes a charge of 20p. The 1,000 motorists who will not pay this price do not, therefore, bring their cars into the City centre.

(b) *Why do 'spivs' obtain such high prices for Cup Final tickets?* To ensure that the regular football supporter who watches his team from the terraces each Saturday shall be able to afford a Cup Final ticket, prices are fixed by the Football Association. Let us simplify the argument by assuming that the Football Association has one price, £1, for the 100,000 tickets, but that a free-market price would be £3. In Fig. 11, when the price is £3 demand equals the available supply of 100,000 but at the controlled price of £1 demand exceeds supply by 150,000.

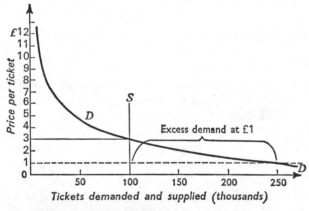

Fig. 11.—Excess demand for Cup Final tickets.

But some tickets are obtained by 'spivs', buyers who wish merely to resell at a profit. These tickets are sold in a free market, where demand and supply determine price. The demand comes from those keen club supporters not lucky enough to be allocated a ticket but willing to pay more than £1. As the price rises, some persons possessing tickets may be induced to sell them to the touts. Thus the demand and supply curves are roughly as shown in Fig. 12, giving a 'spiv-market' price of £10.

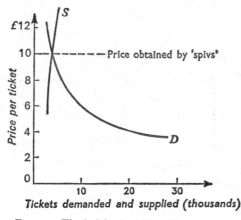

FIG. 12.—The 'spiv' price of Cup Final tickets.

An important conclusion can be drawn from this example: where price is controlled below the market price, only some form of rationing can ensure that everybody gets a share of the limited supply. Normally this is achieved by the Football Association, which, after allocating so many tickets to each finalist, limits each affiliated club to approximately two. The alternative would simply be a 'first come, first served' method of distribution, penalising those who could not queue and increasing the scope for spiv activity. For this reason, when the government controlled prices during the war, it also rationed what it considered were necessities.

(2) It indicates changes in wants

Even if a planning authority organised production, it would still find it advantageous to introduce a modified form of price system. This is because prices are the signals by which the community indicates the extent to which different goods are wanted and any changes in those wants.

Consider how the demand for housing accommodation in London has increased since the war, partly through the pressure of population and partly through the rise in real income. As a result, rents have risen from OP to OP_1 (Fig. 13).

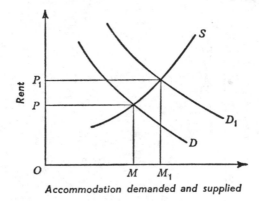

FIG. 13.—The effect on rents of an increase in the demand for accommodation.

(3) *It induces supply to respond to changes in demand*

When demand increases, price rises and supply expands; when demand decreases, price falls and supply contracts. Thus in the diagram above, the increase in price has made it profitable for extra housing accommodation, equivalent to MM_1, to be supplied. This has been achieved by converting existing houses into flats and by building a number of small houses on a site formerly occupied by one large house.

In Chapters 11 and 12 we explain in more detail how supply responds to changes in demand.

(4) *It indicates changes in the conditions upon which goods can be supplied*

Since our resources are limited, more of one good can be produced only at the expense of producing fewer other goods. If the cost of producing a given commodity rises, this should be signalled to consumers who can then decide to what extent they are prepared to pay these higher costs by forgoing other goods. Again this is achieved through price. Assume in Fig. 14 that costs have risen in producing a good x because the raw materials have risen in price. Where demand is depicted by D, most consumers pay the higher costs (price rises by PP_1)

rather than do without the good. Where demand is depicted by D_1, consumers tend to forgo having the good when its price rises (demand falls by MM_1), substituting other goods for it.

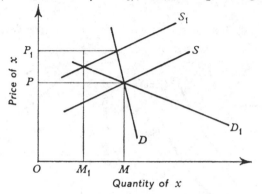

FIG. 14.—The effect of a change in the conditions of supply on price and quantity traded.

(5) *It rewards the factors of production*

When the price of a good rises, producers can afford to offer a higher reward to the factors they use in order to attract them from other uses. Such rewards give the owners of the factors of production spending power. In this way the division (or, as it is more usually termed, the 'distribution') of the cake which has been produced is determined. (Chapter 15 will consider in more detail the rewards to factors of production.)

II. FURTHER APPLICATIONS

(1) *Why do the prices of agricultural products fluctuate more than the prices of manufactured goods?*

Price changes occur because of changes in the conditions of demand and supply. Generally speaking, the conditions of demand for both agricultural products and manufactured goods are, over not too long a period, fairly stable. But the supply of agricultural products, unlike that of manufactured goods, varies from season to season, and, because of weather, plant disease, and farmer's decisions, from year to year. Nor is storage easy, particularly in the case of foodstuffs. Thus the amount of agricultural products coming on the market fluctuates considerably, and so prices also fluctuate. The difference between the two can be seen by comparing tomatoes and carpets (Fig. 15). Whereas the price of tomatoes varies between OP_1 and OP_2, that of carpets remains steady at OR.

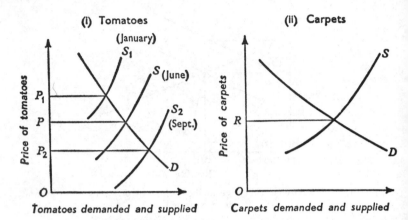

FIG. 15.—Fluctuations in the prices of tomatoes and carpets.

(2) *How would an increase in the demand for cars affect the price of tyres?*

Cars and tyres are 'jointly demanded'. With such goods, prices move in the same direction. This can be seen in Fig. 16. The increased demand for cars leads to an increased demand

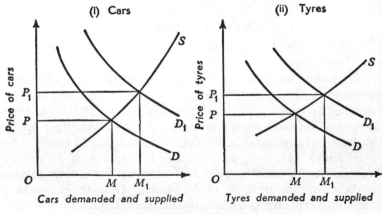

FIG. 16.—Joint demand.

for tyres, and the prices of both rise. (Later it will be shown how slight modifications could be made to the supply curve for tyres to allow for differences in the length of time under consideration (*see* p. 188).)

(3) *How would an increase in the price of petrol affect the price of paraffin?*

Petrol and paraffin are 'jointly supplied'; an increased production of one automatically increases the production of the other. Suppose that demand for petrol increases, but that there is no change in the demand for paraffin. The price of petrol rises from OP to OP_1, and supply expands from OM to OM_1 (Fig. 17). But this means that the supply of paraffin is automatically increased, although there has been no change in

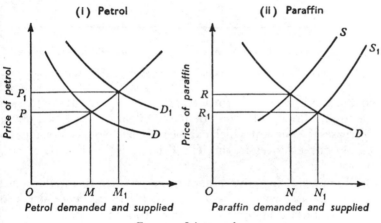

(i) Petrol   (ii) Paraffin

Petrol demanded and supplied   Paraffin demanded and supplied

FIG. 17.—Joint supply.

price. Thus the supply curve for paraffin moves from S to S_1, and the price of paraffin falls from OR to OR_1. In practice it is probable that the oil companies would try to increase the demand for paraffin, e.g. by advertising oil-fired central heating. If this proved successful, the price of paraffin would recover.

(4) *How could the government secure the use of solid fuel rather than oil for central heating?*

Here the government must endeavour to reduce the price of coal and to increase the price of oil by operating on the supply sides. To aid coal, it could give producers a subsidy or reduce railway-transport charges. On the other hand, oil could be penalised by the imposition of a tax, either when it is imported or sold. The position is shown in Fig. 18. Subsidies allow more

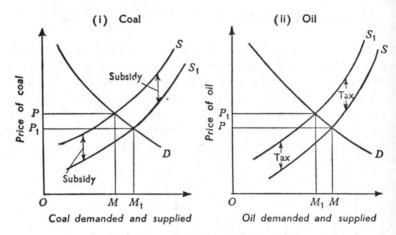

FIG. 18.—The effect on quantity bought of a subsidy and tax.

coal to be supplied at all prices, and the supply curve moves to the right. Price falls, and demand expands. The tax on oil decreases the amount which can be sold at the old prices, and the supply curve moves to the left. Price rises, and demand contracts.

Of course, if the government does not wish to interfere with supply in these ways, it will have to try to influence demand, e.g. by advertising central heating using solid fuel.

CHAPTER 5

A FURTHER LOOK AT DEMAND

I. WHY THE DEMAND CURVE NORMALLY SLOPES DOWNWARDS

OUR conclusion in Chapter 3—that more of a good will be demanded the lower its price—was based solely on our everyday observations of how buyers act in a market. Can we, by explaining *why* people demand more of a good as its price falls, put this conclusion on firmer ground?

The answer is 'yes'; and we shall use what is known as the 'marginal utility theory'. Other theories, such as the indifference curve analysis or revealed preference, may, from the point of view of method, be more satisfying, but the marginal utility theory is shorter to explain and often more useful in future analysis.

Our method of approach will be as follows. Our main interest is in the market demand curve. But the market demand is made up of the demand of all the individuals who comprise the market. If, therefore, we study the behaviour of the individual buyer as he spends his income, and it can be said that other buyers act similarly, we can conclude that the market and individual patterns of behaviour are similar.

Maximising satisfaction

We will assume that every individual has limited resources—represented by a limited money income—and that each acts 'rationally'. 'Rational' must not be interpreted in a value sense as being 'sensible'. It might not be sensible for an individual to spend a large part of his income on cigarettes, but that is up to him. All the economist means by 'rational' is that the individual is consistent in his behaviour in the sense that he tries to get the most out of his limited resources. This is a reasonable assumption. There may be the odd consumer who acts frivolously, but since we are dealing with a relatively large number of consumers in the market, we can think of a typical consumer who does act 'rationally'.

Because resources are limited, buying one good involves going without something else. In disposing of incomes, therefore, persons weigh up the various 'opportunity costs', and try to obtain the maximum satisfaction from their expenditure. Normally their choice does not necessitate making an absolute decision between one good and another, but rather presents itself as whether to have a little more of this by sacrificing a little bit of that.

Here again it might be questioned whether the consumer really does follow this careful procedure. How many people when purchasing a good weigh up its pros and cons and compare it, according to its price, with other goods? Surely, most expenditure is purely automatic? Admittedly, much expenditure is habitual—but this does not mean that people give no thought to it. Our immediate reaction to a selective increase in tax on petrol or cigarettes, for instance, is to ask whether we cannot make do with less. In any case, following a routine for minor matters (including everyday purchases) allows more time for thinking about those things which are outside the usual run of events. Thus while we may not consciously consider the satisfactions to be obtained from other goods every time we buy a packet of cigarettes, we are careful when furnishing a home to weigh up the merits and price of a refrigerator as opposed to a washing-machine.

Questions to be answered

There are three basic questions we have to answer:
(1) What conditions will hold when the consumer has obtained the maximum satisfaction from his limited resources? In other words, what are the equilibrium conditions?
(2) How does the consumer achieve this equilibrium?
(3) What happens when the equilibrium is disturbed by a price change?
Let us deal with each in turn.

Preliminary assumptions

(a) Our consumer is a housewife;

(b) she has a limited housekeeping allowance per week;

(c) she acts rationally to maximise satisfaction from this limited income;

(d) during the period of time under consideration, income and tastes do not change;

(e) she knows how much satisfaction each unit of a good will give;

(f) she is one of a large number of buyers; as a result her demand does not directly affect the price of the good.

(1) *The equilibrium condition*

Our housewife will be in equilibrium when she would not switch a single penny of her expenditure on one good to spending on another.

We can be more explicit by introducing the term 'utility'. In economics, this simply means that a good has the power to satisfy a want. No attempt is made to say whether the good is useful or commendable. That a good has utility merely implies that it is wanted by somebody. Note, too, that we cannot measure utility; like love, pain or fear, it is purely subjective to the individual.

Our housewife, it has been assumed, knows in her own mind how much satisfaction each good affords her—the utility she derives from it. She is in equilibrium, therefore, when she has obtained the greatest possible utility from her income. In other words, her objective is to maximise total utility.

She does this by a careful allocation of her limited income as she purchases a variety of goods. All the time she is asking: 'If I spend a penny more on cheese, will I obtain more or less utility than if I spent the penny on margarine?' She will not be in equilibrium until the utility from the last penny spent on good *A* (in the sense of the penny she only just decided to spend) is equal to the last penny spent on good *B*, and so on. Her adjustment is a borderline one—it takes place at the *margin*.

Note that we did *not* say that she obtained the same utility from the last pound of cheese as she obtained from the last pound of margarine. If, for instance, cheese were four times as expensive as margarine, that would obviously be unreasonable. We should expect four times the amount of utility if we were spending four times on one good what we were spending on another.

Sometimes, however, we cannot buy goods in 'pennyworths' —the good is 'lumpy' and we have to take a whole 'lump' of it or nothing at all. Can we re-state our equilibrium condition to allow for this? We can do so if we first define more carefully this concept of the margin and what we mean by 'marginal utility'.

Each small addition to a given supply of a good is called the *marginal increment*, and the utility derived from this increment is known as the *marginal utility*. Our original condition of equilibrium can therefore be stated as:

$$\frac{\text{The marginal utility of 1p}}{\text{spent on good } A} = \frac{\text{The marginal utility of 1p}}{\text{spent on good } B, \text{ etc.}}$$

But the marginal utility of 1p spent on good A depends on how much of a unit of good A you get for 1p Thus:

$$\frac{\text{The marginal utility of 1p}}{\text{spent on good } A} = \frac{\text{The marginal utility of one unit of good } A}{\text{The number of pennies it costs to buy a unit of good } A}$$

Similarly with good B. Thus our original equilibrium condition can be rewritten as:

$$\frac{\text{The marginal utility of one unit of good } A}{\text{Price of a unit of } A \text{ in pennies}} = \frac{\text{The marginal utility of one unit of good } B}{\text{Price of a unit of } B \text{ in pennies}}$$

That is:

$$\frac{\text{Marginal utility of good } A}{\text{Price of } A} = \frac{\text{Marginal utility of good } B}{\text{Price of } B}$$

Put in another way, if we want to state the equilibrium position by comparing the marginal utilities derived from quantities of different goods, then we have to 'weight' those utilities by the price of the given quantity by dividing it into the marginal utility of that particular quantity.

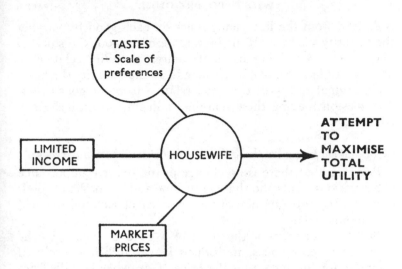

FIG. 19.—Factors affecting the equilibrium of the housewife.

(2) How does the consumer achieve this equilibrium?

The question must now be asked: 'How can our housewife arrange that the utility of the last penny spent on different goods shall be the same?' The answer is to be found in the so-called *law of diminishing marginal utility.* Although wants vary considerably in their nature, they all possess the underlying characteristic that in a given period they can be satisfied fairly quickly. Thus, if a person drinks lemonade to quench his thirst, the first glass will yield him a great amount of satisfaction. Indeed, the second glass may be equally satisfying. But it is doubtful whether he will relish the third glass to the same extent, since his thirst has now been partially quenched. If he continues to drink the lemonade, there will come a time when a glass gives him no additional satisfaction whatsoever and, in fact, might be that he would be better off without it—there is a *disutility.* We can therefore state a general rule that the utility derived from any given addition to a consumer's stock of a good will eventually decline as the supply increase, tastes and the consumption of all other goods remaining unchanged.

This means that our housewife, who knows how much utility she will derive from an additional unit of a good compared with another unit of any other good, can arrange that **equal utility** is derived from the last penny spent on each good by varying the quantity she buys. If she buys more of a good, the stock of other goods remaining fixed, its marginal utility relative to other goods falls. Similarly, if she reduces the quantity she buys, the marginal utility of the good relative to other goods rises. She goes on making these marginal adjustments until she is in equilibrium.

(3) *What happens when the equilibrium is disturbed by a price change?*

Provided that there is no change in the relative importance of her various wants and that her income and the prices of goods remain constant, our housewife's pattern of expenditure will remain unaltered.

But what happens if the price of a good changes? In the language of economists, it disturbs her equilibrium position. Suppose, for instance, that the price of strawberries falls from 20p to 15p per lb., the prices of other goods remaining unchanged. How will this affect her demand for strawberries? We can proceed in either of two ways:

(*a*) The fall in the price of strawberries will enable her to obtain more strawberries than before for every penny, including the last, which she was spending on them. More strawberries usually implies greater total satisfaction. The last penny she was spending on strawberries, therefore, now yields a greater satisfaction than the last penny being spent on other goods. Hence she now reduces the utility obtained from the last penny spent on strawberries by buying more strawberries.

(*b*) The alternative form of the equilibrium condition is:

$$\frac{\text{The marginal utility of last lb. of strawberries}}{\text{Price of lb. strawberries}} = \frac{\text{The marginal utility of } B, \text{etc.}}{\text{Price of } B}$$

A fall in the price of strawberries destroys this relationship; the marginal utility of strawberries to their price is now higher than with goods B, C, etc. To restore the equilibrium relationship, the marginal utility of strawberries must be decreased. Hence our housewife buys more strawberries.

The reasons for this expansion in the demand for strawberries can be analysed more closely. A reduction in the price of strawberries means that our housewife is now able to purchase all the strawberries she had before and still have money left over. This is an *income* effect of a price fall—she can now buy more of all goods, not only of strawberries. But in addition to this 'income effect' of a price fall, more strawberries will tend to be bought because of a 'substitution effect'. At the margin it means that a penny spent on strawberries will now yield more satisfaction than a penny spent on other fruits. Thus strawberries are substituted for other fruits. If strawberries are a good substitute, then marginal utility will diminish comparatively slowly as the consumption of strawberries increases. A given price fall, therefore, will lead to a considerable increase in the quantity of strawberries demanded.

II. EXCEPTIONAL DEMAND CURVES

Normally the demand curve slopes downwards from left to right, showing that demand extends as price falls. It is possible, however, to envisage circumstances in which the reverse occurs—a fall in price bringing about a contraction of demand, and a rise in price an extension.

(1) *Inferior goods*

Certain goods can be termed 'inferior' in that they are bought in large quantities only when a person's income is small, people preferring other goods when their incomes rise. Margarine, bread, cheap cuts of meat, and low-quality floor-coverings are examples.

Now with most goods, e.g. strawberries, demand is likely to increase with a rise in income. The income effect on demand of a price fall will therefore be positive, reinforcing the substitution effect which is always in a positive direction. But with inferior goods the income effect on demand is negative, working in the opposite direction to the substitution effect. Take the case of margarine. A fall in its price would result in a tendency to substitute it for butter; but the income effect would work in the opposite direction, people tending to replace margarine with butter. If the income effect were greater than the substitution effect the net result would be that less margarine would be demanded at the lower price.

The income effect of a price fall will be more significant the greater the proportion of one's income spent on the good. And, if a large part of one's income is spent on an 'inferior' good (as may happen when income is low), the income effect will not only be considerable but negative, possibly outweighing the positive substitution effect. Suppose, for instance, that a person is so poor that he has to spend 40 per cent of his income on bread in order to obtain the necessary calories to live. Now suppose that a loaf of bread falls in price from 10p to 5p per lb. The same amount of bread can now be obtained for only 20 per cent of his money income, the other 20 per cent being available for spending on different goods. In other words, there has been a substantial increase in real income. As he is now better off, it is quite likely that the person will want a more varied diet. Foods, other than bread, will be bought but, since they will yield calories formerly provided by bread, they will tend to replace bread, the demand for which will thus contract although its price has fallen.

The above is really an extreme case. What is an 'inferior' good depends largely upon one's level of income. Take a cheap joint of meat, for instance. To a particular person this may be an 'inferior' good, the negative income effect of a price fall outweighing the substitution effect. But there would also be poor people who could not have afforded this joint at the old price. For them both the income effect and the substitution effect of a price fall would be positive. Thus, when we look at the *market* demand curve (as opposed to an individual's demand curve), we could easily find that it follows the normal shape, showing that more is demanded as price falls.

(2) *Price movements are linked with expectations*

With certain goods, expectations are an integral part of demand. The best example is securities bought and sold on the Stock Exchange where a person's current demand is largely determined by what he thinks will be the price of the security in the future. In this case, a rise or fall in the price of a security may well be associated with a larger or smaller quantity respectively being demanded, for people think that the rise or fall will continue.

(3) Goods having 'snob appeal'

Certain goods, e.g. diamonds, model gowns, and mink coats, may be wanted chiefly for ostentation—the desire to impress others. Should the price of such a good fall so much that it comes within the reach of many more people, original purchasers may no longer want it. Hence total demand could be less. Here again, however, we must distinguish between the individual and market demand curves. Although 'snob' buyers may leave the market when the price of the good falls, it is likely that large numbers of new buyers would enter, thereby adding to demand at these lower prices.

In each of the above types of situation, we have analysed the abnormality of the demand curve as a direct link between price and demand. With all three, however, we cannot ignore the fact that there is a close connection with changes in the conditions of demand. The first has a change in income, the second a change in expectations, and the third a change in tastes. Our theory explaining consumers' behaviour should be able to cope at one and the same time with a change in conditions of demand which are implicit in a change of price. It is a weakness of the marginal-utility approach that it fails to do so.

III. ELASTICITY OF DEMAND

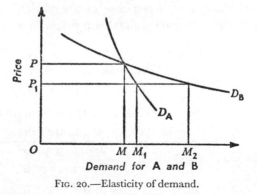

FIG. 20.—Elasticity of demand.

Consider Fig. 20. At price OP, demand for both commodities A and B is OM. But when the price of both falls by PP_1, demand for A expands by only MM_1, whereas that for B

expands by MM_2. In other words, there are differences in the responsiveness of demand to a change in price. We measure the degree of responsiveness by what is known as 'elasticity of demand'.

Measurement of elasticity of demand

Elasticity of demand always refers to the elasticity at a particular price, and in what follows, when we talk about 'elasticity' it will be assumed that there is some price in mind.

Elasticity of demand is defined by comparing the *rate* at which demand expands to the *rate* at which price falls. If the former is greater than the latter, we say that demand is elastic; if it is smaller, we say that demand is inelastic. When they are equal, elasticity of demand is said to be equal to unity. Using this definition, elasticity of demand can be measured in two ways. One is direct, showing the degree of elasticity; the other is indirect, merely indicating whether the demand for the good is elastic or inelastic.

(1) *A direct comparison of the rate at which demand changes with the rate at which price changes*

When we wish to compare *rates* of change, we have to work in terms of proportionate (or percentage) changes. We can therefore define elasticity of demand as the proportionate change in the amount demanded in response to a small change in price divided by the proportionate change in price. That is,

$$\text{Elasticity of demand} = \frac{\text{Proportionate change in demand}}{\text{Proportionate change in price}}$$

$$= \frac{\dfrac{\text{Change in quantity demanded}}{\text{Original quantity demanded}}}{\dfrac{\text{Change in price}}{\text{Original price}}}$$

$$= \frac{\dfrac{\text{New quantity} - \text{Old quantity}}{\text{Old quantity}}}{\dfrac{\text{New price} - \text{Old price}}{\text{Old price}}}$$

We can illustrate by an example from the demand schedule on page 59. When price falls from 5p to 4p, demand for eggs expands from 9,000 to 15,000. Elasticity of demand is thus equal to

$$\frac{\dfrac{6,000}{9,000}}{\dfrac{1}{5}} = \frac{\dfrac{2}{3}}{\dfrac{1}{5}} = 3\tfrac{1}{3}.$$

Similarly, for a fall in price from 2p to 1p, elasticity of demand equals $\tfrac{4}{5}$.

It will be noted that there is a difference in elasticity when we measure for a price rise or a price fall. Thus when price fell from 5p to 4p, elasticity was $3\tfrac{1}{3}$; but when it rises from 4p to 5p, elasticity is $1\tfrac{3}{5}$. The difference occurs because we were measuring the price change from different prices and for a relatively large change. Were the price change only $\tfrac{1}{2}$p instead of 1p, the two results would be more nearly equal. Where the price change is infinitely small, measurement of elasticity of demand is at the same point, and there is only one elasticity.

(2) *A comparison of total outlay as price changes*

For the purpose of economic analysis, it is usually sufficient to refer to elasticity of demand in broad terms. Where elasticity is greater than 1 (the change in the quantity demanded is more than proportionate to the change in price), we say demand is elastic. Where it is less than 1 (the change in the quantity demanded is less than proportionate to the change in price), we say demand is inelastic. If it is 1 (the change in the quantity demanded being proportionate to the change in price), elasticity is described as being equal to unity.

This broad approach can be used to measure elasticity in a slightly different way. If the proportionate expansion in demand is greater than the proportionate change in price, the total amount spent on the good will increase. In other words, demand is elastic when, in response to a fall in price, total outlay increases; or, in response to a rise in price, total outlay decreases. Similarly, demand is inelastic when, in response to a fall in price, total outlay decreases; or, in response to a rise in price, total outlay increases. Demand is equal to unity when, as price changes, total outlay remains the same.

The rule can be remembered as follows:

Price change, then total outlay changes in *opposite* direction— Demand elastic;

Price change, then total outlay changes in *same* direction—Demand inelastic.

Thus, with the demand schedule on p. 59, we have:

Price of eggs (pence)	Demand (thousands)	Total outlay (pence)	
5	9	45,000	Elastic demand
4	15	60,000	
3	20	60,000	Inelastic demand
2	25	50,000	

Between 4p and 3p, elasticity of demand equals unity.

Important points regarding elasticity of demand

(1) *Demand curves are unlikely to have the same elasticity throughout their length.* Thus for the demand schedule on page 59, we have seen that demand is elastic at prices above 4p and inelastic at prices below 3p.

(2) *The important exceptions to the above*, when elasticity of demand is the same throughout the whole length of the curve, are:

(a) *Demand absolutely inelastic*, people buying exactly the same amount of a commodity whatever its price (Fig. 21a).

(b) *Demand perfectly elastic*, people ceasing to buy the commodity at all if its price rises slightly (Fig. 21b). This is the demand curve for his good which faces an individual seller under conditions of perfect competition (*see* p. 169).

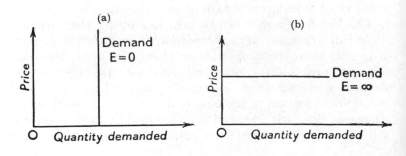

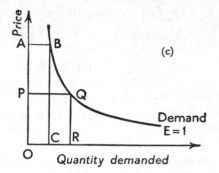

FIG. 21.—Constant elasticities of demand.

(c) *Elasticity of demand equal to unity*, where total outlay is constant at all prices. The curve here is known as a rectangular hyperbola, and all rectangles representing outlay (price × quantity demanded) are equal. For example, rectangle OABC equals rectangle OPQR.

(3) *Any other straight-line demand curve has a different elasticity of demand for each different price.* Take the demand curve D_A (Fig. 22), for example:

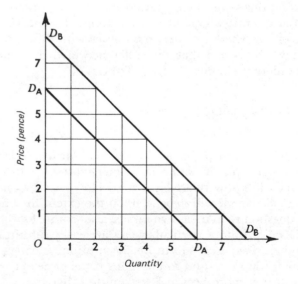

FIG. 22.—Elasticity of a straight-line demand curve.

For a price fall of a penny, (a) at 5p, elasticity of demand is 5; (b) at 2p, elasticity of demand is $\frac{1}{2}$.

The reason for this is that although a straight-sloping line means that demand changes by a constant amount for a given price change, the *rate* at which price itself is falling depends on the price from which we start. This rate will therefore be higher for a given price change the lower the price under consideration.

(4) Usually we cannot compare the elasticities of demand of different goods by comparing the slopes of the respective demand curves. The slope of the demand curve depends not only upon elasticity of demand, but also on the vertical and horizontal scales chosen. Furthermore, even if the same scales are chosen for different commodities, we cannot safely say that, where the demand curve for one commodity slopes more steeply than another, the demand for the first commodity is less elastic. Compare, for example, the parallel demand curves D_A and D_B above. At the same price of 4p, elasticity of demand for commodity A is equal to 2, while for commodity B it is equal to 1.

The reason for the difference is that, although we have taken the same price, we have started measuring proportionate changes in quantity demanded from different quantities. Only at the position where two demand curves with different slopes cut, can we be *certain* that the difference in their slopes will reflect a difference in the elasticity of demand.

Factors determining elasticity of demand

(1) *The availability of substitutes at the ruling market price*

As a good falls in price, so it becomes cheaper relative to other goods. People are induced to buy more of it to replace goods which are now relatively dearer. How far they can carry out this replacement will depend upon the extent to which the good in question is, in their own minds, a substitute for the other goods. Goods within a particular class are easily substituted for one another. Beef is a substitute for mutton, bloaters are a substitute for kippers, and so on. Thus if the price of beef falls, people will buy more beef and less mutton. Between one class and another, however, substitution is more difficult. If the price of meat in general falls, there will be a slight tendency to buy more meat and less fish, but this tendency will be very limited, because meat is not nearly so perfect a substitute for fish as beef is for mutton.

We must be careful, however, over labelling the demand for the accepted necessities of life as 'inelastic' and the demand for luxuries as 'elastic'. With both, the substitution factor may be more important. Thus, although bread is a necessity, at a high enough price demand for it might be elastic because it has to compete with potatoes or cake. Similarly, a Rolls-Royce is a luxury, but demand for it will be inelastic if no substitute gives similar prestige. In any case it is difficult to state categorically which goods are necessities and which luxuries. But we can use the concept of elasticity of demand to help, saying that where the demand for a good is very inelastic over a wide price range, that good can be regarded as a necessity, and vice versa.

(2) *The number of possible substitute uses*

Where a good can be substituted for another good, its demand tends to be elastic. And the more goods it can be substituted for, so the more will demand for it extend as its price falls. Thus reductions in the price of plastics have led to large extensions of demand as they have been substituted for materials used in such articles as enamel bowls, galvanised buckets, paper wrappings, glass garden cloches, wooden toys, and tin containers.

(3) *The proportion of income spent on the good*

When only a very small proportion of a person's income is spent on a good, as for example with pepper, salt, shoe polish, newspapers, and toothpaste, no great effort is made to look for substitutes when its price rises. Demand for such goods, there-fore, is relatively inelastic. On the other hand, when the expenditure on a good is fairly large, as for example with most groceries, a rise in price would provide considerable incentive to find substitutes. Thus supermarkets have succeeded because, when they cut prices, large numbers of customers are attracted from other retailers who are selling the same good at a higher price.

(4) *The period of time*

Since it takes time to find substitutes or to change spending habits, elasticity may be greater the longer the period of time under review. In practice, many firms try to overcome the ignorance or conservatism of consumers by advertising, giving free samples, or making special offers.

(5) *The possibility of new purchasers*

In discussing the possibility of substitution above, we have looked at elasticity of demand from the point of view of the individual consumer. But when we are considering the market demand curve, we must allow for the fact that, as price falls, new consumers will be induced to buy the good. In fact, with many goods, such as cars, television sets, washing machines, etc., of which people require only one, it is the fall in price bringing the good within the range of the demand of new consumers which leads to the increase in demand. Hence a fall in price which induces people in a numerous income-group to buy will result in a considerable elasticity of demand. A fall in price which affects only the higher and smaller income-groups, however, will not produce many new customers and hence the market demand schedule tends to be inelastic in this price range.

Uses of the concept of elasticity of demand

The concept of elasticity of demand must be fully understood, for it figures prominently in both the theoretical analysis of the economist and the practical decisions of the businessman and government. The following are a few examples.

(1) *Theoretical economics*

(a) *To define 'perfect competition' in selling a good.* The economist, in order to explain the working of the economy, usually begins by constructing a model of how it works under theoretical conditions known as 'perfect competition' (*see* pp. 169–73). On the selling side, an essential criterion of perfect competition is that everybody in the market produces so small a quantity of the total supply that no one seller can influence the price of the good by the amount he puts on the market. He has to accept market price as given for any output he might produce. That is, he sees the demand for his good as perfectly elastic (*see* p. 170).

(Similarly, on the buying side, no one purchaser must be able to influence the price by the size of his demand—*see* p. 172.)

(*b*) *As a helpful tool in analysing problems connected with changes in the conditions of supply.* Many problems analysed by the economist can be tackled adequately only by making use of the concept of elasticity of demand. Consider, for example, the question: 'What effect will a rise in wages have on the numbers employed in the car industry?' The answer hinges largely on the elasticity of demand for the product made by that labour. An increase in wages will move the supply curve of the product to the left. Output will contract—but how much it contracts depends upon the elasticity of demand. If demand is elastic, it will contract to OM_1; if inelastic, to OM_2 (*see also* pp. 250–5).

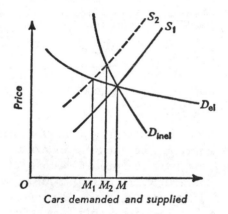

FIG. 23.—Elasticity of demand and a change in the conditions of supply.

(2) *Business decisions*

(*a*) *The supermarket.* The policy of the supermarket rests largely on the high elasticity of demand for its products. When it cuts the price of a good, the supermarket expects a considerable expansion in demand by winning customers from retailers selling at a higher price. Thus it is most successful in selling standardised goods, such as branded groceries, but less successful where customers form a personal attachment to the shopkeeper, as with butchers, tailors, etc.

(b) *The monopolist.* A monopolist is not faced with a horizontal, that is a perfectly elastic, demand curve when selling his product, for the price of the good is affected by the quantity he puts on the market (*see* Chapter 13). Therefore, he looks at the demand schedule for his good and fixes the amount, and thus the price, at which he makes the highest profit.

Let us imagine a football club which is staging a European Cup match. Let us further imagine that there is no comparable attraction within fifty miles and that the price of admission is fixed by the club, which pursues the policy of making as big a profit as possible. Expenses of the club will be roughly the same whether few or many watch the game. The relevant portion of the demand schedule is as follows:

Price of admission (pence)	Number of spectators willing to pay that price	Total outlay by spectators (£)
25	60,000	15,000
50	56,000	28,000
75	50,000	37,500
100	32,000	32,000

The club, therefore, fixes the price of admission at 75p, and the total number of spectators at the game is 50,000.

British Rail, too, have to consider elasticity of demand when fixing fares. Should they, for example, raise fares in order to reduce losses? If, at existing fares, the demand is relatively elastic, then a fare increase would mean that total revenue would fall. Losses would only be reduced if operating costs (through carrying fewer passengers) fell more than revenue.

(3) *Government policy*

Throughout this book we shall find that, in discussing government economic policy, elasticity of demand looms large. For instance, the Chancellor of the Exchequer must always take account of it when considering the effect of imposing a selective tax on a particular good. The demand may be so elastic that the increase in price might cause such a falling-off in the demand for the good that the total tax received was less than formerly. Suppose, for instance, the demand schedule for a commodity is as follows:

Price (pence)	Quantity demanded
20	1,000
30	600
40	200

Assume also that supply is at constant cost and that the market price is 20p at which 1000 units are being sold. The Chancellor of the Exchequer now decides to tax the good, imposing a tax of 10p on each unit. The result is that sales drop to 600 and his total tax receipts amount to £60. Later he goes further, increasing the tax to 20p per unit. This raises the total price of the good from 30p to 40p. Between these two prices, demand is very elastic. Only 200 are now sold, and the Chancellor's tax receipts are reduced to £40. Thus if the Chancellor wishes to raise revenue without increasing VAT he selects a good which has an inelastic demand. This is one reason why tobacco and alcohol bear selective rates of tax. Since they are regarded as luxuries, the higher price which results is not considered to be too serious a burden on the consumer.

Other examples of the application of elasticity of demand to government policy are: (a) How is the burden of a selective indirect tax shared between the consumer and the producer? (See p. 441.) (b) How will a selective tax or subsidy on its products affect the size of an industry? (See p. 439.) (c) Would devaluation be successful in improving the balance of payments? (See p. 494.) (d) Will an improvement in the terms of trade improve the balance of payments? (See p. 450.)

Income elasticity of demand

When we refer to 'elasticity of demand' without qualification, we are speaking, as above, of what is more precisely '*price* elasticity of demand'.

But an increase in real income usually increases the demand for goods to a varying degree. Thus it is possible to speak of *income elasticity of demand*—the proportionate change in demand divided by the proportionate change in real income which has brought it about. If demand increases 20 per cent, for instance as a result of a 10 per cent increase in real income, income elasticity of demand equals 2. Which goods have a high income elasticity of demand depends upon current living standards. In Western Europe today, it is the demand for such goods as cars, washing-machines, dish-washers, central-heating appliances, new houses and personal services which expands the most as income increases. In contrast, necessities, such as potatoes, salt, eggs and soap, have a low income elasticity of demand.

PART III

HOW TO PRODUCE—THE THEORY OF PRODUCTION

CHAPTER 6

THE FIRM

So far we have given only a very approximate explanation of how supply responds to a change in price. For the next seven chapters our task will be to examine the supply curve a little more closely. As with demand, we have to study the actions of individuals (in this case the firms producing goods). By considering the decisions a firm has to make, we try to establish general principles governing its behaviour.

I. THE ROLE OF THE FIRM

Definition of the firm

In Chapter 2 we showed that an economic system consists of two main parts: (1) Households, the units which provide productive resources and consume the goods produced; (2) Firms, the units which hire productive resources in order to produce goods and services. As we shall see, this definition of a firm is very wide, including all forms of organisation from the sole trader to government departments. In the chapters which follow, however, we shall be concentrating on the decisions of firms which produce goods in order to make a profit. Chapters 6 to 10 will be concerned mainly with the decisions on hiring and combining the factors of production. Chapters 11 and 12 will look at problems connected with the size of output. First, however, we must consider what economists are really referring to when they talk about the different 'factors of production' and 'production'.

The factors of production

The classical economists divided the factors of production into four groups—land, labour, capital and organisation. The rewards going to these factor groups were called rent, wages, interest and profit, respectively.

But their narrow classification, based on physical characteristics, has serious weaknesses:

(1) It is over-simplifying the problem to think that all factors can be separated and put into one of the four distinct compartments, land, labour, capital and organisation. These compartments themselves overlap. Land, used in its popular sense, can be improved and increased in quantity by a capital outlay on fertilisers, drainage and irrigation, while much of the acquired skill of a worker can be regarded as a return to the capital investment incurred in training him. Nor can labour free itself entirely from risk-bearing. An engine-driver may find that he has to accept a job at a lower wage should trains no longer be required.

(2) Within each compartment there are wide divergences. An architect is a far different sort of worker from the bricklayer's mate, and the hotel manager to the hotel porter, but the classification lumps them all together under the heading of 'labour' and thereby is inclined to imply that they are all the same. From an economic point of view, one factor is only the same as another in so far as it is a perfect substitute for it or, in other words, if an entrepreneur were indifferent as to which one he used.

(3) The differences between units of a factor in the same group may be greater than the differences between the groups. Thus a bricklayer's labourer is, from an economic point of view, as closely akin to a concrete-mixer as he is to a book-keeper.

The fact is that any form of classification of the factors of production is bound to run into difficulties. Thus present-day economists conduct much of their analysis by talking about factors of production generally—resources which co-operate in the production of goods and services wanted by the community. But they also recognise that certain factors do have some common, broad and important characteristics which permit a general classification useful for purposes of analysis. Unfortunately some obscurity has resulted because the old classical economists' terminology has been retained.

Land now refers solely to the resources provided by nature, e.g. space, sunshine, rain and minerals. In practice, it is treated as a separate factor of production in order to examine the nature of the earnings of any factor which is fixed in supply. Such earnings are termed 'economic rent'.

Labour refers to the actual effort, both physical and mental, made by human beings in production. It is this 'human' element which distinguishes it from other factors, for it gives rise to special problems regarding mobility, unemployment and psychological attitudes.

Capital, as opposed to land, is man-made. Goods can be classified as:

(*a*) *Consumer goods:* those goods which directly satisfy consumers' wants and are in the hands of the consumer, e.g. a loaf, a bicycle, a table.

(*b*) *Producer goods:* those goods which are not wanted directly for their own sake, but for the contribution they make to the production of consumer goods, e.g. buildings, machines, tools, raw materials. Sometimes the same good may be either a consumer good or a producer good, depending on its use. A car, for instance, may be used simply for pleasure, or by a salesman for business.

Capital, as a factor of production, consists of producer goods and stocks of consumer goods not yet in the hands of the consumer. It is treated as a separate factor of production in order to emphasise (*a*) the sacrifice of present enjoyment which is necessary to obtain it, and (*b*) the fluctuations in economic activity which occur because its use extends over a period of time (*see* Chapters 17 and 26).

Enterprise refers to the acceptance of the risks of production which arise through uncertainty. This is a somewhat narrower meaning than that given by the classical economists to the *entrepreneur*—the person or persons who decided what goods to produce and brought the factors of production together to produce them.

Today the role of organising the factors of production is

regarded as a managerial function, which can be performed by a paid manager, that is, by a highly-skilled form of labour. What really distinguishes enterprise from other factors is that it has to carry all the risks of production. How these risks arise will be examined in more detail later. Briefly, they occur because production takes time. The entrepreneur engages labour and buys raw materials and machinery now in order to produce a good which will not be sold until some time in the future. Whether he recovers his costs will depend upon the demand when he comes to sell the good. There may have been a change in tastes in the meantime; or a rival may, through a better process, be putting the good on the market at a lower price. In such ways, an expected profit may turn out to be a loss.

Profit or loss is the reward of uncertainty-bearing. Whoever accepts this ultimate risk is the true entrepreneur—the farmer working on his own account, the doctor who starts his own practice, the persons who buy shares (the 'risk' capital) in a joint-stock company, or the citizens of a state (who gain should a nationalised industry achieve a profit, but ultimately bear any losses made).

Production

Early economists, such as the French Physiocrats of the eighteenth century, considered that only work in the extractive industries (agriculture, mining, and fishing) was productive. Adam Smith, however, went one stage further for he included manufacturing in the term 'productive labour', though he was careful to deny that persons who merely rendered services were productive. In a much-quoted passage he states: 'The labour of the menial servant does not fix or realise itself in any particular subject or vendible commodity. His services generally perish in the very instant of their performance. . . . Like the declamation of the actor, the harangue of the orator, or the tune of the musician, the work of all of them perishes in the very instant of its production.' Nevertheless, the inadequacy of this definition can be realised at once for, according to it, the persons who make the dresses for the actresses and the scenery for the stage are productive, while the actors and actresses themselves are not, and the farmer who grows the food is productive while the cook is not!

To arrive at a more satisfactory definition we have to ask: 'Why do people work? What is the reason for production?' The answer is simple—to satisfy wants. Consequently people who render services must be regarded as being productive. The actor, the soldier, the musician and the shoe-black are all satisfying wants. While the latter satisfies the wants of only one person at a time, the others satisfy the wants of many people at the same time. Similarly in a factory, the clerk who calculates the wages and the boy who sweeps the floor are as productive as the man who makes the nuts and bolts. All are helping to produce the final product—the good which will satisfy wants.

Human wants can take different forms. Most people like a paper to read at the breakfast-table. Thus the newspaper-boy who takes the paper from the shop to the customer's letter-box is productive. Most people, too, prefer to buy their potatoes weekly rather than store the whole of their winter supply from when the crop is lifted in the autumn. Thus the farmer who keeps them in clamps or the merchant who puts them in a shed is satisfying the wants of consumers, and is similarly productive. Utility is created not only by changing the *form* of our scarce resources, but also their *place* and *time*. All these forms of activity are, therefore, productive.

II. THE OBJECTIVES OF THE FIRM

Where production is based on the free enterprise system, a firm's costs have to be covered if it is to stay in business. Thus some regard must be paid to 'profitability'. Indeed, without this the free enterprise system cannot work, for it is through profit (and loss) that supply is adjusted to changes in price.

But, in practice, do firms always seek to *maximise money* profits, particularly in the short run? The answer is 'no'.

Personal factors are sometimes important, especially where the manager is also the owner of the firm. Thus importance may be attached to good labour relations, the welfare of the workers, the desire for power, political influence, personal approbation or simply a 'quiet life'. To cover these other motives, 'profit' would have to be interpreted in a wider sense than 'money profit'.

Where the business is largely run by paid managers, other

motives may dominate. They may follow a 'play-for-safety' attitude rather than take the calculated risks necessary to earn maximum profit. More likely, they will obtain a 'satisfactory' level of profit but, in order to enhance their own positions and salaries, seek to *expand* the firm by maximising sales rather than profit.

Even when there is an emphasis on money profit, a firm may stress its long-term position rather than immediate maximum profits. This situation is applicable when there is an element of monopoly, for then a firm can decide on its pricing policy rather than have it given by competitive market conditions (*see* Chapter 1ʃ). In such circumstances the firm may not adjust price to short-term changes in the conditions of demand and supply. For one thing, there are the administrative costs of printing and distributing new price lists. For another, frequent changes in price tend to offend retailers and may not always please customers.

Finally, a producer enjoying a degree of monopoly has always to assess what the effect of the pursuit of maximum profit may have on his overall position. Will a high price attract new entrants or encourage the development of a rival product? Will it lead to adverse publicity and eventually to government intervention?

Nevertheless, while we must recognise that these other objectives exist, we cannot proceed far with our analysis or obtain any worthwhile principles if we adopt any of them as the main motive force of the firm. In any case, they merely supplement the profit motive. Thus it is useful to start our analysis by saying that firms seek to maximise profits. Having made this assumption, we can then establish principles concerning how the factors of production should be combined and what level of output should be produced.

III. THE DECISIONS OF THE FIRM

To maximise its profits, a firm will have to produce an output which will achieve the largest possible difference between total receipts and total costs. Thus it will always have an incentive to keep the cost of producing a given output to a minimum. This entails a number of decisions:

(1) What legal form shall the business take?
(2) What techniques shall be adopted, and what shall be the scale and scope of operation?
(3) Where shall production be located?
(4) How shall the factors of production be combined?

Such decisions are concerned largely with the factors of production, and will be discussed more fully in Chapters 7 to 10.

But the firm then has to relate costs and receipts, and decide what level of output will maximise its profits. Thus it has a further decision:

(5) What output shall be produced?

This is the question which is discussed in Chapters 11 and 13.

IV. THE LEGAL FORM OF THE FIRM UNDER PRIVATE ENTERPRISE

After deciding what to produce, the entrepreneur must consider what legal form his business shall take and how to raise the initial capital. It may be that the two decisions are closely linked from the beginning. But it must be remembered that, unless the business starts as an offshoot of a parent company, it has to be fairly successful before it can induce outsiders to subscribe capital on a large scale for its development.

Capital is often classified as: (a) fixed capital, and (b) working capital. Fixed capital covers factors which are used many times—factories, machines, land, lorries, etc. Working capital is for purchasing single-use factors—labour, raw materials, fertiliser, petrol, etc.—more or less the factors which are referred to later in this chapter as variable factors.

Finance for *working capital* can be obtained from a variety of sources—the bank, trade credit, advance deposits from customers (e.g. for building a house), hire-purchase companies, factor houses, tax reserves, and inter-company finance. Alternatively, fixed capital may be converted into working capital by hiring plant or renting buildings.

Fixed capital finance is more difficult to raise—people recognise that if they lend for this purpose they have to part with their money for a longer period and accept a greater risk. Thus, as we shall see, it is only when the firm has grown to a certain size that its legal form has much bearing on the ease (and

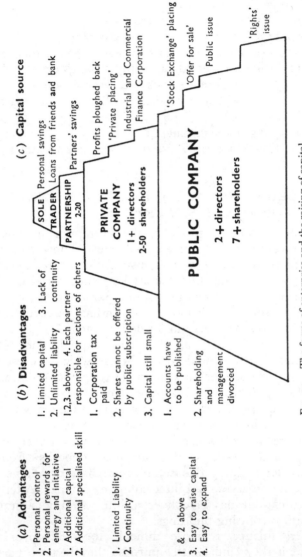

(a) Advantages

1. Personal control
2. Personal rewards for energy and initiative

1. Additional capital
2. Additional specialised skill

1. Limited Liability
2. Continuity

1 & 2 above
3. Easy to raise capital
4. Easy to expand

(b) Disadvantages

1. Limited capital   3. Lack of
2. Unlimited liability   continuity
1,2,3. above. 4. Each partner responsible for actions of others

1. Corporation tax paid
2. Shares cannot be offered by public subscription
3. Capital still small

1. Accounts have to be published
2. Shareholding and management divorced

(c) Capital source

SOLE TRADER — Personal savings
Loans from friends and bank

PARTNERSHIP 2-20 — Partners' savings

PRIVATE COMPANY
1+ directors
2-50 shareholders

Profits ploughed back
'Private placing'
Industrial and Commercial Finance Corporation

PUBLIC COMPANY
2+ directors
7+ shareholders

'Stock Exchange' placing
'Offer for sale'
Public issue
'Rights' issue

Fig. 24.—The forms of enterprise and the raising of capital.

therefore, the cost) with which it can borrow capital. Initially, therefore, it is likely that the legal form of the business will rest primarily on the degree of control which the entrepreneur wishes to exercise personally and the various legal advantages which different types afford. The position is summarised in Fig. 24.

The sole proprietor

The sole proprietor or 'one-man' firm is the oldest form of entrepreneurial organisation. Even today, from the point of view of numbers, small firms predominate, but in their total productive capacity, they are far less important than joint-stock companies (*see* Table 1). Such one-man firms range from the 'rag and bone' man, chimney-sweep and window-cleaner working on his own account to the farmer, shop-keeper and small factory-owner who employ other workers and may even own many separate units. Nevertheless these businesses all have the same characteristic of being owned and controlled by a single person. It is this person's task to make all decisions regarding the policy of the firm, and it is he alone who takes the profits and bears the brunt of any losses which are made. This makes for energy, efficiency and a careful attention to detail.

As a form of entrepreneurial organisation, however, the sole proprietor suffers from three main disadvantages. First, the development of such a firm must proceed slowly because the sources of capital are limited. The success of the venture especially in its early stages, depends very largely on the person in charge, and nobody is likely to provide capital for the business unless he has that confidence in the proprietor which comes from personal contact. Hence the main source of capital is the personal savings of the owner himself, together with such additional sums as he may be able to borrow from relatives or close friends. In time, development and expansion may take place by 'ploughing-back' profits, but this will probably be an extremely slow process and such firms generally remain comparatively small.

The second disadvantage is that, in the event of failure, not only the assets of the business, but also the private assets and property of the proprietor can be claimed against by creditors. In short, there is no limited liability.

Thirdly, there is lack of continuity; on the retirement or death of the owner, a one-man firm may cease to function.

Because of these disadvantages, the sole proprietor form of organisation is, in the main, confined either to those businesses which are just starting up, or to certain industries, such as agriculture and retailing, where requirements of management make the small technical unit desirable.

The partnership

A larger amount of capital is available when persons combine together in a 'partnership', though not more than twenty (ten in the case of a banking concern), may so join. Each partner provides a part of the capital required and shares the profits on an agreed basis. Yet the amount of capital which can be raised in this way is still inadequate for modern large-scale organisations. The result is that partnerships remain relatively small, being particularly suitable to that type of business, such as retailing and the professions (doctors, dentists, consulting engineers and lawyers), where the capital provided is not so much in the form of money as in professional skill and experience, each partner probably specialising in a particular branch.

Moreover, in securing capital through partners, disadvantages are incurred. The risk inherent in unlimited liability is increased because all partners are liable for the firm's debts irrespective of the amount of capital which each has individually invested, and private fortunes may be called upon to meet the demands of creditors. Only if a partner takes no share in the management of the firm, and there is at least one ordinary partner, can the privilege of limited liability be enjoyed. Secondly, any action taken by one partner is legally binding on all the other partners. From this it follows that not only must each partner have complete confidence in the others but that, as the number of partners increases, so does the risk inherent in unlimited liability. Finally, by giving notice to the others, one partner may terminate the partnership at any time, while it is automatically dissolved upon the death or bankruptcy of any one partner. This means that surviving partners have either to buy his share or find a purchaser who is acceptable to everyone. In such circumstances, therefore, the continuation of the business often involves great trouble and expense.

The joint-stock company

The joint-stock company first developed in Tudor times when England's foreign trade began to expand. Instead of a trading ship being owned by one person, it was financed by a number of people who bought 'shares' in a company formed for the purpose. Yet, until the middle of the nineteenth century, people were reluctant to join such companies. The reason was that they enjoyed no limited liability. By purchasing only one share a person risked, not merely the loss of the money invested but, should the company be forced into liquidation, the whole of his private fortune. Moreover, unlimited liability made it virtually impossible to adopt the technique of spreading risks by investing in a number of different companies.

The Industrial Revolution, with the introduction of machines and large-scale organisation, made it essential that more capital should be available to industry. Hence, in order to induce small savers to invest, the privilege of limited liability was bestowed by Act of Parliament in 1855. This is the meaning of the letters 'Ltd' after the name of a company.

Today the joint-stock company is the most important form of business organisation. The advantages it enjoys over the partnership are limited liability, continuity, the availability of capital (since investors can spread their risks and sell their shares easily), and, should the need arise, ease of expansion. Indeed, some kinds of businesses could not be conducted on a small scale. Such businesses have to start from the beginning as joint-stock companies, either being sponsored by important interests, or else developed as subsidiaries of existing large firms.

Against these advantages, however, certain disadvantages, which could add to costs, have to be considered. The chief of these arises under corpora. n tax, to which a small firm becomes liable by trading as a company instead of as a sole trader or partnership. The company's corporation tax could be more than the income tax which would have been paid had the business remained as a sole trader or partnership. Furthermore, any assets of the company which have been built up over the years will increase the value of the original shares (usually owned by the family). When the time comes to wind up the company, e.g. owing to retirement, any increase in the value of the shares will be subject to capital gains tax.

The *finance* of a company is obtained in two main ways: (*a*) by selling 'shares' in the company; (*b*) by borrowing.

(*a*) Shares

A 'share' is exactly what the name implies—a participation in the provision of the capital of a company. Shares may be issued in various units, usually from 5p upwards, and a person can vary the degree to which he participates by the number of units he purchases. The investment of money in a company does involve certain risks, of which two are paramount. The first is that the return on the capital invested may be less than expected because profits are disappointing. The second is that share prices in general may have fallen at the moment when the owner wishes to sell his holding. To minimise these risks, investors usually spread their investments over a variety of concerns and vary the magnitude of the risks undertaken by having a portfolio of shares of different types, debentures and government bonds.

(i) *Ordinary shares*. The dividend paid to the ordinary shareholder depends entirely on the number of shares he owns and on the prosperity of the company. If profits are high, the dividend is usually correspondingly high; if there are no profits, then there is usually no dividend. Moreover, the payment of a dividend to an ordinary shareholder ranks last in the order of priority, while if the company should be forced into liquidation, the ordinary shareholder is repaid only after other creditors have been paid in full. Thus the 'ordinary share' is termed 'risk capital', for its holder bears the risks of the business venture. In return, each ordinary shareholder has a say in the running of the company, voting according to the number of shares held. At the general meeting, directors can be appointed or removed, changes made in the company's method of raising capital and conducting business, and auditors appointed. Thus the ordinary shareholders, because they take the major risks and decisions regarding the policy of the company, are the real 'entrepreneurs'. In practice, however, their rights are rarely exercised. Providing the company appears to be doing reasonably well, few shareholders take the trouble to attend meetings. Moreover, unless the company is very large, the directors are often in a strong position in that they will probably hold or control a large proportion of the ordinary shares. Indeed, at times voting rights are specifically excluded (usually signified by 'A' shares). Hence boards of directors tend to be self-perpetuating.

(ii) *Preference shares.* If the investor wishes to undertake a slightly reduced risk, he can buy a preference share. Such a shareholder is entitled to a dividend payment before the ordinary shareholder, but offsetting this advantage, the dividend is fixed (at a given per cent) no matter how high the profits of the company are. In addition, only in exceptional circumstances, such as when it is proposed to alter their rights or to wind up the company, or when their dividends are in arrears, are these shareholders allowed to vote at ordinary meetings. Should, however, the company be forced into liquidation it is usual for the preference shareholder to rank above the ordinary shareholder in the redemption of capital.

Preference shares may also be 'cumulative'. This means that if the company cannot pay a dividend one year, arrears may be made up in succeeding years before the ordinary shareholders receive any dividend. Since 1965 preference shares have lost popularity through their unfavourable tax treatment (*see* p. 110).

(b) Borrowing

The long-term loans of a company are usually obtained by issuing 'debentures'. These bear a fixed rate of interest (about 14 per cent), irrespective of the profit made by the company. This interest payment is a first charge on the income of the company, and so the risk to the investor of there being no return is not so high. Moreover, should the company fail, debenture-holders are paid out first. In fact, 'mortgage debentures' are secured on a definite asset of the company. One other advantage of debentures is that they are redeemable after a specified period. Should the company be unable to meet its interest charges or to redeem the loan when due, the debenture-holders can force it into liquidation.

Unlike the ordinary shareholder whose investment is bound up with the fortunes of the company, the purchaser of a debenture has eliminated as far as possible the risks attached to the possible failure of the company. In essence, he is merely lending the company money. Hence, he enjoys no ownership rights of voting on management and policy. But a company whose profits are subject to frequent and violent fluctuations is not in a position to raise much of its capital by debentures. Such a method is really suitable only to a company making a fairly stable profit (sufficiently adequate to cover the interest payments), and possessing assets (such as land and buildings), the value of which would not have depreciated a great deal were the company to go into liquidation.

A company having a large proportion of fixed-interest loans to ordinary shares is said to be 'highly-geared'. Such a company will be able to pay high dividends when profits are good, but unable to make a distribution when profits are low. Where profits are expected to rise in the future, therefore, a company may prefer to raise capital for expansion by issuing debentures if the cost of doing so is not too high.

But it is the present-day corporation tax which is the main impulse in this direction. Debenture interest (but not preference-share interest) is included in the costs of a company for the purposes of calculating tax. Thus it reduces taxable profits. On the other hand, if finance is raised by shares, there is no prior interest charge, and profits (which are subject to tax) are that amount higher. This tax advantage has, since the introduction of corporation tax in 1965, led companies to finance capital expansion as far as possible by fixed-interest loans rather than by the sale of shares. Preference shares are now hardly ever issued.

Joint-stock companies are of two main kinds, private and public.

(a) The private company

The organisation of a business as a private company, while conferring the advantage of limited liability, allows it to be privately owned and managed. The formalities involved in its formation are few, but under the Companies Act, 1948, it has to satisfy the following conditions:

(i) Neither shareholders nor debenture-holders exceed 50 in

number; (ii) shares are not offered for sale by public issue; (iii) directors have the power to disapprove any proposed transfer of shares; (iv) none of its shares are held by another company, unless the aggregate shareholding of the two companies does not exceed 50; (v) no corporate body acts as a director; (vi) nobody other than the registered holder has any interest in the company's shares; (vii) no person or body outside the company is in a position to control its policy.

Hence the private company is particularly suitable for either a medium-sized commercial or industrial organisation not requiring finance from the public, or for a speculative venture where a small group of people wishes to try out an idea and is prepared to back it up financially to a definite limit before floating a public company. While private companies are considerably more numerous than public companies, their average capital is much smaller.

The reason why they remain small is often because of the difficulties encountered when they wish to expand. In the past, the chief source of additional capital was the profits which were 'ploughed back' into the business, but today government taxation of profits reduces the funds available. Alternatively, where the company owns its own property, a mortgage can be arranged. If neither of these methods realises sufficient capital, the only alternative is to look round for additional investors. It is at this point that the private company is at a disadvantage. Neither its shares nor debentures can be offered for sale to the public, while any transfer has to be approved by the directors. In short, the shares of a private company tend to be somewhat illiquid. Thus, in order to find the additional investors, it is usually necessary to convert the business into a public company with its shares 'quoted', that is, dealt in on the Stock Exchange.

The formation of such a company, however, is not an easy step. The main obstacle arises from the fact that the costs of a public issue are so high that it is not usually economic to raise less than £150,000. Thus before embarking on such an issue, the company must already have attained a fairly substantial size. The difficult stage in its expansion occurs, therefore, when its capital is in the region of £50,000, for then it is still too small to make a public issue. The gap can be bridged in three main ways. Firstly, it may be possible for a stockbroker to arrange for a life insurance company or an investment trust to purchase shares or debentures. (Such companies are usually in a position to ignore the disadvantages of holding securities of private companies.) Secondly, help might be obtained from the new issue market which has developed considerably over the past thirty years from two main directions. On the one hand, there have come into being a number of issuing houses who specialise in this kind of work. On the other, the merchant bankers, forced to find other outlets for their services when lending abroad was reduced in volume, have devoted their attention to issuing securities for firms at home which require relatively small amounts of capital. Both issuing houses and merchant bankers may themselves provide long- or medium-term capital to bridge the gap prior to making a public issue, though it should be noted that their main work is connected with public issues. Thirdly, there are a number of specialised finance corporations. Thus, for agriculture there is the Agricultural Mortgage Corporation, which will lend on the security of land and buildings. For small firms, the Charterhouse Industrial Development Company and Credit for Industry Ltd are among those who will help with long-term finance. The most important source, however, for such capital is the Industrial and Commercial Finance Corporation, a body backed by the government although mainly financed by the joint-stock banks. Its object is to provide the necessary capital for businesses, not necessarily companies, too small to make a public issue. But in order to obtain a loan, the firm has first to pass a searching investigation regarding its present financial position and business prospects.

(b) *The public company*

Where a large amount of capital is required, for instance above £150,000, it is usually raised by forming a public company (having a minimum of seven shareholders), with its shares quoted on the Stock Exchange. The latter is achieved by sending a letter asking for permission to have the shares 'quoted', that is, dealt in on the Stock Exchange, and this letter will be examined by the Council. If permission is granted, the affairs of the company have to be advertised very fully in at least two leading London newspapers, while if no new issue is being made, a supply of shares has to be made available by existing share-holders sufficient to make dealing and the price fixed realistic.

Once the introduction has been completed, the capital required can be raised by a Stock Exchange 'placing', an 'offer for sale' or a 'public issue by prospectus'. The first is the usual method when only about £150,000 is required, for the costs of underwriting and administration are less. An issuing house, stockbroker or investment company agrees to sell blocks of the shares privately to persons who it knows are likely to be interested in them.

For larger amounts up to £300,000, an offer for sale is a likely method. The shares are sold *en bloc* to an issuing house, which then offers them for sale to the public by advertisement similar to a public issue.

When more than £300,000 is required, a public issue by prospectus is the method usually employed. Here the company's object is to obtain from the public in a single day the additional capital it requires. Hence it must advertise well and price its shares a little on the cheap side. The advertisement is in the form of a prospectus which sets out the business, history and prospects of the company together with its financial standing and the security offered. It must be issued at least three days before the allotment of the securities, so that the prospectus can be adequately examined and reviewed in the financial papers. Attached to the prospectus there is usually an application form which the would-be subscriber completes and sends with his application money (which may be required in full or in part).

In practice the sale is usually conducted through an issuing house, which advises on the terms of the issue. It will also arrange to have the issue underwritten; that is, it will find a number of institutions, such as merchant bankers, who, in return for a small commission, will take at an agreed price whatever part of the issue is left unsold. Nevertheless, such underwriters do not have to rely entirely on permanent investors to buy the securities on the day of issue, for specu-lators, known as 'stags', are usually operating, and they buy the shares hoping to resell them quickly at a small profit. In addition, in recent years, there has been an increasing tendency to give existing shareholders the first option on the purchase of new shares. This is done through a 'rights issue' which offers the right to buy new shares up to a given proportion of shares already held, usually at a favourable price.

Co-operative societies

Although there were many co-operative societies in operation before the Rochdale Pioneers, 1844, it is they who started the modern co-operative movement. The Rochdale Pioneers consisted of a group of 28 artisans, mostly cotton weavers, who, by subscribing a few pence per week, managed to obtain an initial capital of £28, with which they rented a small store in Toad Lane, Rochdale, and started trading with small stocks of flour, oatmeal, sugar, butter and candles. Profits were distributed to members in proportion to their purchases. Today the number of retail co-operative societies in Great Britain and Northern Ireland is 244 with an aggregate membership of nearly 11 million. Capital amounts to £378 million, while the value of trade is about £1,300 million per annum, accounting for nearly 8 per cent of Britain's retail trade. In addition, these retail societies largely provide the capital and control the operation of the Co-operative Wholesale Society.

The minimum shareholding in a retail co-operative society is usually £1. Only if a full share is held does a member enjoy voting rights, but not more than one vote per member is allowed irrespective of the number of shares held. Until fairly recently, the traditional way of paying the Co-op 'divi' was to distribute profits in proportion to the member's purchases over the period. Societies charged the current market price for their goods. Today, however, most societies return the dividend to members through the National Dividend Stamp scheme operated by the Co-operative Wholesale Society. Stamps are given to customers in proportion to their purchases, and a book of stamps can be redeemed for 40p cash or 50p in goods or for 50p deposit in a share account, in which case a bonus of an extra 10p is usually added. Not only has this system allowed the Co-operative shops to compete with the supermarkets and other stores, but it is much cheaper to operate than the old 'divi' method. Nor does the member have to wait at least six months before receiving the dividend, while the national stamp can be gummed in the book irrespective of the source, e.g. petrol stations.

Co-operative societies described above are organised directly by consumers and are therefore called 'consumers' co-operative societies'. Producers also associate together in 'producers' co-operative societies' for the purpose of marketing the produce of their members and sharing the proceeds between them. They are chiefly important in the marketing of agricultural produce, particularly where production is carried on by many small farmers, as in Denmark, New Zealand and Spain. Nevertheless, they have not been developed to any great extent in the United Kingdom. Instead, when marketing difficulties have arisen in agriculture in this country, the government has exercised control through Marketing Boards.

V. STATE ENTERPRISE

We considered in Chapter 2 the various reasons why the state should interfere in the operation of a capitalist economy. Such intervention takes various forms. Sometimes it merely involves modifying the complete operation of the price system, as when subsidies are granted, import duties imposed or prices controlled. At other times, however, the state supervises, or actually undertakes, the production of goods and services. Thus we have producing units ('firms') in the public sector of the economy—government departments, public corporations and local authorities.

With certain goods and services, e.g. defence, the maintenance of law and order, and certain social and welfare benefits (such as health, education and insurance against unemployment, sickness and retirement) there is little disagreement with state provision. But where, for various reasons, the state has taken over industries formerly organised under private enterprise, there has been considerable controversy and opposition. There are arguments in every case for and against. The final decision regarding nationalisation is therefore largely a political one.

In this section we take no sides in the political argument. Instead we simply glance at the possible economic arguments for nationalising certain industries and then consider some of the problems of organisation and operation which have arisen.

Economic arguments for nationalisation

Nationalisation now covers a wide range of industries—the Bank of England, cable and wireless, civil aviation, electricity generation, atomic energy, gas and electricity supply, coal, rail, canal and some road transport, iron and steel. Since these industries differ in such matters as their importance, size, and type of product, not all the economic arguments for and against nationalisation apply equally to each. The following are therefore merely generalised arguments which could, but need not, apply to an individual industry.

(1) *Single control over all the firms in the industry enables the full advantages of large-scale production to be achieved.* Competition between firms may result in their working at less than the optimum size (*see* p. 178) because uncertainty as regards rivals' plans may inhibit investment on a large scale for fear of over-investment. It may also give rise to duplication of research, unnecessary differences in design of tools and product, and inefficiency of operation. The National Coal Board, for instance, has developed a standard pattern of miner's safety helmet, while it has been able to reduce underground haulage on some coal fields by using a nearer shaft (Fig. 25).

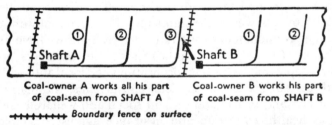

Coal-owner A works all his part
of coal-seam from SHAFT A

Coal-owner B works his part
of coal-seam from SHAFT B

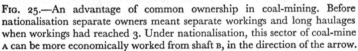

++++++++ Boundary fence on surface

FIG. 25.—An advantage of common ownership in coal-mining. Before nationalisation separate owners meant separate workings and long haulages when workings had reached 3. Under nationalisation, this sector of coal-mine A can be more economically worked from shaft B, in the direction of the arrow.

Similarly, nationalisation secures commercial and financial economies. Thus competitive advertising costs between firms are eliminated, while, in borrowing, a state-owned industry can usually obtain finance more cheaply than a private firm.

(2) *State ownership is essential for the necessary capital investment.* Private owners may not have the resources or may be unwilling to commit themselves to long-term capital outlays. Thus the development of atomic energy has been undertaken by the state, both for security and technical reasons, while, on the railways, the modernisation programme would have been too risky an enterprise under private ownership. Even a loss by the state

could possibly be justified by social benefits, e.g. less congestion on the road network.

(3) *State ownership is a means of controlling monopoly.* Some industries must inevitably be organised as monopolies, either because this power is legally conferred (e.g. public utilities where otherwise chaos might result) or because the economies of large-scale production are so large (e.g. atomic energy, electricity generation). It is argued that the best way of controlling such monopolies is state ownership, for there is then the assurance that they will work in the public interest and not merely for high profits.

(4) *The efficiency of key industries must be guaranteed.* There are certain industries, e.g. iron and steel, power, upon which all other production depends. Others, e.g. atomic research, are vital for defence. Such industries, it is argued, should not be regarded merely as a source of private profit (with their expansion or contraction dependent upon this), but be run by the state in the general interest of the nation, especially as regards full employment and defence requirements.

(5) *Productivity will increase through improved attitudes of employees.* It is argued that workers will enjoy better working conditions, while the fact that the state is the employer and not a company striving for its own profit, will have a psychological result reflected in increased output.

Problems of organisation

Even after it has been agreed that the state should either supervise or undertake the production of goods and services, it still remains to be decided how the management shall be organised. Two fundamental principles, each pulling in opposite directions, need due consideration.

The first principle arises because British democracy requires that, where the state is granted powers, it shall be answerable, in some form or another, for the way in which these powers are exercised. This is known as the principle of 'public accountability'. Our past history has shown that it is not sufficient to assume that the state can always be relied upon to act in the 'public interest'. Often the 'state' consists of a collection of government departments, run by officials who, either misguidedly or wilfully, translate the 'public interest' into policies which suit their own ends. The citizen requires, therefore, some assurance that the powers granted to enable the state to produce goods are not being abused by authoritarianism, inefficiency or monopolistic exploitation.

The most efficient form of accountability is achieved when a government department produces the goods or services. The department usually has a Minister at its head who accepts full responsibility for the work of his department. This Minister is subject to examination in Parliament, and it is his task to explain general policy in debate and to answer questions on even minor details of administration. In finance, too, there is also strict control, for the Treasury is careful to see that money is spent economically and within the limit authorised by Parliament.

Nevertheless, the government department method of organisation or control cannot be used in providing all goods and services. Not only would Parliament be overworked if it tried to exercise detailed control, but the industries would also be the subject of continual political conflict. Above all, while the government department organisation ensures maximum accountability, it has certain weaknesses in providing economic goods and services, weaknesses which become more apparent where it has been or is possible to organise the production through private enterprise. Apart from the inherent deficiencies of the Civil Service (such as lack of initiative, addiction to red tape and the rigid methods of Treasury control of finance), public accountability itself entails some conflict with the second principle, that of 'economic efficiency'.

This principle was discussed in Chapter 2, and it was shown how private enterprise was very effective in solving the two main aspects of efficiency, the estimate of consumers' demand and efficiency in supply. Firms decide what and how to produce. If their decisions are correct, a profit is their reward; if they are wrong, and production is misdirected, then they, and only they, are the losers. Persons who take the risk of producing, therefore, are primarily answerable only to themselves.

But what happens when the department is the producer and its civil servants are accountable to Parliament for day-to-day details of administration? The result is the 'play-for-safety' attitude already commented on. Moreover, accountability through Parliament has additional defects. First, it might lead to difficulties in pursuing long-term industrial and commercial objectives because the Minister in charge is being frequently changed through either reorganisation of the Government or a swing of the political pendulum. Secondly, it is likely that much of the Parliamentary questioning on day-to-day matters would either be irrelevant and ill-informed, because it dealt with a technical matter beyond the understanding of the average Member of Parliament, or even positively harmful, in that it was used solely as an instrument of political opposition.

The result of this conflict between the two principles of public accountability and economic efficiency has been the development of special governmental (sometimes called 'quasi-government') bodies, variously termed commissions, boards, authorities and corporations. Though they differ in the nature and importance of the functions performed as well as in the degree of independence enjoyed, all are subject to some measure of government control. Fig. 26 gives an indication of the nature of their functions.

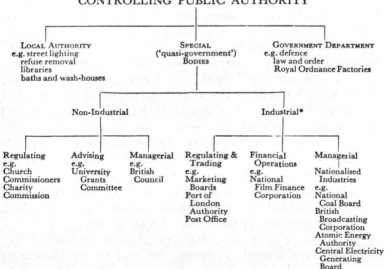

* 'Industrial' in this context means the bodies are connected with a particular industry or serve industry in general.

Fig. 26.—Forms of public organisation for the supervision or provision of goods and services.

The organisation of the nationalised industries

Within the principles outlined above, the organisation of the nationalised industries presents some common features.

(1) The boards are 'bodies corporate'. This means that they have a legal identity and therefore, like a company, have a life of their own, can own property, and sue and be sued in the courts.

(2) The assets of the industry are vested in the board and the nationalising Act usually gives the board instructions as to its general responsibilities. Thus the National Coal Board is charged with the duties of:

(a) working and getting the coal in Great Britain;

(b) securing the efficient development of the coal-mining industry;

(c) making supplies of coal available, of such qualities and sizes, in such quantities and at such prices, as may seem to them best calculated to further the public interest in all respects, including the avoidance of any undue or unreasonable preference or advantage.

(3) A Minister is given an overall control of the board. He exercises, as it were, the shareholders' rights in a company, the 'shareholders' of a board being the community. It is the Minister, therefore, who appoints the board's members, although the nationalising Act usually specifies their general qualifications. In addition, the Minister may give the board directions of a general character as to how they shall exercise and perform the functions with regard to matters which appear to him to affect the national interests. This usually includes authorising capital development, supervising borrowing and appointing auditors. The aim, therefore, is to give the Board freedom in its day-to-day administration with the possibility of some subordination in its general policy. Boards are not subject to Parliamentary questioning on detailed matters of administration, but they are required to submit Annual Reports to Parliament, for which the government usually sets aside a day to debate.

(4) In financial and staffing matters, the boards are free from Treasury control. They are required to pay their way, taking one year with another, free from state subsidy. They engage their own staff, arranging directly, through employees' trade unions or associations, pay and conditions of service.

(5) In order to obviate the necessity of Parliamentary

questioning on matters of detail and to ensure a degree of direct representation by consumers, consumers' councils have been established for the coal, electricity, gas and transport industries. They consist of twenty to thirty unpaid members, appointed, except in the case of Air Transport, by the Minister. Nominations for membership are put forward by bodies whom the Minister selects as being representative of consumers, e.g. local authorities, women's organisations, professional associations, trade unions, and trade associations. The coal industry has two national councils, one for industrial and one for domestic users, but the 'consultative councils' of the other industries are organised on a regional basis. The functions of these councils are:

(a) to deal with complaints and suggestions from consumers, although they are also expected to act on their own initiative in such matters;

(b) to advise both the boards and the Minister of the general views of consumers.

Unfortunately so far, either through ignorance, the remoteness of the offices, or general lack of confidence, little use has been made by consumers of these councils.

In short, therefore, the new public corporations try, as it were, to get the best of both worlds: on the one hand, the world of energetic industrial enterprise found in the private enterprise system; on the other, the world of accountability to the public, to whom it belongs and whom it serves.

The detailed internal organisation of the corporations has varied. Two illustrations will serve to illustrate this point. The Coal Industry Nationalisation Act, 1946, set up a *National* Board consisting of a chairman and seven full-time and four part-time members, with the responsibilities already mentioned. But the rest of the organisation of the coal industry was such as this board should determine. In practice, it has been reorganised from time to time. At present there are 289 collieries, and all but three of these are grouped in seventeen areas, each area controlled by a Director responsible to the N.C.B. The remaining three collieries (in Kent) are controlled by a general manager who is also responsible to the N.C.B. The day-to-day work of running the collieries is under the direction of colliery managers.

It seems, however, that originally the problem of size was

under-estimated, for subsequent nationalising Acts brought an increasing tendency to decentralisation. Thus the Electricity Council and the Gas Council, which were established in 1948, were really only central representative bodies for the industry as a whole, and were composed mainly of the chairmen of the twelve Area Boards, with an independent Chairman or Vice-Chairman appointed by the Minister. In both cases, the nationalising Acts established the twelve Area Boards, and the assets of the industry were vested in them. The Area Boards were also given the *statutory* responsibility for the distribution of electricity and the supply of gas. Each Board adopted its own pattern of organisation and arrangements for fulfilling its statutory obligations.

Circumstances, however, may mean that a new organisation is desirable. Thus the discovery of natural gas meant that its distribution had to be organised centrally. Hence in 1973 the original organisation of the gas industry was scrapped, and the supply of gas was brought under the British Gas Corporation, which took over the assets of the Area Gas Boards.

Economic problems of nationalisation

Apart from problems of a constitutional nature—internal organisation, the exact responsibility of the Minister, the extent of, and opportunities for, Parliamentary review—many economic problems still remain to be resolved.

These problems stem chiefly from the fact that often the nationalised industries are monopolies. On the demand side there is, therefore, some loss of consumers' sovereignty. Initially for instance, a person can choose between gas, electricity, coal and oil when deciding on central heating; but thereafter he is more or less committed. Should he be dissatisfied with subsequent price rises, the ultimate sanction—taking his custom elsewhere—is not available to him. On the supply side, too, there are grounds for concern. Prices are fixed with the object of covering costs, but since prices are fixed on a cost basis, what guarantee is there that costs are kept to a minimum by efficient operation? It is felt that periodic independent efficiency investigations will have to be made. Moreover, in recent years, governments have restricted price rises as part of their anti-inflation measures. This does mean, however, that the corporations cannot fulfil their obligation of paying their way unless they are given subsidies from central government funds.

Problems of scale, e.g. of co-ordination, also arise in managing these vast industries. The result, as we have seen, has been the movement towards greater decentralisation. Yet these same problems exist in the private sector, and there seems little reason why state industry should be inferior in its ability to solve them.

Some critics argue that investment decisions in many of the nationalised industries have not been altogether wise. Thus there has been over-investment in the coal industry and possibly in the railways. Scarce capital could have been better employed elsewhere, e.g. in the construction of motorways. While some error is bound to occur in a dynamic economy (the discovery of North Sea natural gas, for instance, upset the Coal Board's projections of future demand for coal), there is more than a strong suspicion that the nationalised industries came off favourably in the allocation of capital soon after they were created because the government had a vested interest in their success.

Finally, the nationalised industries have not yet really discovered how and when to award wage increases, especially when losses are being made! Threats of strike in these basic industries, e.g. railways, have led to government intervention. The result has been an aggravation of the wage–cost inflationary spiral.

CHAPTER 7

THE ORGANISATION AND SCALE
OF PRODUCTION

WHEN assembling its plant, organising its factors of production and deciding how to get the finished product to the customer, the firm will consider the pros and cons of producing on a large scale and the advantages to be obtained from specialisation.

Because specialisation is the fundamental principle upon which modern production is organised, we begin this chapter by examining it. We do so with particular reference to labour under the traditional heading of 'the division of labour' but, as we shall see, it is equally applicable to machines, localities and even countries.

I. THE DIVISION OF LABOUR

Increased production results when the labour force is so organised that each person is specialising on a particular job. Thus in the simple task of making a table, one man will be sawing the wood, another planing it, a third cutting the joints, a fourth gluing together the various parts, and the last polishing the finished article. This increased production is achieved because:

(1) *Each man is employed in the job in which his superiority is most marked.* Suppose that, in one day, Smith can plane the parts for 20 tables *or* cut the joints for 10, whereas Brown can either plane 10 tables *or* cut the joints for 20. If each do both jobs, their combined production in a day will be 15 tables planed *and* 15 table-joints cut. But Smith is better at planing, while Brown is better at cutting joints. If they specialise on what they can do best, their combined production will be 20 tables planed *and* 20 table-joints cut—an increase in output of a third. Later, when we consider international trade, we shall develop this argument

to show that specialisation can still be advantageous even if one person or country is superior in both lines of production.

Even if initially every worker were equally proficient at the different jobs it would, for the following reasons, still pay to organise them so that they specialised.

(2) *Practice makes perfect, and so particular skills are developed through repetition of the same job.*

(3) *Economy in tools makes possible the use of specialised machinery.* Consider Fig. 27. In (*a*) every man has a saw, a plane, a chisel and mallet, a gluepot and brush, and a polishing cloth. In (*b*) the principle of division of labour has been introduced. One man works a circular saw, another a mechanical plane, a third cuts joints with a special tool (a mortiser), a fourth glues and clamps the tables, and the last uses a sander and polisher electrically powered. These specialised tools are economic

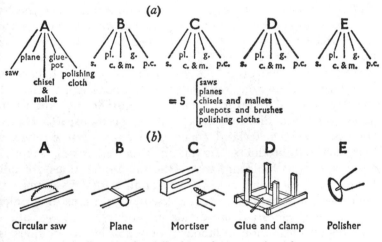

FIG. 27.—Specialisation and economy in tools.

because they are in constant use, and output from them is much greater. Thus, not only does the division of labour set free talented men for research and invention, but it encourages both because the fruits can be used profitably.

(4) *Time is saved through not having to switch from one operation to another.* In the above example, if one man were making the table himself, he would have to put away each different tool after using it. When he specialises, he keeps to the same tool all the time.

(5) *Less time is taken in learning a particular job.* In the making of a table, only one tool and one operation have to be mastered. This makes it easier for labour to move from one industry to another.

(6) *The employer can estimate his costs of production and output more accurately.*

But while it benefits the manufacturer and eventually the consumer, the division of labour has disadvantages both to the worker and to society. The worker may feel that his job is monotonous, while with some occupations, such as paint-spraying, there is increased risk of occupational disease. More-over, the skilled specialist may become redundant when demand falls, and the interdependence involved in our complex organ-isation of the economy can lead to widespread unemployment when a small group of workers goes on strike or a source of raw materials dries up. Finally, standardised products tend to replace the individual work of the old craftsman. Nevertheless it must be emphasised that these drawbacks are but a small price to pay when compared with the great benefits resulting from the division of labour.

Naturally, the degree of division of labour which can be introduced varies from one industry to another. In small or sparsely populated countries, there are insufficient workers to allow a minute division in a number of industries. Hence countries like Switzerland concentrate on a narrow range of manufactured products. Again, in some industries, such as agriculture and building, where the same operations are not taking place each day, many 'Jacks of all trades' are required. Moreover, an exchange system is essential—we must first unite in exchange before we can divide in production. Above all, a high degree of division of labour is only possible where there is a large demand for the product. The complex organisation of car production, for instance, is the result of a mass demand for a standardised product—and one which is largely made up from a multitude of small parts.

II. INTERNAL ECONOMIES

The advantages of large-scale production which a firm can plan to achieve directly by increasing the size of its output are termed 'internal economies'. This is to distinguish them from certain other economies which arise *indirectly* from the growth, not in the size of the *firm*, but in the size of the *industry*. These latter are known as 'external economies' and they will be discussed later.

Following Professor E. A. G. Robinson, internal economies can be conveniently classified under five headings: technical, managerial, commercial, financial and risk-bearing.

(1) *Technical economies*

In the actual making of the good, as distinct from its distribution, economies result when production is on a large scale.

In the first place, production can be broken down into many separate tasks because men can be employed full-time on each. At once all the advantages of the division of labour are achieved. In the production of lower-priced coats, for instance, the multiple tailor employs in his factory a 'flow' method of production. One worker specialises in the actual cutting of the cloth, another tacks the various parts together. Later in the process a girl might concentrate on the making of the button-holes, while another sews the buttons on. The larger the scale of production, the further can the degree of specialisation usually be carried, especially when, as with the motor car, the product largely consists of a multitude of tiny parts.

The larger producer is also able to employ specialised machinery because he can keep it fully occupied. For instance, Ford at Dagenham have sufficient output to keep their own blast furnace at work, whereas a firm producing only a few cars a week could not do this. In the same way, it is only the large firm which can afford to carry out research or to provide canteen and welfare facilities for its employees.

Thirdly, the initial outlay may be lower, and operating costs may be saved by using a large machine even when two or more machines could do the same work. For instance, a double-decker bus can carry twice as many passengers, but the initial cost is not twice as much nor are the running costs doubled, because one driver and one conductor only are still required. It may even be that there is a mechanical advantage in working on a large scale. In farming, for instance, the tendency with modern machinery is for fields to become larger, for less time is wasted in turning the bulkier machines.

Lastly, economies are achieved through linking processes. For instance, in steel-making the large mills can save fuel by rolling the ingots into sheets before they cool.

Generally technical economies fix the size of the unit actually producing, rather than the size of the firm, which may consist of many units. Where technical economies of scale are great, the size of the typical unit will tend to be correspondingly great, as, for example, in the production of cars, sheet steel, gas and electricity. Where, however, increased output merely means duplicating and reduplicating machines then the tendency will be for the unit to remain small. For instance, in farming at least one combine harvester is necessary for about 400 acres. Thus the size of the individual farm tends to remain small, for as yet there are no great technical economies to be derived from large machines. Where few technical economies can be enjoyed and yet the firm is large, consisting, as with chain stores, of many operating units, its size has usually been increased to achieve other types of economy, as follows.

(2) *Managerial economies*

On the managerial side economies may be achieved when output increases because specialists can be fully employed. In other words, the division of labour can be introduced into the task of management. In a shop, for instance, owned and run by one man, the owner, whilst he has the ability to order supplies, manage his books, and sell the goods, has yet to do the trivial jobs of sweeping the floor, weighing articles and packing parcels, jobs which could be done by a boy who had just left school. His sales, however, may not warrant employing a boy. The large business overcomes this difficulty. A brilliant organiser can devote himself wholly to the work of organising, while the routine jobs can be left to a lower-paid worker.

The function of management can itself be divided. Expert administrators can be put in charge of production, of sales, of transport and of personnel departments. The departments themselves might even be sub-divided, the sales department, for instance, being split into sections for advertisement, for exports, and for the study of customers' welfare.

(3) *Commercial economies*

Economies are achieved by the large firm both in buying raw materials and in selling the finished product. Favourable terms may be granted to the large firm placing a large order for materials because such an order is more valuable to the firm producing those materials. It may mean, for instance, that the plant of the latter firm can be worked to capacity, or that the large order to one specification can be turned out without frequent adjustments to machines and tools. This principle of special charges for a bulk order applies in various stages of production. The price of photographs advertising a product, for instance, would be quoted by the photographic firm according to the size of the order, while, for the transport of the finished goods, special rates would probably be obtained by the large firm because costs of transport, especially rail transport, do not increase in the same proportion as the volume of the goods to be transported.

Economies can be achieved, too, in the selling of the product. Very often the sales staff are not being worked to capacity, and hence a far greater quantity of goods can be sold at little extra cost. In any case much less work is involved proportionately in packaging and invoicing a large order than when a similar amount of goods is split up into many orders. Moreover, the large firm often manufactures many products and then one commodity acts as an advertisement for another. Thus Wall's ice-cream is also an advertisement for their pork pies and sausages, while Hoover vacuum cleaners help to sell their washing machines, refrigerators, and hair dryers. In addition, a large firm may be able to sell its by-products, although to a small firm this might be unprofitable. Indeed, one large cinema group has claimed that its box-office takings fail to cover expenses, the over-all profit only being due to its ice-cream sales!

Finally, when the scale of business is sufficiently large, the principle of the division of labour can be introduced on the commercial side, expert buyers and sellers being employed.

These commercial economies represent real advantages to the community, for they help to lower prices through better use of scarce resources. On the other hand, where a large firm is merely using its size to pursue 'monopoly' tactics, lower buying prices of raw materials will simply result in higher prices to other buyers.

(4) *Financial economies*

In raising finance for expansion, the large firm has nearly all the advantages. It can, for instance, offer better security to bankers and, because it is large and well-known, will be able to raise money in shares and debentures at a lower cost than a small firm. There are two reasons for this. First, investors have more confidence in the large, well-known firm. Secondly, they prefer shares which are regularly dealt in and quoted on the Stock Exchange, for then it is comparatively easy and quick, when it is so desired, to dispose of them.

(5) *Risk-bearing economies*

Here we can distinguish three sorts of risk. First, there are risks which can be insured against. With these the small firm is not at so great a disadvantage, for the principle of an insurance company is to enable such firms to secure the advantages of pooling risks on a large scale. The larger the size of this company, the more likely are losses to be spread according to the law of averages. Nevertheless, some undertakings, such as London Transport, are large enough to carry their own risks and can thus save the profits made by the insurance company.

Secondly, certain businesses usually bear some risk themselves in order to increase profits. Here the large firm is at a definite advantage. In banking, for instance, when a run on a bank occurs in a particular locality, a large bank can call in resources from other branches and thus, by meeting all the demands on it, restore the confidence of the public. Similarly, it is rarely the large 'bookie' who has to run for the early train when the favourite wins!

The third kind of risk is one that cannot easily be insured against—risk arising from changes in the demand for the product or in the supply of raw materials, usually referred to as the risks arising through 'uncertainty'.

A large firm may guard against such risks in a variety of ways. To meet variations in demand it can produce more than one product and so, by diversification of output, avoid 'putting all its eggs in one basket'. This was one of the reasons behind the development of mixed farming in England. Or the firm can develop different markets for its product. Hot-water heaters, thermostats and electric-light bulbs are supplied to industrial as well as private users. On the supply side, materials used may be obtained from many different sources, thereby guarding against a crippling loss of vital supplies owing to an increased demand by other users, crop failures, political upheavals or simply the raising of prices by a single supplier. Thus, when cuts occurred in the supply of electrical power, some large firms proved their resourcefulness and foresight by having their own plant installed for generating electricity against such an emergency.

III. THE COMBINATION OF FIRMS

Horizontal and vertical combination

The advantages of large-scale production provide a strong impetus for firms to combine. (A further reason—to establish monopoly power—will be discussed later.)

'Horizontal integration' occurs where firms producing the same product combine under the same management. Thus I.C.T. combined with Plessey and English Electric to form International Computers Ltd, and British Motor Holdings merged with Leyland Motors to form the British Leyland Motor Corporation. 'Vertical integration' consists of the amalgamation

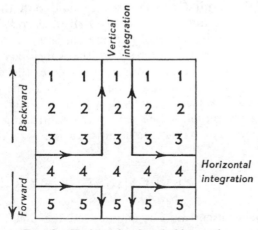

FIG. 28.—Horizontal and vertical integration.

of firms engaged in the different stages of the production of a good. Thus British Motor Holdings took over Fisher & Ludlow, producers of car bodies. Vertical integration may be 'backward', that is, towards the production of the raw material, or 'forward', that is, towards the finished product. In practice, horizontal integration, as opposed to vertical integration, has little relevance to technical economies of scale and is more closely associated with securing monopoly power.

The holding company

Combination may be secured by a complete merger, with the parent company buying all the shares of a smaller firm and absorbing it completely, or by the formation of a holding company in which the parent company owns over 50 per cent of the shares (giving it a 'controlling interest') with the smaller company preserving its identity as a separate trading unit and enjoying considerable independence of action. (Unilever Ltd and Great Universal Stores Ltd are examples of holding companies.)

The latter method, however, is open to misuse. Companies have been formed for monopoly purposes, while by 'pyramiding', a whole group of firms may be concentrated in the hands of few men owning comparatively little capital. Suppose, for instance, that this capital is £100,000. This can be used to control the affairs of a company which has a total capital of £400,000 if only half of this is in the form of ordinary shares. Similarly this capital can be used to hold half the ordinary shares of a company whose capital, half in shares and half in debentures, is in the region of £1,600,000. So the process can be continued. Where the interests of the subsidiary firms are sacrificed to those of the group as a whole, the minority of shareholders in them, who are not members of the controlling group, may suffer. Consequently the Companies Act, 1947 made it easier for the public to be aware of the controlling power of a holding company over its various subsidiaries.

IV. THE PREDOMINANCE OF THE SMALL FIRM

The above discussion has emphasised the fact that certain advantages are possessed by the large firm. Yet when we examine the actual size of firms operating in the United Kingdom, it is remarkable how the small firm predominates. In farming, two-thirds of the total holdings are less than 50 acres in size, while in retailing, nearly three-quarters of all firms consist of only one shop.

But the same applies even in manufacturing where, one would imagine, technical economies of scale would be all-important. Table 1 illustrates this fact.

TABLE 1

SIZE OF MANUFACTURING ESTABLISHMENTS IN
GREAT BRITAIN, 1968

Employees	Number of firms	Percentage of total firms	Number of employees (000's)	Percentage of total employed
1–10	31,627	38	158	2
11–99	37,761	45	1,318	17
100–999	12,797	15	3,538	46
Over 1,000	1,198	2	2,702	35
TOTAL -	83,383	100	7,716	100

Table 1 shows the size of the technical unit, the factory or workshop, in *manufacturing* only. It should be noted that a firm can consist of more than one establishment.

If we ignore this qualification, however, the Table reveals two very important features: (i) the small establishment is typical of manufacturing in Great Britain, over four-fifths employing less than 100 persons; (ii) these small firms employ only one-fifth of the labour force.

Any explanation of the predominance of the small firm, therefore, has to cover two essential facts: (i) small firms are especially important in particular industries, such as agriculture, retailing, building and personal and professional services; (ii) variations in the size of firms exist even within the same industry. Both can be covered by a consideration of particular conditions which can exist in demand and supply.

Demand

The advantages of large-scale production are concerned with *technical* efficiency. But *economic* efficiency relates the conditions of supply to demand. Thus methods of large-scale production are not economically efficient unless justified by the size of the demand.

Some firms, therefore, may remain small simply because the market they supply is relatively small for the following reasons:

(1) The market is limited to local demand for certain goods, e.g. groceries, personal services.

(2) Physical difficulties make the cost of transporting goods long distances excessive, e.g. perishable goods (small market gardeners), bulky goods of comparatively low value (bricks), or where natural difficulties have to be surmounted (water, gas).

(3) Demand is limited to a few articles of one pattern, e.g. highly-specialised machine tools, which are often individually designed.

(4) Product differentiation may split up the market artificially (*see* p. 219).

Supply

Where demand is small, firms are forced to remain small. But even when demand is comparatively large, factors on the supply side may result in that demand being satisfied by a number of small firms, instead of by a few large firms enjoying the advantages of large-scale production. These factors may be classified as follows:

(1) *Institutional.* Friction may prevent growth. Thus, as we have already noted, firms may find it difficult to raise capital at a crucial size simply because institutions do not exist to provide it. On the other hand, with some industries, e.g. retailing and personal services, it is possible to start with little capital.

Taxation, too, may reduce the size of a firm which is personally owned. Thus death duties and capital gains tax may mean that an estate or property holding has to be sold in fragments in order to pay the tax.

Government policy, too, may prevent mergers (*see* p. 213).

(2) *Vertical disintegration is possible.* It may be possible to break down the technical process so that different firms can each perform a small part of the whole task. Thus separate firms may produce a single component, carry out research, advertise, sell by-products, etc.

(3) *Managerial attitudes.* The small owner-manager may not have the ability to supervise a large firm, or may simply not want the extra worry. Or, as in farming and retailing, he may be willing to work long hours (that is, he accepts a lower rate of profit) because he puts a value on being his own boss.

(4) *Diseconomies of scale occur fairly early in the firm's growth.* Such diseconomies can occur because of the lack of adaptability of highly-specialised machines to fluctuations in demand or the higher prices which are sometimes asked when it is known that a large firm (e.g. the government) is buying.

But the main diseconomies occur in management. As the size of the firm increases, the task of management cannot be given to a number of men without creating difficulties. Co-ordination problems arise, and rivalries develop. This means that one person must be in overall command—yet such persons are in very limited supply. In certain industries these difficulties arise earlier than in others. Quick decisions are required where

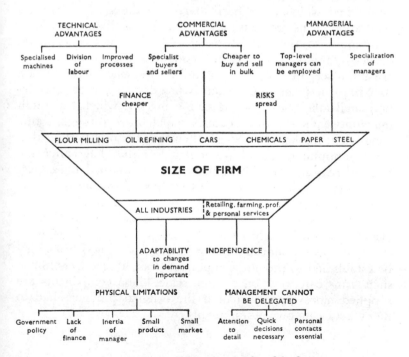

FIG. 29.—Factors influencing the size of the firm.

demand changes quickly (e.g. in the fashion trades), or supply conditions alter (e.g. through the weather in agriculture). Or care may have to be given to personal requirements of customers (e.g. in retailing and services), or to detail (e.g. in agriculture). This may require the close supervision of management, and thus the firm has to be small.

V. EXTERNAL ECONOMIES

Apart from *internal economies*—the advantages which a firm, can obtain for itself by operating on a large scale—economies may result as the *industry* grows in size. The latter are known as *external economies*.

The concentration of similar firms in an area often results in mutual benefits. A skilled labour force is developed; common services, such as marketing organisations, can be set up; roads and social amenities are provided; technical schools are established which cater particularly for the local industry; a reputation for its products may be founded; and ancillary firms may move to the district to supply specialised machinery, collect by-products, etc. While economies of concentration do not influence the firm when planning the scale of production they must be taken into account when deciding where production shall take place, for the saving in costs which can result may outweigh any diseconomies which arise through traffic congestion, smoke, etc. Indeed, they may be so important that firms continue to go to particular localities long after the original reasons why the industry was established there (e.g. abundance of raw materials or power) have passed away.

External economies can also take the form of common information services provided either by associations of firms or even by the government itself.

Finally, as the industry grows in size, specialised firms may be established to provide components for all producers. Since such firms can work on a large scale, these components are supplied more cheaply than if the original producer had to manufacture his own requirements.

CHAPTER 8

THE DISTRIBUTION OF GOODS TO THE CONSUMER

I. THE SCOPE OF PRODUCTION

A manufacturer will have to decide whether to produce one good, or many variations of the same good, or a number of different goods. Whatever his plans, he will still have to decide on how to get his finished goods to the consumer.

He himself may undertake the task. But if he does so, he must be willing to employ salesmen, run delivery transport, carry stocks, organise exports, advertise his product, advise customers, give credit and establish servicing centres. Many of these are highly specialised functions, and full-time experts can only be employed on them if output is large enough. Furthermore, the

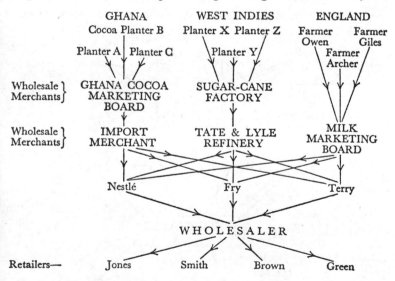

FIG. 30.—The parts played by the wholesaler and retailer in the 'production' of chocolate.

manufacturer's main ability lies in organising the production of the good rather than the selling of it.

The result is that the principle of the division of labour is often applied to the task of getting the good to the consumer. This is achieved by forward vertical disintegration. Just as the manufacturer buys raw materials and components from other producers, so specialists will accept the task of getting his goods to the consumer—the final stage of the whole productive process.

These specialists can perform many different tasks themselves, or each separate task may itself be put in the hands of a specialist. We will simplify, however, and group them together under the headings of 'wholesalers' and 'retailers'. Fig. 30 shows how they fit in to the various stages in the production of chocolate.

II. THE WHOLESALER

The wholesaler buys goods in bulk from producers and sells them in small quantities to retailers according to their requirements. But, to promote this main task, he helps the process of production in a number of ways.

(1) *He economises in distribution*

Since many shops, especially shops which stock a large

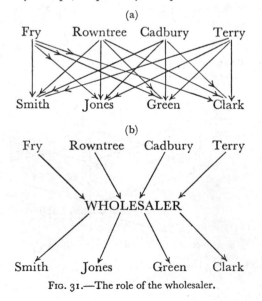

Fig. 31.—The role of the wholesaler.

variety of goods, can order their supplies only in small quantities it is not economical for each producer to sell directly to them. Such a practice would mean employing many salesmen and representatives, packing many separate parcels and making numerous transport journeys in visiting each shop in turn. This fact is illustrated by Fig. 31a, which shows that 16 contacts and van journeys are necessary when 4 chocolate firms deliver directly to 4 retailers.

Fig. 31b on the other hand, shows that, when the goods are delivered in bulk by each to a wholesaler, the number of contacts and journeys is cut down to eight.

In agriculture particularly, where the goods are perishable, it simplifies matters considerably if the farmer, instead of trying to contact retailers himself, can deliver his produce to a wholesaler or commission salesman, for example at Covent Garden, and leave the actual selling to him.

Similarly, in the construction industry, where there are numerous small builders, it is easier for manufacturers to deliver through builders' merchants.

(2) *He keeps stocks*

Consumers like the convenience of being able to go to a shop and obtaining a good just when they require it. This means that stocks have to be held. Often, however, neither the producer nor the retailer has the necessary storage facilities or capital for this, and so it is left to the wholesaler.

In other ways, too, the costs of storage are removed from the producer or retailer. While loss through fire, flood or rats can be insured against, no insurance can be taken out to cover a loss through a fall in demand. Thus a wholesaler, who holds stocks of a good which is liable to go out of fashion, relieves the manufacturers and the retailers of that risk.

The holding of stocks is, in itself, a valuable economic function. Stocks help to even out fluctuations in price resulting from sudden but temporary fluctuations in demand and supply. Thus brick stocks in the hands of merchants are replenished during the winter and run down during the remainder of the year.

(3) *He arranges imports from abroad*

Manufacturers abroad could rarely be bothered to ship small parcels to individual retailers or undertake the foreign currency transactions involved. These tasks are left to a wholesaler, the import merchant, who is known and trusted. Often the import merchant goes abroad to establish and develop trade connections.

(4) *He carries out certain specialised functions*

Not only does the wholesaler advertise goods but, in order to make selling easier, he may process the goods he receives. Thus milk is pasteurised, hams are cooked, tea is blended and sugar is refined, while certain commodities, such as cotton, wheat and wool tops, are graded.

(5) *He is a channel for information and advice*

Suggestions which customers make to the retailer are passed on to the wholesaler, and the latter, especially when he sees that such suggestions are representative of a wide area, passes them on to the manufacturer. Thus the manufacturer discovers how his product could be improved or how he can anticipate fashion changes.

(6) *He assists in the day-to-day maintenance of the good*

With many products, particularly vehicles and machinery, an efficient maintenance service is essential. The manufacturer can be relieved of this task by the wholesaler, who can provide a local and quick maintenance, repair and spare-part service.

III. THE RETAILER

Functions of the retailer

The retailer performs the last stage of the productive process, for it is he who puts the goods in the hands of the actual consumer. His work has been summarised as being 'to have the right goods in the right place at the right time', and his functions, as set out below, are chiefly an enlargement on this. It must be appreciated, however, that, in actual practice, there is not always a clear distinction between the wholesaler and the retailer, and thus it will be found that, in some cases, their functions appear to overlap.

(1) *He stocks small quantities of a variety of goods*

What is the 'right good' depends on the customer, for different people have different tastes, and what suits one may be undesirable to another. Thus having the 'right good' depends largely on having a stock of the different varieties of the good, so that each customer can make his or her individual choice, pay for it, and take delivery there and then. In part, his shop consists of a showroom wherein the customers can examine and compare the different goods one with the other and make their own selection. This is particularly helpful to customers when choosing goods which are only bought infrequently.

The size of the stocks the retailer carries will depend on many factors. Some manufacturers even stipulate that a certain minimum stock shall be carried before they will allow a retailer to sell their goods. Usually, however, it is left to the retailer himself. He will consider the popularity of the product, the possibility of obtaining further supplies quickly, the perishability of the good or the likelihood of its going out of fashion, the season (especially if it is approaching Christmas or if there is a seasonal demand for the good) and the possibility of a future change in its price. Above all, he must allow for the cost, in the form of interest on bank advances, of carrying stocks.

(2) *He takes the goods to where it is most convenient for the customer*

Taking the goods to where it is most convenient for the customer may merely mean that the retailer sets up his shop within easy reach. It is for this reason that we see retailers congregated together in the centre of most towns, though, with goods such as groceries, which are in everyday use, small shops are often dotted around residential districts. Where customers are very dispersed, however, as in country districts, it is quite likely that the retailer will own a 'travelling shop' of some form or another.

While, with the majority of goods, customers take their purchases with them, the retailer may arrange delivery. This occurs with certain goods, such as coal and furniture, where transport is essential, but it also applies where the customer requires the extra convenience of having his goods delivered, as, for example, with milk, the early-morning newspaper, laundry, and groceries supplied by high-class stores.

(3) He performs special services for customers

In the course of his main business, the retailer performs many services for the convenience of his customers all of which help to build up goodwill. The customer is made to feel that he is getting individual attention. Where the good is not in stock, he will order it, and, in other matters where contact with the manufacturer is necessary, the retailer often acts for the customer. Thus goods are returned to the manufacturer for repair, though, in order to effect such repairs more quickly, he may maintain a repair service, e.g. cycle, radio and television retailers.

With many goods, too, such as fishing tackle, photographic equipment, musical instruments, machinery and sports gear, he can often provide special advice. Indeed, some manufacturers insist on their retailers having technical competence.

Finally, for the greater convenience of customers, goods may be sent on approval or credit facilities arranged through hire purchase, special credit accounts, etc.

(4) He advises the wholesaler and manufacturer

A retailer maintains close contact with his customers. From them he discovers, either through a chance remark in the course of conversation or by direct suggestion, how a good could be improved or what type of good there is a large demand for. This information finds its way to the manufacturer, who will probably act upon it, and eventually the modification or the new good will be produced.

Types of retail outlet

Retailing might be widely defined to include all shops, mail-order firms, garages, bus companies, launderettes, betting shops or indeed any organisation which sells products or services to the consumer. It is usual, however, to take a narrower view and to confine retailing to shops and mail order outlets. These can be classified as follows.

(1) Independents

These are mainly small shops with no other branches, and they account for just under half of the total sales through shops. Yet, in spite of their advantages of individual attention to customers, 'handy' locations for quick shopping trips, and the willingness of owners to accept a lower return for the benefits of being one's own boss, these independents are steadily losing ground to the larger stores.

A major bid to avert the decline has come through the voluntary chains, such as Spar, Mace and Wavy Line, of which over 32 per cent of independents are members. While retaining their independence, members buy in bulk from the wholesaler (often at times and at minimum quantities dictated by him) and use common advertising and display techniques.

(2) Multiples

These can be defined arbitrarily as organisations of ten or more shops. Some, such as Mothercare and Dorothy Perkins, sell a particular type of good. Others, such as Littlewood, Woolworth, Boots, and Marks and Spencer, have a fairly extensive range of products. Together they comprise over 35 per cent of the market.

Their chief advantages are that they can obtain the economies of bulk buying and centralised control, eliminate the wholesaler, invite instant recognition through their standardised shop fronts, and establish a reputation through brand names.

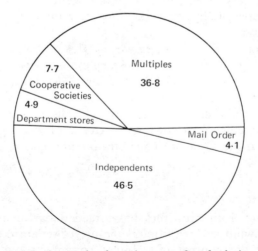

FIG. 32.—Retail sales: market shares (per cent of total value), 1970. (Source: Department of Trade and Industry.)

(3) Supermarkets

These may be defined as self-service shops with a minimum selling area of 2,000 sq. ft. While organisationally they would count as multiples, their share of the food trade warrants separate attention. In 1973 they accounted for half the grocery trade and nearly a third of total retail food sales.

The field is led by the four major retail grocery chains: Tesco, Sainsbury, Allied Suppliers and Fine Fare. They thus secure the benefits of economies of scale, low labour costs, a clear and attractive display of merchandise and bulk buying to the extent of their own labelling (e.g. Sainsbury's cornflakes, Tesco coffee). As a result they have gained ground rapidly through highly-competitive prices.

Indeed, many of these self-service organisations have extended their activities beyond groceries, to clothing and hardware for example, where profit margins are usually higher.

(4) Hypermarkets

Urban congestion, lack of adequate parking space and rising land prices or rents have made the High Street an increasingly expensive place from which to sell goods. The American and, to an increasing extent the European answer to these problems has been the very large (20,000–40,000 sq. ft.), 'out-of-town' shopping centre or 'hypermarket' to cater for the car-borne weekly shopper.

In the United Kingdom, however, the development has been slow. This is mainly because planning permission for such schemes is not readily forthcoming. The Department of the Environment continues to keep a watchful eye on the expansion of these space-consuming establishments, largely with the problems of 'down-town decay' and spoiling of the countryside in the forefront of environmental cost considerations.

(5) Department stores

Competition from multiples has forced department stores to alter somewhat the traditional picture of separate departments under the control of a buyer enjoying some degree of autonomy (which led to the epithet 'many stores under one roof'). Instead, a more streamlined approach with an increasing degree of bulk-buying by central office, more self-service, and extended credit facilities have allowed them to retain about 5 per cent of the market.

The main groups are Debenhams, House of Fraser, John Lewis Partnership, Great Universal Stores, and Sears Holdings.

(6) *Co-operatives (see* pp. 114–15)

(7) *Mail order*

While retail sales in general rose by about 27 per cent between 1966 and 1971, mail-order business increased by 32 per cent. By 1975 mail-order houses are expected to have 6 per cent of the market.

The five major companies: Great Universal Stores, Littlewoods Mail Order, Grattan Warehouses, Freemans and Empire Stores sell by agency and illustrated catalogues, purchases usually being arranged through weekly interest-free payments. Over one-half of all sales are accounted for by women's clothing and household goods.

Factors affecting the type of retail outlet

Over the last twenty years, the pattern of retailing has moved away from the small, independent shop towards the larger organisation, notably the multiples, supermarket chains and mail order firms. This trend reflects a greater emphasis on competition through lower price rather than by better service.

The larger firms are in a strong position to cut prices. Not only do they obtain the advantages of large-scale production (particularly those of selling a whole range of goods and of buying in bulk), but they can use their bargaining strength to secure further price discounts from manufacturers. Indeed, the largest may force the manufacturer to supply goods under the retailer's 'own-brand' label at a price below that at which other retailers can buy the manufacturer's national brand. Moreover, since the large retailer caters for a whole range of shopping, e.g. food, they can attract customers into stores by 'loss-leaders'.

Economic factors influencing this trend have been:

(1) *Increased income*, which has led to a swing in expenditure towards the more expensive processed foods and towards consumer durable goods.

(2) *An increase in car ownership*, which has enabled people to move from the city centre to the outer suburbs. Shops have followed, not only to be near their customers, but also to obtain larger sites with parking facilities. In doing so, they avoid the high rents and congestion of city centre sites.

The car has also made customers more mobile, enabling them to travel to good shopping centres where they can purchase all their requirements at a single stop.

(3) *An increase in the number of married women going to work*, which has promoted the demand for convenience foods and labour-saving devices. It has also led to the reduction of the number of shopping expeditions which can be made, and this trend has been helped by the wider ownership of refrigerators and deep-freezers.

These factors are likely to remain important in the future. It seems probable, therefore, that new supermarkets will take the form of discount stores or hypermarkets selling a wider range of products whose profit margins are larger than those on groceries. Moreover, if planning permission is forthcoming, these new stores will develop outside the town. Cash-and-carry warehouses may also be open to those consumers who can buy in bulk and transport their goods.

Such changes are likely to be at the expense of the medium-sized business, for the retail trade will largely consist of small local retailers offering convenience services and the large out-of-town shopping centre.

IV. THE FUTURE OF THE MIDDLEMAN

Criticisms of middlemen

The people who come between the actual manufacturer and the consumer, the wholesalers and retailers, are often referred to as 'middlemen', though more usually the term is applied only to the wholesaler. Criticism of them is frequent. Many critics argue that middlemen take too large a share of the selling price of the good and that, if they were eliminated by the manufacturer establishing direct contact with consumers, prices could be reduced.

But, as we have seen, wholesalers and retailers perform essential functions, and if a producer does not sell through them, he has to perform these functions himself. Unless his output is large enough, this would be uneconomic. The fact is that, through these middlemen, producers obtain the advantages of specialisation and large-scale production in marketing products. This form of forward vertical disintegration is, therefore, usually the cheapest way of getting the good to the consumer.

However, this general case for middlemen does not mean that all criticism of them is unjustified. Sometimes their profit margins are too high. This may occur through the perpetuation of antiquated methods or by the playing-off by a single middleman of one small producer, such as a farmer, against another (hence the formation of producers' co-operatives).

The elimination of the wholesaler

In recent years, there has been a tendency for the whole-saler to be eliminated. This has been due to: (i) the growth of large shops, such as the co-operative society, multiple store and supermarket, which can order in bulk; (ii) the development of road transport, which reduces the necessity of holding large stocks; (iii) the desire of manufacturers to retain some control over retailing outlets in order to ensure that their products are pushed or that a high standard of service, freshness, etc., is maintained; (iv) the practice of branding many products, which eliminates many specialised functions. In other cases, however, the elimination of the wholesaler has been confined to those goods which are of high value, such as furniture and television sets; to circumstances where the producer and retailer are close together, as with the market gardener who supplies the local shop; and cases where the manufacturer does his own retailing.

On the other hand, the wholesaler has, as we have seen, responded to this challenge by developing in two main directions: (*a*) the cash-and-carry warehouse, sometimes called 'the retailers' supermarket'; (*b*) becoming the organiser of a voluntary chain of retailers, who are supplied, and to some extent controlled, by him.

Direct selling by manufacturers

Selling direct to consumers by the manufacturer occurs chiefly where: (*a*) he wishes to push his product (e.g. beer and footwear), or to ensure a standard of advice and service (e.g. sewing machines); (*b*) the personal service element is important (e.g. made-to-measure clothing); (*c*) he is a small-scale producer-retailer, often selling a perishable good (e.g. cakes and pastries), or serving a local area (e.g. printing); (*d*) so wide a range of goods is produced that a whole chain of shops can be fully stocked (e.g. Lyons, Manfield shoes); (*e*) the good is highly technical or made to individual specifications (e.g. machinery).

CHAPTER 9

THE LOCATION OF PRODUCTION

A FIRM has to decide where to produce. It will reach its decision by considering: (a) the advantages of producing in different areas; (b) the level of rents in these different areas. Thus, although the rent of sites in an area may be high, it can pay a firm to go there if the advantages of that particular area mean that other factors cost less.

I. THE ADVANTAGES OF DIFFERENT LOCALITIES

These can be classified as: (1) natural, (2) acquired, (3) government-sponsored.

(1) *Natural advantages*

Costs are incurred both in assembling the raw materials and in distributing the finished product to the consumer. In manufacturing some products, the weight of the initial raw materials is far greater than that of the final product. This is particularly true where coal is used as the source of heat and power, e.g. in iron and steel production (Fig. 33). Here transport costs are saved by producing where raw materials are found (e.g. on coal- and iron-ore fields), or are easily accessible (e.g. near a port).

On the other hand, with some industries the costs of transporting the finished product are greater than those of assembling the raw materials, e.g. ice-cream, furniture, beer, mineral waters, metal cans, and glass containers. With these, it is cheaper for a firm to produce near the market for its goods. Thus, whereas Stewarts and Lloyds has one main plant for producing steel tubes at Corby, Northamptonshire, where the

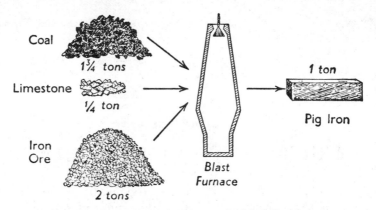

FIG. 33.—The production of pig-iron—a 'weight-losing' industry.

iron ore is mined, T. Wall has ice-cream factories close by most large concentrations of population, and Metal Box manufactures its containers in over forty factories scattered throughout Britain.

Generally speaking, transport improvements and new developments (e.g. electrical power) have helped firms to move away from their sources of raw materials. The tendency now, therefore, is for firms to concentrate, not on the coalfields, but on the outskirts of areas of high population which provide both a supply of labour and a market for the finished good.

Besides accessibility to raw materials and nearness of markets, suitability of climate is a further natural advantage which may have to be considered when locating production. Indeed, in agriculture, it is usually decisive, provided soil conditions are not adverse. But even in industry, climate may add to the advantages of an area. Thus the humidity of the atmosphere in Lancashire and West Yorkshire assisted in the spinning and weaving processes in the production of cotton and woollen cloths until these conditions were produced artificially.

Under the heading of 'natural advantages' we can also include an abundant supply of cheap, unskilled labour. This may be important in attracting certain industries, e.g. in Malta and Hong Kong.

(2) *Acquired advantages*

Improved methods of production, the development of transport, the provision of alternative sources of power and new inventions may bring about a change in the location of industry since they alter the relative importance of natural advantages. Thus, as high-grade iron-ore fields became exhausted and improved techniques reduced coal consumption, the pig-iron industry has shifted from the coalfields to the low-grade iron-ore fields of the East Midlands, for it is now cheaper to transport the coal required than the iron ore. Similarly improved transport may upset the relative pulls. By transporting coal and iron ore to Dagenham, the Ford motor company is able to produce pig-iron on a *consumption* centre. Finally new inventions, such as 'humidifiers' for producing a damp atmosphere, and water-softeners, help to relieve an industry from dependence on the natural factors of a particular locality.

Yet we must not overstress the importance of the above changes. Even when natural factors have entirely disappeared, an industry often continues to be located in the same region. Thus the steel industry persists in most of its older centres and cotton production still concentrates in Lancashire. Indeed, it has been said that the ability of a locality to hold an industry greatly exceeds its original ability to attract it. This is due to the acquired or 'man-made' advantages which arise as the industry expands. Such advantages were largely considered in Chapter 7 when we studied the external economies of concentration. They include a skilled labour force, communications, marketing and commercial organisations, nearby ancillary industries (either to achieve further economies of scale or to market by-products), training schools, etc., in the locality, and a widespread reputation for the products of the region. All help to lower the costs of production, thereby making the locality attractive to new firms considering where to produce a particular good.

(3) Government-sponsored advantages

The heavy concentration of firms in certain districts can have harmful social effects—traffic congestion, smoke pollution, a lack of open spaces, strain on the public transport system during peak hours, etc. Above all, when an industry becomes localised in a particular area, a serious unemployment situation can arise if there is a fall in demand for its products. Thus, over the last fifty years, some of Britain's older industries (e.g. cotton, shipbuilding and jute) have declined, and coal has been replaced by oil as a source of power. This has led to unemployment in Lancashire, the North-East Coast, Northern Ireland, Central Scotland, South Wales and a number of other districts, for newer industries have preferred to go to the Midlands and South-East England.

The government, therefore, has had to interfere in the decisions of firms when siting their plants. So far it has not resorted to compulsion, although it has refused to give Industrial Development Certificates in the areas of already high employment. Instead it has offered financial inducements—investment grants, regional employment premiums and tax concessions—to attract firms to those areas where unemployment is most severe, the 'Assisted Areas' (*see* Chapter 27).

Such financial advantages would have to be considered by a firm when deciding where to site its factory.

II. THE LEVEL OF RENTS IN DIFFERENT AREAS

In addition to the advantages of being in a particular locality, a firm will also have to consider the cost of land there relative to the cost of land elsewhere.

The cost of the land will be decided by the price system. Other firms, possibly from other industries, may be looking for the same site advantages. Thus the cost (that is, the price) of the land will be fixed by competition among the various firms wanting to go there, and it will settle at the highest price which the keenest firm has to pay—its opportunity cost.

Now the firm that can pay the most will be the one which values its advantages the highest compared with the advantages of land elsewhere. Thus, early in its history, it seemed that the cotton industry might settle on the Clyde, for the locality had all the natural advantages of South-East Lancashire. But it also had deep water—and shipbuilding firms were prepared to pay extra for this advantage. For cotton manufacturers this extra cost of a site on the Clyde was greater than any disadvantage of being in Lancashire. Thus shipbuilding firms settled along the Clyde, while cotton firms concentrated in Lancashire.

In the final analysis, therefore, it is not the absolute

advantages of a district which decide where a firm locates its production, but the advantages relative to those of every other district. Many industries, for instance, would be able to use cheap, unskilled labour. But an industry whose outlay on unskilled labour formed a high proportion of its total costs would, other things being equal, be able to bid more for land in an area of cheap, unskilled labour than where the cost of such labour was a comparatively minor item. And, in any town centre, we see the same principle at work—shops oust other businesses, and houses are converted into offices.

III. CONCLUSIONS

A firm will normally choose a site where the benefits are greatest compared with its cost. Where it is producing in a comparatively new industry, natural advantages will play an important part.

Even so, we cannot assume that, outside the heavy industries, they will be decisive. Thus the Barlow Report on the Distribution of the Industrial Population, 1940 quotes a Board of

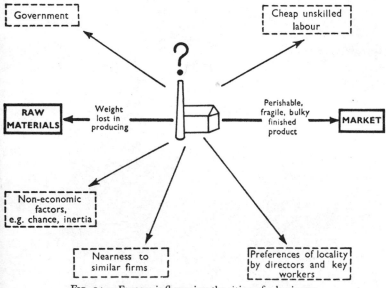

FIG. 34.—Factors influencing the siting of a business.

Trade statement which emphasises the important part which even historical accident may play. This statement even goes as far as to assert that the cotton industry first 'settled in Lancashire for no particular reason, except perhaps that the woollen industry was already there, the foreigners were kindly received and that Manchester had no corporation' (thereby being free from restrictive practices). Similarly, the British Leyland Motor assembly plant was established at Cowley chiefly because William Morris, its founder, had a cycle business in Oxford.

In time, the original natural advantages may pass away, especially as electricity displaces coal. Yet firms may still go to the original areas because of the acquired advantages which have developed over time. Nevertheless, emancipation from a coalfield site has enabled many firms to go nearer their markets. On the other hand, some of these 'footloose' firms have located in certain districts, particularly in the south-east of England, largely because the managing directors (or their wives) have preferred living there!

The various factors influencing location are summarised in Fig. 34.

CHAPTER 10

COMBINING THE FACTORS OF PRODUCTION

EVEN the simplest form of production requires at least two factors of production. Thus the manna which fell from Heaven, although a free gift of nature, needed labour to collect it (Exodus 16). Nevertheless, factors can usually be combined in different proportions. The same amount of concrete can be mixed by having many men with just a shovel apiece or by having only one man using a concrete mixer.

Each entrepreneur, therefore, when planning production, has to decide how much of each factor he will use, for his object must be to combine his factors of production so that a given outlay on them will yield the maximum output. Can we discover any general principle governing his decision? Let us start by examining how *physical* yields vary as factors of production are combined in different proportions.

I. THE LAW OF DIMINISHING RETURNS

What happens to total output when the supply of any factor is held fixed while the quantities of other factors are increased is described by the 'law of diminishing returns', first formulated by the classical economists in the middle of the nineteenth century. For our exposition of the law we shall assume:

(1) production is by two factors only;
(2) all units of the variable factor have the same efficiency— one unit is a perfect substitute for another;
(3) there is no accompanying change in techniques or organisation.

Given these assumptions, the law can be stated as follows: if one factor is held fixed, but additional units of the varying factor are added to it, eventually the extra output resulting from an additional unit of the varying factor will become successively smaller. Since the additional output resulting from an extra unit of the varying factor is known as the 'marginal product', the law refers to eventual diminishing marginal productivity.

The law can be illustrated by following the classical economists' assumptions that land is the fixed factor and that the number of labourers employed on this fixed amount of land is varied. Suppose potatoes are being produced. Table 2 shows a purely hypothetical yield.

TABLE 2

VARIATIONS IN OUTPUT OF POTATOES RESULTING FROM A
CHANGE IN LABOUR EMPLOYED

Number of men employed on the fixed unit of land	Total output	Yield (cwt.) Average output	Marginal
1	1	1	1
2	8	4	7
3	27	9	19
4	40	10	13
5	$47\frac{1}{2}$	$9\frac{1}{2}$	$7\frac{1}{2}$
6	54	9	$6\frac{1}{2}$
7	60	$8\frac{4}{7}$	6
8	65	$8\frac{1}{8}$	5
9	69	$7\frac{2}{3}$	4
10	71	$7\frac{1}{10}$	2
11	71	$6\frac{5}{11}$	0
12	66	$5\frac{1}{2}$	-5

Notes:
  (a) *Total output* is the total yield (cwt.) from all factors employed.
  (b) *Average output* refers to the average yield per man. It therefore equals

$$\frac{\text{total output}}{\text{number of men employed}}$$

  (c) *Marginal output* refers to the marginal yield (cwt.) to labour, and equals the addition to total output which is obtained by increasing the labour force by one man. That is, marginal output equals total output of $(n+1)$ men – total output of n men.
  (d) There is a fundamental relationship between average output and marginal output. Marginal output equals average output when the latter is at a maximum (Fig. 35). This relationship is bound to occur. So long as the

marginal output is greater than average output, the return to an additional labourer will raise the average output of all labourers employed. On the other hand, as soon as the marginal output falls below average output, the additional labourer will lower the average output. Hence when average product is neither rising nor falling, that is, at its maximum, it is because marginal product equals average product.

This relationship can be made clearer by a simple example. Suppose Boycott has played 20 innings and that his batting average is 60 runs. Now if in his next innings he scores more than 60, say 102, his average will increase—to 62. If, on the other hand, he scores less than 60, say 18, his average will fall—to 58. If he scores exactly 60 in his twenty-first innings, his average will remain unchanged at 60.

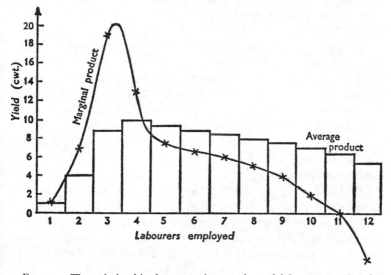

Fig. 35.—The relationship between the number of labourers employed, average output and marginal output.

Our example shows that the physical productivity of a factor can be varied by combining it in different proportions with another factor. Thus when 4 men are employed on the fixed piece of land, the marginal output is 13 cwt.; when there are 8 men, the marginal output is only 5 cwt. The maximum return per labourer is achieved when there are 4 labourers to the given plot of land. Diminishing returns occur because labour is an imperfect substitute for land. The result is that when we increase the number of labourers, total output increases, but at a diminishing rate. We can only maintain the maximum return per labourer by increasing the amount of land—8 would need double the amount of land. Otherwise eventually, after 3 labourers, the extra return resulting from an additional labourer becomes progressively smaller. When 11 labourers are employed, they start to get in one another's way. The marginal product is nil, and thereafter becomes negative. Total output is then declining absolutely.

Some important points regarding the law of diminishing returns

In order to avoid any misconceptions, it is helpful to call attention to certain fundamental points regarding the law of diminishing returns.

(1) The units of the variable factor are homogeneous. The marginal product of labour does not fall because less efficient labourers are being employed. Diminishing returns occur because more labourers are being employed on a fixed amount of land—and, through physical considerations, labour is an imperfect substitute for land. (If it were otherwise, all the world's food supplies could be grown on a garden plot: extra land would not be necessary, since output could be increased merely by adding men).

(2) The law applies only if one factor is held fixed. (If both factors can be varied, we have a change of 'scale').

(3) The law is not applicable if the factors can only be combined in fixed proportions. If, for instance, you must have one labourer to one shovel to obtain any output, then merely increasing the number of labourers by one will add nothing to output; the marginal product is nil. For the law to hold, the proportions in which the factors can be combined must be variable. For this reason, the law is often referred to as the law of variable proportions.

(4) The law does not formulate any *economic* hypothesis or theory. It is merely technical, stating physical relationships. While the physical productivity of an extra labourer is important to a farmer in deciding how many men to employ, it will not *determine* his decision. We also have to know the cost of an extra labourer relative to the cost of an alternative factor. That is, we have to consider economic data as well as technical relationships.

(5) There are no changes in techniques.

The practical applications of the law of diminishing returns

The law is significant both in our everyday life and in the theoretical analysis of the economist.

First, it helps to explain the low standard of living in many parts of the world, particularly the Far East. Increasing population is cultivating a fixed amount of land. Marginal product, and thus average product, are falling—and so, therefore, is the average standard of living.

Secondly, it shows how an entrepreneur can arrive at an equilibrium position in purchasing his factors of production. So far we have assumed that we have just two factors, land and labour, and that land is fixed. But suppose that there is another variable factor, say capital. Now the farmer will have to decide how he will combine labour with capital.

He will want to ensure that a given outlay on them will yield maximum output. This is essentially the same problem that faced the consumer when allocating his expenditure. And, in the same way that a consumer could adjust his marginal utility by adding to or subtracting from the amount of a commodity possessed, so the entrepreneur can adjust the marginal productivity of a factor by varying the amount of it which he uses with another factor. In other words, factors can be substituted at the margin. For instance, the same amount of wheat can be produced by employing many men and little land (intensive farming) or by using few men and much land (extensive farming). Thus the law of diminishing returns fulfils a parallel role to the law of diminishing marginal utility—they both show how yield at the margin can be varied. (Theoretically there is a difference in that, while we cannot measure marginal utility, we can measure marginal productivity either in physical or money terms.)

II. THE OPTIMUM COMBINATION OF VARIABLE FACTORS

The solution to the problem of how to obtain the maximum yield from a given outlay on variable factors is also similar to that of the consumer seeking to obtain the maximum satisfaction from the expenditure of his limited income. The consumer considers the utility of a particular unit of a good relative to its price. Similarly, how much of each factor an entrepreneur employs when it is variable will depend upon its productivity relative to its cost.

Let us go back to our example of labour and capital which are being used to produce a given product—potatoes. The entrepreneur will be in equilibrium, that is, he will cease to rearrange the combination of labour and capital, when, for the last pound spent on both, he obtains the same amount of product. Suppose, for instance, the last pound's worth of labour is yielding a greater physical quantity of potatoes than the last pound spent on capital. It will obviously pay the entrepreneur to transfer the last pound from capital to buying more labour, for this will increase his total physical yield.

But labour and capital are obtained in different units, the units being of different prices. Thus we cannot compare directly the productivity of one man with that of one unit of capital, say a mechanical hoe; we must allow for their respective prices. If the cost of one man is only a third of the cost of a mechanical hoe, then the marginal product of a man need only be one-third of the hoe's to give the same yield for a given expenditure. Thus the entrepreneur will be in equilibrium in combining factors which can be varied when he has established the fundamental relationship:

$$\frac{\text{Marginal product of factor } A}{\text{Price of factor } A} = \frac{\text{Marginal product of factor } Z}{\text{Price of factor } Z}$$

A corollary of this is that, like the housewife in purchasing her goods, the entrepreneur will tend to buy more of a factor as its price falls, and less as it rises. Suppose the wage rate rises, but the marginal product of labour remains unchanged. The fundamental relationship stated above has now been destroyed. To restore the position it is necessary to raise the marginal product of labour and to lower that of capital. The law of diminishing returns shows how we can do this—by combining less labour with more capital. In short, a rise in wages without a corresponding increase in the productivity of labour will tend towards the substitution of machinery for labour.

The above argument helps to explain why in Britain more

capital is combined with a given amount of labour in agriculture compared with Ireland; relative prices are different. Similarly, if land is variable as well as labour, agriculture will be extensive where land is relatively cheap (as in Canada) and intensive where it is relatively dear (as in Britain).

A third application of the law of diminishing returns is to show how costs vary with changes in output when one or more factors are fixed. It is to this problem that we now turn.

CHAPTER 11

DECIDING ON THE MOST PROFITABLE OUTPUT

I. THE COSTS OF PRODUCTION

Costs as alternatives forgone

SUPPOSE a man sets himself up as a shopkeeper selling sweets. Suppose, too, that he invests £500 of his savings in the business, and that over a year his receipts are £5,000 and his outgoings £3,500. It is probable that he would say that his profits over the year were £1,500. But are they really? The economist would answer 'no'.

The reason for this is that the economist is not so much concerned with money costs as with opportunity costs—what a factor could earn in its best alternative line of production. As we shall see, this concept of costs has a bearing on: (*a*) the economist's concept of 'profits'; (*b*) the extent to which production should be carried on in the short period when certain factors cannot be transferred to an alternative use.

Opportunity costs and profit

The £3,500 money outgoings of the shopkeeper above can be regarded as 'explicit costs'. But, when we look at costs as alternatives forgone, we see immediately that the shopkeeper has certain 'implicit costs'. This is because, although he uses his own capital and labour, both could earn a reward in alternative lines of production. Say, for instance, his capital could be invested elsewhere at 7 per cent. There is thus an implicit cost of £35 a year. Similarly with his own labour. His next most profitable line, we will assume, is as a shop-manager earning £900 a year. There are thus £935 implicit costs in addition to the explicit costs to be taken from his revenue.

Normal profit

But we have not finished yet. The shopkeeper knows that even in running a sweet business there is a certain amount of 'hazard' through uncertainty—a hazard which he avoids if he merely works for somebody else. The shopkeeper must therefore anticipate at least a certain minimum profit, say £65 a year, before he will be prepared to set up business on his own, that is, before he will become an entrepreneur. If he does not make this minimum level of profit, he feels he might just as well go into some other line of business or become a paid shop-manager. Thus another type of cost (which we call 'normal profit') has to be allowed for—the minimum return which keeps an entrepreneur in a particular industry after all other factors have been paid their opportunity cost. Normal profit is a cost because if it is not met the supply of entrepreneurship to that particular line of business dries up.

We have, therefore, the following costs: explicit costs, implicit costs, normal profit. Anything left over after all these costs have been met is 'abnormal', 'super-normal' or 'pure' profit. In terms of our example, we have:

		£	£
Total revenue			5,000
Total costs:	explicit	3,500	
	implicit	935	
	normal profit	65	
			4,500
Abnormal profit			500

Fixed costs and variable costs

For the purposes of our analysis, we shall classify costs into *fixed costs* and *variable costs*.

Fixed costs are those costs which do not vary in direct proportion to the firm's output. They are the costs of indivisible factors, e.g. buildings, machinery, vehicles. They arise because, for technical or other reasons, such factors have to be engaged in a certain size or quantity but, once engaged, they can be used over a period of time at no further cost. Even if there is no output, fixed costs must be incurred, and they remain the same, even if output expands rapidly.

Variable costs, on the other hand, are those costs which vary directly with output. They are the costs of the variable factors, e.g. operative labour, raw materials, fuel for running the machines, wear and tear on equipment. Where there is no output, variable costs are nil; as output increases, so variable costs increase.

In practice it is difficult to draw an absolute line between fixed and variable costs; the difference really depends on the length of time in mind, as follows. When current output is not profitable, the entrepreneur will have to contract production. At first, overtime work will cease; if necessary, workers will be paid off at the end of the week. In time, more factors become variable—administrative staff, salesmen, research workers—and if receipts still do not justify expenditure on them, they too can be dismissed. A factor becomes variable as soon as a decision has to be taken as to whether or not it shall be replaced, for then alternative uses of the factor have to be considered. Eventually, machines have to be replaced; even they have become a variable cost. A decision may now have to be taken as to whether it will be profitable to remain in business.

The distinction between fixed and variable factors and costs is useful in two ways. First, in economic analysis, it is a means of distinguishing between differences in the conditions of supply which arise as we vary the period of time under consideration. The economist divides time into the *short period* and the *long period*. The short period is defined as a period when there is at least one fixed factor. While, therefore, supply can be adjusted by labour working overtime and more raw materials being used, the time is too short for altering fixed plant and organisation. Thus in the short period, because some factors are fixed, the entrepreneur cannot achieve his best possible combination for a given output. The long period, however, is sufficiently long for supply to be adjusted, not only by altering the variable factors, but also the fixed factors; here, therefore, supply can make a full response to a change in demand. Factors can once more be combined in the best possible way and, as we shall see, at a given price more can be supplied.

Secondly, as we shall see later, the distinction between fixed and variable costs is fundamental when the entrepreneur is considering whether or not to continue producing in the short period. In the long period, all costs of production, fixed and variable, must be covered. But, in the short period, fixed costs still remain even if there is no production. They have been paid once and for all simply because it was necessary to have some 'lumpy' factors even before production could start. Only variable costs are saved by ceasing to produce; and so, provided these are recovered by receipts, the entrepreneur will continue to produce. Anything that he makes above such costs will help to recoup his fixed costs.

II. HOW DO COSTS BEHAVE AS OUTPUT EXPANDS?

The relationship between the costs of production and a diminishing marginal product

In our discussion of the law of diminishing returns, we referred to quantities of factors and their yield in physical terms only. This was necessary to show how the return to a factor varies when it is combined in different proportions with other factors.

However, in his endeavour to make as large a profit as possible, the entrepreneur is concerned not so much with physical quantities of factors and their yield, but with those quantities translated into money terms. He can then see directly the relationship between costs and receipts at different outputs and is thus able to decide what output will give the maximum profit (*see* Table 2). Our first task, therefore, is to find out how costs are likely to change as output increases. We shall assume perfect competition in buying factors of production —the demand of each firm is so small in relation to total supply that any change in demand will not directly affect the price of those factors.

In the short period there are, by definition, bound to be fixed factors. And, in the law of diminishing returns, we found that, when a variable factor was applied to a fixed factor in increasing quantities, for a time the marginal product might increase but eventually would diminish.

How will this affect costs as output expands? Let us assume that two factors are being used, one of them fixed. If each additional unit of the variable factor costs the same, but the output from each additional factor is increasing, the entrepreneur is obtaining an increasing amount of output for any given additional expenditure on the variable factor. In other words, the cost of each additional unit of output is falling as output expands. When the marginal product of the variable factor is diminishing, the cost of an additional unit of output is rising. (The reader can test this for himself by giving the fixed factor a price, say £10, each unit of the variable factor a price, say £4, and each unit of output a price, say £1, for converting the total product at different amounts of the variable factor into total revenue. Table 2 for diminishing returns can be used.) The cost of producing an additional unit of output is known as *marginal cost* (MC).

The above conclusions can be represented diagrammatically (Fig. 36).

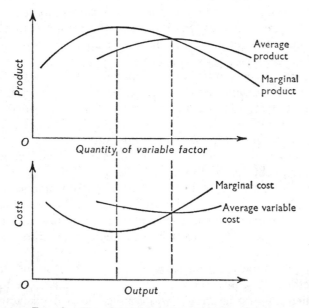

Fig. 36.—The relationship between returns and costs.

Cost schedules

Table 3 illustrates this relationship between output and costs. The figures, which have been kept as simple as possible, are for an imaginary firm, A. Cluck, maker of hen-houses. Fixed costs (FC) amount to £1,000 and, as variable factors are added, output expands. At first there is an increasing marginal product; as a result MC is falling. This has its effect on average total cost (ATC) until approximately 75 units are being produced. From then onwards, as the fixed factors are being worked more intensively, diminishing returns cause the ATC curve to rise.

TABLE 3

COSTS OF A. CLUCK, MAKER OF HEN-HOUSES (in £)

Output per year (units)	Fixed Cost (FC)	Total Variable Cost (TVC)	Total Cost (TC)	Marginal Cost (MC)	Average Fixed Cost (AFC)	Average Variable Cost (AVC)	Average Total Cost (ATC)
0	1000	—	—		—	—	—
				20			
10	1000	200	1200		100	20	120
				14			
20	1000	340	1340		50	17	67
				10			
30	1000	440	1440		$33\frac{1}{3}$	$14\frac{2}{3}$	48
				10			
40	1000	540	1540		25	$13\frac{1}{2}$	$38\frac{1}{2}$
				$13\frac{1}{2}$			
50	1000	675	1675		20	$13\frac{1}{2}$	$33\frac{1}{2}$
				$18\frac{1}{2}$			
60	1000	860	1860		$16\frac{2}{3}$	$14\frac{1}{3}$	31
				24			
70	1000	1100	2100		$14\frac{2}{7}$	$15\frac{5}{7}$	30
				30			
80	1000	1400	2400		$12\frac{1}{2}$	$17\frac{1}{2}$	30
				39			
90	1000	1790	2790		$11\frac{1}{9}$	$19\frac{8}{9}$	31
				51			
100	1000	2300	3300		10	23	33
				66			
110	1000	2960	3960		$9\frac{1}{9}$	$26\frac{8}{9}$	36
				84			
120	1000	3800	4800		$8\frac{1}{3}$	$31\frac{2}{3}$	40

Notes:
(1) TC of n units = FC + VC of n units.
(2) MC is the extra cost involved in producing an additional unit of output. That is, MC of the nth unit = TC of n units − TC of $n-1$ units. Here output is shown in units of 10, so that this difference in total costs has to be divided by 10.

(3) AFC of n units $=\dfrac{FC}{n}$.

(4) AVC of n units $=\dfrac{TVC \text{ of } n \text{ units}}{n}$.

(5) ATC $=\dfrac{TC \text{ of } n \text{ units}}{n}$.

(6) MC and ATC and AVC bear the same relationship as marginal product and average product; that is, MC cuts both ATC and AVC when these two are at a minimum. The same reason applies as in our earlier example of marginal product and average product.

These curves can be plotted on a graph (Fig. 37).

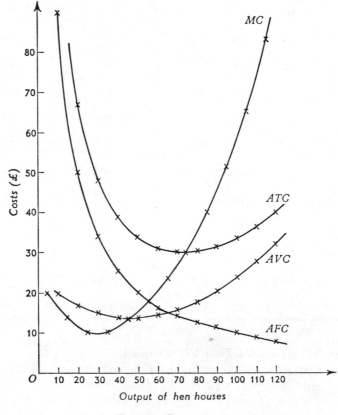

Fig. 37.—Cost curves.

The following relationships between the curves should be noted:

(1) AFC and AVC added vertically give ATC.

(2) AFC is a rectangular hyperbola, since AFC × units of output $= k$ (a constant).

(3) The MC curve cuts both the AVC and the ATC curves when they are at a minimum.

(4) Minimum AVC occurs at a smaller output than minimum ATC. AVC is at a minimum when the return to the *variable* factor only is at a maximum. But when we are considering ATC the cost of the fixed factor also has to be taken into account, and AFC continues to fall even after AVC begins to rise. While AFC is falling at a greater rate than AVC is rising, ATC will continue to fall.

III. PERFECT COMPETITION

In order to assess whether a firm is maximising its profits we have to know:

(a) the price at which it can sell different outputs and the price at which it can buy different quantities of factors of production;

(b) whether it is free to enter another industry where it can make higher profits.

Both considerations involve us in a study of the degree of competition which exists.

The degree of competition can vary. But we have to start our analysis somewhere, and so, to begin with, we make the simplifying assumption that there is 'perfect competition'—the highest degree of competition possible. For the rest of this chapter and the next, therefore, we shall be building up a model under the assumptions of perfect competition. Later these assumptions can be modified to bring the model closer to real life by allowing for forms of 'imperfect competition'.

The conditions necessary for perfect competition

For perfect competition to exist, certain conditions must hold. These are:

(1) A large number of relatively small sellers and buyers

The first condition is that there must be a large number of sellers relative to demand and a large number of buyers relative to supply.

If there are a large number of sellers relative to demand in the market, any one seller will know that, because he supplies so small a quantity of the total output, he can increase or decrease his output without it having any significant effect on the total supply, and therefore on its price in the market. In other words, he has to take the market price as given and can sell any quantity at the ruling market price. In short, he is a 'price-taker'.

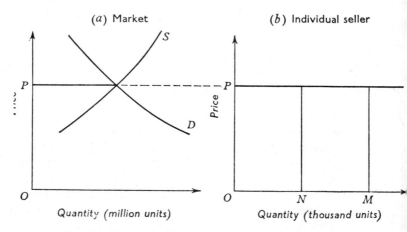

FIG. 38.—The firm's demand curve under perfect competition.

This is illustrated in Fig. 38, where (*a*) shows market price *OP* determined by the demand for and supply of the goods of the industry as a whole. But the industry supply is made up of a thousand producers, each, we will assume, of about the same size. Each individual producer, therefore, sells such a small proportion of the total market supply, that he can double his output from *ON* to *OM* or halve it from *OM* to *ON* without affecting the price at which he sells his units. (Fig. 38*b*.)

In other words, in perfect competition, a seller is faced with an infinitely elastic demand curve for his product. If, in our example, he charges a higher price than *OP*, nobody will buy from him; if he charges less than OP, he will gain no advantage and will not be maximising his revenue, for he could have sold all his output at the higher price, OP.

The difference between perfect and imperfect competition on the selling side can be seen in Fig. 39.

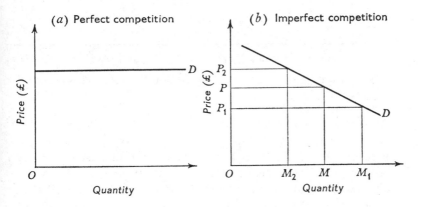

FIG. 39.—The firm's demand curve under perfect and imperfect competition.

The producer in (b) sells such a large proportion of the market supply, that a change in his output affects the price he receives for his product. When he supplies OM, the price is OP. If he increases his supply to M_1, the price falls to OP_1. Similarly, if he decreases his supply to OM_2, the price rises to OP_2. Or, such a producer can, instead of fixing the quantity, fix price and leave the market to decide how much it will take at that price. But he cannot fix both price and quantity at the same time. We can call such a producer a 'price-maker'.

Similarly, on the buying side, purchasers of goods and of factors of production are faced with an infinitely elastic supply curve. For example, one producer can increase his demand for a factor of production but the price of the factor does not rise as a result (Fig. 40a below). Here the producer's demand is so small relative to the market supply that he can buy all the labour he requires at the prevailing market wage rate OW. On the other hand, in (b) the producer employs such a large proportion of the market supply of labour that, when he takes on more workers, the wage rate rises.

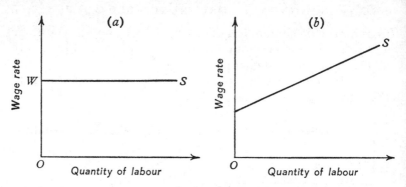

FIG. 40.—The supply of a factor under perfect and imperfect competition.

(2) *Homogeneous product*

Buyers must regard the product of one producer as being a perfect substitute for that of another, and purchase solely on the basis of price. This means that if one producer raises his price, all consumers immediately buy from his competitors. Where goods are graded, e.g. wheat and cotton, there is identity of product in the same grade.

But such identity of product does not exist where there is a real or imaginary difference (e.g. a special wrapping or brand name) or where reasons other than price (e.g. goodwill) influence buyers. Here an individual producer can raise his price without necessarily losing all his customers. To some extent, therefore, there is a downward-sloping demand curve for his product.

(3) *Perfect knowledge*

There are two aspects of perfect knowledge:
- (a) Sellers and buyers must know the prices being asked in other parts of the market so that they can act accordingly;
- (b) in order to make free entry effective, a would-be producer must also know what profits are being made by other producers and the profit he could reasonably expect to make.

(4) *Free entry*
- (a) If the number of sellers is to remain large, there must be free entry to the industry for other producers. Otherwise

existing firms could combine to influence price or they could grow in size as existing firms leave the industry.

(b) Free entry allows the profit motive to function. If demand increases, causing the price of a product to rise, the possibility of profits will attract other entrepreneurs into that industry. Likewise, if the demand falls, losses sustained by some entrepreneurs will cause them to leave the industry.

(5) *Perfect mobility of the factors of production in the long period*

A change in the demand for a product must, in the long period, result in factors of production being transferred from one line of production to another. Moreover, all factors, including entrepreneurship, must be equally available to all firms. As we shall see, however, in real life this does not occur. Entrepreneurs do not possess perfect knowledge. Therefore they have to estimate, and in this some are better than others.

(6) *No transport costs*

This is not an essential condition, but it will simplify our analysis.

In real life all these conditions never apply simultaneously. It must therefore be emphasised again that the assumption of perfect competition is primarily an analytical device to enable us to arrive at some fundamental conclusions.

IV. THE SHORT-PERIOD EQUILIBRIUM OUTPUT OF THE FIRM UNDER PERFECT COMPETITION

Since the firm is seeking to maximise its profits, its equilibrium output will be that amount where the difference between total revenue and total costs is greatest. At this output, the firm will have no incentive to increase or decrease production.

The firm, therefore, will be concerned with two broad questions:

(a) How much will it obtain by selling various quantities of its product?

(b) How much will it cost to produce these different quantities?

At first sight it may seem that maximum profit will occur at that output where average cost is at a minimum. But this is unlikely to be so. The real question which the entrepreneur will be continually asking is: 'If I produce a further unit of output, will it cost me less or more than the extra revenue I shall receive from the sale of it?' In other words, he concentrates his attention at the margin. If an extra unit of output is to be profitable, then the extra revenue he obtains for it must be greater, or at least equal to, the extra cost of producing it. That is, *marginal revenue* (the revenue received from the last unit of output) must at least equal *marginal cost* (the cost of producing the last unit of output).

Under perfect competition, the producer will obtain the market price for his good, whatever his output. In other words, marginal revenue (MR) = price; thus the price line is also his MR curve (*see* Fig. 41).

Furthermore, under perfect competition, the prices of factors of production do not rise to the firm as it demands more. But MC eventually rises because, in the short period, there are fixed factors, and so diminishing returns set in.

The equilibrium output of Mr Cluck

Let us return to our imaginary firm. Assume that the market price of hen-houses is £45. We can impose this MR curve on the cost curve diagram (Fig. 41).

Now at any output where MR (price) is above MC, Mr Cluck can increase profits by expanding output. Where MC is above MR (price), Mr Cluck can increase profits by contracting output. His equilibrium output, therefore, is where MR (price) equals MC; that is, at an output of 90 units. (The reader can check this by seeing whether, from the total costs given in Table 3, the difference between total revenue and total costs would be greater at any other output.)

There are two provisos to the above generalisation:

(1) The MC curve must cut the MR curve from below. (It is possible for the MC curve to cut the MR curve at a smaller output while it is falling, but in this case the firm could increase profit by expanding output.)

(2) Current revenue must cover current costs overall. Now 'current revenue' is simply the number of goods currently

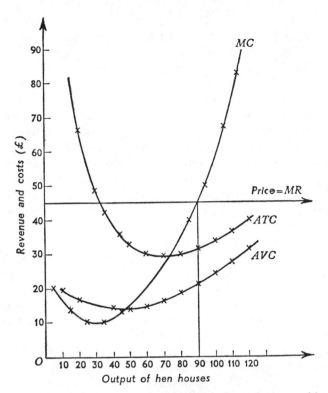

FIG. 41.—The equilibrium output of the firm under perfect competition.

produced times their price. But what do we mean by
current costs? The simple answer is that they depend
upon the period of time we have in mind. This is because
the businessman (and the economist) are concerned not so
much with costs that have been incurred in the past,
but with what it costs in the present to hold factors in
their present use—their opportunity cost. Here, therefore,
we divide our analysis into the short period and the
long period.

The short-period 'shut-down' price

An entrepreneur will only *start* to produce if he expects that
his total revenue will be sufficient to cover:
 (i) the cost of replacing his fixed factors;
 (ii) the cost of his variable factors, e.g. labour, raw materials;
 (iii) normal profit.

We will imagine that he does think he can make a 'go' of it. He buys highly specific machinery (fixed costs) which, we will assume for the sake of simplicity, has no value to anybody but himself, together with labour and raw materials (variable costs), and starts producing.

But, as time goes by, he finds that his original expectations are not being fulfilled. The price at which he can sell his good is lower than he estimated. Although he is covering the cost of his variable factors (those which vary directly with the size of his output), he sees that the margin above this cost will be insufficient to cover fully the replacement cost of his machines by the time they wear out. In other words, the business as a whole will prove unprofitable.

This is where the idea of opportunity costs must once more be introduced. Suppose our entrepreneur stops production. What will he save? Obviously he will save the cost of those factors, the variable costs, which vary proportionately to output. But will he save anything on his machines by not using them? The answer is 'no'—because they have no alternative use, they cannot be transferred elsewhere. Their opportunity cost is zero; in other words, there is no cost of using them! There is nothing he can do now about past expenditure on those machines. In economics, as in other walks of life, 'bygones are forever bygones'. Not using the machines now, cannot recoup past expenditure. He is stuck with them, for better or worse.

Consequently our entrepreneur takes a philosophic view of the situation. He has some perfectly good machines which, if he uses, will not add to his costs a bit. So, provided the cost of labour, raw materials, etc.—the variable factors—is being covered, he goes on producing. Anything he makes above the cost of these factors will contribute to the cost of his fixed factors.

How can we tell if variable costs are being covered? Simply by looking at the AVC curve. If we take Mr Cluck as an example, a price of £13·50 for a hen-house would just enable him to produce in the short period. Here his MC would equal his MR, and, with an output of 45 units, his TVC would just be covered. Any price lower than this, however, would mean that an output where MC = MR, total receipts (price × output) would be less than TVC (AVC × output). He could not make a 'go' of it even in the short period; and so we can call £13·50 the 'shut-down' price. At any price above £13·50 an output where MC = MR will give him a surplus above his TVC, and this will help him towards paying off his FC.

V. THE LONG-PERIOD EQUILIBRIUM OF THE FIRM AND INDUSTRY

In the long period, all factors are variable. This has two effects:

(1) The *firm* can vary the size of its plant in order to obtain a given output at the lowest possible cost.

(2) New firms can obtain plant in order to enter the *industry;* or alternatively, firms need not renew plant and can leave the industry.

We shall develop each of these effects in turn.

The firm

The firm must have started off with some plant, and, in deciding on its size, have taken into account the advantages of producing on a large scale. But it may have misjudged its future sales. They may be larger than originally expected; as a result, plant capacity is too small. On the other hand, sales may have been overestimated; as a result, plant capacity is too large.

Let us assume that Mr Cluck has underestimated what he can sell. As a result of starting with too small a plant for his output, he has had to work it more intensively by increasing his variable factors—labour, etc. That is, he is working under conditions of diminishing returns.

But in the long period he can remedy this situation. He decides to enlarge his capacity, to combine more capital with labour. This gives him the chance to acquire more specialised machines, for these are justified by the larger output. Probably, too, he will be able to introduce more division of labour.

Thus, as we saw in Chapter 7, as the scale of output increases, costs per unit fall. In other words, up to a certain point (an output of *OM* in Fig. 42), additions to plant produce new short-run cost curves for any given capacity, each lower than the other. Here there are increasing returns to *scale*.

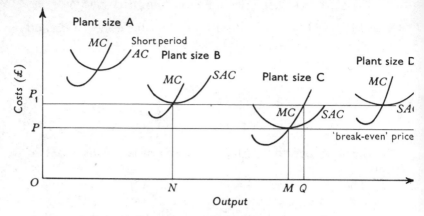

FIG. 42.—Increasing and decreasing returns to scale.

Beyond output OM, decreasing returns to scale set in. As we have seen, this could arise through the increased difficulties of making decisions, or, in other words, through the fixed nature of entrepreneurship. And, from OM onwards, these diseconomies resulting from the fixed nature of management outweigh any economies still being achieved of a technical, commercial, financial or risk-bearing nature. Thus, although plant is adjusted to cope with a larger output, the minimum average cost per unit possible is still higher, even in the long period, than at a smaller output.

The optimum size of the firm

In the above example, the firm's long-period costs of production per unit are at a minimum when output is OM. This is known as the optimum size of the firm; it is its *most efficient* size.

As we have seen, this 'most efficient' size varies from one industry to another. When technical economies of scale are important, as for instance in the production of steel and cars, decreasing costs occur over a large output. On the other hand in some industries, such as farming and retailing, reductions in average cost which may be obtained by working with large machines are exhausted at a relatively small output. From then onwards, only economies of a commercial, financial, risk-bearing, or managerial nature can be secured. But as output increases, management problems are more likely to arise.

Personal attention to detail is impossible, quick decisions are more difficult, and flexibility is lost. As a result, diseconomies occur and, eventually, these diseconomies outweigh the economies of increased size, thereby producing increasing costs. The optimum size is thus a compromise of forces pulling in opposite directions.

In practice, the optimum size of a firm is not a fixed one. Not only do the relative prices of different factors of production change (resulting in changes in the shape of the cost curves), but techniques are improved (again changing the position of the curves). Hence the concept of an optimum size of firm is basically theoretical; it is, as we shall see, the size to which firms tend to conform in the long period as, in their efforts to survive, they compete with other firms.

The industry

We now have to consider the effects of competition between firms. In the long period, not only can existing firms alter the size of their plant to secure greater efficiency, but new firms, observing the super-normal profits being earned by firms already producing, will be able to obtain plant to enter the industry. Output will increase.

But this increased supply by the industry will cause the market price to fall. That is, the horizontal price line facing the individual firm will fall in the long period, e.g. from OP_1 (Fig. 42). Furthermore, this adjustment will continue until no abnormal profits are being made, for only then will there be no incentive for firms to enter the industry.

If one firm is more efficient than the others, it will be making abnormal profits. This could occur, for instance, because it was producing OQ with plant size C, when other firms were each only producing ON with plant size B. In the long period, some of these firms would increase their size of plant towards plant size C. As a result of the increased supply, price would fall. Firms failing to adjust towards the more efficient size would be forced out of business.

Thus competition forces existing or new firms towards plant size C, and increased output forces price down to OP. If there were a higher price, some firms could be making abnormal profits, and new firms entering would increase supply and force down the price. On the other hand, if price were less than *OP*, no firm could break even in the long period when all factors had to be paid their current price. *OP* is therefore referred to as the 'break-even' price.

To summarise: in the long period and assuming conditions of perfect competition, each firm will be producing at the 'optimum' size *OM* and the price of the product will be *OP*. Each firm, too, will be in equilibrium at output *OM* because price equals marginal cost. The industry is in equilibrium because: (*a*) each firm is in equilibrium; (*b*) there is no incentive for firms to enter or leave the industry, because no abnormal profits or losses are being made.

We can illustrate the above from Mr Cluck's cost curves (Fig. 37). Let us assume that he chose the optimum size of plant in the first place—all firms have to conform to his cost curves in the long period or go out of business.

In the long period, all costs must be covered—but with no abnormal profits if the industry is to be in equilibrium. This will occur when Mr Cluck's output is 75 units and the market price of hen-houses is £30. Here total revenue (£30 × 75) equals total cost (average cost × output, that is £30 × 75). £30 is thus the 'break-even' price.

CHAPTER 12

THE SUPPLY CURVE OF THE INDUSTRY UNDER PERFECT COMPETITION

I. INTRODUCTION

So far we have concentrated our attention on the behaviour of the firm. But the individual firm is only one of a large number comprising the industry. To obtain the supply curve of the industry, therefore, we have to add together the supply curves of these firms. This will give us the market supply curve, the one which interacts with the demand curve to fix price.

In practice, the term 'industry' presents difficulties. In everyday speech, 'industry' includes firms producing goods which differ slightly, e.g. cars, washing-machines, furniture, etc. But the reader is reminded that, when we defined perfect competition, we assumed a homogeneous product. Our definition of an industry, therefore, must be the group of firms producing the total amount of an identical good supplied to the market. Variations in this definition can be allowed for later (*see* Chapter 14).

We total the output of the individual firms at different prices to obtain the market supply schedule. Generally speaking, more is supplied the higher the price. But why this is so differs in principle according to whether we are considering the short or the long periods. Each must, therefore, be examined separately.

II. THE SHORT PERIOD

In the short period, firms can adjust their output by varying the amount of the variable factors (raw materials, operative labour, etc.) which they combine with their fixed factors. But no new firms can enter the industry, because they cannot obtain plant. Thus the short-period supply curve is explained simply by the way firms' outputs respond to a change in the price of the good produced.

Consider, for example, Mr Cluck's cost schedules, Table 3. At any price below £13·50 per hen-house he will stop production, because his TVC are not covered. At higher prices however, he will produce an output where price = MC. The MC curve, therefore, is his short-period supply curve as follows:

Price (£)	Outputs (units)
13·50	45
18·50	55
24	65
30	75
39	85, and so on.

Suppose, for the sake of simplicity, that the industry consists of three other firms each less efficient than Mr Cluck. Their outputs (starting from minimum AVC) are given under A, B and C in the following schedule:

Price (£)	Firm A	Firm B	Firm C	Mr Cluck	Total
13·50	—	—	—	45	45
18·50	—	—	45	55	100
24	—	45	55	65	165
30	50	55	65	75	245
39	55	65	75	85	280

This is shown graphically in Fig. 43. The MC curves of the four firms are summed horizontally to obtain the short-period supply curve of the industry.

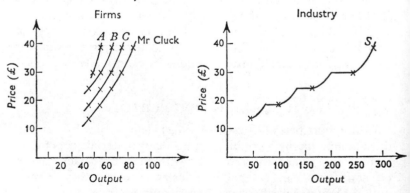

FIG. 43.—The short-period supply curve of the industry.

It will be observed that the supply curve derived above is not smooth, but stepped. This is because we have taken only four firms. If there had been very many firms each differing only slightly in efficiency, we should have had a much smoother curve.

Since all firms under perfect competition must produce where MC is rising, their output will be greater the higher the price. Thus the short-period market supply curve rises from left to right, showing that more is supplied the higher the price.

III. THE LONG PERIOD

The long-period equilibrium of the firm

Our discussion of the firm showed that, in the long period, each existing firm (including any attracted into the industry) will be producing at its optimum size *OM* and at a price *OP* where total costs are just covered (Fig. 42). Now since new firms can come into the industry on identical terms, there would be a long-period supply curve for the industry which will be perfectly elastic at price *OP*. In other words, the supply curve would be horizontal.

But such a conclusion can be arrived at only on the very theoretical assumptions of perfect competition. In particular, this assumed that:

(*a*) each firm is so small that its demand for a factor does not affect the price of that factor;

(*b*) there is perfectly free entry into the industry.

A rigid acceptance of these conditions, however, is impossible. First, it creates a theoretical difficulty—if all firms are at the peak of efficiency since they are operating at minimum average cost, which goes out of business if the price of the goods falls slightly? Secondly, it leads to a conclusion—that supply can be increased indefinitely at constant cost—which is most unlikely. We can overcome both objections by making either of the above assumptions more realistic.

The price of factors of production and the size of the industry

While an individual firm may be so small that its demand will not affect the price it has to pay for factors of production, the collective action of all firms in the industry will have repercussions. In the past, we have referred to these 'industry results' as *external* economies and diseconomies of scale.

Now it could happen that, as the industry expands, there are external economies of scale—growing reputation, skilled labour availability, transport improvements, etc. These will tend to lower the cost curves for individual firms as the output of the industry expands. On the other hand, there may be diseconomies which will raise costs. One such likely result of the expansion of the industry will be an increasing price of the factors of production. Given full employment, as the size of the industry's output expands, higher rewards will have to be paid to attract factors from other industries.

In practice, therefore, at the same time as the increased supply resulting from the entry of new firms tends to lower the price of the product, the costs curves of the firm are tending to be pushed down by external economies and pushed up by external diseconomies of scale. In other words, external economies will make for increased supply at a lower cost— there are decreasing costs to the industry; external diseconomies will make for increased supply at a higher cost. The actual slope of the long-period supply curve—downwards or upwards—will depend upon the balance between the two.

Suppose, for instance, that the entry of a fourth firm, *D*, to the industry in Fig. 44 drives up the prices of the factors of production without giving any external economies. As a result the cost curves of all firms move from (*a*) to (*b*), each firm in (*b*) having a higher minimum average total cost. This gives a new supply for the industry M_4 at a higher price OP_1, as compared with the previous supply M_3 at a price OP (Fig. 44*c*). That is, there is an upward-sloping industry supply curve.

Perfectly free entry

Even if there were no institutional barriers to entry into an industry (e.g. through cartel or other agreements or through conditions imposed by the government), the condition of free entry is effective only if:

(*a*) there is perfect knowledge;

(*b*) factors of production are perfectly mobile and equally available to all firms.

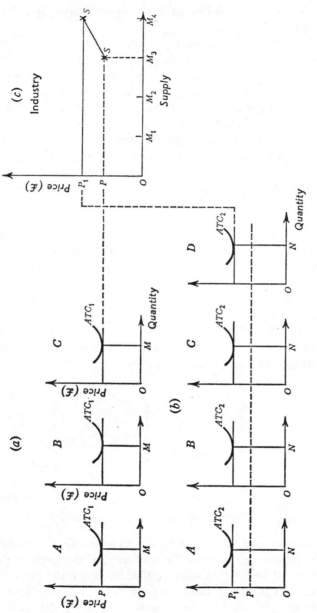

FIG. 44.—The long-period supply curve of the industry.

As soon as either of these conditions is relaxed, firms of differing degrees of efficiency will result.

Is it likely that these conditions will apply as regards entrepreneurship? The answer is 'no'. Our assumption of 'perfect knowledge' means that entrepreneurs outside the industry are aware of any super-normal profits being earned by existing firms, of the prices of all factors of production, and of all the different ways in which the good can be produced.

Obviously, the extent of such knowledge is so vast that entrepreneurs must differ in the degree to which they possess this knowledge. And this disparity becomes even more marked when we introduce dynamic considerations. Fluctuations in demand, improvements in techniques, and changes in the relative prices of factors of production are continually giving rise to changes in the conditions of demand and supply. Entrepreneurs, therefore, have to plan ahead according to their estimates. Some entrepreneurs will make more accurate estimates than others.

What this means is that equally efficient entrepreneurs are not available to all firms. At any one time, therefore, some firms are making super-normal profits of varying degrees, while others are marginal in that they are just making normal profits. Diagrammatically, the situation is shown in Fig. 45.

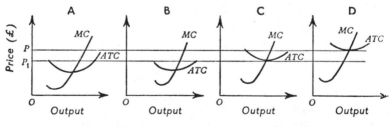

Fig. 45.—Differences in efficiency of entrepreneurs.

Firm D, the highest cost firm, is also a marginal firm—it is only just induced to stay in the industry by the present price OP, and it will be the first to leave the industry if the price falls, e.g. to OP_1. If the price falls below OP_1, Firm C will leave the industry, and so on. Once again, therefore, we can plot the supply of the industry at different prices. This will give a supply curve sloping upwards from left to right.

IV. ELASTICITY OF SUPPLY

Definition of elasticity of supply

Normally more of a good will be supplied the higher the price offered. The extent to which supply extends for a given price rise is indicated by the elasticity of supply. In Fig. 46, for a rise in price from OP to OP_1, supply extends from OM to OM_1 with S_1 and to OM_2 with S_2. At price OP, therefore, S_2 is said to be more elastic than S_1.

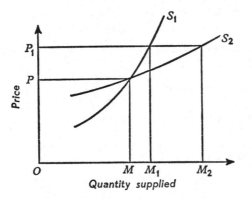

FIG. 46.—Elasticity of supply.

More precisely, the elasticity of supply of a good at any price or at any output is the proportional change in the amount supplied in response to a small change in price divided by the proportional change in price. In the supply schedule on p. 62, for instance, when the price of eggs rises from 5p to 6p, supply expands from 32,000 to 40,000. Elasticity of supply is, therefore, equal to:

$$\frac{\dfrac{8}{32}}{\dfrac{2}{10}} = \frac{5}{4}$$

As with elasticity of demand, we say that supply at a given price is elastic if elasticity is greater than 1, and that it is inelastic if elasticity is less than 1.

Limiting cases

There are two limiting cases of elasticity of supply which are of economic significance:

(1) *Elasticity of supply equal to infinity*

The main uses of this concept are: (*a*) where a single producer demands so small a proportion of a factor of production that he can obtain an infinite amount at a given price—that is, there is perfect competition in buying factors of production; (*b*) where production takes place at constant cost. In both cases, the supply curve is horizontal (Fig. 47*a*).

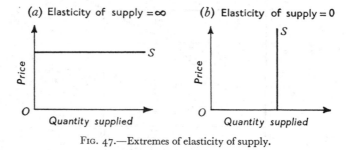

FIG. 47.—Extremes of elasticity of supply.

(2) *Supply absolutely inelastic*

Here a good is fixed in supply whatever the price offered (Fig. 47*b*). It applies to rare first editions and Old Masters, and, by definition, to fixed factors in the short period (*see* p. 176).

Whereas elasticity of demand equal to 1 was significant because it described the case where total expenditure on the good remained constant at all prices, unitary elasticity of supply has no such significance. (Any straight line passing through the origin will give a supply curve with a constant elasticity of 1, for such a line describes a situation where supply always changes in the same proportion to a given price change.)

Factors determining elasticity of supply

Elasticity of supply is determined by: (1) the period of time under consideration; (2) the relationship between the individual firms' minimum supply points; (3) the cost of attracting factors from alternative uses. We shall consider each in turn.

(1) *Time*

Marshall analysed supply under three periods:

(*a*) *Momentary equilibrium*. Here the supply is fixed, and elasticity of supply = 0. An example is perishable fish on a Friday. With many goods, some increase in supply can take place by (i) drawing on stocks, or (ii) switching factors of production from one product to another (where a firm makes two or more different products).

(*b*) *Short-period equilibrium*. Usually a variation in supply means that there must be some change in the factors of production employed. But this takes time—and the period differs between one factor of production and another. In the short period, as we have seen, it is possible to adjust supply only by altering the variable factors (raw materials, labour, etc.).

(*c*) *Long-period equilibrium*. Other factors, the fixed factors (e.g. land already sown, capital equipment, etc.), can be altered in the long period. Only in the long period, therefore, can a full adjustment of supply to a change in price take place. Elasticity is greater in the long period.

This is because the difference between the short and the long periods has an important effect on costs. Since, in the short period, supply can be expanded only by adding to the variable factors, it means that, unless there is surplus capacity, the best possible combination of the factors of production cannot be achieved. Too many of the variable factors are being applied to the fixed factors, and the law of diminishing returns operates. Increased production, in other words, is obtained only by decreased efficiency, and we have increasing marginal cost.

In the long period, because all factors can be varied, the optimum combination can be achieved. Increased efficiency produces a smaller rise in costs per unit as output expands. But it may take a long time before this position is reached. Expanding rubber production, for instance, takes seven years, while new trees mature.

It follows that, because the supply curve of an industry consists of the *MC* curves of the firms in it, a given rise in price will produce a smaller expansion of supply in the short period than in the long period. The longer the period of time under consideration, the greater elasticity of supply will tend to be. If we refer to Fig. 46, S_1 could well represent the short-period supply curve, and S_2 the long.

(2) *The relationship between the firms' minimum supply points*

The supply curve is obtained by aggregating the supply of the individual firms. If these firms each offer a supply to the market at more or less the same minimum price, then supply will tend to be elastic at that price. Similarly at higher prices— the greater the number of firms coming in, the greater the elasticity of supply.

If, on the other hand, the entry of firms is spread over a wide range, supply will tend to be less elastic.

(3) *The cost of attracting factors of production*

In order to expand production, additional factors have to be attracted from other industries. For an industry as a whole, this means that, even in the long period, higher rewards will have to be paid. What we have to ask, therefore, is: How much of a factor will be forthcoming in response to a given price rise? In other words, what is the elasticity of supply of factors of production? And, more significant, what are the influences determining this elasticity?

In answering this question, we can first consider what happens when one particular industry, e.g. office-building, wishes to expand. Let us concentrate on one factor of production, labour. As the demand for building labour increases, so the wages of building labourers rise. But they rise, not only to the office-building industry, but to all other industries using it —house-building, road-construction, public works, etc. How will it affect these industries?

First, they will try to substitute other factors (e.g. cement-mixers, bulldozers, etc.) for the labour which now costs more. Is such substitution physically possible? If so, how elastic is the supply of these alternative factors? Will their price rise sharply as the demand increases? If physical substitution is fairly easy, and the supply of alternative factors is elastic, it will mean that a small rise in wages will release much labour for the office-building industry.

Secondly, higher wages will lead to increased costs in building houses, constructing roads, etc. The supply curve of these products, therefore, moves to the left, and, the higher the proportion of wages to total costs, the further will it move. The extent to which it leads to a reduced production of these alternative goods will depend upon the elasticity of demand for them. If elasticity is high, the small rise in the price of the good will cause a considerable contraction of demand, and labour will be released for office-building. If, on the other hand, demand is inelastic, even a considerable rise in wages will have little effect on the output of houses, etc., and the increase in the supply of labour to office-building will be correspondingly small.

We see, therefore, that the two main influences affecting the elasticity of supply of a factor to a particular industry are: (*a*) the degree of substitution by other factors; (*b*) the elasticity of demand for the alternative goods it produces (*see also* p. 253).

Practical uses of the concept of elasticity of supply

(1) *The elasticity of supply of a good is a major factor in determining how much its price will alter when there is a change in the conditions of demand.*

This is apparent in the following examples:

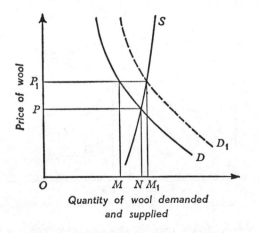

FIG. 48.—The effect of a government's stockpiling wool.

(*a*) *Why was there such a large rise in the price of wool at the outbreak of the Korean war in 1950?* The Korean war led to a stockpiling of basic commodities, including wool, chiefly by the U.S.A. In Fig. 48, suppose the U.S.A. wishes to stockpile MM_1 amount of wool. Normal demand is represented by the curve *D*. Thus the price is *OP*. Demand now increases by MM_1 at all prices, and is shown by the new demand curve D_1. Price rises from *OP* to OP_1, at which price less wool (*OM*) is demanded by normal commercial users, and MM_1 is stockpiled by the U.S.A. The comparatively large rise in price is chiefly the result of the inelastic supply, though it should be noted that had demand been more elastic, the price rise would not have been so great.

(*b*) *How would the price of cane sugar be affected in the short period and the long period if the demand for sugar increased?* Once again we can assume a fairly inelastic demand curve for sugar. The original price is *OP* (Fig. 49). Demand then increases from *D* to D_1. The supply of cane sugar in the short run is inelastic, for supply can be expanded only by adding labour, fertilisers, etc. Price, therefore, increases to OP_1. But in the long period more land can be planted with sugar cane. Supply is, therefore, more elastic, and is represented by the curve S_1. The long-run price falls to OP_2.

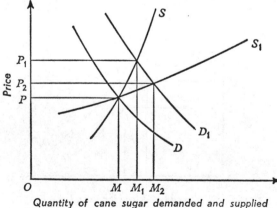

Quantity of cane sugar demanded and supplied

Fig. 49.—Changes in the price of cane sugar over time in response to a change in demand.

(c) *Why does the price of butter fluctuate more than the price of margarine?* Generally speaking, the prices of primary products tend to fluctuate between wider limits than the prices of manufactured goods. This is because (i) demand is often more inelastic for primary products, and (ii) supply is usually more inelastic, particularly in the short period. We shall concentrate on supply.

Margarine is processed chiefly from vegetable oils. If the price of margarine falls, these oils can be transferred to other uses, e.g. soap manufacture. The supply of butter, on the other hand, depends chiefly on the number of cows. If the price of butter falls, roughly the same amount of milk still has to be processed into butter, for other outlets are very limited. No real change can take place in the number of cows for some time. This would still apply should the price of butter rise. In short, the supply of butter is more inelastic than the supply of margarine, and the price varies more for a given change in demand (Fig. 50). The price of margarine rises from OP to OP_1, whereas that of butter moves from OP to OP_2.

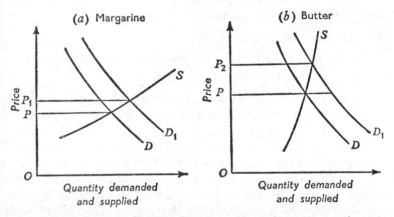

FIG. 50.—Changes in the prices of margarine and butter in response to a change in demand.

The general rule is: a change in the conditions of demand or supply will tend to produce wide fluctuations in price but small fluctuations in the quantity bought, where supply or demand respectively are inelastic; and small fluctuations in price but wide fluctuations in the quantity bought, where supply or demand respectively are elastic.

(2) *The elasticity of supply is significant with regard to taxation*

(a) Where the supply of a good is inelastic, the Chancellor of the Exchequer can impose a tax on the producer without it having a great effect on the amount of the good offered for sale. Suppose, for instance, that a man owns a field which is suitable only for sheep-grazing, and that the most any farmer will pay him for the use of this field is £10 a year, which the owner accepts. Now suppose that the government puts a tax of £5 a year on this type of land. This means that the owner will have to pay the tax out of his own pocket, for the farmer will pay no more, and the land cannot be put to any other use. In fact, the government could tax almost all the rent away before it would make any difference to the number of sheep being grazed on it; but, if all the rent went on tax, the owner might leave the land standing idle (*see* p. 268).

(b) The relative elasticities of demand and supply determine the proportion of a selective indirect tax borne by the producer as compared with the consumer (*see* p. 441).

V. THE VALUE OF THE ASSUMPTION OF PERFECT COMPETITION

Since conditions of perfect competition are so rarely met with in real life, it might be asked why economists should choose the assumption for purposes of analysis.

The first reason is that model-building has to start at a simple level. From this first step modifications can be made to the original assumptions to make the model conform more closely to real life. We can illustrate by an example from the physical sciences. The physicist tells us that a body falling freely to earth will accelerate at 32 feet per second per second. But, by inserting the word 'freely', he eliminates any resistance by the air or other force. Yet such a condition does not apply to the real world; it can only be produced artificially. On the other hand, it provides the fundamental 'bench-mark'. From it he can proceed to work out the rate at which different objects, e.g. a parachute, would fall when allowance is made for air resistance, etc. In exactly the same way the analysis of a private enterprise economy operating under conditions of perfect competition provides a simple jumping-off board from which more complex situations can be analysed as the conditions of perfect competition are relaxed.

The second reason for assuming perfect competition follows from the first. Since certain assumptions have to be made when beginning to build a model, it is desirable to be as realistic as possible, even though they will be modified later. Now, an alternative model could start from monopoly—one seller. Yet, as we shall see later, there can be no absolute monopolist, since all goods are to some extent competitive with each other. In real life, too, a deviation from perfect competition is probably a much nearer approximation than a deviation from monopoly.

Lastly, perfect competition does provide some indication of economic efficiency. Production, for instance, takes place where price (what consumers are prepared to give up at the margin) equals marginal cost (what it costs in factors of production to produce this marginal increment). Moreover, in the long period, production also takes place at minimum average total cost; no super-normal profits are being made. The conditions necessary for perfect competition, e.g. mobility of the factors of production and perfect knowledge, can often be promoted by a government seeking to improve the efficiency of an economic system.

On the other hand, we must not go so far as to say that complete perfect competition would provide maximum economic efficiency. For one thing, it considers only private costs and benefits. But there are likely to be social costs and benefits. Thus it may be efficient for society to produce where marginal cost exceeds price if, as for instance with an underground railway line, there is also a social benefit. Above all, our analysis of perfect competition has been conducted for purely static conditions. It may be that some other market form is more adaptable to future change or more conducive to innovation and therefore to growth.

CHAPTER 13

MONOPOLY

I. IMPERFECT COMPETITION

What do we mean by imperfect competition?

In Chapter 11 we stated the assumptions of perfect competition and examined their implications. What happens if *any* of these assumptions is broken?

(1) *Many small sellers and buyers*

Suppose that, instead of many sellers, there are only a few, or even one. Each seller now provides a substantial part of the market supply. As a result, the market price will be affected whenever he varies the amount he supplies of the commodity. In other words, he is faced with a downward-sloping demand curve (*see* p. 171).

Similarly, on the buying side, when any buyer takes a significant proportion of the total market supply, he will be faced by a rising supply curve.

In both cases we have some element of 'imperfect competition'. As we shall see, a downward-sloping demand curve has particular significance as regards marginal revenue.

(2) *Homogeneous product*

Products may not be homogeneous. The seller may split up the market to some extent by (*a*) product differentiation, or (*b*) goodwill. The result will be that even though he raises his price a little, he still retains some of his customers. Again he faces a downward-sloping demand curve. Nevertheless, there may still be freedom of entry to the 'industry' (*see* Chapter 14).

(3) *Perfect knowledge, free entry, and perfect mobility of the factors of production*

A breach of any of these conditions can give rise to demand

or supply curves which are not perfectly elastic. Consumers, for instance, may not have complete knowledge of prices ruling elsewhere, e.g. in retail markets. Thus sellers can raise their price without losing all their custom. Similarly, there may not be free movement into the industry. This may arise again because outside firms may not have complete knowledge of the profits being made by existing firms. Or entry may be legally prohibited or made impossible by the inability to obtain essential factors of production. In such cases, existing firms can combine to exert some control over the market supply.

Thus, whenever any of our assumptions of perfect competition is broken, some form of 'imperfect competition', indicated by a downward-sloping demand curve or an upward-sloping supply curve facing the individual seller or buyer, results.

Forms of imperfect competition

There are many 'shades' of imperfect competition. At one extreme, we have a single producer of a certain product; at the other, the only difference from perfect competition is that firms in the industry are each producing a slightly different brand. The first we call 'monopoly', the second 'monopolistic competition'. In between, we can have just a few sellers of the same or of a slightly different product—'oligopoly'. When sellers are so few, each has to take into account the reactions of rivals to his own pricing or output policy. Various assumptions can be made, giving many possible solutions. This puts a consideration of oligopoly outside the scope of this book. The broad market forms are shown in Fig. 51.

II. WHAT DO WE MEAN BY 'MONOPOLY'?

Comparison with perfect competition

Under perfect competition, there are many sellers each producing a very small amount of the total supply of a homogeneous product. The result is that each producer is faced with an infinitely elastic demand curve. It would be nice, therefore, if, at the other extreme, we could define a monopolist, which literally means 'one seller', as a producer who is faced with an absolutely inelastic demand curve.

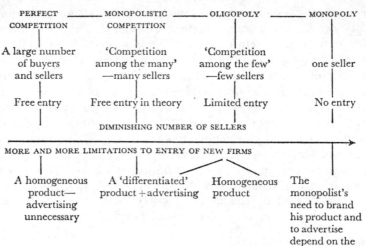

FIG. 51.—Market forms.

Unfortunately this is impossible. Because income is limited, goods compete with each other for this income. To a greater or lesser degree, therefore, all goods are substitutes for each other.

Has the monopolist's demand curve constant elasticity of 1?

It has been suggested, therefore, that the only true monopolist is one who sold all goods and therefore obtained all consumers' spending. The demand curve facing him would then be of unit elasticity at all prices. Any rise in the price of goods would simply mean that, although less were bought, total expenditure would remain the same.

But if we follow this argument through we can see that this definition is untenable for two reasons:

(a) Any reduction in output will result in the same receipts, but lower costs. Where, then, does the reduction stop?

(b) What the monopolist pays to the factors of production (his costs) is also the income of households (Fig. 90) which they spend on the goods he produces (*see* Chapter 26). If he goes on reducing output (in order to lower costs), where do his receipts come from?

Monopoly in practice

Since, therefore, a theoretical definition of monopoly is impossible, we have to consider the situation from a practical point of view. While to some extent all goods are substitutes for each other, there may be essential characteristics in a good or group of goods which give rise to gaps, as it were, in the chain of substitution. If one producer can so exclude competitors that he controls the supply of such a good, he can be said to be a 'monopolist'. Were he to raise the price of his good, customers could not turn to the products of his competitors; nor would they find it easy to substitute related goods. Depending on the extent of the price rise, some customers may cease to demand the good, but not all. The demand curve facing the monopolist, therefore, slopes downwards from left to right. In other words, elasticity of demand is something less than infinity—the actual degree of elasticity depending on how much price must rise before customers are driven to purchasing the nearest alternative.

In practice 'pure' monopoly is seldom found in real life. But one producer may dominate the supply of a good or group of goods. Monopoly legislation in the United Kingdom now considers that, where a dominant seller controls one-quarter of the market, he can be considered to be a 'monopoly'.

III. FOUNDATIONS OF MONOPOLY POWER

A monopolist is the sole supplier of a good for which there are no very close substitutes, and who can exclude competitors. His control over the supply of a good may be either in its production or sale. The sources of this power can be classified under four main headings:

(1) *Immobility of the factors of production*

Immobility of the factors of production means that new competitors cannot compete with existing suppliers. Such immobility may arise through:

(a) *Legal prohibition of new entrants.* James I granted mono-polies as a means of raising revenue, but today prohibi-tion of entry of new firms is chiefly confined to the 'public utility' undertakings, e.g. water supply, docks and harbours, and the nationalised industries, e.g. coal-mining, gas, electricity, radio and television broad-casting, postal services and telephones. For technical reasons, the provision of such goods and services is not suitable to open competition, especially as they are important to the community as a whole.

(b) *Patents, copyrights and trademarks,* with the object of promoting invention and the development of new ideas.

(c) *Government policy of establishing single buying and selling agencies,* e.g. marketing boards.

(d) *Control of the source of supply by one firm,* e.g. minerals, mineral springs, specialist workers (e.g. Dior dress-designers), trade unions and professional associations.

(2) *Ignorance*

A monopoly may persist largely through the ignorance of possible competitors. On the one hand, they may not realise that abnormal profits are being made by the existing firm (whose published profits may not reflect its actual profits); on the other hand, they may not be able to acquire the necessary 'know-how', such as is required, for instance, in involved technical processes.

(3) *Indivisibilities*

The original firm may have been able to build up its size gradually, whereas new firms, in order to compete in costs, have to start on the scale already reached by the established firm. Raising the large sums of capital required may prove difficult to new firms.

In some cases, too, the efficient scale of plant may be so large relative to the market that there is only room for one firm. This applies to many of the public utilities, e.g. transport, water, electricity generating, telephones, etc.

(4) *Deliberate policy to exclude competitors*

Restriction of competition falls into two main groups. On

the one hand we have the sources of monopoly power described so far. These have, as it were, resulted indirectly rather than from any deliberate action by producers. In fact, such monopolies can almost be described as 'spontaneous'. We must contrast these 'spontaneous' monopolies with the second kind —those which are artificially created with the deliberate object of making abnormal profits by restricting supplies. There is 'contrived scarcity' (Professor Samuelson).

It is essential to recognise the distinction between the two groups when it comes to formulating policy. While the 'spontaneous' monopolies may still abuse their fortunate position in order to make high profits, there is some element of inevitability about them, and the general policy towards them must be one of control rather than destruction. On the other hand, monopolies which have arisen with the specific object of following restrictive practices detrimental to the consumer should, where possible, be broken up. In practice, however, as we shall see later, it is often difficult to draw a distinct line between the two different kinds of monopoly. A firm may increase the scale of its production, or firms may combine, with both of two objects in view—increased economies of scale and the forcing out of competitors to achieve greater control of total supply.

Deliberate action to exclude competitors may take various forms. Competitors may be bought out by 'take-over' bids, or there may be a combination of firms producing or selling the same good. This applies also to the sale of services. Trade unions are primarily combinations of workers formed with the object of obtaining higher wages and improved conditions of work (see Chapter 16). Moreover, certain professions, such as medicine, the law, accountancy and engineering, also have their associations which regulate qualifications, methods of entry, professional conduct and often the scale of fees to be charged. Inasmuch as they can regulate the supply of these services by limiting entrants or by fixing a scale of fees, they must be regarded as a form of monopoly.

Some practices to exclude competitors are highly questionable, taking the form of vicious temporary price-cutting, agreements in submitting tenders, intimidation of buyers by threats to cut off the supply of another vital product, etc.

IV. THE EQUILIBRIUM OUTPUT OF
THE MONOPOLIST

The effect of the downward-sloping demand curve on marginal revenue

Consider Fig. 52 below. In (*a*) the producer is selling under conditions of perfect competition. His MR, his addition to total receipts from selling an extra unit, is equal to the full price at which the extra unit sells. For the fourth unit it is the shaded area *A*.

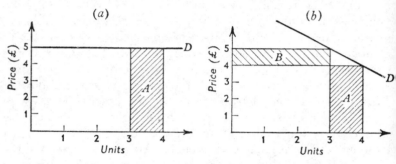

Fig. 52.—Marginal revenue under conditions of perfect and imperfect competition.

In (*b*), however, the producer is selling under conditions of imperfect competition. If he wishes to sell a fourth unit, for example, he must lower his price from £5 to £4. But this lower price applies not only to the fourth unit but to the first three units as well. Thus, his net addition to receipts is equal to what he gets for the fourth unit, *A*, less what he loses on the three previous units, *B*. Under imperfect competition, therefore, MR is always less than price at any given output.

The relationship between costs, revenue and output of a monopolist

Let us consider another hypothetical builder of hen-houses, A. Rooster. To simplify, we shall assume that he has identical cost curves to A. Cluck. But he differs in that he makes a special type of hen-house, very popular in a certain district. A patent enables him to exclude competitors. In short, in this particular market, he is a monopolist. Since what he supplies is also the market supply, the number he puts on the market affects the price. Thus if he produces only 20 hen-houses a year, they will fetch £79 each; if he increases his total output to 90, the price per hen-house will drop to £44.

A. Rooster has the same problem as A. Cluck—to decide on the output which will give him the maximum profit. But he has an extra complication on the revenue side—as output increases, price falls, not only for the last unit of output but for the *whole* output. The result can be seen in his marginal receipts (Table 4).

TABLE 4

COSTS, RECEIPTS, AND PROFITS OF A. ROOSTER, MANUFACTURER OF HEN-HOUSES (IN £)

Output per year (units)	Total	COSTS Average Total	Marginal	Price per unit	RECEIPTS Total	Marginal	PROFITS
0	1000	—	—	—	—	—	-1000
			20			84	
10	1200	120		84	840		-360
			14			74	
20	1340	67		79	1580		240
			10			64	
30	1440	48		74	2220		780
			10			54	
40	1540	38½		69	2760		1220
			13½			44	
50	1675	33½		64	3200		1525
			18½			34	
60	1860	31		59	3540		1680
			24			24	
70	2100	30		54	3780		1680
			30			14	
80	2400	30		49	3920		1520
			39			4	
90	2790	31		44	3960		1170
			51			-6	
100	3300	33		39	3900		600
			66			-16	
110	3960	36		34	3740		-220
			84			-26	
120	4800	40		29	3480		-1320

These figures are plotted in Fig. 53.

By inspection we can see that the maximum profit is made when 65 hen-houses are being produced per year. At this output, MR, as in perfect competition, equals MC (both £24 at 65 units). But MR is no longer equal to, but is less than, price (£56·50). Total receipts are £3,672·50 and total costs £1,982·50 (by interpolation). This gives a maximum profit of £1,690.

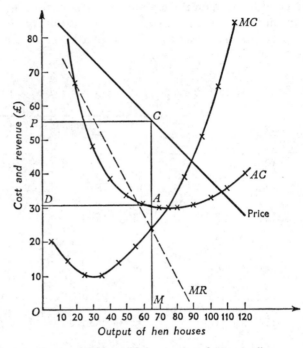

Fig. 53.—The equilibrium output of a monopolist.

Alternatively, we can use ATC and price per unit to calculate profit at an output of 65 units. In Fig. 53, total receipts equal the rectangle *OMCP* (output × price) = 65 × £56·50; total cost equals the rectangle *OMAD* (output × average cost) = 65 × £30·50. Thus profit is the difference between these two rectangles, the rectangle *DACP* = 65 × £26 = £1,690.

Some important analytical points concerning the monopolist

(1) MR *is related to elasticity of demand*

As we have seen, demand is elastic when, as a result of a fall in price, total expenditure increases. In terms of MR, demand is elastic when MR is positive. Similarly, demand is inelastic when MR is negative. This is shown in Fig. 54, where we have assumed a straight-line demand curve for simplicity.

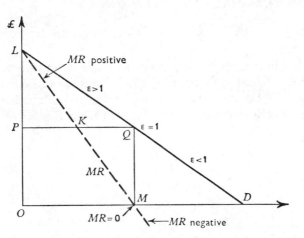

Fig. 54.—Elasticity of demand and the monopolist's output.

From Fig. 54 we can draw the following conclusions:

(a) A monopolist will never produce at a price where demand is inelastic. (Here his MR is negative; so he can increase his total revenue by reducing output).

(b) Where a monopolist has no marginal costs (e.g. the owner of a mineral spring gushing from the earth), his MC curve will be horizontal along the x-axis. He will produce, therefore, where elasticity of demand equals unity.

(c) Where a monopolist has marginal costs, he will always produce at a price where demand is elastic. (If MR = MC, MR must be positive too.)

(2) *With a straight-line demand curve, the* MR *curve bisects the horizontal distance between the price axis and quantity demanded*

This can be proved as follows:

Total revenue = the sum of the revenues for each unit of output = LOM at output OM.

Total revenue = price × output = $POMQ$ at output OM.

Therefore $LOM = POMQ$.

But area $POMK$ is common.

Therefore LPK is equal in area to QMK. But identical angles are equal. Therefore $\triangle LPK$ is congruent with $\triangle KMQ$. Therefore $PK = KQ$. Thus $OM = MD$.

(3) *The greater the absence of substitutes, the greater the power of the monopolist to make profits*

While the monopolist will never produce at an output where demand is inelastic, the greater the inelasticity of demand, the greater will be his power—a higher price will drive fewer purchasers elsewhere. This can be seen from Fig. 55.

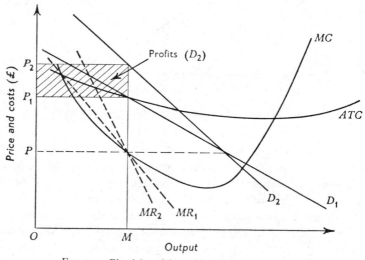

FIG. 55.—Elasticity of demand and monopoly profits.

At any given price above OP, D_1 is more elastic than D_2. At output OM, MR is the same from (2) above. Suppose the monopolist's MC curve cuts these MR curves at output OM. This will give the same equilibrium output for both D_1 and D_2. But the price he will charge will be OP_1 for D_1, and OP_2 for D_2. His profits are therefore greater for D_2 (shaded) than for D_1 (nil).

(4) *The monopolist can produce at an output where* MC *is falling even in the long period*

At an output where MC is falling, AVC must be greater than MC. Under perfect competition, therefore, an output where price = MC (falling) must mean that TVC are greater than TR.

With monopoly, however, MR is below price. Thus a profit is still possible provided ATC at the equilibrium output, e.g. OM (Fig. 55), is less than the price at which the monopolist sells.

(5) *It is impossible to derive a supply curve for the monopolist*

Under perfect competition, MC is equated with MR to obtain equilibrium output. Since the producer is faced with a demand curve of infinite elasticity, MR also equals price. There is thus a direct relationship between the amount supplied and price.

A monopolist, too, equates MC and MR, but now MR is less than price. Now the MR corresponding to a given price depends upon the elasticity of demand at that price. It is possible, therefore, to have many different outputs at the same price, or many different prices for the same output. Thus we cannot show a *unique* supply at any given price as we can under perfect competition.

This can be illustrated from Fig. 55, for at the output OM different elasticities of demand give different prices. The reader can construct a similar diagram showing different quantities supplied by the monopolist for the same price according to differences in elasticity of demand.

(6) *There is no difference between the monopolist's long-period and short-period equilibrium positions*

Under perfect competition, the existence of profits in the short period attracts new entrants, and super-normal profits are competed away. Under monopoly, the producer is the industry, and, by definition, no new firms can enter. Thus, even in the long period, the monopolist's profits remain.

V. PUBLIC POLICY AND MONOPOLY

Monopoly and perfect competition

Monopoly is an emotive word. It is often assumed that the monopolist, in seeking to maximise his profit, will always carry out policies inimical to the consumer. The argument goes somewhat as follows.

Where there is perfect competition, output for all firms in the industry will take place where price $=$ MC, that is at OM (Fig. 56). Moreover, in the long period, this will be the output where, for all firms, ATC is at a minimum. In this situation, production is carried to the point where the cost of an extra unit just equals the value which consumers place on that extra unit in the market place, that is MP.

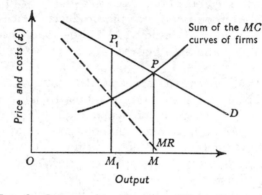

FIG. 56.—Output under perfect competition and monopoly.

Now suppose a cartel takes over the marketing of the products of all the individual firms. In order to maximise its profits, it will only sell an output where $MC = MR$, that is $OM_{\scriptscriptstyle \rm I}$, and at a price $MP_{\scriptscriptstyle \rm I}$. Thus consumers get less of the product and at a higher price than under perfect competition; factors of production are not fully allocated according to the wishes of consumers.

Criticisms of the above argument

While there may be much truth in this argument, it is not infallible. For one thing, it makes certain implicit assumptions; for another, it ignores dynamic considerations.

Its chief assumption is that the competitive industry's supply curve will be the same as the MC curve of a single firm supplying the whole market. But this is unlikely to be so. As we have seen, a single firm may be able to achieve economies of scale which are not open to the comparatively small firms which comprise the competitive industry. Such economies arise through indivisibility of plant, increased division of labour, improved co-ordination, and greater investment (since there is now no fear of over-capitalisation of the industry through rival firms carrying out similar investment).

It is probable, therefore, that the monopolist will, at the relevant market output, have lower costs than firms producing under conditions of perfect competition. Indeed, we can envisage a situation where, even though the monopolist is producing at his maximum profit output, the consumer nevertheless obtains more of the product and at a lower price than under perfect competition. Thus, in Fig. 57, perfect competition between firms would give an output of OM at price OP. But, since the monopolist has lower cost curves, he would produce OM_1 at a price OP_1 (and still be making super-normal profits!). It is this consideration—rationalisation—which even led to government encouragement to firms to combine production, e.g. computers (I.C.L.)

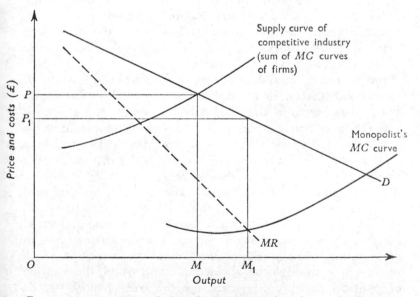

Fig. 57.—A monopolist producing a larger output and at a lower price than a perfectly competitive industry.

Secondly, our competitive model was purely static in its approach. Profits were maximised on the basis of given prices of products and factors. No consideration was given to other influences on the growth of firms over time.

But the *development* of firms depends upon innovation and investment in research. Thus we have to ask the question: 'Are firms more likely to innovate and spend on research if, by the grant of monopoly powers, they can be assured of the rewards of their spending?' In other words, are monopolies more conducive to growth than perfect competition? We cannot develop the argument here, but the mere existence of the Patents Acts suggests that there is some truth in it. On the other hand, there have been instances where monopolies have bought up patents in order that they shall *not* be developed in competition with them.

The control of monopoly

Monopolies can be divided into two groups: (*a*) the 'spontaneous', which arise through indivisibilities or through government policy, e.g. the Patent Acts, nationalisation, rationalisation; (*b*) the 'deliberate', which have come into being with the principal object of eliminating competition in order to make super-normal profits.

But such a division does not make the first group 'white' or the second 'black'. In the first place, our analysis has shown that, no matter how the monopoly has arisen, it still has an interest in restricting output if it is seeking to maximise its profits. Secondly, while a monopoly may be 'deliberate', there may yet be attendant benefits for some of the reasons already given. All we can say is that some control of monopoly is desirable, but that it must usually be done on an empirical basis. The degree of monopoly power has to be established and the benefits weighed against the possible economic and social disadvantages—restriction of output, a waste of resources in maintaining the monopoly position (e.g. by advertising), a lack of enterprise through the absence of competition, the exertion of political pressure to secure narrow ends (e.g. by trade unions), and a redistribution of wealth from consumers to the monopolist.

As a result, monopolies in the United Kingdom are regulated rather than prohibited. Yet any policy is fraught with difficulties. An exact assessment of the public benefits and disadvantages resulting from a monopoly is impossible. Very often, too, the decision as to whether a monopoly is useful or anti-social in character depends on circumstances and therefore varies from one period to another (note the fostering of monopolies in the 1930s). Moreover, if legislation is proposed, the term 'unfair competition' has to be closely defined by lawyers, though, for the purposes of control, it really requires an elastic interpretation based on economic issues. Lastly, government policy in another field may influence the problem of monopoly. Thus tariff protection, by restricting competition from abroad, enhances the possibility of establishing monopolies in the home market.

Broadly speaking, policy can take three main forms:

(1) *State ownership*

When it is important not to destroy the advantages of monopoly, the problem may best be solved by the state taking it over completely; the public then appears to be effectively protected. Freed from the incentive of the profit motive, there should be no tendency for the state-owned monopolies to make high profits. Should, however, such profits be made they would eventually be passed on to the public in lower future prices, or in relief of taxation.

In practice, however, profits may be masked by inefficiency in operation or by the payment of wages to employees above the current economic level. Consequently, provision must be made for the examination of the prices charged by an independent council and for efficiency checks by independent experts.

(2) *Legislation and administrative machinery to regulate monopolies*

This method is usually employed when it is desired to retain monopolies because of the benefits they bring but leave them fairly free to operate under private ownership. It was the policy consistently followed in Germany before the war, but not until 1948 did the United Kingdom set up machinery for investigating monopolies.

The Monopolies and Restrictive Practices Act, 1948, set up a Monopolies Commission, the members of which were appointed by the President of the Board of Trade. Under the terms of the Act, the Board of Trade could, whenever it

appeared to the Board that in the supply, processing or export
of goods not less than one-third was in the hands of one concern or group acting to restrict competition, refer the matter
to the Commission. The Commission could be told either to
ascertain facts only or to go further and assess the effect of
the monopoly on the public interest and recommend appropriate action. Upon the Commission's report, the Minister
could issue an Order declaring certain arrangements or practices illegal. No criminal proceedings, however, could be
brought under the Order, but the Crown could seek an
injunction. Subjects investigated include: supply of electric
lamps, household detergents, colour film, flat glass, chemical
fertilisers and wallpaper; tendering practices by builders in
the Greater London Area; collective discrimination; restrictive practices in the professions.

The Act was subject to two main criticisms. First, it
specifically excluded investigation of the nationalised industries and trade unions. Secondly, it did not possess any
'teeth', only civil action following the breach of a Ministerial
Order. Nevertheless, publicity, rather than direct action
following an adverse report, usually influenced firms to mend
their ways.

(3) *Breaking up or prohibition of the monopoly*

Where the monopoly is on balance detrimental to consumers,
policy can take the form of breaking it up or prohibiting it by
legislation. Thus the state can reduce the period for which
patents are granted or make their renewal more difficult.
Similarly, it may pass Company Acts requiring firms to publish
profit statements, so that other firms can ascertain quickly if
super-normal profits are being made.

Alternatively, the state can outlaw attempts to eliminate
competition, whether by unfair practices, the formation of
cartels or restrictive agreements. Total prohibition was the
policy at one time followed by the U.S.A. The Sherman Act,
1890, made every contract or combination in restraint of trade
illegal and any attempt to monopolise trade a misdemeanour.
Yet difficulties arose which made it hard to enforce. Some
administrations acted vigorously, while others were passive.
Again, the purposes of the Act were often frustrated because of

the difficulty experienced by lawyers in assessing economic conditions and terms. Above all, after a monopoly had been successfully prosecuted, it often found alternative means of circumventing the law, such as by substituting 'gentlemen's agreements' in place of written contracts. In practice, while the Act may have deterred the creation of new monopolies, it did not succeed in breaking up those which already existed.

In the United Kingdom, largely through the publicity resulting from an investigation by the Monopolies Commission into certain restrictive practices, a Restrictive Trade Practices Act was passed in 1956.

This Act: (a) allowed manufacturers and traders to enforce *individual* resale price maintenance through the ordinary civil courts; (b) banned the *collective* enforcement of resale price maintenance through such practices as private courts, stop lists and boycotts; (c) required other restrictive pacts, such as common price and level tendering, to be registered with a new Registrar of Restrictive Trading Agreements, appointed by the Crown; (d) appointed a new Restrictive Trade Practices Court. The Court sits as three-member tribunals consisting of at least one judge and two lay members and for a practice to be allowed, it must be justified as being 'in the public interest' according to any of seven closely defined 'gateways'. The tribunal's decision is made on a majority basis.

But the 1956 Act still permitted individual suppliers to enforce resale price maintenance for their own products. This was amended by the Resale Prices Act, 1964, which made minimum resale price maintenance illegal, except for goods approved by the Court. To be approved, the resulting benefits to consumers must outweigh any detriments.

The Monopolies and Mergers Act, 1965, strengthened and extended the legislation on monopolies. It permitted the Board of Trade to refer a merger or proposed merger to the Monopolies Commission where the merger would lead to a monopoly (at least one-third of the market) or would increase the power of an existing monopoly. The Act also increased the government's powers to enforce the findings of the Commission (for example, by giving it powers to prohibit mergers or to dissolve an undesirable monopoly).

The Fair Trading Act, 1973, introduced a new concept

with regard to monopoly and consumer protection. Unlike the earlier Monopolies Acts, whose primary concern with monopolies was whether they might be harmful to economic efficiency and thus not in the 'public interest', the object of this new Act has been stated to be to 'strengthen the machinery of *promoting competition*'. The Act:

(1) Creates an office of Director-General of Fair Trading. Not only does the Director take over the functions of the Registrar of Restrictive Trading Agreements, but also those of the Department of Trade and Industry with regard to discovering probable monopoly situations or uncompetitive practices. Thus the Fair Trading Office will become a new central source of information and advice for Ministers on consumer protection, monopoly, mergers, and restrictive practices.

(2) Empowers the re-named Monopolies and Mergers Commission to investigate local as well as national monopolies, and extends their powers of inquiry to the activities of nationalised industries, and even to investigate restrictive labour practices (though with limited follow-up powers).

(3) Reduces the criterion for a monopoly situation to a one-quarter (minimum) market share.

VI. DISCRIMINATING MONOPOLY

A discriminating monopolist is one who can, and does, sell the *same* product at different prices to different consumers.

Examples of discriminating monopoly are: (*a*) a doctor who varies his fee for the same treatment according to his estimate of the wealth of his patient; (*b*) a car manufacturer who sells cars in export markets at a lower price than on the home market (even allowing for differences in taxation); (*c*) electricity taken during the night for heat-storage and charged at a lower tariff than that consumed during the day; (*d*) a small builder's merchant who charges the professional builder less for paint and wall paper than he does the 'do-it-yourself' amateur.

The necessary conditions for discriminating monopoly

For discriminating monopoly to be practicable, certain conditions must be fulfilled:

(1) *There must be some imperfection in the market.* Under conditions of perfect competition, discrimination is impossible. But where there are different markets, or where parts of the market are separated by transport costs, consumers' ignorance, or national barriers, sellers can exercise some control over each market, or each part of the market, separately.

(2) *Elasticities of demand in the markets must be different.* This means that the demand curves must slope differently. As a result, different prices will be charged by the monopolist in order to maximise his profits.

(3) *No 'seepage' is possible between markets or different parts of the market.* If an exporter in one country, for instance, sells his good much more cheaply in another country, then either transport costs or physical controls must prevent reimport to the country of origin.

The equilibrium position of the discriminating monopolist

Suppose that a discriminating monopolist is faced with two markets, *A* and *B*. The demand curves for each of these markets are shown in Fig. 58. In order to maximise his profits he will have to decide: (*a*) the total output he will produce; (*b*) how to divide this output between the two separate markets; (*c*)

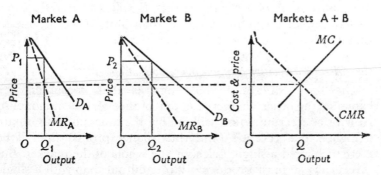

Fig. 58.—The equilibrium output of a monopolist who sells in different markets.
Notes:
(1) For simplicity, straight-line revenue and cost curves have been assumed.
(2) Demand is more elastic in market B at all prices.

what price to charge in each market. We shall examine each problem in turn.

(*a*) *What shall be his total output?* Since we assume that the product is homogeneous, the monopolist must consider his MC for the *whole* output irrespective of which market it is sold in. This MC he will equate with the combined MR curve of the two markets (CMR). This curve is found by adding the two MR curves—the output of market *A* for any given MR is added to the output of market *B* for that MR. This is repeated for all values of MR. Thus in Fig. 58, the monopolist will produce *OQ*. At that output the addition to his cost of producing the last unit just equals the addition to his revenue from selling that unit in either market.

(*b*) *How shall he divide this output between the two markets?* The monopolist will maximise profits by equating the MC of the *whole* output with the MR in market *A* (MR_A) and the MC of the *whole* output with the MR in market *B* (MR_B). This means that he will sell OQ_1 in market *A* and OQ_2 in market *B*, for the combined output at *OR* (where MR equals marginal cost) is obtained by summing the output in *A* and in *B* at *OR*. MR must be the same in both markets, for it has to be equated with the same MC, *OR*. In any case, if it were not the same, the monopolist could increase profits by transferring output from where marginal revenue was lower to where it was higher.

(*c*) *What will be the price in each market?* This, too, can be seen from the diagram. An output of OQ_1 in market *A* will sell at OP_1; an output of OQ_2 in market *B* will sell at OP_2. Since demand is less elastic in market *A* than in market *B*, a smaller quantity is sold and at a higher price in *A* than in *B*.

Can price discrimination be in the interest of consumers?

The term 'discrimination' suggests that consumers are exploited in order to increase the profits of the monopolist. Now price discrimination will enable the monopolist to obtain a higher total revenue (and thus higher profits) than if he merely charged a single price for the whole of the market. But this means he must produce a larger output than with a single price. He is able to do this because, by being able to separate the markets, he does not force down the price in one market by selling extra goods in another market. Indeed, if there were different markets for all units of his product (that is, 'perfect discrimination'), the marginal revenue for each good would be the price at which it sold. The monopolist's output would then be identical with the perfectly competitive output (Fig. 59).

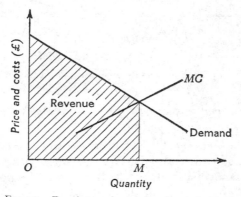

FIG. 59.—Receipts under 'perfect discrimination'.

Two points of significance to the consumer follow from this.

(1) *Price discrimination may make it possible to supply a particular market*

Two examples come to mind. British Rail charge all passengers at so much per mile. Main line services are profitable at the standard rate; many local services are not. Local lines are therefore being closed down. It is possible, though, that local passengers would be willing to pay higher fares to maintain the service.

Or we can consider a doctor whose services are demanded by both wealthy and poor patients. Their demand curves, D_1 and D_2 respectively will, with price differentiation, allow the monopolist doctor to supply OM_1 at price OP_1 to the wealthy patients and OM_2 at price OP_2 to the poorer patients. But if he has to charge a single price (and wishes to maximise his profits), he will supply OM at a price OP—and this only to his wealthy patients. This is because his total demand curve is still D_{1+2} but, without price discrimination in separate markets, a negative MR_1 outweighs increased revenue from D_2 at the price and output where that becomes effective, OK (Fig. 60).

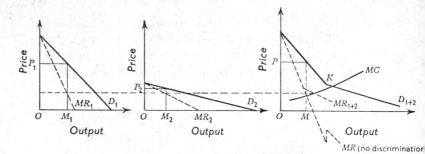

FIG. 60.—How price discrimination allows an extra market to be supplied.

(2) *Price discrimination may make it possible to supply a good when no
single price would cover total costs*

Suppose the demand for the product and the costs of producing are as shown in Fig. 61. Where a single price is charged,
no firm could cover its total costs. But it may be possible for a

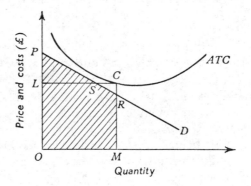

FIG. 61.—The possibility of supply with price discrimination.

firm (e.g. a public utility) to charge discriminating prices and
thus cover its costs. If the monopolist could discriminate
perfectly between every purchaser, he could produce an output
up to the point where $\triangle SRC = \triangle PLS$, for $LOMC$ are his total
costs and $POMR$ would be his total revenue.

CHAPTER 14

MONOPOLISTIC COMPETITION

Competition in real life

PERFECT competition, we have seen, occurs where identical goods are made by a large number of producers and there is completely free entry to the industry. The opposite market condition, monopoly, is possible where a good which has no close substitutes is made by a single producer who can prevent competitors entering the industry.

Thus perfect competition and pure monopoly are the limiting cases at each end of the scale of competition. But neither situation is found frequently in the real world. What is more usual is an industry where there are elements of both competition and monopoly. The industry consists of many firms each making a product which differs only in detail from that of its rivals. Each firm, since its product is not homogeneous with that of other firms, enjoys some monopoly power. On the other hand, because there is no real gap in the chain of substitution, there is competition from other firms. What we really have is a number of small 'monopolists' competing with one another— 'monopolistic competition'. How does it come about?

Conditions giving rise to monopolistic competition

On the demand side, we have a situation which is closely akin to monopoly. Few goods are completely homogeneous. Indeed, nearly every producer tries deliberately to give his product some distinction from those with which it competes. This 'product differentiation', as it is called, takes various forms. Special characteristics of the good are extensively advertised, competitions are run periodically, free gifts are offered, distinctive wrappings are used. Or, quite simply, the brand name is splashed across television screens and street hoardings in the hope that constant repetition will lead consumers to prefer the good. Apart from product differentiation, a seller may depend upon 'goodwill' (arising through habit or social contacts), rather than the actual price charged, to retain customers.

Whichever method is used, product differentiation or goodwill, the result is the same. The producer is not faced with a market demand which is outside his control. If he raises his price, some of his customers will buy the brands of his competitors. But not all his customers will do this. Some will consider other brands inferior, and only a large price rise will induce them to change. Similarly, if he lowers his price, he will attract only a limited number of customers from his rivals. In short, the producer of a brand good or a seller possessing goodwill is, like a monopolist, faced with a demand curve which slopes downwards from left to right. Nevertheless, demand tends to be elastic. Although there are not perfect substitutes available, there are fairly good ones—the different brands of rival producers.

On the supply side, because entry to the industry is possible, the situation is similar to perfect competition. Where one producer can be seen to be making abnormal profits, existing producers tend to copy his product and new competitors start producing a somewhat similar brand.

The equilibrium of the industry under monopolistic competition

We simplify the analysis by making two important assumptions: (*a*) individual producers can obtain all their supply of any factor at a given price; (*b*) external economies do not affect costs as the number of firms in the group increases. While the latter can be allowed for by subsequent modification, the former is to some degree unrealistic. The industry consists of many, but not an infinite number of, firms. The demand of one firm for a factor of production, therefore, may be sufficient to affect its price. Nevertheless, our assumption enables us to analyse a situation where all firms can, in the long period, achieve identical cost curves, and where cost curves will not rise as new producers enter.

(1) *The short period*

In the short period, existing firms cannot increase production by employing additional fixed factors, nor can new firms enter.

Each firm, therefore, is a little 'monopolist', having a down-ward-sloping demand curve for its product and producing where MC equals MR. Price, however, will be greater than MR, and abnormal profits are made.

(2) *The long period*

In monopolistic competition, the full long-period equilibrium position is possible only when both firms and the industry are in equilibrium. Whereas for each firm the condition of equilibrium (MR = MC) will apply whatever the output, for the industry we must allow, as with perfect competition, for the entry of new firms and for increased production by existing firms. This is where monopolistic competition differs essentially from monopoly; with the latter, *one* firm is *the* industry.

The increase in supply in the long period will lead to a fall in the price of the good, and the demand curve facing each producer shifts its position downwards to the left, for more producers are now dividing up the total market. At the same time, it is likely that the demand curve will become more elastic, for all products of the group will tend to become more similar to that of the most successful. In other words, each brand becomes a better substitute for other brands.

This will continue until abnormal profits have disappeared. Each firm will be earning only normal profits. (In practice the full equilibrium position is unlikely to be reached. Differences between firms will persist, and most will be earning small abnormal profit.)

A comparison of the equilibrium position of the firm in the short period and the long period under monopolistic competition is shown in Fig. 62. In the short period, output is OM, where MR = MC. But the inability to add to fixed factors means that abnormal profits exist, equal to $ABCD$. In the long period, the entry of close substitutes causes the AR curve to fall. Abnormal profits disappear, and the equilibrium output is OM_1, where MC = MR, and AC = AR.

Certain points regarding this long-period equilibrium should be noted:

(a) No abnormal profits are made; as in perfect competition, there is free entry to the industry.

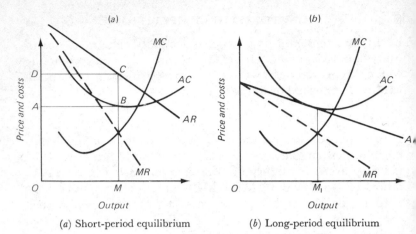

(a) Short-period equilibrium   (b) Long-period equilibrium

Fig. 62.—Monopolistic competition: equilibrium of firms in the short and long periods.

(b) The same conditions of full equilibrium hold as in perfect competition—MC = MR (equilibrium of the firm), and AC = AR (equilibrium of the industry). That both conditions hold at the same output is due simply to a mathematical relationship. At an output less than OM_1, AC is falling more rapidly than AR. This means that MC must be pulling down AC more than MR is pulling down AR. In other words, MC must be less than MR. At any output greater than OM_1, AC is rising more rapidly than AR. MC must therefore be greater than MR. The only point where AC and AR are falling at the same rate is at output OM_1 where they are tangential, and here MC is neither less nor greater than MR—it is equal to it.

(c) Price is greater than MR—a result of the falling AR curve.

(d) The equilibrium output is less than that under perfect competition. This again is the result of the downward-sloping AR curve, which can be tangential to a U-shaped average-cost curve only at an output less than the minimum average cost.

The economic and social effects of monopolistic competition—the 'wastes of competition'

(1) *Even in the long period firms operate at less than the optimum size*

Under perfect competition, not only are abnormal profits eliminated, but in the long period each firm is producing where AC is a minimum—the optimum output. At this output, factors of production are combined in the correct proportions and the full advantages of large-scale economies are achieved. What happens under monopolistic competition is that firms operate at less than their optimum size and thus there is some waste in the way in which factors of production are used. If the same total output were produced by fewer firms, each could operate at the optimum output, and factors of production could be released for production elsewhere.

But we should not assume from the above argument that monopolistic competition is necessarily a 'bad' thing. Not every consumer will want to buy goods which are identical with those bought by other consumers. Different individuals have slightly different tastes. Thus waste in the use of the scarce resources can be regarded as the part of the price that has to be paid for variety of choice.

(2) *Costs are incurred in competitive advertising*

Perfect competition assumes perfect knowledge and homogeneous goods. Advertising is, therefore, unnecessary. If any one firm incurred costs in this way, it would benefit no more than its rivals.

In practice, however, knowledge is not perfect, and most firms marketing a new product have to spend money in bringing its merits to the notice of the public. Such costs are as justifiable as those incurred in the actual production of the good. Indeed, they may even be beneficial in that, by expanding demand, they allow the advantages of large-scale production to be achieved.

But 'informative' advertising forms only a small proportion of modern advertising. The main object is to *persuade*. Firms, having made their product somewhat different, then incur large costs in advertising this difference and in persuading the customer that their brand of good is superior to other brands. Put in economic terms, they aim at decreasing the elasticity of demand for their particular product as well as shifting the demand curve to the right. In reality, there may be little basic difference between brands—but labour and other scarce resources are wasted in trying to convince the public that it is otherwise.

In practice it is not always easy to draw the line between informative and persuasive advertising. What is 'one man's meat is another man's poison'; and if you adhere to the principle of allowing people to exercise freedom of choice, then you must accept the concomitant—that they are open to be persuaded. What consumers lack is knowledge of the good, and they are thus easy victims to the pressures of advertising. Today there is only a private body, the Consumers' Association (*Which?*), to report on goods to subscribers.

PART IV

FOR WHOM? HOW THE FACTORS OF PRODUCTION ARE REWARDED—THE THEORY OF DISTRIBUTION

CHAPTER 15

THE MARGINAL PRODUCTIVITY THEORY OF DISTRIBUTION

I. INTRODUCTION

WE now consider how the various factors of production are rewarded. This is often referred to as the Theory of Distribution for, under a free price system, how the total product is distributed between persons will depend upon what they receive when they sell the various factor services they own.

Our approach will be as follows. The price of a factor service is determined, like that of a good, by demand and supply. First, therefore, we look at the demand for and supply of factor services in general. That will be the concern of the rest of this chapter.

But, as we have seen, factors can be classified according to certain broad and important characteristics. In the chapters which follow, therefore, we shall examine how these special characteristics influence the return to these different factors.

Before proceeding, however, two important points must be made:

(1) Some factors are consumed in one use (e.g. raw materials), while others are durable, rendering services over a period. In what follows we are examining the price of the *service* rendered by a factor, not the factor itself, although of course the two are directly related. This proviso must be borne in mind when, in what follows, we abbreviate by talking about the 'price of a factor of production'.

(2) Here we are concerned only with the price of factors in a given industry, occupation or district. In other words, we examine how the price of a factor is fixed in a particular market. Analysis by ordinary demand and supply curves is therefore possible. When, as in Chapter 26, it becomes necessary to examine the economy as a whole, we have to abandon this partial-equilibrium analysis for a more general one, and we then speak of labour, capital, investment, wages and the rate of interest in broad terms.

II. THE MARGINAL PRODUCTIVITY THEORY: PERFECT COMPETITION

The marginal productivity theory is primarily concerned with what determines the *demand* for factors of production. It shows that, under perfect competition, an employer will always pay a reward to a factor equal to the full value of its contribution to the product. Its most serious weaknesses are that in the real world perfect competition seldom prevails and that it tends to ignore the supply side. Nevertheless, it does give precision to what determines the demand for a factor, and thus some examination of the theory is a necessary preliminary to a more detailed discussion of the rewards of individual factors in the real world. It is a general theory applying to all factors of production. Illustration, however, is usually in terms of labour and wages, and we shall adopt this practice in the explanation which follows.

Demand of the individual firm

The demand for a factor is made up of the individual demands of all the firms using it. Our first task, therefore, is to ask why a firm demands labour and how much it will demand.

Demand for a factor comes from entrepreneurs. It is a *derived* demand—the factor is not wanted for its own sake, but simply because it can contribute to the production of particular goods. Hence the actual price which an entrepreneur is willing to pay for a factor depends upon the addition to his receipts which results from the employment of a particular unit of that factor. By examining this idea in more detail, precision can be given to what constitutes the demand for a factor. Let us begin by making the following assumptions:

(1) There is perfect competition in the market where the product is sold.

(2) There is perfect competition in buying the factor—with labour, each firm is so small relative to the size of the market that it cannot, by varying its own demand, alter the wage rate.

(3) All workers offering the particular type of labour are homogeneous.

(4) In changing output, only the quantity of labour employed is varied; all other factors remain fixed in supply.

The law of diminishing returns (Chapter 10) showed that, as additional quantities of a variable factor (labour) are added to a fixed factor (land), the marginal return (physical product) of that variable factor would eventually decline. The analysis was conducted in terms of the physical returns to factors (Table 2, p. 156), and columns (1) and (2) of Table 5 overleaf are extracted from that earlier table.

But when demanding labour (or any other factor), the entrepreneur is not so much interested in the marginal physical product as in the amount of money he will receive from the sale of that product. He pays for a factor because it contributes to his ultimate receipts. What he has to ask, therefore, is: 'How much will tótal revenue increase if I employ an additional worker?' The value of this contribution to total revenue of an additional factor is known as its *marginal-revenue product* (MRP).

The MRP depends not only on the marginal physical product, but also on the price at which the product sells. Under perfect competition, the producer can sell any quantity at a given price. Hence the MRP is equal to the marginal physical product × the price of the product. Thus, in Table 5, by assuming that potatoes sell at £1 per cwt., we can arrive at the MRP in column (3). For example, when 2 labourers are employed, the total physical product is 8 cwt., which at £1 a cwt. yields a total revenue of £8. When 3 men are employed, the total physical product is 27 cwt., giving a total revenue of £27. The MRP of the third man is thus £19. Table 5 gives the MRP for each additional man, and the figures are plotted in Fig. 63. The MRP curve shows the increase in total revenue as each extra worker is added to the labour force.

TABLE 5

SCHEDULES OF MARGINAL PHYSICAL PRODUCTIVITY AND
MARGINAL-REVENUE PRODUCTIVITY OF LABOUR—PRODUCT
SOLD UNDER CONDITIONS OF PERFECT COMPETITION

Number of men employed (1)	Marginal physical product (cwt. potatoes) (2)	Marginal revenue product (£) (3)
1	1	1
2	7	7
3	19	19
4	13	13
5	$7\frac{1}{2}$	7·50
6	$6\frac{1}{2}$	6·50
7	6	6
8	5	5
9	4	4
10	2	2
11	0	—

How the farmer decides on the number of men he will employ can be seen from this example. He will employ an extra labourer so long as the resulting addition to total revenue is greater than the cost of employing the additional worker. In our example, because labour is the only variable factor, the farmer is equating MR and MC.

MR is shown by the marginal-revenue-productivity curve. But what of MC, the cost of engaging each additional labourer? Here it must be remembered that we have postulated perfect competition in buying factors of production. This means that the farmer's demand for labour is so small relative to the market that he cannot directly influence the price of labour. He has to accept the market wage rate as given, and, at this ruling wage rate, the supply of labour to him is perfectly elastic. MC and AC are one and the same thing, and are represented by a horizontal straight line equal to the wage rate (Fig. 63).

The entrepreneur, therefore, equates MRP and the wage

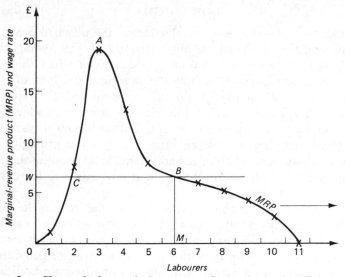

FIG. 63.—Changes in the marginal-revenue product as the number of labourers is increased.

rate. Thus, in Fig. 63, if the wage rate were £6·50 per week, the farmer would engage 6 workers. If fewer men, say 5, were employed, he could add more to receipts than to costs by taking on another worker, for the MRP (£7·50) would exceed MC (£6·50). On the other hand, if 7 men were employed, the farmer would be paying the seventh man 50p more than he was contributing to receipts.

Some difficulties examined

It might be asked whether the entrepreneur can always estimate the marginal-revenue productivity of each factor of production. The following two cases are particularly difficult.

First, with certain factors, such as clerks, teachers, policemen, etc., there is no definite and immediate physical product resulting from their work. How then can the marginal physical product, and thus their marginal-revenue productivity, be measured? The answer is simply that they cannot be—but that does not alter the fact that, in practice, an entrepreneur proceeds to engage factors as though he can so estimate.

Secondly, how do we separate the contribution of factors when, for technical reasons, they have to be combined in fixed proportions? In our example this difficulty does not arise.

Because labour is the only variable factor, the physical product of an additional worker is measured simply by seeing the difference he makes to the total product. Even when there is more than one variable factor, the marginal product of one factor can be estimated if it is possible to hold the other factors fixed while the one is varied. But where a driver and a lorry, a miner and a pick, or a carpenter and a plane have always to be combined together in a fixed ratio, there is the difficulty of distinguishing how much of the additional total product should be attributed to the extra labourer and how much to the extra machine or tool employed.

In practice this problem arises only in the case of labour, for it is usually possible to vary the proportion of capital employed by such means as giving the driver a larger lorry, replacing the miner's pick with a pneumatic drill, or providing the carpenter with a mechanical plane. But where an addition to labour necessitates an automatic addition to capital equipment, the marginal-productivity theory comes up against a real obstacle. All we can do is to measure the MRP to each factor in turn by deducting from the MRP of the whole unit the cost of all the other factors. This will give us what we can call the 'marginal net revenue product' of the particular factor.

III. THE DETERMINATION OF THE PRICE OF A FACTOR SERVICE

Like all other prices, the price of a factor service is determined by demand and supply.

Demand

The concept of marginal-revenue productivity gives precision to what basically determines the demand of an individual firm for a factor.

The *position* of the demand curve of the individual firm will depend upon:

(1) *The physical productivity of the factor*

Productivity could be increased through: (*a*) additional capital being combined with labour, though in the short period some labour might be displaced; (b) technical progress and improved organisation, e.g. increased division of labour, though here again there may be some initial unemployment; (c) higher wages increasing the efficiency of undernourished or discontented workers ('the economy of high wages').

(2) *The price of the product that the factor is producing*

A rise in the price of the product resulting from an increase in demand would raise the marginal-revenue productivity of labour (*see* p. 232).

(3) *The prices of other variable-factor services employed by the firm*

In our example above, we assumed that there was only one variable factor. But most firms employ, even in the short run, many variable factors—skilled workers, unskilled workers, fuel, raw materials, etc. In order to obtain the maximum return from a given outlay, the entrepreneur has to combine his variable factors so that:

$$\frac{MRP_A}{Price\ A} = \frac{MRP_B}{Price\ B} \ \cdots \ \frac{MRP_Z}{Price\ Z}$$

(*See* p. 160.) It is obvious, therefore, that if the prices of other services, e.g. B, rise, the demand curve for A (when A can be substituted for B) will move to the right. Similarly, if the price of B falls, the demand curve for A will shift to the left.

• Two complications, however, we have so far avoided—the shape of the *demand* curve and imperfect competition in the demand for a factor. Both will be postponed until we consider trade union activity in the next chapter.

The *industry's demand curve* for a factor service is the sum of the demands of the individual firms. This would be a simple horizontal addition at each given price if we assumed that the price of the product remained unchanged as the quantity of the factor demanded by firms increased. But it is much more realistic to assume that, as firms obtain more of the factor service, the supply of the product will increase and its price fall. The result will be that the industry's demand curve for a factor will fall more steeply than the curve obtained by a straightforward addition of the firms' marginal revenue curves.

Supply

By the supply of a factor we mean the amount which is offered as the reward is varied. Usually we should expect a higher price to expand supply, for factors would be attracted from other industries and occupations. Thus the supply curve normally slopes upwards from left to right (Fig. 64).

Nevertheless, the actual shape of the supply curve, that is, the elasticity of supply, will vary according to (*a*) the nature of the factor, and (*b*) the period of time involved. It is considered in the chapters which follow, where each class of factor is dealt with separately.

Demand, supply, and the price of the factor

The reward of a factor, in this case the wage rate, is determined by the interaction of demand and supply. Thus in Fig. 64, with demand curve D and supply curve S, the wage rate is OW.

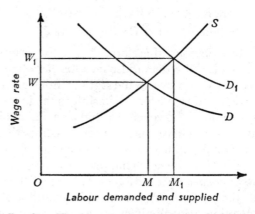

Fig. 64.—The determination of the price of a factor.

A change in the price of the product will affect the marginal-revenue productivity of the factor. This will be reflected by a change in the position of the demand curve. Suppose, for instance, that the price of the product rises. This will mean that the demand curve for labour will shift to the right, say from D to D_1. As a result, the wage rate is higher, OW_1, and the number of men employed increases from OM to OM_1.

CHAPTER 16

LABOUR AND WAGES

I. WHY LABOUR IS TREATED AS A SEPARATE FACTOR OF PRODUCTION

LABOUR is the effort, both physical and mental, made by human beings in production. It is the 'human' element which is important.

Compare labour with a machine. A machine can be reproduced fairly easily and quickly. When set to work, its output is automatic and exact. A machine, too, can be moved without difficulty from one place to another. It is purely passive and cannot combine with other machines to withhold work. And, if not required, it can be stored without deteriorating (although it may become out-of-date).

But none of these statements is true of labour. Because people have feelings and emotions, they respond differently from machines. First, the overall supply of labourers does not depend upon the return to labour. Other factors are more important in deciding how many children parents have. Secondly, the effort of labour is not geared automatically to the reward offered. A contented worker will produce more than an unhappy one; loyalty to a firm, rather than a high rate of pay, may be the decisive factor in inducing an employee to work overtime. On the other hand, the method of payment may affect effort, while raising wages may result in less work being offered! Thirdly, labour does not move readily, either occupationally or geographically, in response to the offer of a higher reward. It is said to be 'immobile', and often the immobility results from strong human contacts. Fourthly, workers can combine together in trade unions and withhold their labour in an endeavour to obtain better conditions of employment. Finally, if unemployed for long periods, workers deteriorate physically and mentally.

The problem of unemployment is examined in Chapters 26 and 27. In this chapter we shall look at the other peculiarities of labour.

II. METHODS OF REWARDING LABOUR

Working for an employer usually eliminates 'risk-bearing'

Some people are self-employed—window-cleaners, plumbers, solicitors, doctors, etc. As such they are really 'entrepreneurs', taking the rewards if demand is high, but accepting the risks of being unemployed or of working for a low return.

The great majority of workers, however, contract out of risk, accepting a wage instead. This wage is received whether or not the product of their labour is sold.

Occasionally, an element of risk-bearing is incorporated in the wage agreement, e.g. by commission payments, bonus schemes, and profit-sharing arrangements. Nor must we forget that when a worker is trained for a particular industry, his fortunes are to a large extent bound up with those of that industry. Engine-drivers, for instance, may have to work in other occupations at lower pay with the closing down of many lines. Unless a worker is completely mobile, geographically and occupationally, he cannot entirely eliminate the economic risks which are inherent in any dynamic economy.

Wages and salaries

The period of the contract between employer and employee varies. Key research workers or managers may have a contract extending over a number of years. Administrative staff are usually paid a 'salary' on a monthly basis. Clerks, typists, lorry-drivers, and most manual workers are paid a weekly wage, at least a week's notice terminating employment being required. In other occupations the work may be by the day (e.g. dockers, bricklayers, painters), or even by the hour (e.g. casual agricultural labourers), though arrangements guaranteeing a minimum number of hours per week are increasing.

The wage rate and earnings

In what follows, reference will be mainly to the *wage rate*—the sum of money which an employer contracts to pay to a worker in return for services rendered. Such a definition includes salaries as well as wages, and makes no distinction between time- and piece-rates.

Earnings are what the worker actually receives in his pay-packet (his 'take-home' pay) plus deductions which have been made for insurance, income tax, superannuation, etc. In practice earnings often exceed the rate agreed to for a given period of time because this basic rate may be supplemented by overtime working, piece-rates, or bonus payments.

Time- and piece-rates

Wage rates may be calculated on a time or piece basis, or on a combination of both.

(1) Time-rates

Time-rates are more satisfactory than piece-rates where:

(a) A high quality of work is essential, e.g. computer programming.

(b) The work cannot be speeded up, e.g. bus-driving, milking cows.

(c) There is no standard type of work, e.g. certain car repairs.

(d) Care has to be taken of delicate machinery, e.g. hospital medical tests.

(e) Output cannot be easily measured, e.g. teaching, police duties.

(f) Working long hours may undermine health, e.g. laundry work.

(g) The labour is by nature a fixed factor which has to be engaged whatever the output, e.g. clerical and selling staff.

(h) Periods of temporary idleness necessarily occur, e.g. repair work.

On the other hand, time-rates have certain disadvantages:

(a) There is a lack of incentive for better workers.

(b) Supervision of workers is usually necessary.

(c) Agreements can be undermined by working to rule and 'go-slow' tactics.

(2) *Piece-rates*

Where output is both measurable and more or less proportionate to the amount of effort expended, piece-rates are possible. It is not essential that each individual worker's output should be capable of exact measurement. So long as the output of the group of which he forms a part can be assessed, he can be attributed with a part of that group product.

The advantages of piece-rates are:

(*a*) Effort is stimulated.

(*b*) The more efficient workers obtain a higher reward.

(*c*) The need of constant supervision and irksome time-keeping is eliminated.

(*d*) Interest is added to dull, routine work.

(*e*) Workers can proceed at their own pace.

(*f*) A team spirit is developed where workers operate in a small group.

(*g*) Workers are encouraged to suggest methods of improving production.

(*h*) The employer's costing calculations are simplified.

(*i*) Output is increased, and the more intensive use of capital equipment spreads overheads.

We see, therefore, that piece-rates have advantages for both the employee and employer. Moreover, the lower prices which result benefit the community as a whole. Nevertheless, for the following reasons, they are often disliked by trade unions.

(*a*) Workers may over-exert themselves.

(*b*) Where piece-rates have to be varied according to local conditions or different circumstances, e.g. capital per employee, negotiations for a national wage rate are difficult.

(*c*) Variations in piece-rates from one place to another undermine union solidarity.

(*d*) The union may lose control over the supply of labour, and this makes it difficult to take strike action or to apportion work in periods of unemployment.

(*e*) Piece-rates are subject to misunderstanding, e.g. an employer who installs a better machine may be accused of cutting the rate if he does not attribute all the increased output to the effort of labour.

(*f*) Some employers, too, have found that piece-rates have disadvantages, for workers resist being shifted from tasks in which they have acquired dexterity (and which therefore produce high piece earnings) even though the current needs of the factory organisation require such a transfer. Thus employers find that piece-rates lead to a loss of control over their employees, and many prefer to pay high time-rates to obviate this.

(3) *Combined wage and piece-rates*

When deciding the basis of the wage rate, both employees and employers want certain guarantees. Workers have a minimum standard of living to maintain, and they desire protection against variations in output which may be outside their control, e.g. weather conditions. On the other hand, the employers who provide expensive equipment must ensure that the machines are used for at least a given period of time. The net result is that piece-rates are usually incorporated in a wider contract which provides for a minimum basic wage and a stipulated minimum number of hours.

III. THE TOTAL SUPPLY OF LABOUR

By the supply of labour we mean the number of hours' work offered. There are two separate problems to be considered: the total overall supply of labour available, and the supply of labour to a particular industry, occupation or locality. Here we consider the first.

The total supply of labour will depend upon:

(1) *The size of the population*

The size of the population sets an obvious limit to the total supply of labour. But while it is influenced by economic factors, e.g. through the birth-rate and immigration, it is doubtful, especially in more advanced economies, whether economic factors are of paramount importance.

(2) *The proportion of the population which works*

The working population, the proportion of the population which forms the labour force, is determined chiefly by the age distribution, social institutions and customs, the wage offered and, to a lesser extent, by the numbers who can live on unearned incomes.

In the United Kingdom the size of the working population depends largely on the numbers within the 16–65 age-group, for attendance at school is compulsory until reaching 16 years of age, while at 65 years of age (60 years for women) the state provides retirement pensions. The extent to which women, especially married women, enter paid work depends partly on the wage rate offered and also on custom and opportunity. Both custom and opportunity can vary from one time to another and from one place to another, even within the same country. Finally, greater equality of wealth and income, achieved largely by taxation, decreases the numbers who do not need to work because they have independent means.

(3) *The amount of work offered by each individual labourer*

Higher rates of pay usually induce a person to work overtime, the increased reward encouraging him to substitute work for leisure. But this is not always so. In addition to the substitution effect, there is also the income effect, and the latter may outweigh the former (*see* p. 83). A higher wage rate enables the worker to maintain his existing material standard of living with less work, and he may prefer extra leisure to more goods. Thus while it is usual to depict the supply curve of labour as in Fig. 65*a*, it is possible that it may follow the shape of the curve in Fig. 65*b*.

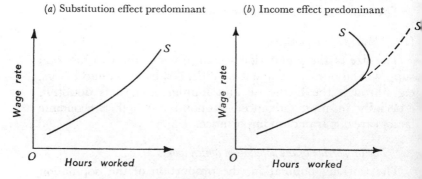

(*a*) Substitution effect predominant   (*b*) Income effect predominant

FIG. 65.—The relationship between the wage rate and hours worked.

IV. THE WAGE-RATE IN A PARTICULAR INDUSTRY, OCCUPATION OR LOCALITY

In theory the wage rate in a particular industry, occupation or locality will be determined as shown in Chapter 15 by demand and supply. The demand will depend upon the MRP; the supply will depend upon the wage rate being offered.

In practice this merely provides us with a first approach to the problem, for other considerations have to be taken into account:

(1) While marginal productivity explains differences in demand for different types of labour, more important may be immobilities which split up supply. It is these which have to be considered when we examine the supply of labour to particular industries, occupations or localities.

(2) The strength and militancy of the respective trade unions will influence relative wage rates.

(3) Interference by the government through a prices and incomes policy will modify the extent to which trade unions can secure wage increases.

In this section we shall consider the influence of immobilities. In the two following sections we shall look at the influence of trade unions and the government.

The wage rate and the immobility of labour

The supply of labour will depend upon:

(1) *The response of existing labour to a higher wage rate*

In the short period, an industry may find that the supply curve of labour corresponds to curve S in Fig. 65b. This was the experience in coal-mining where, as wages increased, miners preferred to enjoy more leisure. In the long period, however, higher wage rates should attract labour from other industries, with the result that the long-period supply curve follows the dotted line, S_L.

(2) *The cost of attracting labour from alternative uses or localities*

Unless there is unemployment, the supply of labour in a particular use can be expanded only by increasing the wage offered. This will attract labour of the same or of a nearly similar kind from other industries, occupations or localities.

The extent to which this happens depends upon the elasticity of demand for the products in these alternative sources. If demand is inelastic, higher wages can be offered to hold on to labour, and thus the supply of labour will expand little in response to the wage rise.

(3) *The mobility of labour*

A rise in the price of a factor should attract it from alternative uses or localities. This may take time, but it is achieved in the 'long period'. With labour, however, there are particular obstacles to moving, and these may mean that the long period is delayed indefinitely. Such obstacles provide frictions to the full operation of the price system. When they cannot be overcome, the effect is to split up the market into a number of separate occupations and localities with barriers around each.

Thus differences in the wage rates between occupations or between localities for the same occupation can frequently be explained by differences in the supply rather than by differences in demand. We are dealing not with one market for labour but with a number of fairly distinct markets.

What are these major barriers? What are the causes of the 'immobility of labour', as it is usually termed?

A worker may be required: (1) to shift his job from one industry to another; (2) to change his occupation; (3) to move his home to a different district. Often conditions dictate that all three types of change take place at the same time, but this is not necessarily so. Each presents its own obstacles to the worker in his efforts to change his job.

(1) *Obstacles between industries*

Provided that it does not involve a change of occupation or district, a worker can usually move his job from one industry to another fairly easily. Clerks, typists, storemen, lorry drivers and porters, for example, are found in most industries. But middle-aged and older workers may experience difficulty. Prejudice or tradition in certain industries may also prove to be obstacles. Women drivers, for instance, would find it difficult to become taxi drivers in London. Moreover, a worker's loyalty to a particular firm may prevent him from looking for another job,

even though he has suffered a cut in wages, though obviously
this does not apply if he is unemployed.

(2) *Obstacles to a change of occupation*

In changing occupations, obstacles may be encountered in
both moving out of the old occupation or in entering a new
one. They arise because:

(*a*)   a high natural ability is required in certain occupations;

(*b*)   training is costly and takes time;

(*c*)   trade-union or professional-association regulations prohibit entry except under certain stringent conditions;

(*d*)   the job in question is repugnant, or alternatively, occupations, e.g. the Church, art, and acting, are so pleasant
that workers are not drawn into another occupation by
the offer of a higher wage rate;

(*e*)   workers may be too old to learn a new job;

(*f*)   workers may prefer to remain unemployed in alternative
occupations rather than accept a wage below a 'recognised minimum';

(*g*)   there is discrimination on account of sex, colour, social
class, or religion.

(*h*)   workers are ignorant of wage rates and opportunities in
other occupations.

Of the above, the greatest obstacle to occupational mobility
is natural ability. In this respect it should be noted that there
can be more mobility between occupations, e.g. storeman and
clerk, requiring the same level of innate ability than between
doctors and dockers, where there are marked differences in the
natural ability and training required. The first is sometimes
termed 'horizontal' occupational mobility; the second, where
there are non-competing groups of workers, 'vertical' mobility.

(3) *Obstacles to a change of district*

When it comes to moving from one part of the country to
another, workers have to overcome both real and psychological
obstacles. These include:

(*a*)   the costs of moving, which to many workers represent a
considerable capital sum and are incurred even if the
worker owns his own home;

(*b*)   the difficulty of securing accommodation elsewhere on comparable terms, particularly for council and rent-controlled tenants;

(c)   social ties of friends, clubs, Church, etc.;

(d)   family ties, such as the children's education;

(e)   imperfect knowledge of vacancies or wages paid in other localities;

(f)   prejudice against certain parts of the country, people at present generally preferring to live in the south-east of the country, rather than in the industrial north.

In Chapter 27 we shall consider some of the ways in which the government tries to reduce occupational and geographical immobility. Here we merely note its effects. Even if there is competition between employers, differences in supply will lead to differences in the wage rates between occupations (provided there is no counterbalancing difference in demand) and between localities even for the same occupation. Thus solicitors earn more than their clerks because: (i) on the demand side, the services of solicitors are valued more highly; (ii) on the supply side, the supply of solicitors is small compared with clerks, for more natural ability and longer training are required.

V. TRADE UNIONS: THE PROCEDURE OF COLLECTIVE BARGAINING

Trade unions have many functions. These include:

(1)   An improvement in working conditions;

(2)   Educational, social and legal benefits for members;

(3)   The improvement of standards of work;

(4)   Obtaining an increase in pay for members by collective bargaining;

(5)   Co-operation with the government of the day in the furtherance of economic policy.

In this chapter we shall be concerned mainly with the last two functions.

The process whereby workers settle the conditions of employment with employers jointly through their trade union is known as 'collective bargaining' and, except when the rate of inflation has become critical, the government has followed the principle of allowing negotiations by the two sides to proceed on a voluntary basis. For its smooth working, however, certain conditions should be fulfilled. The first is that it must be pursued with good sense on both sides. This is helped considerably if already within the industry there has been built up a tradition of good relations between the employers and the workers. Good sense is further enhanced when there is some accepted objective measure (such as a cost of living index, the wage rates paid in other grades of work and in other trades, or the profits being made by the industry) to which wage rates can be linked. Then negotiation from an agreed starting-point is possible, as opposed to a heated wrangle where each side tries to grab the best possible terms by threats based upon its strength in the prevailing economic conditions. Secondly, collective bargaining works better when both sides consist of strong organisations. If all employers in the industry are linked in an association they know that they will not have to face under-cutting of wage rates by outsiders, and if the union can speak for and preserve discipline amongst all its members, the employers know that the agreement will be honoured. Un-official stoppages damage the reputation of the trade union, and in order to avoid them it is essential that there is regular contact between the employer and the union, prompt investigation of grievances at workshop level and that members understand and follow the procedure for settling disputes.

Thus we come to the third requirement for a smoothly working system of collective bargaining—an accepted procedure between the parties for dealing with questions as they arise. Such a procedure should, without being so prolonged that it frays patience, exhaust all possibilities of reaching agreement peaceably. A strike or lock-out should come about only after the procedure has been followed to its finality. We can therefore distinguish two stages in the procedure: (1) negotiation; (2) the settlement of disputes.

(1) *Negotiation*

Broadly speaking, the machinery for negotiation falls into three groups.

(a) *Voluntary negotiation between the unions and employers' organisations.* Generally the government has left it to the parties concerned to work out their own procedure for negotiation and the settlement of disputes. Today this voluntary machinery covers over 60 per cent of the insured workers of Great Britain. Because the organisation of the different unions varies considerably, especially in the older basic industries, the recognised procedure differs according to the particular industry and trade, and, as in the engineering and shipbuilding industries, this procedure may contain no agreement upon arbitration when a wage claim is rejected. Most industries, however, have some national joint council or committee, completely independent of outside assistance, which thrashes out agreements on matters affecting working conditions—wages, hours, holidays, factory conditions, discipline and the allocation of work amongst the various trades.

(b) *Joint Industrial Councils.* The more standard form of voluntary negotiating machinery is through the system of Joint Industrial Councils. These councils are composed of representatives of both employers and workers in the industry, and their task is to consider regularly such matters as the better use of the practical knowledge and experience of the workpeople, the settlement of the general principles governing the conditions of employment, means of ensuring the workers the greatest possible security of earnings and employment, methods of fixing and adjusting earnings, piece-rates, etc., technical education and training, industrial research, improvement of processes and proposed legislation affecting the industry. Although Joint Industrial Councils are sponsored by the government they are not forced upon any industry, and some of the more important industries, such as the iron and steel, engineering, shipbuilding and cotton, which had already developed their own procedure for negotiation, did not form Joint Industrial Councils. Nevertheless, in 1973, there were in existence some 200 Joint Industrial Councils or bodies of similar character.

(c) *Wages Councils.* In some industries and trades, where organisation of workers, of employers, or of both is either non-existent or ineffective, the government has had to depart from the principle of leaving negotiating machinery to be established on a purely voluntary basis. Government interference first started in 1909 when Trade Boards were set up to fix minimum time- and piece-rates for the 'sweated' trades, such as bespoke tailoring, paper-box making, machine-made lace and net finishing, where home-workers were being paid exceptionally low wages. In the course of time these Boards were increased in number and in 1945 were renamed Wages Councils with their powers and scope still further extended. Today (October, 1973) there are 53 such Wages Councils in operation covering the clothing, textile, food and drink and metalware industries, together with distribution, catering, road haulage and other services. The Councils are appointed by the Secretary of State for Employment after consultation and are composed of equal numbers of employers and workers' representatives together with not more than three independent members. Their task is to fix minimum remuneration and conditions regarding holidays and a minimum week, which, if the Minister approves, become the subject of a Wage Regulation Order, enforceable by law. In addition, they may advise the Minister regarding problems affecting labour in the industry.

In agriculture, wages are fixed by machinery, similar to the Wages Councils system, set up by special legislation. Thus, in all, about 20 per cent of insured workers are covered by schemes of statutory wage regulation, as opposed to the 65 per cent where negotiation is on a voluntary basis.

(2) *The settlement of disputes*

So far we have discussed the different forms of machinery which are used for negotiating wage rates, etc., by employers and workers. Where this machinery fails to produce an agreement, it is advantageous if agreed procedures exist for ending the deadlock. Usually, however, no step towards intervention is taken by the Department of Employment until the negotiating system has been fully used.

In its first moves the Department acts as it were as a broker between the two parties, under the provisions of the Conciliation Act, 1896, and the Industrial Courts Act, 1919. Three methods can be employed: conciliation, arbitration or special inquiry.

(a) *Conciliation.* The department's conciliation and advisory service keeps in constant touch with the course of relations between employers and workers at all levels. Where there is a dispute it may, in certain circumstances, help the two parties to reach an agreement.

(*b*) *Arbitration.* Where both parties agree, disputes may be referred to *voluntary* arbitration, either by a single arbitrator, by an *ad hoc* board of arbitration, or by the Industrial Arbitration Board, a permanent tribunal established under the Industrial Courts Act, 1919. The board is presided over by an independent person appointed by the Secretary of State, normally assisted by a member representing employers and one representing workers.

Although its decisions are not enforceable at law, it has won a reputation for being fully independent, and hence it is only very rarely that disputants have refused to accept its findings.

The Terms and Conditions of Employment Act, 1959, allows claims by trade unions registered under the Industrial Relations Act, 1971, to be made to the Secretary of State, that a particular employer is not observing the terms or conditions of employment established for the industry. It can then be referred compulsorily to the Industrial Arbitration Board for a legally binding award.

(*c*) *Inquiry and investigation.* The Secretary of State has power under the Industrial Courts Act to inquire into any trade dispute, whether existing or apprehended and, if he thinks fit, to appoint a Court of Inquiry or a less formal Committee of Investigation. Neither is a conciliation or arbitration body, but either may make recommendations upon which a reasonable settlement of the dispute can be based. Usually, however, they are a means of informing Parliament and the public of the facts and causes of a major dispute, and are only set up when no agreed settlement seems possible.

The Industrial Relations Act, 1971

In spite of the machinery already described, the number of man-days lost through strike action showed an increasing trend between 1963 and 1971. Particularly alarming was the number of strikes which took place without the backing of trade union headquarters or without exhausting the agreed or customary procedures in the industry or workplace, and the concentration of a high proportion of these strikes in a limited number of important industries.

The object of the Industrial Relations Act, 1971, therefore, was to provide a new legal framework for industrial relations. While it is designed to retain the voluntary principle of collective bargaining, it seeks to modernise the conditions in which collective bargaining operates.

The main provisions are:

(1) *Registration of trade unions and employers' associations*

New and existing legal privileges were granted to those trade unions and employers' associations whose rules and standards meet the specified standards and who voluntarily register themselves with the Registrar of Trade Unions and Employers' Associations.

Registration was a move against unofficial strikes. Now only registered trade unions and their officials are legally entitled to induce a breach of contract in order to further an industrial dispute.

(2) *Redress for employers and employees for unfair industrial practices*

Written collective agreements are presumed legally binding unless otherwise specified. Unfair industrial practices include threatening a strike to force an employer to discriminate against an individual on the grounds of his non-membership of a union and 'blacking' the products of a firm involved in a strike.

Similarly, certain employers' practices, for example, threatening a lock-out, are made illegal.

(3) *The setting-up of a National Industrial Relations Court*

This is presided over by a judge of the High Court and includes members with special knowledge or experience of industrial relations. It hears appeals from industrial tribunals with regard to contracts of employment, redundancy payments and complaints of unfair industrial practices.

(4) *The possibility of a 'cooling-off' period of up to 60 days and a secret ballot*

In disputes where industrial action could cause an emergency situation, the Secretary of State may apply to the

N.I.R.C. for an order suspending such industrial action for a period of up to 60 days. He may also apply for a ballot to be held amongst all workers involved to discover whether in fact a majority are in favour of the strike.

Under the Act the government has drawn up a Code of Industrial Relations Practice which gives guidance on the conduct of industrial relations, concerning such things as, for example, more formal means of communication between management and workers, greater re-training to prevent redundancies, the provision of occupational pension and sick pay schemes. However, the Code is not enforceable.

In practice, the Act cannot claim to have met with much success. The T.U.C. has declined to participate, even suspending member unions who registered. Nor did the 'cooling-off' period and ballot in the 1972 rail strike affect the eventual outcome.

VI. TRADE UNIONS AND WAGES

The question must now be answered—how, and to what extent, can trade unions secure increases in the wage rate for their members?

We shall assume that the trade union has a strong membership—practically 100 per cent. Workers can thus bargain collectively. As a result, instead of there being a number of sellers of labour in competition with one another, wages are negotiated through one seller, the trade union, which thus becomes a monopolist in selling that particular type of labour.

Broadly speaking, there are three ways in which a trade union can secure a wage increase:

(1) *It can support measures which will increase the demand for labour*

An increase in the demand for labour will come about if the MRP curve is raised. This will result either from a rise in the price of the product or from an improvement in the physical productivity of the workers. Thus the National Union of Mineworkers not only backs the campaign advertising the advantages of solid fuel for central heating, but supports the National Coal Board's exhortations to miners to improve output per man-shift.

The situation is illustrated in Fig. 66. As marginal-revenue productivity rises from MRP to MRP$_1$, wages of existing workers, ON, rise from OW to OW_1. Alternatively, if there were

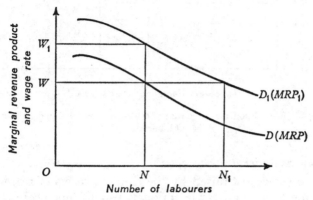

Fig. 66.—The effect of a change in marginal-revenue productivity on the wage rate.

unemployment, extra men, NN_1, could be employed at the previous wage rate.

(2) *It can restrict the supply of labour, allowing members to compete freely in fixing remuneration with employers*

Where a trade union or professional association is sufficiently strong to limit entry, it may also stipulate a minimum wage rate or scale of charges. But it need not do so. The supply of plumbers and electricians, for instance, is restricted by apprenticeship regulations, but many work on their own account and negotiate their own rewards. Similarly, solicitors, doctors, surgeons, accountants and surveyors are given suggested scale fees by their respective associations, but these are not rigidly enforced.

We can, therefore, analyse this method of securing a wage increase by the simple demand-and-supply approach (Fig. 67). Trade-union action reduces the supply of workers in a particular occupation from S to S_1; the wage rate rises from OW to OW_1.

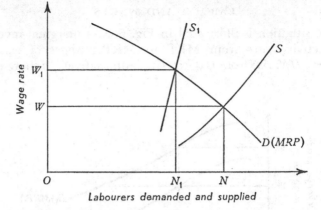

FIG. 67.—The effect on the wage rate of trade-union restriction of the supply of labour.

(3) *It can fix a minimum wage rate*

Where wages are raised by the simple process of restricting entry, the individual trade union is usually not greatly concerned about the overall numbers employed. It works simply on the principle that, assuming demand remains unchanged, greater scarcity leads to a higher price.

Most trade unions, however, are faced with a more difficult problem. While they may secure a higher wage rate for their members, their success may turn to ashes in the mouth if, as a result, many members are sacked. Herein is the rub. What we really have to ask, therefore, is *under what conditions can a trade union obtain higher wages for its members without decreasing the numbers employed?*

Once again we have to consider conditions of competition.

(*a*) *Perfect competition in both selling the product and buying labour.* In the short period, even if there is perfect competition, an entrepreneur may be making abnormal profits. Here a strong trade union could, by threatening to withhold all its labour, force the employer to increase wages to the point where the whole of his abnormal profits disappear.

But this could not be permanent. The long-period equilibrium position is one in which there are no abnormal profits and the wage rate is equal to the MRP. A higher wage will represent a rise in costs. Some employers will now be forced out of business (*see* p. 186) and remaining firms will have to reduce their demand for labour until once again the MC of labour (the wage rate) is equal to the MRP. Thus, in Fig. 67, we will assume that OW is the original wage rate fixed by competition and ON the number of men employed—the trade-union membership. Suppose the trade union stipulates a minimum wage of OW_1. In the long period, employment will then be reduced to ON_1. Given a downward-sloping MRP curve, this will always be true. Where there is perfect competition both in selling the product and in buying labour, a trade union can successfully negotiate an increase in wages only if there has been increased productivity; any increase without this will merely lead to members becoming unemployed.

The amount of unemployment resulting from such a rise in wages depends upon the elasticity of demand for labour. This will vary according to:

(i) *The physical possibility of substituting alternative factors*

As the price of one factor rises, other factors become relatively cheaper and the tendency is to substitute them for the dearer factor. Thus, if wages rise, entrepreneurs try to install more machinery and labour-saving devices; that is, they replace labour by capital. But because different factors are imperfect substitutes for each other, such substitution is limited physically. Indeed, if they have to be employed in fairly fixed proportions, little or no substitution is possible. As we saw in Chapter 5, the extent to which substitution can take place largely determines the elasticity of demand.

The degree of substitution is shown by the slope of the marginal-productivity curve. Where labour is added to another factor, but is a poor substitute for it, marginal productivity falls steeply; where it is a fairly good substitute, marginal productivity falls more gently. Thus in Fig. 68a, labour is not a good substitute for land, and marginal-revenue productivity falls steeply as the number of men employed increases. Demand for labour is therefore inelastic, and a wage fall of WW_1 leads to only NN_1 extra men being employed. Compare this with Fig. 68b, where labour and land are better substitutes. Here the same wage fall leads to a much larger number of men being employed.

It should be noted that, since the possibility of substitution

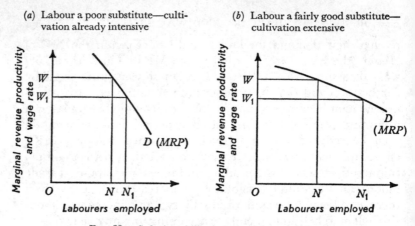

(a) Labour a poor substitute—cultivation already intensive

(b) Labour a fairly good substitute—cultivation extensive

Fig. 68.—Substitutability between labour and land.

increases over time, the longer the period under consideration, the greater will be the change in the labour force.

(ii) *The elasticity of supply of alternative factors*

Under conditions of perfect competition, the cost of a factor to an individual firm will not rise as the firm's demand for that factor increases (*see* p. 171). But when we are analysing a rise in the wage rate of the workers of an *industry*, we must recognise that the whole industry will now be demanding the alternative factors in order to substitute them for labour. This increased demand will affect the price of the alternative factors, and a higher price will have to be paid in order to attract a greater supply. This increase in price of the alternative factors also limits the extent to which substitution is carried out. Thus if the supply of the alternative factor is perfectly elastic, only the physical considerations referred to above will affect the demand for it; if, on the other hand, supply is inelastic, then it is likely that the quick rise in its price will soon make it uneconomic to substitute it for labour. Once again, the elasticity of supply of the alternative factors will be greater the longer the period of time under consideration.

Where unemployed labour exists, two conditions prevail which make it difficult for a trade union to obtain a wage increase without reducing the level of employment: (i) a high degree of substitution existing between the union labour and the alternative factor, unemployed labour, particularly if the work performed is unskilled; (ii) an infinite elasticity of supply of the alternative factor, unemployed labour, at least for a time. Hence trade unions are weak in periods of unemployment.

(iii) *The proportion of labour costs to total costs*

The proportion of labour costs to total costs has two effects. First, if labour costs form only a small percentage of total costs, demand for labour will tend to be inelastic, for there is less urgency in seeking substitutes (*see* p. 91). Secondly, if labour costs form a small percentage of total costs, as in steel production, a rise in wages will produce only a small movement of the supply curve of the product to the left. The opposite applies in each case.

(iv) *The elasticity of demand for the final product*

The effect of a rise in the wage rate will be to decrease the supply of a good at each price; that is, the supply curve moves to the left. Hence the market price of the good rises. We have to ask, therefore: 'How much will the demand for the good contract as a result of this rise in price?' Once again we are back to the practical application of elasticity of demand.

If demand is elastic (D_{el}), the quantity of the good demanded will contract considerably, from OM to OM_1. This will mean a large reduction in the numbers employed. On the other hand, if demand is inelastic (D_{inel}), there will be no great contraction

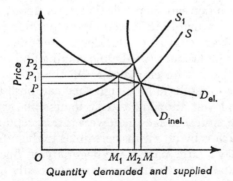

FIG. 69.—The extent to which demand for the product contracts as a result of a wage increase.

in the quantity demanded—only to OM_2. Here people are willing to pay a higher price for the good (OP_2), and this will cover the increase in wages. In other words, the marginal-revenue productivity of labour has risen.

Elasticity of demand depends mainly on the availability of substitutes. Thus demand in export markets is usually more elastic than in the home market, for with the former there are often many competing alternative sources of supply from firms in other countries. Consequently, if an industry sells a high percentage of its output abroad, e.g. scientific instruments and machine tools, the trade union is limited in its ability to secure a wage increase.

(b) *Imperfect competition.* If there is imperfect competition in selling the product or in hiring labour, the firm is likely to be making abnormal profits. Here it may be possible for the trade union to wring increased wages from the employer without loss of employment. Since it is a monopolist in the supply of labour, the union can insist that the firm shall employ *all* or none of its members at the new wage rate. Thus the firm may be forced to employ workers beyond the point where MRP = MC. The difference would come from abnormal profits, with the firm working on the principle that 'half a loaf is better than no bread'.

In these circumstances, there is a whole range of possible wage rates between the minimum which the workers are prepared to accept and the maximum which employers are prepared to give rather than lose all their labour. The success of the trade union will depend, therefore, upon: (i) the extent to which it can maintain its monopoly position by preventing employers from engaging blacklegs, non-union workers, or other substitute labour; (ii) the bargaining ability of its leaders relative to that of the employers. On the one side, the union leaders have to estimate how high they can push the wage rate without employers allowing a strike to take place; on the other, the employers must judge the lowest rate acceptable without a strike. As each is by no means certain as to the other's strength, bluff will play a large part in the negotiations. Such factors as a large order book for the firm's products, costly capital equipment standing idle, or a wealthy strike fund will obviously strengthen the union's hands. Should a strike actually take place, it is usually because of misjudgement by one side; it is doubtful whether either really gains in the long run by strike action. Thus the strike is a form of 'blood-letting', allowing one or both sides to reassess the position prior to further negotiations.

VII. TRADE UNION CO-OPERATION WITH THE GOVERNMENT IN THE DEVELOPMENT OF ECONOMIC POLICY

While the improvement of the conditions of work for its members still remains the primary task of a trade union, the time has passed when it can act independently of government policy, especially as regards full employment. Accordingly, trade unions are consulted by the government on economic policy and, individually, usually have a voice in saying how industry can be made more efficient. Indeed, through the National Economic Development Council, permanent arrangements exist for consultation at the national level between the government, the Confederation of British Industry and the T.U.C.

Full employment means that the government has to formulate a national wages policy. Labour is in a strong bargaining position, and the tendency is for each union to exploit the situation in order to obtain a wage increase for its own section of workers. Unless this increase is accompanied by increased productivity or can be met by a reduction in profits, such a rise in money wages of a particular industry will lead to some increase in the price of its goods.

Initially this rise represents an increase in real wages to the particular workers concerned since it is likely that they will spend only a fraction of their incomes on the goods they produce. But this is not the end of the story. Workers in other industries have not only suffered a relative decrease in money wages, but the rise in the price of the good in the industry where there has been a wage increase represents a decrease in their real wages. The result is that they too ask for increased wages, and these are granted by employers who know they can raise prices (for the extra money wages now being paid by most employers will ensure that the goods are bought at these higher prices).

Thus we have the spiral of wages and prices chasing one another. In the United Kingdom this process has usually resulted in balance of payments difficulties, since British exports cannot compete in world markets, and imports increase as foreign goods become cheaper than home-produced goods. As a result successive governments have had to take action.

Originally, voluntary restraint was urged upon trade unions generally. But when this was not forthcoming both the Labour government in 1966 and the Conservative government in 1972 had to take legal powers.

At this point it is worth noting that in applying policies of wage increase restrictions, the element of 'fairness' plays a prominent role. There is thus discrimination in favour of lower-paid workers on ethical and social grounds. This means that today not only does the government exercise a considerable influence over the general level of money wages but also that, even as regards relative wages, the demand and supply mechanism is an incomplete explanation.

CHAPTER 17

CAPITAL AND INTEREST

I. CAPITAL

What is 'capital'?

A SCHOOLMASTER earns, say, £40 a week. He also has £400 in the National Savings Bank, yielding him £14 per annum interest (or just on 27p a week). We can say, therefore, that his total *income* is £40·27 *a week*, or £2,094 *per annum*; his *capital* assets are £400.

Thus we see that, whereas *income* is a *flow of wealth* over a *period of time*, *capital* is a *stock of wealth* existing at any one *moment of time*.

This broad definition of capital, however, has slightly different meanings when used by different persons. The ordinary individual, when speaking of his 'capital', would include his money assets, holdings of securities, his house, and possibly many durable goods, such as his car, television set, cine-camera, etc. (sometimes referred to as 'consumer's capital'). The businessman would count not only his real assets (such as his factory, machinery, land, stocks of goods, etc.), but add any money reserves ('liquid capital') held in the bank and titles to wealth (such as share certificates, tax-reserve certificates, government bonds, etc.).

But the economist considers capital chiefly as a form of wealth which contributes to production. In other words, he is concerned with capital as a *factor of production*, that is, as something real and not merely a piece of paper. It is the factory and machines, not the share certificates (the individual's entitlement to a part of them), which are vital to him.

This has two effects. First, in defining capital, he concentrates his attention on all producer goods and any stocks of finished consumer goods not yet in the hands of the final consumer. Secondly, in calculating the 'national capital', he has to be careful to avoid double-counting. Titles to capital —shares, bonds, savings certificates, National Savings, Treasury bills, other items of the National Debt—must be excluded. Share certificates merely represent the factories, machinery, etc. which have already been counted. Government debt refers to few real assets, for most has been expended on shells, ships, and aircraft in previous wars. Its effect is really to establish a debt from one person in the country to another, with taxation redistributing income (in the form of interest) to those who hold government bonds. The only exception regarding titles to wealth is where a share or bond is held by a foreign national, or conversely, where a British national holds a share or bond representing an asset in a foreign country. We then have to subtract the former and add the latter when calculating national capital. Foreign shares or bonds held by British nationals, for example, can always be sold to increase our real resources (as they were during the war).

Naturally, 'social capital' (roads, schools, hospitals, municipal buildings, etc.) which belongs to the community at large is just as much capital as factories, offices, etc. And, in order

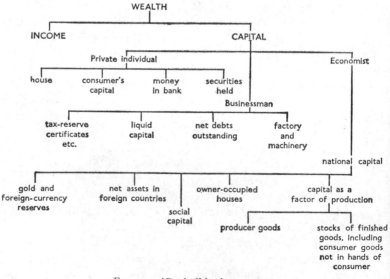

Fig. 70.—'Capital' in the economy.

to be consistent, owner-occupied houses have to be included,
for they must be treated in the same way as houses owned by
a property company.

Capital as a factor of production

When the economist refers to 'capital', it is usually in the
sense of *wealth which has been made by man for the production of
further wealth*. This is because capital plays such an important
part in increasing production, and, therefore, in improving
living standards. It is in this sense that the term is used from
now on.

Increased   production   occurs   because   capital—tools,
machines, irrigation works, communications, etc.—greatly assists
persons in their work. Indeed, with modern electronic equipment, machines often take over the actual work. As the use of
capital increases, there are three possible gains. First, more
current goods can be produced. Between 1963 and 1971 the
North Nottingham area of the National Coal Board increased
its production of coal by 1 million tons. But over that period
the number of miners dropped by over 2,000. There was thus
an increased output per man-shift, due almost entirely to the
introduction of machinery into the pits. Secondly, instead of
simply producing more current goods, people can be released
to produce new goods. And, thirdly, people can, as an alternative to more goods, enjoy increased leisure.

The accumulation of capital

If capital is so important in adding to our well-being, why
do we not have more of it? The answer is simply that we can
accumulate capital only by postponing current consumption.
In everyday language, more jam tomorrow means less jam
today. The accumulation of capital represents an opportunity
cost over time—consumption now or greater consumption
later? A simple example will make this clear.

Suppose a peasant farmer has been tilling the ground with a
primitive spade. By working twelve hours a day he can cultivate
two acres. Obviously, if he had a plough which could be drawn
by his oxen it would help him considerably. How can he
obtain it? Three ways are open to him:

(1) He could reduce the land he cultivates to 1½ acres. This

would reduce his tilling time by three hours, and he could use this time to make the plough.

(2) He could reduce his leisure and sleeping time from twelve to eight hours a day. This would give him an extra four hours for making the plough.

(3) He might decide not to consume some of the produce already harvested, exchanging it instead for a plough.

What is important to notice is that, whichever method is chosen, some present sacrifice is necessary. With (1) and (3) he has to reduce his standard of living by having less to eat. With (2) he has to forgo some leisure. In short, he has either to draw in his belt or work harder. But the reward of such sacrifice comes when he has the plough at work. Then, with twelve hours' work a day he can cultivate 4 acres; his standard of living has doubled.

One other point emerges from this illustration. If, owing to the poverty of the soil, sixteen hours were required to dig his two acres, our farmer would have found it much more difficult to obtain his plough. He would have to be careful not to reduce his consumption of food below the subsistence level. Yet he would now have fewer surplus hours each day which could be devoted to making the plough. In other words, the more fertile his land, the easier it is for him to increase his income. In economics the maxim 'to him that hath shall be given' often holds. Thus a country with a very low standard of living finds it difficult to build up the capital which would improve its living standards and it is for this reason that any aid which can be given to poor countries is so valuable.

Naturally our farmer will have to devote time to repairing the plough. So long as his capital equipment is capable of cultivating 4 acres, we can say that it is being 'maintained intact'. If it is being increased or replaced in a more efficient form so that more acres are cultivated, capital is 'being accumulated'. Where it is not being maintained (as in wartime), capital is being 'run down' or 'depreciated'.

In practice it is unusual for the same people to devote so much time to producing consumer goods and so much to the production of capital. Instead, production is organised by applying the principle of the division of labour—some people specialise in consumer goods and others in capital goods.

We can now see why most governments encourage investment, the process of producing capital. Where the proportion of productive capacity devoted to investment falls, there may be serious consequences for living standards in the future. More important, the poverty of many countries is chiefly the result of their lack of capital. Hence Russia, China, India, and Cuba have directly restricted present consumption so that capital development may proceed rapidly under Five-Year Plans.

II. INTEREST

Investment, that is adding to capital goods or stocks, usually first involves obtaining liquid capital. Interest, expressed as a rate, is the price which has to be paid for this liquid capital. What we shall examine here is the rate of interest which has to be paid for liquid capital in a *particular* use or industry. We shall *not* discuss what determines the *general* level of interest in the economy.

The *demand for liquid capital* arises because it is necessary or advantageous to use capital in production. The farmer who sows his seed in the autumn and harvests the crop in the summer is using capital in the form of seed. Similarly, a manufacturer needs capital in the form of a factory and machines because, provided demand is large enough, it is cheaper to produce in this way.

Now as we saw when examining the peasant's decision to make a plough, the accumulation of capital can come about only by postponing present consumption. This can be done directly by the producer himself. The farmer could have obtained his seed by putting aside a part of the previous year's harvest; the manufacturer could have secured his capital by carefully saving income in previous years—income which was probably the profit of a smaller business. If, however, the farmer or manufacturer is unable or unwilling to forgo current consumption himself, he can produce only by borrowing funds from other persons who have so saved, repaying them later when the product is sold.

Suppose a farmer calculated that he can increase his profit by spending £200 on a cow now. To avoid complications, let us also assume that he considers that in eight years' time, when the cow ceases to be worth milking, he will be able to sell it for beef for £200. Assume that the increase in profit (yield from the extra milk less labour and feeding costs) is estimated to be £80 for the year. He would then be willing to borrow the money to buy that cow so long as the interest he had to pay was not more than £80, that is, not more than 40 per cent. If he bought another cow, the net addition to receipts might be only £76, for the third cow £72, and so on. It is possible, therefore, to draw a curve showing the expected addition to profit which the farmer estimates he will receive through adding another cow to his herd. We can call this curve the 'marginal-revenue-productivity-of-capital' curve, and the farmer will go on borrowing capital until the rate of interest equals the marginal-revenue product of capital. Hence at different rates of interest, different quantities of capital will be demanded.

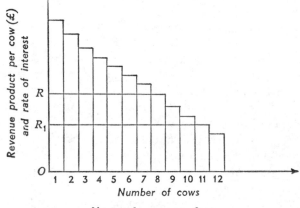

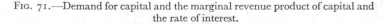

Note: each cow costs £200.

Fig. 71.—Demand for capital and the marginal revenue product of capital and the rate of interest.

Thus in Fig. 71, when the rate of interest is OR, the farmer will borrow capital to buy 8 cows. If the rate falls to OR_1, he will borrow sufficient capital to buy 11 cows. One point must be emphasised. Because he is producing in advance, the farmer has to base his demand for capital on the *prospective* money yield resulting from its use. His expectations are thus all-important, and we shall have more to say on this subject later.

The sum of the demand curves for liquid capital from all the firms in the industry gives the demand curve for the industry, though some allowance could be made for a fall in the price of the good produced by the capital equipment (*see* p. 231).

The *supply* of liquid funds for *one* use can only be obtained by bidding them away from alternative uses. How much has to be paid for a given quantity relative to other uses will depend upon:

(1) whether lenders consider more or less risk is involved;
(2) the period of the loan, people preferring to lend for a short period rather than a long one;
(3) the elasticity of demand for the product to which capital contributes in alternative uses.

Generally speaking, however, we can expect more liquid capital to be forthcoming the higher the rate of interest offered. We therefore have an upward-sloping supply curve. Thus the rate of interest is fixed by the interaction of the demand and supply curves.

Once again, however, we must point out that this is only a partial explanation of the determination of a rate of interest. It does not tell us why, for instance, £10 million of liquid capital should be forthcoming at 10 per cent rather than at 6 per cent or at 14 per cent. This will depend upon the general level of interest rates. To discover what determines this bench-mark we have to look at the nature of money and government policy (*see* Chapters 20 and 23).

CHAPTER 18

LAND AND RENT

I. 'LAND' AND 'RENT' AS GENERAL TERMS

The everyday meaning of 'land' and 'rent'

To the economist, the terms 'land' and 'rent' have a special meaning. This is just as well, for in everyday speech each can imply different things. Thus if I buy land for farming, it will probably include buildings, fences, a water supply and a drainage system, all of which are really capital. Similarly, I can rent things other than land—a house, television set, gasmeter, building equipment, shooting rights, etc. Rent in this sense simply means a periodic payment for the use of something. It can be termed 'commercial rent'.

Usually, however, rent does refer to payment for the use of a piece of land and, before we consider 'land' and 'rent' in their special economic sense, we must ask what determines how much rent is paid to a landlord.

The rent of land in a particular use

The problem is similar to the determination of the return on any factor service; and the answer follows the same demand-and-supply analysis. The demand for land, as with other factors, is a derived demand and therefore depends on its marginal-revenue productivity. The curve slopes downwards from left to right chiefly because, as output from land increases, the price of the product falls. On the supply side, land, like labour, can usually be put to alternative uses—building factories or houses, growing wheat or barley, raising cattle or sheep, and so on. A given piece of land will be transferred to its most profitable use. If, for instance, the price of cattle rises and that of wheat falls, some land will be transferred from arable to pasture farming. Should the price of cattle rise still further, more land will be transferred, and so on. We can thus draw a supply curve for land in a particular use. It slopes upwards from left to right. The interaction of the demand and supply curves will give the rent actually paid (Fig. 72).

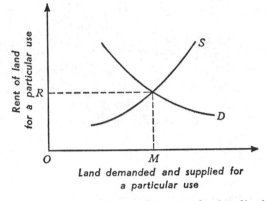

FIG. 72.—The determination of the rent of a plot of land.

Of course, this assumes: (a) that the landlord can vary the rent charged any time the demand for and supply of his particular type of land alters; and (b) that land can be transferred fairly quickly to a different use. The first assumption is complicated by the fact that rents are usually fixed for a period of years. Only when the contract expires is the landlord free to adjust the rent. The second assumption implies that we are concerned only with the long period in our analysis. But what of the short period when land is a fixed factor? An analysis of this situation is basically what we are concerned with in the remainder of this chapter.

II. ECONOMIC RENT—LAND AND RENT TO THE ECONOMIST

Ricardo's views on 'land' and 'rent'

To explain the special meaning which economists today give to the terms 'land' and 'rent', we have to examine the views of Ricardo, a classical economist of the early nineteenth century. He was concerned, not with the rent paid to land for a particular purpose, but with the rent paid to land as a whole.

Moreover, just as in Chapter 6 we defined land as 'the resources provided by nature' (thereby eliminating improvements by man through the addition of capital), so too it was the 'original and indestructible powers of the soil' that Ricardo emphasised. He pointed out that land in this sense was given freely by nature; its total supply was fixed once and for all.

In this respect, he argued, land was different from the other factors of production, capital and labour. When the price of capital rose, people would be induced to postpone present consumption; the supply of capital would expand. Similarly, a rise in wages would be an inducement to rear and train more children. On the other hand, should the price of capital and labour fall, supply would contract. If no price at all were offered, there would be no supply. Both capital and labour, therefore, have a supply price.

But with land as a whole—in the sense of space and natural resources—the same amount is available whatever the price offered. An increase in price cannot bring about an expansion of supply; on the other hand, if the price fell to zero, the same amount would still be available. Land as a whole, therefore, has no supply price.

To appreciate Ricardo's reasoning, we have to remember that he was trying to prove that the value of a good was determined by the quantity of labour embodied in it, or what was virtually its cost of production.

Both labour and capital had a cost which had to be covered by the price of the good produced. But what about land, for which there was no cost? Ricardo saw that the price of corn had risen considerably since the Napoleonic Wars, a rise which was certainly not due to any increase in either wages or interest. Yet land, the other factor, had no supply price!

The return to land was, therefore, simply the difference between the price of the product and the payments of wages and interest. Rent was merely a surplus. If the price received for the product was high, there would be more left over as rent; if the price was low, there would be less for rent. Rent did not determine the price of the good produced; instead, the opposite was true—rent was determined by price.

'Land' and 'rent' in economic theory today

On the ambiguities of Ricardo's reasoning we need not dwell. First, it can be argued that the total supply of land is fixed only in the short period; in the long run improved farming techniques and developments in transport are constantly increasing the amount of land which can be put to economic use. Indeed, in this respect there is little difference between land and other factors of production, which likewise can only be increased in the long period. Over a certain period of time—the short period, whatever that may be in months or years—all are fixed in total supply. Secondly, land, like other factors of production, has alternative uses. It can be used to produce different crops, or as a site for different buildings. The cost of putting it to one use is the yield that could have been obtained had it been employed in another way. Thus, in order to secure it for one purpose, a producer will have to pay a sufficient price to attract it from its best alternative use. It is this allocation of land between its different uses which is the main concern of the economist.

The nature of the return to a fixed factor

But Ricardo did point out an essential truth—that the return to a factor fixed in supply, that is, whose supply is absolutely inelastic, will vary directly with variations in the price of the good produced by it. We can illustrate this more clearly by a simple example.

Let us assume: (*a*) a given plot of land on which only potatoes can be grown; (*b*) only land and labour are necessary to grow potatoes; (*c*) the supply of labour for growing potatoes is perfectly elastic because only a small proportion of the total labour force is required.

The return to this plot of land will depend entirely on the price of potatoes. This can be seen from Fig. 73.

When the marginal-revenue product of labour is shown by the curve QN, at a wage of OP, OM men are employed. The value of the total product is $OMNQ$; the wage bill is $OMNP$ and the return to the plot of land PNQ. If now the price of potatoes increases, the marginal-revenue product of labour rises, in Fig. 73, to Q_1N_1. OM_1 men are now employed at a wage bill of OM_1N_1P: (Each worker still receives the same wage, OP, because the supply of this type of labour is perfectly elastic.) But the return to the given plot of land has increased to PN_1Q_1. The opposite would apply if the price of potatoes fell.

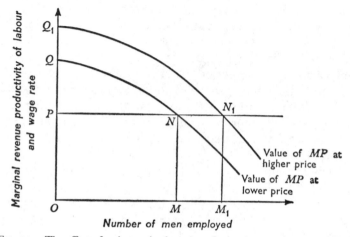

Fig. 73.—The effect of a change in the price of a product on the rent of land.

What practical conclusions can we draw from the above simple analysis? First, because the plot of land will grow only potatoes, it will be cultivated so long as the value of the total product is sufficient to pay the wage bill. In other words, at the lower price a lump-sum tax on the plot up to QPN could be levied without affecting the output. This is the basis of the much-proposed tax on land. Secondly, the return to land as we have analysed it above—rent in its economic sense—is purely a surplus. It arose because, by definition, our plot of land was confined to one particular use—growing potatoes. The supply of this land offered for sale or hiring will not be affected by a price, simply because nobody has any other use for it. In short, it has no opportunity or transfer cost.

Economic rent

The principle of rent being a surplus resulting from the fixed nature of land has a more general application. Economists have adopted Ricardo's concept of land as being symbolic of all factors which, in some way or another, are fixed in supply. The return to such factors is usually discussed under the headings of 'economic rent' and 'quasi-rent'.

'Economic rent' is the term used to describe the earnings of any factor over and above its supply price. Put in another way, it is any surplus over its transfer earnings—what it could obtain in its next most profitable use (its 'opportunity cost', in our earlier terminology). How this idea can be applied generally will now be explained.

The actual rate of return to a factor is the price per period of time at which it is now selling its services. For example, the return to a plasterer is his wage, say £60 per week.

But what is the opportunity cost? Simply what has to be paid to retain it in its present use—that is, sufficient to keep it from going to the best alternative use. Take our plasterer, for instance. His next best occupation may simply be plasterer's labourer, earning £15 per week. He would offer his services as a plasterer, therefore at anything above £15 per week.

A second plasterer, however, may be a competent bricklayer, and as such earn £20 per week. He will only offer his services as a plasterer, therefore, if at least £20 per week is offered. And so we could go on. The supply curve to the industry is thus an 'opportunity cost' curve (Fig. 74).

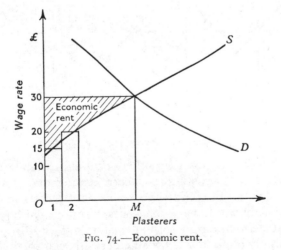

FIG. 74.—Economic rent.

If in Fig. 73 we now insert the demand curve, we can obtain the current wage rate to the industry, £30, when OM plasterers will be employed. But all plasters receive this wage rate. Thus the first plasterer receives an economic rent of £15, the second £10, and so on. The total economic rent received by plasters as a whole is shown by the shaded area.

What determines the size of economic rent?

The size of economic rent earned by a particular type of factor depends upon the elasticity of supply of that factor and how the particular type of factor is defined.

(1) *The elasticity of supply*

Elasticity of supply is determined largely by the period of time under consideration and immobilities, some of which cannot be eliminated even in the long period. Both will affect economic rent.

Let us assume that, in the short period, the supply of plasters is fixed; there is insufficient time for them to move into alternative occupations or for others to move in. In short, there is no alternative occupation—they can either work as plasters or not at all. Thus all their earnings are economic rent (Fig. 75*a*).

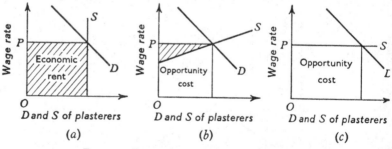

FIG. 75.—Economic rent and elasticity of supply.

In the long period, however, other occupations can be trained as plasters, and existing plasters can move elsewhere. Sufficient has to be paid—the opportunity cost—to retain plasters. Thus we have a long-period supply curve of plasters, and economic rent is smaller (Fig. 75*b*).

If the supply of plasters became perfectly elastic, then economic rent would disappear (Fig. 75*c*). Thus economic rent depends upon a less than perfectly elastic supply curve to the industry.

Sometimes the degree of immobility between different uses or occupations persists indefinitely. Building sites for offices in the City of London, for instance, earn rents far in excess of what they could obtain in their best alternative use, say for houses. Simply because such sites are very limited in supply, competition for office accommodation has forced up the rents of these sites far beyond the possible price which houses could offer. A large part of their earnings, therefore, is 'economic rent'.

Sometimes, too, we refer to the 'rent of ability'. Many pop singers, film stars, barristers and surgeons have a talent which, to all intents and purposes, is unique, for it cannot be duplicated by training others. Their high earnings, therefore, are almost wholly in the nature of 'economic rent'.

(2) The definition of an 'occupation', etc.

If we adopt a wide definition of our factor, e.g. land as a whole, the distinction is between employing it or idleness, and thus the whole of its earnings is economic rent. This is what Ricardo had in mind.

If, however, our definition is narrower, e.g. land for a particular use, such as for growing wheat, then the opportunity cost will be larger (e.g. growing barley) and economic rent smaller. Similarly, we could distinguish between cabinet-makers and carpenters, surgeons and doctors, etc. Each would give a smaller 'economic rent' than if the distinction were simply between cabinet-makers and labourers, surgeons and teachers, etc.

Likewise, economic rent will be different whether we are looking at it from the point of view of the industry or the firm. The industry is unlikely to have a perfectly elastic supply curve; thus there will be some element of economic rent in its payment to the factors it hires. The firm, however, will face, in perfect competition, a perfectly elastic supply curve. In this case it will pay the transfer cost to all factors (whose best alternative is another firm); there is thus no economic rent.

Quasi-rent

For fixed factors, particularly capital equipment, what the firm has to pay to retain them will vary according to the period of time.

In the short period, capital equipment is, by definition, fixed in supply. There is no transfer price. More capital equipment cannot be added; nor can existing equipment be diminished. The entrepreneur, as we have seen, will continue to work his capital equipment so long as total earnings just cover the cost of his variable factors (*see* Chapter 11). Any earnings above variable costs will be in the nature of a residual which helps towards the cost of the fixed factors. The size of this residual depends upon the price at which the product sells.

This can be seen immediately if we refer to Fig. 41. Were the demand for hen-houses to increase, the price would rise, say to £60, and production would be expanded to the point where once again price equalled marginal cost, that is, to 100 units. The increased cost of such production would be equal to the increase in total cost, that is £510. But total receipts would have increased by £1,950, and so the fixed factors earn an additional return—the increase in 'abnormal profit', equal to £1,440.

As time passes, however, we move into the 'long period'. If the product has been selling at a high price, the return to the capital equipment will have been high, and this will induce entrepreneurs to produce and install additional equipment. On the other hand, if the price of the product was low, existing capital equipment will either be transferred to its next most profitable use, or, when it wears out, simply not be replaced. In the long period, therefore, earnings of fixed factors are, under perfect competition, equal to their transfer cost; economic rent is eliminated.

To distinguish between economic rent which is more or less permanent and that which disappears over time, the latter is often referred to by economists as 'quasi-rent'. It is not a true rent, for the high return earned by such factors leads to an increase in their supply, and this eliminates the economic rent they earn. True rent refers only to factors which are fixed in supply; even if their earnings are high, identical factors are not forthcoming, and so economic rent persists.

CHAPTER 19

ENTREPRENEURSHIP AND PROFIT

I. ENTREPRENEURSHIP

The identity of entrepreneurship and risk-bearing

FOR production to take place, land, labour and capital (including raw materials) must be brought together and set to work. Whoever undertakes this task is often described as 'the entrepreneur'. Economic analysis, however, is better served if a somewhat narrower meaning is given to the term.

The entrepreneurial function can be broken down into two parts. First, there is the task of co-ordination—bringing the factors of production together and setting them to work. Secondly, there is accepting the risk of buying or hiring factors to produce goods which will not be sold until some time in the future—when they come to be realised, receipts may not cover costs.

In practice, it is not always easy to separate co-ordination and risk. A farmer, for instance, not only manages and runs his farm, but also accepts the risk involved in deciding what to produce. On the other hand, in a joint-stock company most of the work of co-ordination is left to a paid board of directors, with a chairman or managing director playing the major role. Even British Rail, a public corporation, has a paid manager. With a joint-stock company, the risks of the business are borne by the ordinary shareholders; with a public corporation, they are carried by the taxpayers. But neither shareholders nor taxpayers exercise control over the running of the business except in a most remote way.

The function of co-ordination, therefore, can be fulfilled by a paid manager who is given a regular salary. In this respect, management is simply an exceptionally highly skilled form of labour. It is convenient if we regard it as such.

This means that we must narrow our concept of enterprise to cover only the bearing of the risks of the business which are associated with ownership.

The nature of risks

A businessman is always open to the risk of fire, accidents to employees, theft, damage by storm, etc. But these risks are calculable. A mathematician can work out, for instance, what likelihood there is of a building catching fire during the course of the year. He cannot say which building will be destroyed in this way, but he does know that on average, say, one out of every ten thousand will be. Such risks, therefore, can be insured against. They are thus reduced to a normal cost, and the businessman contracts out of the risk involved.

Certain risks, however, are not calculable—they cannot be reduced to a law of averages. Nobody, for instance, can forecast with certainty how many cold drinks will be sold in Britain next summer. That will depend upon the weather. Similarly, it might be thought that square toes will be the fashion for ladies' shoes within six months. But again there is a chance that this will not be so. The risk of demand being different from that estimated cannot be reduced to a mathematical probability. Such a risk, therefore, cannot be insured against; it must be accepted by those persons whose money is tied up in producing goods for which the demand is still uncertain.

These uninsurable risks are inherent in a dynamic economy. Modern methods of production take time. When an entrepreneur engages factors of production, therefore, it is an act of faith—faith in his estimate of the demand for the product some time ahead. But demand can never be completely certain. People have freedom of choice, and their tastes may change. Many of the factors affecting demand fluctuate even over a relatively short period of time. It is similar on the supply side. Techniques do not stand still; new methods discovered by a rival may mean that, by the time an entrepreneur's product comes on the market, it is undersold by a cheaper or better substitute of a competitor.

Thus there is always some degree of uncertainty, and this involves risk. It is a risk which must be shouldered by those who back with their money the decision as to what shall be produced. The true entrepreneurs, therefore, are those who accept the risks of uncertainty-bearing.

II. PROFIT

How profit differs in nature from other rewards

The reward of uncertainty-bearing is 'profit'. But profit differs from the earnings of other factors of production. First, profit may be negative. Whereas wages, rent and interest are paid as part of a contract at the time of hiring, profits are received some time in the future, and then only if demand has been more or less correctly estimated. Where the entrepreneur has been far too optimistic, a loss is made. Secondly, profit fluctuates more than the other rewards. While the latter are adjusted over time, it is profit which feels the immediate impact of booms and slumps. Hence, in a boom, profits rise faster than wages, interest and rent; in a slump, they fall more severely. Thirdly, unlike wages, interest and rent, which are contractual and certain payments, profit is simply a residue. Its size is most uncertain—for it depends on how the good sells some time in the future.

Differences in the concept of the term 'profit'

We must be careful to distinguish four different concepts of the term 'profit':

(1) *Profit in its everyday meaning*

In its general use, profit means simply the difference between total receipts and total costs (*see* p. 162). But because the economist defines cost in terms of alternatives forgone, he would amend this idea of profit by deducing, first, the return which the entrepreneur would have received on his capital had it been used elsewhere, and secondly, the value of the entrepreneur's labour in the best alternative line of business.

(2) *Normal profit under perfect competition*

Because uncertainty cannot be eliminated from a dynamic economy, there must be a return to induce people to accept the responsibility of bearing uncertainty. This is true even in the long period. Thus there must be a rate of profit—the price which equates the demand for and supply of entrepreneurship. In the long period under perfect competition, any rent element from profit is eliminated. We then have 'normal profit'—the cost which has to be met if the supply of uncertainty-bearing is to be maintained.

Two modifications should be noted. First, industries differ as regards the uncertainty involved. Where fashions or techniques change frequently, for instance, uncertainty is greater. This would tend to reduce the supply of entrepreneurship in such industries at any given level of normal profit, and thus for them normal profit must be higher. Secondly, the elimination of the rent element in profit in the long period assumes that entrepreneurs can be obtained of equal ability. In practice this is not so. Thus there will always be some entrepreneurs earning a rent of ability (super-normal profit) even in the long period.

(3) Abnormal or super-normal profit

Under perfect competition, the entrepreneur is able to make abnormal profits for a period because other entrepreneurs cannot enter into competition with him. Certain factors are fixed in supply. Thus workers are immobile, and so it may be difficult to obtain immediately certain skilled operatives. More important, machinery takes time to produce, and for a time those entrepreneurs already possessing it will make abnormal profits. Such profits, therefore, are really the return to factors fixed in supply over the short period. To some extent they are in the nature of rent—quasi-rent—for they are the earnings on the fixed factors and disappear in the long period.

(4) Monopoly profit

With monopoly, competitors can be excluded. Certain factors, e.g. diamond-mines, know-how, patents and copyrights, are fixed to the monopolist. Even in the long period, competitors cannot engage such factors, and so abnormal profits persist. The profits of the monopolist, therefore, are closer to economic rent than to quasi-rent.

The functions of profit in a private-enterprise economy

The word 'profit' is often spoken of in terms of abuse, and persons who make large profits are likely to be regarded as social pariahs. But usually there is little justification for such an attitude, for profits are inseparable from the private-enterprise economy and are vital in making that system work.

We must emphasise, however, that we are discussing only profits under conditions of perfect competition. Given these conditions, abnormal profit is eliminated in the long period (*see* Chapter 11). Only normal profit—which is really a cost to cover uncertainty-bearing—remains.

Monopoly profit, on the other hand, is not eliminated, even in the long period. Entry into the industry is not free; consequently, profits are not competed away. It may be that monopoly profits stimulate research and allow an industry to expand. But where scarcity has been deliberately brought about, they simply represent an economic rent earned at the expense of consumers by the monopolist owners. Government action, therefore, is usually aimed at eliminating monopoly profits, and we shall have nothing further to say about them.

Where there is perfect competition, the functions of profits are as follows:

(1) *Normal profits are necessary to induce persons to accept the risks of uncertainty*

Because uncertainty is implicit in a dynamic economy, some reward is essential to ensure a supply of entrepreneurs to industry. This reward is known as 'normal profit'. Without such profit, no production would take place. It is thus a cost, as essential as the payment of wages to labour.

(2) *Abnormal profits indicate to entrepreneurs which industries should expand and which should contract*

When an entrepreneur produces a good which proves to be popular with consumers, it is reflected in its selling price, and therefore in his profits. As a result, he receives abnormal profit over and above normal profit. This is an indication that more factors should be brought into the industry to expand output to meet the wishes of consumers.

On the other hand, should the entrepreneur overestimate demand, he may incur a loss. Consumers have shown that they do not want the good, and production should contract.

(3) *Abnormal profits encourage entrepreneurs to increase production of a good*

Profits not only indicate that consumers want more of a good; they are the inducement to entrepreneurs to produce those goods. As we saw in Chapter 11, abnormal profits act as the spur for existing firms to increase capacity and for other entrepreneurs to enter the industry. On the other hand, when losses are being incurred, firms go out of production and the industry contracts. Thus losses are as important as profits in the operation of the private-enterprise economy.

(4) *Abnormal profits provide the resources for expansion*

An industry making abnormal profits can secure the factors which are necessary to further expansion.

In the first place, profits can be used to provide further capital ('ploughing back'), and shareholders will respond to a request for further capital (usually made through a 'rights' issue). Similarly, new firms can enter the industry, because investors will purchase the shares or debentures of a company intending to operate in an industry where the level of profits is relatively high.

Secondly, profits enable expanding firms to offer higher rewards to land, labour and capital than can be earned in the declining industries. In this way factors of production are moved according to the wishes of consumers. Eventually, under perfect competition, profits are competed away.

(5) *Profits ensure that production is carried on by the most efficient firms*

In a perfectly competitive industry, the firm making the largest profit is the one whose costs are lowest. It will have an incentive to expand production and, if necessary, can afford to pay more for factors in order to do so. Less efficient firms must copy its methods, for otherwise they cannot retain factors. Still worse for them, the increased output of the more efficient firm will eventually lower the price of the product. As a result, inefficient firms find that profits become negative—a loss is made.

Thus it can be seen that, under a private-enterprise system the drive is provided by profits—and the fear of losses. Whether

the desire for personal gain is the best of motives may be open
to doubt. But, human nature being what it is at present, it is
still the most effective. Uncertainty exists in any dynamic
economy, and so there is bound to be scope for profits whether
production is organised by private enterprise or by the state.
What we have to ask, therefore, is: 'When no personal gain or
loss is involved, is there the same incentive to maximise profits
or to avoid losses?'

It must be pointed out, too, that under perfect competition,
profits are self-destructive. Moreover, in the process of elimination, industry is made more efficient.

It is wrong, therefore, to regard profits as being somewhat
immoral. The exception is monopoly profits, which do not
disappear and do not motivate a full distribution of the factors
of production according to the wishes of consumers.

PART V

MONEY AND FINANCIAL INSTITUTIONS

CHAPTER 20

MONEY AND THE RATE OF INTEREST

I. THE FUNCTIONS OF MONEY

What is money?

IT is possible to exchange goods by a direct swap. But barter, as direct exchange is usually termed, is comparatively rare in the modern world. Consider this advertisement in *Exchange and Mart*: 'Ever Ready battery portable in exchange for any pedigree bitch up to two years.' The formidable difficulties in the way of such an exchange are obvious.

In an economy where there is a high degree of specialisation, exchanges must take place quickly and smoothly. Hence we have a 'go-between'—money—a common denominator for all goods. The product of specialised labour is sold, that is, exchanged for money, and this money is then used to buy the many different goods and services required.

Anything which is generally acceptable in purchasing goods or settling debts can be said to be money. It need not consist of coins and notes. Oxen, salt, amber, woodpecker scalps and cotton cloth have at times all been used as money.

In fact, the precise substance, its size and shape, are largely a matter of convenience and custom. But whatever is used, it should be immediately and unquestionably accepted in exchange for goods and services. Thus the use of the particular good should be backed by custom, and people must feel that it will retain its value by remaining relatively scarce.

Legal tender

Sometimes an attempt is made to confer acceptability by law. In the United Kingdom, notes have unlimited 'legal tender', in that a creditor must accept them in payment of a debt. But a commodity does not have to be legal tender for it to be money. Nor does legislation ensure that it will be acceptable. In Germany, after World War II, cigarettes were preferred to the Reichsbank mark in payment for goods.

Precious metal as money

Most commodities used as money in the past have proved unsatisfactory, especially as exchange economies have developed, for they did not completely overcome the difficulties of barter. Oxen, for instance, were bulky to transport, deteriorated over time, and were costly to store. Moreover, not only were they rarely uniform in size or quality, but they could not easily be divided to purchase goods of small value.

Hence, precious metals eventually replaced other goods as money. Later, in order to simplify transactions, metals were minted into coins of different weights and shapes. The exact amount of money required could now be found by counting instead of by weighing.

Paper money

In England, precious metals and coins were used almost exclusively as money until the middle of the seventeenth century. However, in 1640, Charles I appropriated £130,000 worth of gold held for merchants in the Tower of London. Thereafter gold and silver bullion plate were kept in the strong rooms of the goldsmiths. Eventually, receipts for these deposits were accepted in exchange for goods, and so withdrawal of the actual gold and silver became unnecessary.

This was the origin of the banknote, and paper currency soon began to form an increasing proportion of British money. The paper from which notes are made is comparatively worthless. But people who receive notes are confident that others too will accept them. Notes possess, therefore, the essential characteristic of money—general acceptability. This is true even though, since 1931, it has not been possible in the United Kingdom to exchange notes for gold at the Bank of England.

The functions of money

Money, it is usually stated, performs four functions:

(1) It is *a medium of exchange*, the oil, as it were, which allows the machinery of modern buying and selling to run smoothly.

(2) It is *a measure of value and a unit of account*, making possible the operation of a price system and automatically providing the basis for keeping accounts, calculating profit and loss, costing, etc.

(3) It is *a standard of deferred payments*, the unit in which, given stability in its value, loans are made and future contracts fixed. Without money, there would be no common basis to allow for dealing in debts—the work of such institutions as insurance companies, building societies, banks, and discount-houses. By providing a standard for repayment, money makes borrowing and lending much easier.

(4) It is *a store of wealth*, the most convenient way of keeping any income which is surplus to immediate requirements. More than that, because money is also the medium of exchange, wealth stored in this form is completely liquid. That is, only money of all possible assets can be converted into other goods immediately and without cost. Indeed, it is this 'liquidity' which is the most distinctive characteristic of money, and it results in money playing an active, rather than a merely neutral, part in the operation of the economy. We must, therefore, give it further consideration.

II. THE DEMAND FOR MONEY

What do we mean by the 'demand for money'?

Most people would regard a miser as a crank. To the ordinary person, money is wanted not just for counting or to be gloated over, but to be spent on food, clothes, holidays, a car and all the other things which can be enjoyed. In short, it would seem that money is useful only when we are getting rid of it.

But there is somewhat more to it than that. Money was defined as anything generally acceptable in settling debts. But why is it 'generally acceptable'? Simply because everybody has confidence that other people will accept it *immediately* whenever they wish to buy something. Money is, as we have seen, perfectly liquid.

Moreover, no other form of wealth is liquid to the same degree as money. Assets kept in the deposit account of a bank are subject to seven days' notice of withdrawal. Equities and bonds have to be sold before anything else can be bought, and this involves payment of broker's commission and maybe a capital loss. Or, if a house, car or piano are to be exchanged for something else, it usually means finding a cash purchaser first. Only money can be changed into some other form of wealth without cost or delay.

People want a money balance, therefore, because it is a perfectly liquid asset. It is in this sense that there is a 'demand' for money—*to hold perfectly liquid reserves*. We must now examine why people should want such reserves.

Why people demand money

Lord Keynes gives three main reasons for holding money:

(1) The transactions motive

Both consumers and businessmen hold money to facilitate current transactions.

Most consumers receive the bulk of their income weekly or monthly. On the other hand, payments for food, travel, and pleasure have to be made each day. Thus a part of money income has to be held throughout the week or month to cover these everyday purchases. How much will this be?

Suppose that a man is earning £26 a week, all of which is being spent. He receives £26 on the Friday which begins the week, and by the following Friday he will have nothing left. Thus his average holding of money is £13. Should it now be decided to pay him monthly, and his spending habits remain the same, his average holding of money, either in cash or in his current account at the bank, would rise to £52. In the same way, if his income doubled but was still fully spent, the amount of money he held would double.

Similarly, a businessman requires money to pay wages, purchase raw materials, and meet other current expenses.

There may be special reasons why the demand for money for the transactions motive may suddenly increase; it does, for instance, at Christmas and the holiday periods, or if there is a flurry of activity on the Stock Exchange. Usually the underlying determinants are fairly stable. With consumers, these are the length of time between successive pay-days and the level of income and prices; with businessmen, it is the size of turnover. It can be seen, therefore, that the community's demand for money for transactions purposes will be roughly in proportion to the size of the national income.

It should be noted that the value of transactions for which money is required is much greater than the value of money national income. For instance, if the cost of goods to a shop-keeper (including his shop expenses) is £100, and he sells them for £110, the income he makes from the transaction is £10, whereas £210 in money was required to effect the necessary exchanges. In addition, money is required for what are basically non-income-creating transactions, e.g. switching securities.

(2) *The precautionary motive*

Apart from expenditure on regular, everyday purchases, money is required to cover events of a more uncertain nature which may easily occur—illness, accident, unemployment, defects in the car or household appliances, and snap decisions to obtain a cash bargain. Hence both consumers and business-men usually keep some extra reserve of cash for a 'rainy day' or to make a favourable purchase. The amount held will depend mainly on the outlook of the individual, how optimistic he is both as regards events and the possibility of borrowing at short notice should the need arise. But, taking the community as a whole, the amount set aside for the precautionary motive is, in normal times, likely to be tied fairly closely to the level of national income.

Keynes terms tne money held for the transactions and precautionary motives as 'active' balances. The size of such balances is chiefly dependent on the level of income.

(3) *The speculative motive*

Usually the amount of money in existence exceeds what is necessary to satisfy the demand for active balances. But any surplus must be held by somebody, for it must be somewhere! Why, however, should people wish to hold 'idle' balances?

The immediate response of the reader might be 'why not?'

As we have seen, money has no carrying costs (e.g. storage, maintenance) and is perfectly liquid. Of all assets, only money confers complete manœuvrability.

But holding wealth in the form of money has the disadvantage that *it does not provide a yield*. (In periods of inflation, there is the added disadvantage that the value of money is falling, but we can ignore this complication for the time being.) Furniture, jewellery, works of art, etc., afford pleasure; a house can be lived in or rented out. With shares, there is usually a dividend; with bonds, a fixed rate of interest. There is thus an opportunity cost of being liquid—the yield forgone. To simplify, let us refer to this yield as 'the rate of interest'.

Thus, while people might desire liquidity, they have also to think of the cost involved. The higher the rate of interest, the greater the cost of remaining liquid. As the rate rises, so fewer people will be prepared to pay the 'price'; in other words, they will be tempted out of holding money. Thus demand for idle balances is closely related to the rate of interest—the higher the rate, the greater the cost of holding money and so the less will money be demanded.

But the complete answer is less simple than this. Holding money, as opposed to securities, permits speculation. Keynes considers that the main reason why people hold idle balances is for purposes of speculation. Such speculation arises as follows.

On any given day it is quite usual for the prices of some securities to rise while those of others fall. But there are periods when the prices of almost all securities move in more or less the same direction. To simplify our explanation, however, we shall concentrate our attention on undated government bonds (fixed-interest-bearing securities); this eliminates time and risk complications.

If people think that the price of bonds is going to rise, they will buy bonds now. Should their forecast prove correct, they will make a capital gain. Similarly, if they think that the price of bonds is going to fall, they will sell bonds. Now the lower the price of bonds, the more will people think that the next likely move will be in an upward direction. As the price rises, so more people will gradually come round to the view that the price is so high that a fall is likely to occur. It follows, therefore, that when the price of bonds is low, people prefer bonds to liquidity;

but as the price of bonds rises, people move out of bonds in order to hold money.

However, the price of bonds varies proportionately but inversely with the rate of interest. Thus if the current rate of interest is 2½ per cent, £100 3½ per cent War Loan would be worth £140 on the Stock Exchange, but if the rate were 7 per cent, it would be worth only £50.

Thus it is possible to relate the demand for money, not only to the price of bonds, but also to the rate of interest. When people are speculating against the future price of bonds they are speculating against the future rate of interest. Hence we can rewrite our original proposition as: when the rate of interest is low (the price of bonds is high), people will prefer to hold money; when the rate of interest is high (the price of bonds is low), people will not wish to hold money. This relationship between the current rate of interest and the demand for idle balances is shown in Fig. 76.

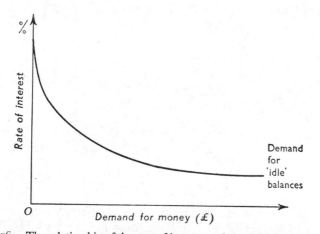

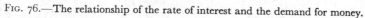

FIG. 76.—The relationship of the rate of interest and the demand for money.

It should be noted that there is nothing sinister about this speculation on the future rate of interest. Speculation must occur where there is an element of uncertainty and where it is important to the holder of a bond whether its market price rises or falls while it is in his possession. He will compare the interest he is likely to earn on the bond over a period with the possibility of any loss in its capital value. If the latter outweighs the former, he will prefer to hold money.

Whereas the level of income, the main factor influencing the demand for money for the transactions and precautionary motives, is fairly stable, people's expectations of the future rate of interest, the determinant of liquidity preference for the speculative motive, is far more liable to change. It is this speculation, therefore, which Lord Keynes considers as exercising the dominating influence on the level of the rate of interest.

The demand for money and saving

It must be emphasised that the demand for money and saving are quite different things. Saving is simply that part of income which is not spent, and the influences determining it are analysed in Chapter 26. Saving adds to a person's wealth. Liquidity preference is concerned with the form in which that wealth is held. The motives for liquidity preference explain why there is a desire to hold some wealth in the form of cash rather than in goods affording utility or in securities earning income.

III. THE SUPPLY OF MONEY

The supply of money consists of the following:

(1) Coins

These are insignificant in volume, amounting in 1973 to £365 million. They are convenient for small, everyday transactions.

(2) Notes

From the seventeenth century, paper currency began to form an increasing proportion of British money. Today (Aug. 1973) the value of notes in circulation is £4,545 million. Whenever the note issue exceeds £1,575 million, the Treasury has to make and lay before Parliament a Statutory Order which has to be renewed after two years. This is a relic of the days when Parliament exercised a strict control over the 'Fiduciary Issue' —the note issue in excess of the value of gold held by the Bank of England. Today, however, less emphasis is put on the necessity of checking the issue of notes as a guard against inflation (*see* pp. 324, 336). Instead, notes, like coins, are regarded as the small change of the monetary system, and so sufficient are always made available for the practical convenience of the public.

(3) *Bank deposits*

While purchases of everyday goods—groceries, bus-rides, cigarettes, petrol, laundry, etc.—are usually paid for in coins or notes, about 80 per cent (in value) of all transactions are effected by cheque. When a person writes a cheque, he is instructing his bank to transfer deposits standing in his account to the person to whom he owes money. Bank deposits, therefore, act as money.

A large part of these deposits are 'created' by the bank. How banks create deposits and how they can be controlled will be described in the following two chapters.

Other forms of money

There is really no hard and fast dividing line between what is money and what is not. 'True money' confers complete *liquidity* on its holder and, in the last resort, only banknotes and sovereigns do this, for other coins are limited in legal tender. But when considering what serves as money in our economy, the more practical approach is to start from the idea that 'money is what money does'. Is it accepted in payment for goods? If so, it is acting as money. Cheques, as we have seen, are money for this reason, although they represent nothing more than deposits in a bank. Yet, in advanced economies, cheques form the major part of 'money' in use.

And, pursuing our argument in the same direction, we find other instruments of credit which, although not 'true money' in the sense that they can be spent anywhere in their present form, nevertheless fulfil the functions of money, if only within a limited sphere. But we must be careful to see clearly how and when they add to the money supply. Deposits can be 'created' by banks only because their clearing system enables them to economise in cash (*see* Chapter 22). In this the banks hold a unique position; other forms of credit add to the money supply only when they are not covered by cash held idle to an equal amount. Thus, when a person buys a postal order to cover his 'pools' entry, the cash he pays in may be put into circulation again by the Post Office before the order is presented by the pools firm. Thus, to some extent, postal orders can form an addition to the money supply, for they are doing the work of money. This is true, too, of other instruments of credit—bills of exchange (especially those 'negotiated', that is, passed on to a third party to settle a debt), trade credit (particularly when deals between firms are allowed to cancel credit, or if the entitlement to payment is transferred to a third party) and book entry settlements replacing cash (as occurs, for example, when there is a vertical amalgamation of firms).

'Near' money

We can carry the above idea further. Any assets possessed can usually be turned into money eventually. Liquidity, therefore, is largely a matter of degree, often depending upon the organisations which exist whereby such assets as government securities, shares in public companies, insurance policies and building society loans can be made liquid. Thus in recent years, traders have become more liquid by the development of factor houses to which trade debts can be sold immediately for cash. While assets may have to be sold at some capital loss, they do afford some degree of liquidity to the holder. A person possessing first-class shares, for instance, would not need to keep so large a cash balance for the precautionary motive, for he could always sell some in an emergency. In short, the existence of 'near' money means that the demand for 'true' money can be correspondingly less. We shall assume that this has been allowed for in our demand for money curves, which therefore depict the demand for 'true' money.

IV. THE RATE OF INTEREST

The classical economists' views

We are now in a position to consider the problem postponed in Chapter 17: 'What determines the overall level of interest rates in the economy?' Or, as it is more usually put: 'What determines the *pure* rate of interest?'

The rate of interest is the price which has to be paid for a loan of liquid capital. The classical economists explained it, therefore, in terms of the demand for and supply of loanable funds. Because investment is profitable, entrepreneurs demand funds for investment. The lower the rate of interest, the greater the number of investment projects which are profitable. Thus total demand for liquid capital consists of the sum of the demands of the individual entrepreneurs at different rates of interest.

The *supply of liquid capital* comes from persons willing to forgo present consumption in order to enjoy it at some future date. To most people, 'a bird in the hand is worth two in the bush'. The classical economists argued, therefore, that in order to persuade people to overcome the inclination to consume immediately, a reward in the form of interest had to be offered. The higher the rate of interest, the greater would be the inducement to postpone current consumption, and so the greater would be the supply of loanable funds. Thus we have a supply curve for liquid capital sloping upwards to the right.

The rate of interest, the price of liquid capital, is fixed by the interaction of demand and supply—at the point of intersection of the two curves.

The classical economists' explanation of the rate of interest is too simple.

First, it ascribes to the rate of interest a greater influence on the volume of investment and saving than is justified. Other factors, notably the level of income, are more important (*see* pp. 366–82).

Secondly, since investment and saving as conceived by the classical economists would be fairly stable, their theory cannot explain why fairly short-term variations in the rate of interest occur.

Thirdly, it offers no explanation of how the government has been able to influence the rate of interest in recent years.

Lastly, and most important, it assumes that the whole of income saved is actually lent to entrepreneurs. But besides being reluctant to save, people are reluctant to lend. They prefer to keep their assets liquid in the form of money. It is on the fact that money is a *liquid* asset that the modern explanation of the rate of interest hinges.

The rate of interest as a monetary phenomenon

Income not spent by an individual is said to be 'saved'. But even after he has saved a part of his income, he still has to choose what assets he will hold. This is because assets differ in the qualities they possess, particularly as regards lender's risk, liquidity and yield.

The greater the lender's risk, the higher the yield required, other things being equal. The exact difference in yield between different types of risk will be decided in the market. We can eliminate this complication by concentrating attention at the extreme end where risk of non-payment of interest and capital are nil—government securities.

Liquidity and yield, too, are usually related inversely. Illiquidity has to be compensated for by a high yield. Complete liquidity, conferred only by money, involves total loss of yield.

But since liquidity is a desirable attribute in an asset, money can be regarded as an acceptable way of holding wealth in comparison with interest-yielding assets. A person, therefore, has to arrange his portfolio of assets according to the emphasis he puts on liquidity as opposed to interest yield. To eliminate the complication of loans of differing periods, we shall assume that all securities are undated government stock, which we shall term 'bonds'. Thus there are only two kinds of asset which a person may hold in storing his wealth—bonds and money. The price of bonds will also give us the rate of interest on riskless, undated securities (see p. 287).

On the capital market there will be bonds offered for sale. Some will come out of the existing stock held by people; others will be new bonds arising from current government borrowing. But their price will be determined by demand and supply, just as the price of rubber, tin, wool, cotton and any other commodity is in their respective markets.

People holding money bid on the capital market for the bonds offered. How much money they have will depend upon the total supply of money in the economy and how much they want to hold for the transactions and precautionary motives. At the end of a day's dealing, all bonds may have changed hands. But this need not be so. If the price of bonds is low, some would-be sellers may prefer to hold on to them. On the other hand, if the price of bonds is high, some would-be purchasers may prefer to retain their money.

But, at the end of the day's dealings, a price will have been found at which people have finished dealing—nobody will wish to exchange more bonds against money, and nobody will wish to exchange more money against bonds. There is equilibrium at this price. This price is the inverse of the current 'pure' rate of interest—the bench-mark referred to in Chapter 17.

The Keynesian emphasis on particular determining factors

It can be seen from the above that a change in the demand for money relative to bonds, given the stock of money and of bonds, will bring about a change in the rate of interest. Thus if it becomes less attractive to hold money, the rate of interest would fall.

But changes in the relative quantities of money and bonds, that is, in the sizes of the stocks of each, will also produce variations in the rate of interest. If, for instance, the quantity of money increased and the demand for money and the stock of bonds remained unchanged, it would mean that more money was being offered against bonds, with the result that the price of bonds would rise. Looked at in an alternative way, the owners of wealth could not, at the given rate of interest, be induced to hold the whole stock of money. Thus there would have to be a reduction in the inducement *not* to hold money, that is, in the rate of interest. Similarly, if the quantity of bonds increased, the demand for bonds and the supply of money remaining unchanged, the price of bonds would fall. Looked at in an alternative way, it would mean that at the given rate of interest owners of wealth could not be induced to hold the whole stock of bonds. Hence the inducement to hold bonds, that is, the rate of interest, would have to rise. In practice, stocks, both of money and of bonds, are not subject to great variations except over fairly considerable periods of time.

The supply of money is controlled by the government (*see* Chapter 23). The supply of bonds coming on to the market comes chiefly from existing stocks of old bonds. In comparison, the flow of new bonds on to the market is small. Current government borrowing would therefore have little impact on the rate of interest. Thus, Keynes considers, it is much more realistic to analyse the rate of interest from the point of view of the variable which is most likely to change over the short period—the demand for money. And here he stresses the role of speculation.

In the market for bonds there will be many persons whose main interest will be in their future price. Indeed, as we have seen, Keynes thinks the speculative element dominates all other considerations. If so, then the demand for bonds is largely the result of the present price of bonds. Or, the demand for money is primarily a function of the rate of interest.

Instead of approaching the rate of interest through the demand and supply of bonds, therefore, it is possible to approach it through the demand for and supply of money, the alternative asset.

The demand for money depends upon the level of income (transactions and precautionary motives) and the rate of interest (speculative motive), though modern thought would not separate them completely, for people can economise on active balances when the rate of interest is high. But we can combine the demand for each in a single demand curve, adding the demand for active balances (which is largely unaffected by the rate of interest) to the demand for idle balances (which is influenced by the current rate of interest).

This is shown in Fig. 77. The demand for money for active balances is shown by the distance of the vertical sections of the demand curve from the y-axis. Thus if income increases from Y to Y_1, the increase in the demand for active balances is equal to the horizontal difference between the two. To this demand for active balances must be added the demand for idle balances—the sloping portion of the curve.

The supply of money is fixed by the government and the banking authorities (see Chapter 23). Suppose it is equal to ON. If the level of income is low, Y, there is less demand for active balances and thus more available for idle balances. The rate of interest is therefore only 4 per cent. With a higher level of income, Y_1, more money is demanded for active balances. This leaves less for idle balances and the rate of interest rises to 6 per cent. And so on.

A smaller supply of money, ON_1, would produce a rate of interest of 6 per cent with Y.

As we shall see, the level of income is influenced by the level of saving and investment. It is through their effect on income that saving and investment have an impact on the rate of interest.

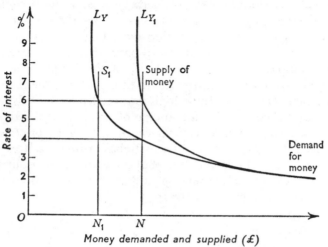

FIG. 77.—The determination of the rate of interest.

The structure of interest rates

It merely remains to remove our earlier simplification that the only type of security in existence is bonds. In practice people can put their money into a range of securities each varying in the degree of liquidity and lender's risk involved. These securities can, however, be regarded as fairly close substitutes for one another, and there will be a rate of return on each depending on the demand for that type of security and the supply of it. These rates will be interrelated because, since they are close substitutes, the demand for one type of security will be affected by the rate of return on the security most similar to it. For instance, a rise in the rate of return on short-dated government stock will cause a movement of funds to it from its immediate close substitutes, such as Treasury Bills. This sets up a ripple running through the whole structure of interest rates until eventually equilibrium has been restored. Of course, this ripple could easily start by a change in the demand for or supply of money. It is likely to have its first effect on short-term (three-month) securities, and eventually the long-term rate is brought into line, though this may occur only over a considerable period of time.

Generally speaking, differences in the rate of interest reflect either differences in liquidity (the period of the loan), or differences in lender's risk, or both. However, in periods of steadily rising prices, with people expecting these price rises to continue, fixed-interest-bearing securities cease to be such good substitutes for equities (ordinary shares) because the earning power, and thus the value, of the former does not increase in sympathy with the rise in prices. Hence the demand for ordinary shares may be so high that the lender's risk is more than outweighed by the advantage of an 'inflation hedge'— holding a security whose capital value will rise as prices rise. As a result, the rate of return on first-class ordinary shares (the 'blue chips') may be lower than that on government securities, a situation known as 'the reverse gap' or 'the cult of the equity' and one which has existed since 1953.

CHAPTER 21

THE MONEY MARKETS AND THE CAPITAL MARKET

In Chapter 17 we saw that capital is demanded because of the contribution it makes to production. Hence liquid capital, that is loans of money, is required by producers—manufacturers, traders and the government—for varying periods of time. Such funds are provided by persons who not only save a part of their income, but lend all or some of these savings.

Finance is required for different purposes, by different persons and for varying periods of time. Thus there is a great variety in the institutions providing such loans and in the types of loans arranged. As with goods, markets have sprung up to bring together buyers and sellers.

We shall discuss the subject, however, under the following headings:

    (i)   the Money Markets, which deal in short-term loans;

   (ii) the Capital Market, where medium- and long-term capital is raised;

 (iii) the joint-stock banks, which are the major source of working capital, and which exercise a major influence on the system through their ability to create credit;

 (iv) the Bank of England, which exercises overall control on behalf of the government.

In this chapter we are concerned with the first two. For convenience, we also include a description of the work of the Stock Exchange, although this is mainly a market in existing securities and only indirectly helps in providing new loans.

None of the Money Markets or the Capital Market have any formal organisation in the sense that buyers and sellers meet regularly in a particular building to conduct business. Instead they are merely a collection of institutions connected, in the case of the Money Markets, by dealings in bills of exchange and short-term loans and, more loosely in the case of the Capital Market, in channelling medium and long term finance to those requiring it. The complete structure is shown in a very simplified form in Fig. 78.

Not only are there Money and Capital Markets but, within each, there is further specialisation. This will be illustrated later. But, in order to explain: (a) the nature of markets in finance; (b) how the City of London acquired its expertise;

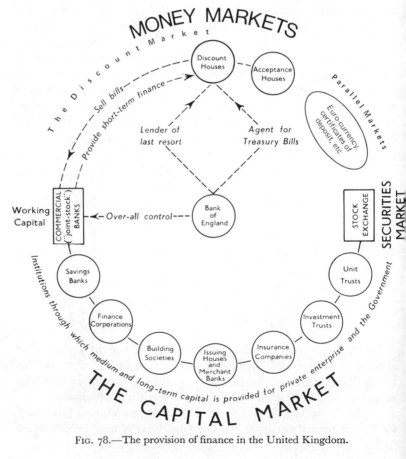

FIG. 78.—The provision of finance in the United Kingdom.

(c) how the Bank of England enters into the market, we commence by looking at the traditional London Money Market or, as it would be more precisely described today, the Discount Market.

I. THE DISCOUNT MARKET

The Discount Market is composed of the discount houses and 'running brokers', the acceptance houses or merchant banks, the commercial banks and the Bank of England. All are linked by the various dealings in bills of exchange (Fig. 80). We shall show the connection for the commercial bill as used in foreign trade.

The generally accepted custom of business is that an importer is allowed a period of grace, usually three months, before payment for goods is required. This is arranged through a bill of exchange as follows.

Suppose A is exporting cars from London to B in New York to the value of £10,000. When A is ready to ship his cars, he draws up a bill of exchange, as shown in Fig. 79. This is sent to B together with copies of the shipping documents, such as the bill of lading and insurance certificate, to show that the cars had actually been placed aboard the ship. On receipt of

---

£10,000

A's address

25 April 1974

Three months after date, pay to me or to my order Ten Thousand Pounds, value received.

(Signed) 'A'

To 'B',
B's address.

FIG. 79.—A commercial bill of exchange.

the bill, B 'accepts' it, by writing 'Accepted' and his signature across the face of the bill, and then returns it to A. This acceptance of the bill by B is the condition for handing over the original bill of lading, the documentary title to the cars.

A can now do one of three things: (i) he can hold the bill until it matures three months after the date of acceptance; (ii) he may be able, after endorsing it, to get another merchant to take it in settlement of a debt which A owes; or, (iii) he can sell the

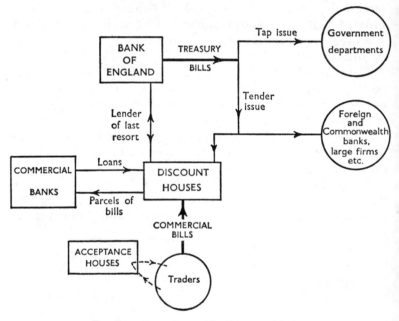

FIG. 80.—Operations of the Discount Market.

bill to somebody, usually a discount house, having money to spare for the purpose.

Discount houses

The probability is that A will choose the latter course. So, after endorsing it, he takes it along to one of the eleven discount houses operating in the City of London. Here it will be bought at less than its face value, the exact amount paid depending on the length of time it still has to run to maturity, the prevailing short-term rate of interest in the Money

Markets, and the opinion of the discount house as to B's financial standing. Suppose the bill has still three months to run and that the prevailing rate of interest on that class of bill is 8 per cent, the Discount House will pay £9,800 for it. This process is known as 'discounting'. It is obvious that through these arrangements the bill of exchange has advantages to all concerned. The exporter A can quickly regain liquidity by selling the bill, while B obtains three months' credit, during which time it is probable that he will be able to sell the cars which he has imported.

Discount houses do not usually hold bills for their full currency. Instead commercial bills are assembled in 'parcels' and sold to the commercial banks who like to have so many falling due each day. There are a few 'running brokers' who act as agents in the process of discounting, etc.

Acceptance houses

If B is a well-known firm of high financial standing, the accepted bill is, from the risk point of view, almost as good as cash. However, as bills are drawn on firms in all parts of the world, it may well be that little is known about B's financial standing. The result is that the discount house is either chary of discounting the bill or will only do so at a fairly high rate of interest. Nevertheless, the difficulty can be overcome by getting a firm of international repute to 'accept' it. This means that such a firm will make itself responsible for payment should B default. It is obvious that any firm accepting such a bill must have adequate knowledge of the creditworthiness of the particular trader upon whom the bill is drawn. Such knowledge is possessed by the merchant banks, such as Lazards, Barings and Rothschilds, who commenced as traders but later specialised on financing trade in particular parts of the world. In their capacity of accepting bills, such merchant banks are known as 'acceptance houses', and for the service they charge a small commission of about ¾ per cent, which is willingly paid by the person wishing to discount a bill because the rate of discount on a 'bank bill', that is one bearing the name of an acceptance house, is lower than on a 'trade bill' (a bill accepted only by a trader) or on a 'fine trade bill' (where the merchant is of good standing).

In recent years the business of accepting has declined. This has been due to: (*a*) the diminished use of the commercial bill in international trade; (*b*) the decline of London as the world centre for financing foreign trade, which has resulted from the reduced share of the United Kingdom in world trade and a certain loss of faith in sterling; (*c*) the increased competition of the commercial banks in the business of accepting bills, largely through the development of the 'reimbursement credit', which works in the following way. B, the importer, induces his own bank in New York to secure an acceptance credit for him in London, which means that he can instruct A to draw the bill on the London branch of his own bank or on a London bank or acceptance house. The New York bank makes itself responsible for the payment of the bill, and so all the London bank or acceptance house has to do is to satisfy itself as to the financial standing of the New York bank. This simpler procedure means that reimbursement credits can be granted at very low rates of interest.

The Treasury Bill

The operations of the discount and acceptance houses have been described with relation to the commercial bill of exchange, for it was in dealing with this type of bill that they developed. But, as already noted, the use of commercial bills declined after 1914. This, however, coincided with a large increase in the amount of government borrowing by means of Treasury Bills. A Treasury Bill is really a bill of exchange drawn by the Treasury on itself, usually for a period of three months (91 days), though occasionally two-month bills (63 days) are issued. Since such bills are only a short-term loan, they represent the government's cheapest method of borrowing, the interest being just over 10 per cent. Treasury Bills are issued in denominations of £5,000 upwards, and since the minimum is for £50,000 they are primarily for the institutional investors.

The impact of recent developments

Recent developments have had repercussions on both the discount houses and merchant banks. The government has reduced its dependence on short-term borrowing (see page 425). Furthermore, the restrictions on the lending powers of the banks before 1971 led to the development of other means of short-term borrowing, e.g. internal commercial bills, local authority bills, certificates of deposit, etc.

Dealings in these short-term instruments are now, therefore, the mainstay of the *Discount Houses*, though they still tender for Treasury Bills.

The functions of the *merchant banks* have also changed. The work of accepting is not required for Treasury Bills or for most of the new short-term instruments as the standing of the borrower is generally known to be first-class. Instead, they arrange and underwrite new issues, advise on the terms of 'take-overs' and mergers, and pay dividends to stock-holders as they fall due. They compete in specialist fields, e.g. property development, in domestic banking business, and also act as trustees and manage investment portfolios. Other functions have resulted from their overseas trading connections. Thus they have important business in the bullion and foreign exchange markets.

The commercial banks

The commercial banks fulfil two main functions in the Discount Market—providing funds to the discount houses and holding bills to maturity.

The discount houses do not themselves possess the huge financial resources necessary to purchase all the bills, commercial and Treasury, which are offered to them. They overcome this difficulty, however, by borrowing money from the commercial banks at a comparatively low rate of interest. Then, by discounting at a slightly higher rate, they make a small profit. The banks are willing to lend at a low rate because the loans are of short duration, often only a day at a time. This more than compensates the banks for the low yield for, should there be a particularly heavy demand for cash from their ordinary customers, they have an asset which becomes liquid in a day or so. They can therefore economise in cash held in reserve. From the point of view of the discount houses, the trouble involved in its daily renewal and the slight risk of its non-renewal is compensated for by the comparatively low rate of interest charged when secured by Treasury Bills or first-class bills of exchange. When the banks are calling in existing loans, money is said to be 'tight', and when lending is expanding, money is said to be 'easy'.

The commercial banks can earn a higher rate of interest if they themselves hold both commercial and Treasury Bills for a part of their currency. Indeed, there is no reason why they should not tender for Treasury Bills, though by convention they refrain from doing this. Instead, after the discount houses have held the bills for about four weeks leaving them with two months to run, the banks purchase them according to their requirements.

The Bank of England

The Bank of England enters into the structure of the Discount Market as follows.

First, it is the agency by which the government issues Treasury Bills. This issue is achieved by two methods, 'tap' and 'tender'. Government departments, the National Savings Bank, the Exchange Equalisation Account, the National Insurance Funds, and the Bank of England Issue Department, all of whom have funds to invest for a short period, can buy what bills they want at a fixed price, that is 'on tap'. This price is not published.

The discount houses and anyone else who wishes to apply (such as Commonwealth and foreign banks) obtain their issue by 'tender'. Every Friday, the Treasury, acting through the Bank of England, invites tenders for a specified amount of bills, usually between £200 and £300 million. Until 1971, the discount houses tendered as a 'syndicate' at a single rate. As part of the new policy of Competition and Credit Control (CCC), they now compete in their tenders, though they have agreed to 'cover' the whole of the issue.

Secondly, the Bank of England is the 'lender of last resort'. When the discount houses are pressed for money because the commercial banks will not renew their 'call money', the Bank of England will lend to them at the official 'minimum lending rate', which replaced the old bank rate. It is convenient, however, if we postpone further discussion of this function until the position of the Bank of England as a central bank has been considered.

II. PARALLEL MONEY MARKETS

With the traditional sources of finance (particularly the clearing banks) becoming increasingly restricted by the monetary authorities in recent years, there was a ready demand even for short-term funds. Here the City of London has showed its adaptability. Specialist Money Markets developed to meet the specific requirements of particular borrowers and lenders. Indeed, the existence of such markets encourages funds to be lent short-term for they enable lenders to regain liquidity should they so desire.

The following are the most important of these comparatively new markets:

(1) *Inter-bank deposits*

Because money at call and bills of exchange have always been acceptable to the Bank of England as part of the liquidity ratio, clearing banks tended to be connected mainly with the Discount Market.

Until 1971, however, the other banks—Scottish banks, merchant banks, British overseas banks and foreign banks— were not subject to a liquidity ratio. Brokers therefore established a market so that those banks having funds surplus to their immediate requirements were able to lend to those who had immediate outlets for such funds, the rate of interest obtained being higher than in the Discount Market. Now that the non-clearing banks are subject to reserve ratio requirements, the clearing banks also have begun to participate directly in the market.

(2) *Local authority deposits*

Local authorities, which now obtain most of their funds on the open market, are willing to make use of very short-term money. Brokers now exist for placing such short-term funds from banks, industrial and commercial companies, charitable funds, etc., with the local authority. Such brokers also deal in longer term local authority bonds.

Today the market is integrated very closely with the inter-bank market as funds from the latter are very often deposited in the former.

(3) *Negotiable certificates of deposit*

Certificates of deposit enable the banks to borrow for periods from three months to five years. They are similar to a bill of exchange drawn on the bank by itself. They have the advantage over the ordinary time deposit in that a bank feels under an obligation to repay the latter to a customer virtually on demand, thereby inhibiting medium-term lending. To the lender, they offer a higher rate of interest, while the market that has developed still provides them with liquidity. This market is largely comprised of the Discount Houses and the banks. It originated in dollar certificates, but sterling certificates of deposit were introduced in 1968 and today comprise two-thirds of the market.

(4) *Euro-currency balances*

Euro-currency deposits are simply funds which are deposited with banks outside the country of origin but which continue to be designated in terms of the original currency.

The most important Euro-currency is the dollar. As a result of the United States' continuing adverse balance of payments, branches of European banks have built up dollar balances as customers were paid for exports. These balances are offered to brokers in London (where interest rates are higher than can be earned in New York), and are placed mainly with companies or banks (e.g. Japanese) operating on an international scale to finance foreign trade or investment.

While the dollar still dominates the market, other European currencies are now dealt in, chiefly the Deutschemark and the Swiss franc.

(5) *Other markets*

Smaller specialist markets have developed in *Finance House deposits* and *Inter-company deposits*. Thus Finance houses have obtained funds by issuing bills which are accepted by banks and discount houses. Similarly, in periods of tight credit, firms which are short of finance turn towards other companies which temporarily have funds to spare.

III. THE CAPITAL MARKET

The unique machinery of the money markets developed in order to supply trade and the government with the short-term finance each requires. Industry, on the other hand, usually obtains its short-term or 'working' capital (to purchase raw materials, pay workers and maintain stocks) from the commercial banks (to be described later), although there are other sources (*see* p. 103).

Long-term capital (to finance investment in buildings, machinery and government projects) is obtained through the Capital Market. As can be seen from Fig. 81, this consists of the suppliers of long-term capital on the one hand and those

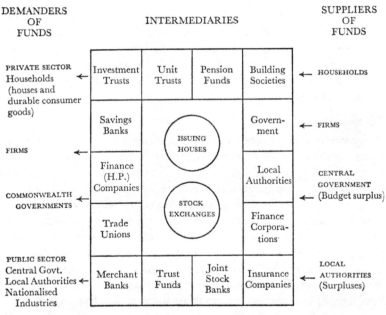

Notes:
(1) Arrows merely indicate direction, not particular intermediaries.
(2) Intermediaries collect relatively small amounts of capital, which are channelled to where they are wanted.
(3) Some intermediaries are mainly concerned with old issues.
(4) Issuing houses assist the movement of funds; Stock Exchanges provide a market in old securities and thus encourage the provision of new funds.

FIG. 81.—The Capital Market.

308 MONEY AND FINANCIAL INSTITUTIONS PART V

requiring such capital on the other, the two being connected by a number of intermediaries, usually of a specialist nature. Many of these intermediaries were described when the methods by which such capital was raised were discussed in Chapter 6. Here we look briefly at the work of the others.

Insurance companies

Insurance companies receive premiums on the various types of risk insured against. Some of these premiums, such as those received for insuring ships and property, are held only for relatively short periods having, apart from the profit made, to be paid out against claims. But with one group of insurance, life, endowments, annuities, etc., premiums are usually held for a long time before the final payment has to be made. Hence insurance companies have large sums of money to invest in long-term securities. These investments are spread over British Government and other public stocks, the shares and debentures of various companies, property, and mortgages. Today 'institutional investors', of which insurance companies are the most important, supply the bulk of savings required for new issues.

Investment trusts

Investors usually try to avoid 'putting all their eggs in one basket' by having an interest in the securities of many different types of enterprise. However, such spreading of risks requires some special knowledge of investment possibilities and, above all, sufficient resources. The small investor can overcome these two difficulties by buying shares in an investment trust. This invests its capital over a wide range of companies and, after paying expenses of management, the net yields from its various investments are distributed in the usual way as a dividend on its own shares. Thus investment trusts are not 'trusts' in the legal sense, but merely companies formed for the purpose of investment.

Unit trusts

Unit trusts are a development of the investment trust idea. But they differ in two main respects. First, they are trusts in the legal sense of the term. Trustees are appointed, while the trust deed often limits investments to a specified range of securities.

Unit trusts now specialise in their holdings, e.g. metals and minerals, bank-insurance, property, energy, cross-Channel, capital growth, income, etc. Secondly, the aggregate holding is split into many 'units' of low nominal value. Thus even a small investment covers the whole range of securities. Many unit trusts have schemes linked with assurance, savers subscribing on a regular, usually monthly, basis.

While most of the unit trust funds are used to purchase existing securities, they do make capital available for new investment, particularly when they take up 'rights' issues by companies whose shares they already hold.

Savings banks

The National and Trustee Savings Banks provide savings facilities, particularly for persons with a small income. Savings, however, are limited to a total holding of £10,000 per person. The savings deposited are invested in securities prescribed for the trustees, mostly government and similar securities.

Trust, pension and trade union funds

All these accumulate income which is reinvested in government securities, property, shares, etc.

Building societies

These have a specialised function—the supply of long-term loans on the security of private dwelling-houses purchased for owner-occupation, though sometimes they lend on the security of farms or industrial or commercial premises. Their funds are derived chiefly from money invested in them by the general public, but their shares are not dealt in on the Stock Exchange, being available for cash upon notice. Their liquid reserves are usually invested in trustee savings.

Finance corporations

The part played by the Industrial and Commercial Finance Corporation and the Finance Corporation for Industry in providing funds for industry has already been described (Chapter 6). There are, however, other somewhat similar corporations, whose funds are subscribed by different sources— the banks, the public and the government—which specialise in particular fields, e.g. the Agricultural Mortgage Corporation, the National Film Finance Corporation, the Exports Credit Guarantee Department of the Department of Trade and Industry.

Capital for small firms may also be provided by the Charterhouse Industrial Development Company and Credit for Industry Ltd, both of which were set up in 1934.

Finance companies

These borrow savings from the public and obtain loans from banks in order to finance hire-purchase of both consumer goods and machinery. But when hire-purchase has been restricted, many finance companies have switched to financing house purchase. The rates at which they borrow are comparatively high because of the greater lending risks involved, and for a similar reason the rates at which they lend are high. Many joint-stock banks now own a considerable proportion of the equity of certain finance companies, e.g. Mercantile Credit, Lombard Banking, United Dominions Trust.

IV. THE STOCK EXCHANGE

Origin

In the same way that organised *produce* markets were set up for buying and selling such commodities as wheat, tea, wool and cotton, so organised markets were eventually established for buying and selling 'securities', that is, claims to loans or shares. Although there are 'stock exchanges' in most of the larger cities of the United Kingdom, the London exchange is by far the most important and henceforth will be referred to as 'the Stock Exchange'. A glance at the financial page of any daily newspaper will reveal the nature of the securities dealt in. They consist chiefly of British funds (government stock and the stock of the nationalised industries); Commonwealth and foreign government stock; corporation stock (issued by local authorities, such as the Greater London Council, or by public utility undertakings, such as the Thames Water Authority); and the stocks and shares of all types of industrial and commercial companies.

It was not until the second half of the seventeenth century

that a recognisable stock market began to function, although joint-stock companies had existed for a hundred years, the first in England being the Russia Company, 1553. The stock of these companies was dealt in, and additional dealings took place in, government-sponsored lottery tickets, in seamen's pay tickets and, above all, in loans contracted by Charles II and James II from the goldsmiths. A large part of the money borrowed by them was never repaid, and this formed the nucleus of the National Debt of £644,000, officially recognised in 1688 by William III. Since that date the National Debt has, despite variations in its importance, largely been the mainstay of the Stock Exchange.

The first settled premises were established in 1773 and over the door were inscribed the words 'The Stock Exchange', showing that it was now a formal institution. The present site in Capel Court was occupied in 1801, and in 1803 the first Official List of prices appeared.

Members and their work

The Stock Exchange is privately owned, and the 'proprietors' are the members who between them hold the shares which originally provided the capital to purchase the site and buildings and later extensions. Today the affairs of the Stock Exchange are controlled by an elected Council, consisting of thirty-six members.

Members are either 'brokers' or 'jobbers', but they are not allowed to act in both capacities.

The *stockbroker* acts as the agent for the public, receiving and executing business according to the instructions of his clients and advising them on their investments. He earns commission on the business he transacts, but he is not allowed to advertise. In effect, he acts as the link between the investing public, who wish to buy and sell securities, and the *jobber*, the actual dealer and 'wholesaler' who buys and carries a stock of securities in order to resell them later. The difference between broker and jobber is best shown by an example.

Mr A, any member of the public, wishes to buy 500 25p ordinary shares in Bovis Limited. He therefore phones or writes to his broker (or to his bank manager who will contact the broker who acts for the bank), giving him the necessary instructions. He will either name the maximum price at which he will buy or instruct the broker to buy at the lowest price possible. The broker will then leave his office and go to the 'House' in order to carry out these and other instructions which he has received. He finds his way to that part of the 'House' occupied by the jobbers who specialise in the leading industrial ordinary shares. The broker approaches a jobber and enquires the price of 25p Bovis Ordinaries, but he does not say whether he wishes to buy or sell. Suppose the jobber replies: 'Two-seventy-four to two-seventy-eight'. This indicates that he is prepared to buy at the lower and to sell at the higher price. The difference between the two prices is known as the 'jobber's turn' and is the normal source of the jobber's profit, the size of spread depending on the jobber's estimate of the risk involved in dealing in that particular security. The broker

INVOICE No.   1475   To. Mr A.N. Other
BARGAIN DATE   Client No. 436485
AND TAX POINT
   3rd April 1973

WE THANK YOU FOR YOUR INSTRUCTIONS AND ADVISE HAVING **BOUGHT** FOR YOUR ACCOUNT SUBJECT TO THE RULES AND REGULATIONS OF THE STOCK EXCHANGE

AMOUNT	STOCK OR SHARES	PRICE	CONSIDERATION		
500	Bovis Limited Ordinary 25p Shares	278p	1390	00	N
	TRANSFER STAMP		14	00	N
	CONTRACT STAMP			30	N
	COMMISSION 1¼% on money		17	37	T
	TOTAL V.A.T. @ 10%		1	74	
	FOR SETTLEMENT 17th April 1973	£	1423.41		

Spencer Thornton & Co.
MEMBERS OF THE STOCK EXCHANGE

CONTRACT NOTE AND TAX INVOICE FOR SERVICES RENDERED   WE RECOMMEND THAT THIS DOCUMENT BE RETAINED FOR FUTURE REFERENCE can accept the price, try to get the jobber to lower his price or else move on to other jobbers in the hope of doing better. Let us suppose that he considers 278p satisfactory. He then informs the jobber that he wishes to buy 500 shares, the bargain is struck, and both broker and jobber make notes in their dealing books. The broker, having arranged the deal, sends to Mr A, or to the bank acting for him, a contract note (see opposite page).

The transfer stamp represents revenue charged on all transfer deeds (except British Government stocks). It is charged only on purchases. All bargains have to be settled on the next 'Account Day' which usually falls fortnightly on a Tuesday, though government and municipal stock is 'for cash', meaning that settlement is immediate.

Economic functions

There is a widespread view that brokers and jobbers are parasites who make money by speculating at the expense of the public. Such a view, however, merely reveals ignorance of the real functions of the Stock Exchange. It is true that the facilities offered by the Stock Exchange do provide openings for speculation. The fortnight's grace before settlement is made enables a speculator to buy securities at the beginning of the Account, sell them again within fourteen days and take the profit (or loss), without ever having put up any money. A speculator who buys securities because he thinks the price will rise is said to be a 'bull'. He is thus an optimist, buying shares, not because he wants to keep them, but because he hopes to sell them at a profit. On the other hand, a speculator who is a pessimist is known as a 'bear', and he sells securities he does not possess at the beginning of the Account period because he expects the price to fall before the time for settlement. Sometimes, if a person's credit stands high with his broker or if he can put up security, he may be permitted to 'carry over' his commitments from one Stock Exchange Account to the next. Such a transaction is known as a 'contango'.

The difficulty concerning speculation is that both optimism and pessimism are contagious and the market becomes extremely susceptible both to panic and over-confidence. Indeed, the effect of the initial outlook, whether of optimism or pessimism, is to cause prices to take the very direction in which they were expected to go. For instance, persons who expect the price of securities to rise bid for those securities, *thereby* sending up their price. The result is that, particularly in the past, there have been numerous speculative booms and slumps, when stocks and shares were written up and down, not with any real change in the legitimate expectation of income from them, but with waves of confidence or mistrust which swept over the great financial centres of the world. Two such booms ended with the South Sea Bubble (1720) and the Wall Street crash (1929). It is hoped that speculative booms and slumps will be far less prevalent in the future, for in recent years the Stock Exchange Council has carried out important reforms in order to check abuses.

Nor must we forget that speculation has certain advantages. Expert professional operators, such as the jobbers, tend to steady prices through their function of holding stocks. This also permits securities to be bought and sold at any time, thereby making them more liquid. The great difficulty occurs in distinguishing harmful speculation from genuine investment, for with all investment there is a certain element of risk. In any case the magnitude of the speculative business must not be over-estimated. The majority of business represents genuine investment conducted on behalf of investment trusts, insurance companies, building societies and private individuals.

The truth is that, for the following reasons, an organised market in securities is an indispensable part of the mechanism of a capitalist economy.

(1) *It facilitates borrowing by the government and industry*

If people are to be encouraged to lend to industry and the government by the purchase of securities, they must be satisfied that they will subsequently be able to sell easily those investments which they no longer wish to hold. Such an assurance is afforded to any holder of a fairly well-known security by the Stock Exchange, for it provides a permanent market bringing together sellers and buyers.

Thus, indirectly the Stock Exchange encourages savers to lend to the government or to invest in industry. Indeed, if a new issue receives a Stock Exchange quotation, the chances of its success are considerably enhanced.

(2) *Through the jobbers, it helps to even out short-run price fluctuations in securities*

Whilst the jobber himself may often speculate, in the short run he acts as a buffer to speculation by outsiders. This is because he does not merely 'match' a buyer with a seller but acts like a wholesaler, holding stocks of securities. Since he specialises in dealing in certain securities, he obtains an intimate knowledge of them. Thus when the public is pessimistic and selling, he may be more optimistic in his outlook and consider that the drop in price is not likely to continue. He therefore takes these securities on to his book. Similarly, when the public is rushing to buy, he will, when he considers the price has reached its zenith, sell from his stocks. The effect in both cases is to even out the fluctuations in price for, in the first case, he increases his demand as supply increases, and, in the second, he increases supply as the demand increases.

(3) *It advertises security prices*

The publication of current Stock Exchange prices enables the public to follow the fortunes of their investment and to channel their savings into profitable enterprises.

(4) *It protects the public against fraud*

The Official List of securities is a guarantee that securities listed are reputable. Permission to deal is not given to members unless the Council is satisfied on this score, and it may be withdrawn if any doubts arise about the conduct of a company's affairs. Moreover, the Council insists on a high standard of professional conduct from its members. Should any member default, the investor is indemnified out of the Stock Exchange Compensation Fund.

(5) *It reflects the country's economic prospects*

The movement of the market acts as a barometer which points to the economic prospects of the country as 'set fair'—or otherwise!

CHAPTER 22

JOINT-STOCK BANKS

By far the largest part of the business of the commercial banks today is carried on by the 'Big Four'. Thus, unlike the systems of other countries, such as the U.S.A., which are composed of a large number of unitary small banks, the United Kingdom has only a few large banks, each having a network of branches throughout the country.

This system of branch banking has two main merits. The first is that the larger unit of operation can enjoy the advantages of large-scale production. The second, and more important, is that there is less risk of failure when financial reserves are concentrated in a large bank than where the banking activities for a particular locality are conducted by a small bank. The fortunes of the small bank are tied up with the fortunes of the locality which, especially if the main activity is farming, may be liable to periodic fluctuations. In short, with a large bank, risks are spread geographically. On the other hand, the large unit has to suffer disadvantages on the managerial side, for usually loans of any size have to be sanctioned by Head Office. This is in sharp contrast to the position of the small unit which can grant even large loans on the spot according to its own judgement, based on its knowledge of local conditions.

I. THE CREATION OF CREDIT

The cheque system

Joint-stock banks are really companies which exist to make profits for their shareholders. They do this by borrowing money from 'depositors' and relending it at a higher rate of interest to other persons. Borrowers are private persons, companies, public corporations, the money market and the government. The more a bank can lend, the greater will be its profits.

Persons who hold a current account at a bank can settle their debts by cheque. This is a very convenient form of payment. Cheques may be sent safely through the post, can be written for any amount to the nearest penny, obviate carrying round large sums of money, form a permanent record of payment, and serve as receipts, for the cancelled cheque is eventually returned through the banking process to the person drawing it.

But the use of cheques is, as we shall see, advantageous not only to its customers but to the bank itself. Thus, in order to advertise their business, to induce customers to pay by cheque rather than by cash, and to encourage people to keep sums of money with them, banks perform many services (often free of charge) outside their main business of borrowing and lending money—keeping accounts, making standing-order payments, providing night-safe facilities, paying bills by credit transfers, purchasing securities, transacting foreign work, storing valuables, acting as executors, etc.

The cheque as a substitute for cash

The extension of the cheque system has led to a reduction in the use of cash. Suppose that I have paid £100 into my banking account. Imagine, too, that my builder banks at the same branch and that I owe him £50. I simply write him a cheque for that amount, and he pays this into the bank. To complete the transaction, my account is debited by £50, and his account is credited by that amount. What it is important to observe, however, is that in the settlement of the debt no actual *cash* changes hands. A mere book entry in both accounts has completed the transaction.

Perhaps my builder will, towards the end of the week, withdraw some cash to pay his workers' wages. But it is likely that most of his payments, e.g. for building materials, petrol, and lorry servicing, will be by cheque. Similarly, while from the £50 still standing to my account I may withdraw some cash to cover everyday housekeeping expenses, the probability is that many of my bills, e.g. club subscription, half-yearly rates, hire-purchase instalments on the car, mortgage repayments, will be settled by cheque or by a credit transfer directly from my account. Furthermore, even where cash is withdrawn, it is often compensated for by cash being paid in.

With the development of the cheque system, the proportion of cash which is required for transactions has decreased. Let us assume a simple model in which the banks operate free of government control but have discovered that in practice only 10 per cent of their total deposits need be retained in cash to cover all demands for cash withdrawals. In short, only £10 of my original deposit of £100 is needed to form an adequate cash reserve.

The creation of credit

It is obvious, therefore, that £90 of my original cash deposit of £100 could be lent by the bank to a third party without me or anybody else being the wiser. What is not quite so obvious is that the bank can go much further than this—and does!

Let us assume that there is only one bank and that all lending is in the form of advances to the public. When a person is granted a loan by his bank manager, all that happens is that the borrower's account is credited with the amount of the loan or, alternatively, he is authorised to overdraw his account up to the stipulated limit. In other words, a deposit is created in the name of the borrower by the bank.

When he spends the loan, the borrower will probably do so by cheque. If this happens, there is no immediate demand for cash. There is no reason, therefore, why the whole of my cash deposit of £100 should not act as the safe cash reserve for deposits of a much larger sum created by the bank's lending activities. But the bank must not overdo this credit creation. To be safe, our model has assumed, cash must always form one-tenth of total deposits. This means that the bank can grant a loan of up to £900. Because it is the only bank, there is no need to fear that cheques drawn on it will be paid into another bank and eventually presented for cash.

The process of credit-creation is illustrated in Fig. 82. X pays £100 in cash into the bank. This allows the bank to make a loan of £900 to B. B now settles his debts to C and D of £400 and £500 respectively by sending them cheques. These cheques are paid into the bank. C withdraws cash rather heavily, £70; but this is compensated for by D, who only withdraws £20 in

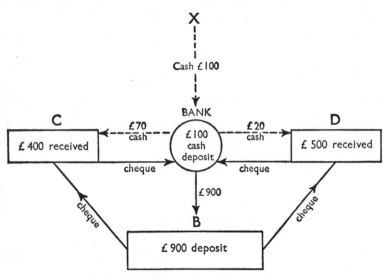

FIG. 82.—How a bank creates credit.

cash. This leaves £10 cash—enough to cover the average withdrawal which X is likely to make. At the same time as these cash withdrawals are being made, other cash is being paid in, thereby maintaining the 10 per cent ratio.

In practice there are many banks, but for the purpose of credit creation they are virtually one bank, because they are able to eliminate a large demand for cash from each other by their clearing arrangements through the London Clearing House. While this consists of only six banks (the 'Big Four' dominating), other banks can do their clearing through one of these. Moreover, banks keep in line with one another as regards their credit creation. Were one bank to adopt, say, a 6 per cent cash ratio, it would find that because its customers were making such a large volume of payments to persons who banked elsewhere, it would be continually called upon to settle a debit with the other banks in cash at the end of the day's clearing. Its cash reserve at the Bank of England would therefore fall so low that it would have to modify its lending policy.

The effect of lending on the bank's balance-sheet

Suppose that the receipt of the £100 in cash and the loan to B are the sole activities of the bank so far. We ignore shareholders' capital. Its balance-sheet will then be as follows:

Liabilities	£	Assets	£
Deposits:			
Deposit Account	100	Cash in till	100
Current Account	900	Advances	900
	1,000		1,000

The advance to B is an asset; it is an outstanding debt. On the other hand, his account has been credited with a deposit of £900—just as though he had paid it in. It can be seen, therefore, that *every loan creates a deposit.*

II. CONSIDERATIONS DETERMINING A BANK'S LENDING POLICY

In practice the structure of the bank's assets is more varied than that above. This can be explained as follows.

Creating deposits in order to lend at a profit entails certain risks. In the first place, the loan may not be repaid. Secondly, and more important, there may be a run on the bank for cash, the original depositor wishing to withdraw his £100, or B, C, and D requiring between them an abnormally large amount of cash. Any suggestion that the bank could not meet these demands would lead to such a loss of confidence in the bank that other depositors would ask for cash, and the bank would have to close its doors.

Hence, although a permanent cash reserve ratio must always be retained, a bank must have a second and third line of defence so that in an emergency it can raise cash easily and quickly. This means, therefore, that it must not lend entirely by means of advances, for these are usually required by the borrower for a minimum of six months and even longer. Some loans must, if possible, be made for a shorter period—even for as little as a day at a time.

On the other hand, the shorter the period of the loan, the smaller will be the rate of interest that the bank can charge. Yet it wants profits for its shareholders to be as high as possible.

The bank, therefore, is limited in its lending policy both quantitively and qualitatively. Not only must credit be restricted to a multiple of the liquid reserves, but it must afford adequate *security, liquidity, and profitability.*

As regards security, the bank endeavours not to lend if there is any risk of inability to repay. Default on a loan represents a serious error of judgement by the bank manager. While it usually requires collateral, e.g. an insurance policy, the deeds of a house, or share certificates, this is regarded more as a weapon to strengthen its demand for repayment against an evasive borrower than as a safeguard against default. Collateral therefore really assists liquidity; if there were a risk of outright default, the bank would not lend.

Liquidity and profitability pull in opposite directions—the shorter the period of the loan, the greater the bank's liquidity, but the less it will earn by way of interest. The difficulty is resolved by a compromise: (1) loans are divided among different types of borrower and for different periods of time; (2) the different types of loan are kept fairly close to carefully worked out proportions. In short, the bank, for financial prudence, maintains a 'portfolio' of assets. Later we shall see that the monetary authorities dictate a minimum percentage of liquid assets.

III. THE DISTRIBUTION OF A BANK'S ASSETS

We can see how, in practice, a bank reconciles the aims of liquidity and profitability by studying its assets. This is possible because, apart from its cash, buildings, and goodwill, loans represent its sole assets. Just as 'sundry debtors' appears on the asset side of a firm's balance sheet, so debts outstanding to a bank represent assets to it. The position is shown in Fig. 83. *Money at call and on short notice* consists of short-term loans to discount houses which enable them to discount bills of exchange and hold them for a month or so before passing them on to the banks. *Bills*, which are mostly Treasury Bills, are obtained chiefly from the discount houses (though some may be discounted directly for customers) and are held for the remainder of their currency—usually two months. *Investments* are medium-

and long-term government securities bought on the open market. *Advances*, to nationalised industries, companies and personal borrowers, are the most profitable (1 to 3 per cent above base rate) but also the least liquid of all the bank's assets. The main object of bank advances is to provide the working capital for industry and commerce. The type of loan preferred is 'self-liquidating' within a period of about 6 months. A good example of such a loan is one made to a farmer, who borrows at the beginning of the year in order to buy seed and

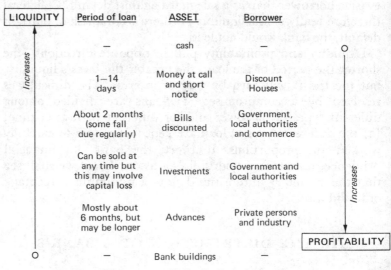

FIG. 83.—The nature and distribution of a bank's main assets.

fertilisers and to pay wages, and repays the loan when the harvest has been sold. Similarly, a manufacturer may borrow to employ additional labour and raw materials just prior to Christmas in order to increase production. When he receives payment for those goods some time later, the cheque will be paid into his account, thereby enabling him to repay the overdraft. It is evident, though, that until such payment is received by the borrower, there is little possibility of the bank's being able to get its money back.

Generally banks have refrained from providing long-term capital for firms, leaving this to the agencies in the Capital

Market. In recent years, however, they have engaged in financing some long-term capital projects, such as the building of additional factory accommodation and the purchase of farms and houses. These fixed assets are the security required, although the bank's main consideration is whether or not the venture is likely to succeed.

It must be emphasised that, apart from cash and bank buildings, these assets are covered only by credit created by the bank. For example, Treasury Bills and government securities are paid for by cheques which will increase the accounts of the sellers. If they are new issues, there is an addition to the government account at the Bank of England; if they are old issues, the bank is virtually taking over from somebody else a loan already made to the government. In writing these cheques, the bank increases its liabilities, for book-entry deposits have to be created to cover them. This 'pyramid of credit', created to buy earning assets and to make loans upon a minimum $12\frac{1}{2}$ per cent (1973) liquid assets basis, is shown in Fig. 84.

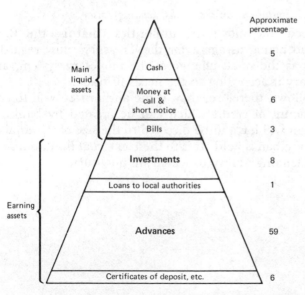

FIG. 84.—The pyramid of bank credit (18 July 1973). The remainder consisted of Special Deposits (4 per cent), items in transit, etc. (Source: Bank of England *Quarterly Bulletin*.)

IV. MODIFICATION OF THE CASH-RATIO APPROACH

The importance of liquid assets as a whole

Our model of how a bank creates credit has followed traditional lines: credit bears a fixed relationship to the cash reserves. This approach is the easiest to understand and underlines the main principles involved.

However, while the basic principles of credit-creation still hold true, some modification is necessary to allow for modern banking practice.

Today, banks are more concerned with their general liquidity position when deciding on their lending policy than with the one item, cash. This tendency of cash to lose significance originally stemmed from the introduction of the Treasury Bill which, through government support, became almost as good as cash. Improved markets for loans, e.g. the parallel money markets described in Chapter 21, also increase liquidity and, as a result, such loans can be regarded as 'near money'.

External limitations on the banks' lending policy

Indeed, the monetary authorities (that is, the Bank of England acting as agent for the Treasury) now regard cash simply as the small change of the monetary system, and so they vary it according to the needs of trade.

It follows, therefore, that, if the authorities wish to control the amount of credit which can be created by banks, their attention will have to be directed to the size of the total assets which the banks hold. It is to these external limitations on the banks' lending ability to which we now turn.

CHAPTER 23

THE BANK OF ENGLAND

THE Bank of England, established by Act of Parliament in 1694, remained a joint-stock company until nationalisation in 1946. But, although started as a private enterprise, the Bank of England has, for the past 200 years, followed policies which have placed the needs of the country as a whole before its own financial interests. Nationalisation merely formalised its position as a 'central bank'—the institution which, on behalf of the government, exercises the ultimate control over the policies of the joint-stock banks and other financial institutions. In the words of the Radcliffe Report, 'The Bank of England stands as the market operator between the public sector (to which it belongs) and the private sector.' The whole of its capital stock is now owned by the state, and its affairs are regulated by a Court of Directors, consisting of a Governor, a Deputy-Governor and sixteen Directors appointed by the Crown, though not more than four of the Directors can be full-time officers. The members of the Court are distinguished men in financial, industrial and commercial affairs, and it is usual for the full-time members to be professional bankers with experience of work in the Bank of England.

I. FUNCTIONS OF THE BANK OF ENGLAND

We need deal only briefly with most of the Bank's functions.

(1) *It issues notes*

The Bank of England is the only ultimate source from which the private sector can obtain cash. It obtains coins from the Royal Mint, but issues notes itself. The *Fiduciary Issue* (the amount by which the note issue is allowed to exceed the Bank's holding of gold) has ceased to have any relevance. Since 1939, the gold reserves of the Bank have been held in the Exchange Equalisation Account, and thus today the notes issued are backed almost entirely by Treasury Bills and other marketable government securities.

While in England and Wales the Bank of England is the sole note-issuing authority, Scottish and Northern Irish banks can issue their own notes, though most of these have to be covered by Bank of England notes.

(2) *It is the government's banker*

The government has always been the most important customer of the Bank of England. As a result the Bank has acquired the functions of a 'central bank' (*see* p. 325). But it also performs many tasks for the government which spring from the normal banker–customer relationship:

(a) It keeps the central government accounts (the Consolidated Fund and the National Loans Fund) and the accounts of many government departments.

(b) It gives assistance by means of 'Ways and Means' advances if the account goes temporarily 'into the red'.

(c) It manages the government's borrowing through the issue of Treasury Bills and government stock. This involves arranging new issues and conversions, paying interest, keeping the registers, and recording transfers.

(d) It advises the government on financial matters.

(3) *It is the bankers' bank*

The next most important customers of the Bank of England are the joint-stock banks. The London clearing banks hold about half their cash reserve at the Bank of England, and they use the Bank very much as a private customer uses his bank. In particular, they:

(a) draw notes and coin from their balances at the Bank as required;

(b) set off the net payment which has to be made to other banks as a result of the day's clearing by drawing on the balance held at the Bank of England;

(c) take advice on financial matters from the Bank.

(4) *It manages the Exchange Equalisation Account* (see p. 488)

(5) *It protects the gold and dollar reserves*
   (*a*) It determines the minimum lending rate.
   (*b*) It administers foreign exchange control. Under the Exchange Control Act, 1947, the Treasury can control payments out of sterling into other currencies. The administration of this control rests with the Bank of England. The task is performed chiefly by issuing regulations to the joint-stock banks. Thus a bank is restricted in the amount of sterling it can exchange for foreign currency on behalf of a customer.
   (*c*) It arranges loans from other central banks to strengthen the United Kingdom's reserves.

(6) *It has financial responsibilities internationally*
   (*a*) The Bank of England maintains close contact with the central banks and monetary authorities of other countries, chiefly with the aim of bringing greater stability to international monetary affairs.
   (*b*) It provides banking services for the central banks of non-sterling countries, e.g. holds and manages their holdings of sterling.
   (*c*) It participates in the work of certain international financial institutions, such as the Bank for International Settlements, the International Monetary Fund, the International Bank for Reconstruction and Development, the European Monetary Agreement.

(7) *It manages the monetary system of the United Kingdom in accordance with government policy*

The Bank of England is the central bank of the monetary system of the United Kingdom. It is therefore responsible for seeing that the monetary system of the country is working in harmony with government economic policy. In broad terms, this means varying the cost and availability of credit.

Where people (entrepreneurs and private persons) can obtain credit on relatively easy terms, the demand for goods (both producer and consumer goods) will normally increase. If there is unemployment, this is a good thing, for the economy will expand and idle resources be put to work. If there is already full employment, the supply of goods cannot be expanded, and prices rise.

The Bank of England, therefore, has frequently to adjust the supply of credit to the prevailing economic situation as seen by itself and the Treasury, though the latter will have the last word. While the impact falls most directly on the joint-stock banks, the main providers of credit, it is felt by other credit-granting institutions, such as hire-purchase finance companies, insurance companies, building societies, and firms giving trade credit.

II. MONETARY POLICY BEFORE 1971

Impact of policy on the joint stock banks

Prior to 1971, the monetary authorities paid more attention to keeping down interest rates rather than limiting the *overall* supply of credit. Moreover, their operations concentrated almost exclusively on the clearing banks, the largest single source of credit.

By mutual agreement, the interest rates which banks paid on deposit accounts and those they charged for advances were fairly rigidly linked to 'bank rate'. Bank rate was announced by the Bank of England each Thursday; it was the rate of interest it would charge to the discount houses as the 'lender of last resort'. This weapon, therefore, gave the Bank of England some control over the cost of credit supplied by the *clearing banks*. In addition to this, the Bank of England used other weapons (described later) to 'squeeze' the banks from time to time.

The result of this government policy, however, was that the rate of interest charged by the clearing banks was usually less than the equilibrium rate which would have been arrived at in a free market. Thus there had to be some form of 'rationing' of bank loans, and this was done on instructions from the Bank of England. Exporters were given priority; property developers, in comparison, came near the bottom of the queue. The ultimate weapon of the Bank of England, therefore, was its instructions to the banks.

Weaknesses of the above policy

One advantage of selective credit control is that it can be made discriminatory in order to reinforce government policy objectives, for example by encouraging exports. But as a workable monetary policy it suffered from the weaknesses of all price controls:

(1) *Controls are not popular with those responsible for operating them*

The clearing banks disliked refusing loans to some profitable customers while having to give credit to others. Above all, they felt that, in comparison with other suppliers of credit, they were being discriminated against. They thus had to bear the main burden whenever credit was squeezed.

(2) *Controls are eventually circumvented*

As we have seen there are a number of fairly close substitutes for 'true' money (that is, cash and clearing bank deposits). As the Radcliffe Report (1959) pointed out, it is not simply the amount of money in existence but the overall liquidity position of the economy which is really relevant to monetary policy. Such liquidity is influenced by the existence of many kinds of credit and financial institutions. In practice, therefore, the Bank of England's control of 'true' money simply led to an expansion of 'near' money.

One way in which this expansion came about was by foreign banks, e.g. Chase Manhattan and First National, developing their activities in the United Kingdom. But many internal financial institutions extended their financial operations. Thus finance companies, which could outbid the banks for deposits, were able to grant credit other than through hire purchase, while insurance companies lent against policies. In addition, liquidity was improved through the development of other money markets which the squeeze largely inspired.

Indeed, the clearing banks themselves took defensive action, acquiring specialised subsidiary agencies, e.g. finance companies. Thus, in effect, they operated a divided structure. The main business in deposits and in 'traditional lending' was done through the parent institutions, with their widespread branches. The more competitive business in large deposits at higher rates for less orthodox and more varied forms of lending was undertaken by their subsidiaries, usually operating from a single office.

These developments gave rise to problems of control. Mainly because of their specialised operations, foreign banks and these other financial institutions were less susceptible to traditional instruments of credit control. Their operations, therefore, were a loophole which seriously limited the ability of the authorities to control credit creation and necessitated increasingly severe restriction on the clearing banks which were amenable to control.

III. COMPETITION AND CREDIT CONTROL (CCC)

Credit control

The authorities, therefore, eventually came to the view that in order to control the general level of spending in the economy it was desirable to do more than merely restrict the supply of credit granted by the clearing banks. What had to be limited was the overall total supply of money and credit instruments from *all* agencies.

Accordingly, the government now decides on the general level of credit (that is liquidity), which it considers is desirable at any one time to regulate the level of activity in the economy. The various credit-granting institutions are then allowed to compete amongst themselves, through the rate of interest offered, for a share of this credit supply. In other words, there has been a move towards a more effective market mechanism.

Competition

Under this new policy of competition the discount houses have agreed not to tender as a syndicate at the weekly tender for Treasury Bills, but to bid competitively. Collectively, however, they would still cover all bills offered. And the London and Scottish clearing banks similarly abandoned their collective agreements on interest rates. Each bank now expresses its lending rates in relation to a *base rate*, which it fixes itself in the light of its own policy and market considerations.

Thus ended the fixed link between the old 'bank rate' and the clearing banks' interest rates. Such influence as bank rate had exerted internally, therefore, largely disappeared. Consequently, in October 1972, the term was dropped, to be replaced by a 'minimum lending rate' as the last resort rate (see later).

However, probably more important as regards competition was the decision to extend credit control to all banks, instead of applying it merely to the clearing banks as formerly. Moreover, other financial institutions, such as discount houses and finance companies, were brought within the scope of the new policy. This means that henceforth the clearing banks can compete with other lending institutions without their hands being tied behind their backs.

We must now examine the new policy more closely, describing the methods by which the authorities manage to control the overall supply of credit.

IV. THE WEAPONS USED BY THE BANK OF ENGLAND TO CONTROL THE SUPPLY OF CREDIT

(1) *The minimum reserve assets ratio*

The foundation of the policy by which the supply of credit is controlled rests in the ability of the Bank of England to dictate to the banks and other lending institutions the minimum liquidity ratio which they shall maintain.

Each bank is required to observe a minimum reserve ratio (at present $12\frac{1}{2}$ per cent) of 'eligible reserve assets' to 'eligible liabilities'.

'*Eligible reserve assets*' comprise:

(a) balances with the Bank of England, other than special deposits;

(b) Treasury Bills;

(c) company tax reserve certificates;

(d) money at call with the London money market;

(e) local authority bills eligible for re-discount at the Bank of England;

(*f*) commercial bills eligible for re-discount at the Bank of England (up to a maximum of 2 per cent of eligible liabilities);

(*g*) British government securities with one year or less to go to reach final maturity.

Broadly, this list is similar to those items which the clearing banks were formerly allowed to regard as liquid assets. But there are important differences. For example, cash in bank tills is no longer regarded as an eligible reserve asset, while the 2 per cent ceiling on commercial bills limits the bank's ability to acquire liquid assets from this source. On the other hand British government securities with a year or less needed to reach final maturity is a newcomer to 'liquid' assets.

'*Eligible liabilities*' refer broadly to net bank deposits (excluding foreign currency deposits and deposits having an original maturity of over two years).

It is important to note that this ratio applies to *all* banks, not merely to the clearing banks as previously.

Special arrangements apply to some other groups of institution. Until July, 1973, member firms of the London discount market were required to maintain at least 50 per cent of their funds in defined 'public sector assets'. The range of such assets was wider than that prescribed for the banks. It included local authority bonds and stocks and government-guaranteed stocks with up to five years to run to maturity. This requirement ran into practical difficulties, and so it was replaced by a new control which limits a discount house's holding of assets other than 'public sector assets' to twenty times its capital and reserves. The discount houses are also required to apply each week for a total amount of Treasury bills sufficient to cover the amount offered at the tender. (This they have always done in the past. Now they must bid for the bills competitively instead of at a common, agreed price as they used to.)

For other finance houses (except small ones with liabilities of less than £5m.), the minimum reserve assets ratio is fixed at 10 per cent (as compared with 12½ per cent generally). Calls for special deposits will normally be at the same rate as for banks, but in some circumstances could be at a higher rate.

However, a distinction must still be drawn between those financial institutions subject to control under the new arrangements (such as the finance houses) and those which are not. Some institutions, which are strictly neither banks nor finance houses are able to perform some banking roles because they advance loans, e.g. insurance companies which permit clients to borrow on life assurance policies. Such institutions were outside the old regulations and their lending activities were of some concern to the monetary authorities as the scale of their operations grew. Under the new arrangements, the line of demarcation between 'other banks', finance houses and other financial institutions still remains indistinct as far as credit creation is concerned, so that problems of regulation of financial institutions such as insurance companies are likely to persist.

(2) *Open market operations*

While the minimum reserve assets ratio provides the base for monetary policy, marginal adjustments to the money supply can be made by 'open market operations'.

This works on the basis that any reduction in the eligible reserve assets held by the banks will, with a liquidity ratio of $12\frac{1}{2}$ per cent, cause a reduction of total deposits by eight times, and vice versa. A weapon of monetary policy which can therefore be used is to vary the banks' holding of liquid assets.

This the Bank of England achieves by buying or selling government securities in the open market. Suppose, for instance, it sells long-term securities. The increase in the supply offered lowers their price (that is, raises the rate of interest) until the total offering has been bought by the banks or by their customers. But cash will be necessary to pay for them, and so the banks' cash balance at the Bank of England falls. In other words, the liquid reserve assets held by the banks are reduced and, if previously they were fully lent, they will be forced to squeeze their advances.

Or the Bank of England may put the pressure on the short-term end of the market by varying the size of the Treasury Bill offer at the weekly tender. Inasmuch as these bills are bought initially outside the banks, the cash balances of the bank's customers are likely to fall and hence, also, the cash of the banks.

(3) Funding

A deliberate policy of converting government short-term debt into long-term debt is known as 'funding'. It is achieved by open market operations as described above over an extended period. What happens is that the Treasury Bill offer for tender is reduced, the government raising the finance it requires by selling medium and long-dated securities instead.

(4) Special deposits

More fundamental changes in the supply of credit can be effected through calls for 'special deposits'.

This policy originated in 1960. Banks are required to deposit with the Bank of England a given percentage of their total eligible liabilities. These special deposits do not count as part of their liquid assets, though they earn interest at the current Treasury Bill rate.

The weapon of 'special deposits' has certain advantages:

(a) The percentage of special deposits called for can be sufficiently high to make it difficult for the banks to maintain their $12\frac{1}{2}$ per cent liquidity ratio.

(b) When the banks are put on a tight rein in this way, marginal adjustments by way of open market operations and funding become more effective.

(c) The reduction in the banks' liquidity is achieved without the dislocation of large scale funding operations.

(d) The banks cannot afford to sell investments provided the Bank of England stays out of the market. The impact of special deposits must then eventually result in the banks' having to reduce 'advances'.

(5) Requests

When CCC policy was originally introduced, the intention seemed to be to leave the allocation of credit available to be controlled by market forces.

But unlike selective credit controls, the market is not discriminatory—credit is simply allocated according to whether people are prepared to pay the equilibrium price. In practice, while property developers could pay high rates for funds, the expectations of firms regarding the profitability of capital goods were not sufficiently optimistic for entrepreneurs to pay the going equilibrium rate to obtain funds to purchase such goods. Yet it was investment spending in capital goods that the government was anxious to revive. To some extent, therefore, it had to revert to the old policy of issuing instructions to banks, requiring them to discriminate against property developers when granting loans.

Moreover, as, under the new policy, interest rates rose, depositors in building societies switched funds to more profitable outlets. In order to compete for funds, therefore, the building societies were forced to raise their deposit rates and therefore their mortgage rates. The government did not wish to see the mortgage rate charged to house-owners at too high a level, and so in September, 1973, banks were instructed not to pay more than $9\frac{1}{2}$ per cent on loans of less than £10,000. This was to allow the building societies to compete with the banks—but, nevertheless, the latter raised their mortgage rate to 11 per cent.

(6) Directives

By section 4(3) of the Bank of England Act, 1946, the Bank of England can, if so authorised by the Treasury, issue directions to any banker for the purpose of ensuring that effect is given to its requests and recommendations. So far this power has not had to be used, the banks preferring to heed the requests of the Bank of England, rather than being forced into obeying them.

(7) Minimum lending rate

Having lost its significance as a reference point for other interest rates when CCC was introduced, bank rate was abolished in October 1972. There is still, however, a 'last resort' rate, officially known as the 'minimum lending rate', at which the Bank of England will come to the assistance of the discount houses. This minimum lending rate, normally fixed weekly on a Friday, is at $\frac{1}{2}$ per cent above the average rate of discount for Treasury Bills, rounded to the nearest

¼ per cent above. Thus the minimum lending rate is less active than the old bank rate. Nevertheless, it must be remembered that, since the government controls the supply of Treasury Bills, it can influence in some measure the average rate of discount and so indicate the general direction in which it wants short-term rates of interest to move.

Indeed, the monetary authorities have reserved themselves the right to announce the minimum lending rate on a Thursday (as with the previous bank rate). Such a move, however, must be regarded as being abnormal. It would probably only be used when the Bank of England wished to publicise its intentions regarding the future long-term rate, chiefly as a means of influencing the flow of short-term funds in or out of the United Kingdom.

Conclusion

It is unlikely that a single weapon will be used exclusively in pursuit of monetary policy, since one reinforces the other. And the Governor of the Bank of England has commented on the Bank's objectives as follows: 'It is not expected that the mechanism of the minimum asset ratio and special deposits can be used to achieve some precise multiple contraction or expansion of bank assets. Rather the intention is to use our control over liquidity, which these instruments will reinforce, to influence the structure of interest rates. The resulting changes in relative rates of return will then induce shifts in the asset portfolios of both the public and the banks' (Bank of England *Quarterly Review*, June 1971).

PART VI

THE GOVERNMENT AND THE ECONOMY

CHAPTER 24

THE NATIONAL INCOME

IN Chapter 2 we summarised the various objectives of government policy. While some of these, e.g. the development of certain industries, the control of monopolies or the protection of workers in 'sweated' industries, can be achieved by intervention in particular parts of the economy, certain broad objectives, e.g. full employment, a stable price level, a healthy balance of payments and adequate growth, require government regulation of the economy as a whole.

But, to be successful, such regulation must be based on adequate information. Hence measurements are made of a variety of items and published yearly in the Blue Book on National Income and Expenditure. Later we shall indicate how these figures can be used to plan the economy. For the time being we are concerned with the overall figure—the level of the national income.

I. THE PRINCIPLE UPON WHICH CALCULATION OF THE NATIONAL INCOME IS BASED

Income, as we have seen, is a flow of wealth (goods and services) over a period of time. If our income rises, we can enjoy more goods and services.

But, to enjoy goods, they must be produced. A nation's income, then, is basically the same as its output over a period. Thus national income is the total money value of all goods and services produced by the country during the year. The question is: 'How can we measure this money value?'

We can approach the problem by studying the different ways in which we can arrive at the value of a table.

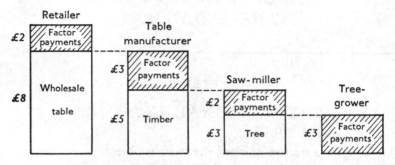

FIG. 85.—Value of total product equals sum of values added by each firm.

Fig. 85 shows that the value of the table can be obtained by taking the value of the final product (£10) or by totalling the value added by each firm in the different stages of production. Thus the output of the tree-grower is what he receives for the tree (£3) which, we will assume, cost £2 in wages to produce, leaving £1 profit for him. The output of the saw-miller is what he receives for the timber (£5) less what he paid for the tree. Again, this output (£2) is made up of wages and profit. And so on. The total of these added values equals the value of the final table. Thus we could obtain the value of the table by adding the *output* of the tree-grower (forestry), the outputs of the saw-miller and table manufacturer (manufacturing) and the output of the retailer (distribution).

We could have added up these individual outputs in a different way. Instead of putting them in industry categories, we could have added them according to the type of factor payment—wages, salaries, rent or profit. This gives us the *income* method of measuring output.

Thus, if we assume (*a*) no government taxation or spending, (*b*) no economic connections with the outside world, we can obtain the national income either (1) by totalling the value of final output during the year or, what is the same thing, by totalling the value added to the goods and services by each firm, or (2) by totalling the various factor payments during the year—wages, rent, profit.

There is, however, yet another method of calculating the national income. The value of the table in Fig. 85 is what was spent on it. If the table had sold for only £9, that would have been the value of the final output. The final factor payment—profit to the retailer—would have been only £1 (assuming that the wholesale price had remained unchanged). It follows, therefore, that we can obtain the national income by totalling *expenditure* on final products over the year.

It must be emphasised that the money values of output, income and expenditure are *identical by definition*. They simply *measure* the national income in different ways. This was shown by the fact that factor payments were automatically reduced by £1 when the table sold for £9 instead of £10. It can be further illustrated by looking at expenditure in more detail.

Assume the value of the national output (consisting of consumer goods and capital goods) is £1,000 million. Factor payments (wages, rent, profit) must therefore equal £1,000 million. Suppose, however, that the spending of households on consumer goods (consumption) and the spending of firms on capital goods (investment) does not amount to the income each has received. The result is an addition to stocks—'unintentional' investment by firms which have, as it were, 'bought in' some of their products.

To summarise, the national income is the national output—the total value of all goods and services produced by the country during the year. We can regard it as:

(1) the cost of the national output expressed as the earnings (wages, rent, profit) of all the factors of production combining to produce it;

(2) the total amount spent on final goods and services for consumption and investment purposes during the year;

(3) the total of the values of the goods and services produced by the various industries, public authorities, etc., during the year.

Before we proceed to examine in more detail the actual process of measuring these three identities, it is convenient if first we consider some of the general difficulties which arise and how they are overcome.

II. NATIONAL INCOME CALCULATIONS
IN PRACTICE

General difficulties

Difficulties arise in all calculations of the national income because of the following:

(1) *The necessity of having to make arbitrary definitions*

(a) *Production.* In calculating the national income, only those goods and services which are paid for are normally included. Because calculations have to be made in money terms, the inclusion of other goods and services would involve imputing a value to them. But where would you draw the line? If you give a value to certain jobs which a person does for himself—growing vegetables in the garden, cleaning the car, painting his house—then why not include shaving himself, cleaning his shoes, driving to work, etc.?

On the other hand, excluding what a person does for himself may have the effect of distorting national income figures. As the division of labour develops and the number of exchanges consequently increases, a country's national income can rise although there may have been no addition to real output! (*see also* pp. 349 and 350).

An imputed money value is included for certain payments in kind which are recognised as a regular part of a person's income earnings, e.g. goods produced and consumed by a farmer; food, etc., of the Forces and of domestic servants.

(b) *The value of the services rendered by consumer durable goods.* A table, T.V. set, dish-washer, car, etc., render services for many years. Should we not, therefore, give a yearly value to such services? Once again we face the difficulties mentioned above of imputing a value and knowing where to stop. A toothbrush, pots and pans, all render services over their life! All such goods, therefore, are included at their full value when they are bought, and subsequent services are ignored.

The one exception is owner-occupied houses. Here the rateable value provides a basis for an imputed value. Including a notional rent keeps owner-occupied houses in line with property owned for letting (income shown as rents or profits of companies) and prevents the national income falling as more people become owner-occupiers!

(c) *Government services.* Education and health services, although provided by the state, are obviously no different from similar services for which some persons pay. Consequently, they are included in national income at cost. But how should we view the work of persons maintaining law and order and defence? A policeman, for instance, when helping children to cross the road is providing a consumer service. But at night his chief task may be guarding banks and factories against theft, and in doing so he is really furthering the productive process. Strictly, therefore, to avoid double-counting, this part should be excluded from output calculations. Nevertheless, because in practice it is impossible to differentiate between the two activities, all the policeman's services, and indeed all government services (including defence) are included at cost in the national output (*see also* p. 349).

(2) *Inadequate information*

The sources from which data are obtained were not specifically designed to provide information for national income calculations. Thus not only do income-tax returns fail to cover the small-income groups, but they err on the side of understatement. Similarly, the Census of Production and the Census of Distribution are only taken at approximately five-year intervals. The result is that many figures must simply be estimates based on samples.

Information, too, may be incomplete. Income-tax returns would not show income from state-owned property or profits of public corporations.

But it is 'depreciation' which presents the major problem, for the figure given by companies, etc., is really only a book figure determined by tax regulations. There is no accurate figure for real depreciation, and thus it is largely the practice now to refer to Gross National Product rather than to National Income (*see* p. 346).

(3) *The danger of double-counting*

As we shall see, care must be taken to exclude transfer incomes when adding up national income (*see* p. 343), the contribution to production made by other firms when calculating national output (*see* p. 344) and indirect taxes when calculating national expenditure (*see* p. 344).

A fourth way in which a form of double-counting can occur is through 'stock appreciation'. When there is a rise in the general level of prices, the value of stocks of raw materials and goods rises. While this adds to the profits of firms holding such stocks, it represents no increase in real output. Such gains must therefore be deducted from the income and output figures.

(4) *Complications arising from relationships with other countries*

Methods of calculating national income must take into account the effects of international trade and international indebtedness.

(a) *Trade*. British people spend some of their income on foreign goods, while foreigners buy British goods. In calculating national *expenditure*, therefore, we have to deduct the value of goods and services imported (since they have not been produced by Britain) and add the value of goods and services exported (where income has been earned by factors in Britain).

(b) *Indebtedness*. If, within a family, a father increases his son's pocket-money, it does not increase the family income. Instead it merely effects a redistribution, the father having less and the son more. But if the boy's income is suddenly augmented by a wealthy aunt who makes him a regular allowance, then the family income is increased. Similarly with the nation; while transfer incomes do not increase national income, payments by foreigners do. These payments arise chiefly as interest and dividends from loans and investments made abroad. They can be regarded as payments to factors owned by British people but situated abroad, e.g. the paper factories of Bowater Ltd. in Canada and the U.S.A. Similarly, interest and dividends have to be paid to foreigners who have invested in Britain. Net income from abroad (receipts less payments) must, therefore, be added to both domestic expenditure and output.

If the calculation has been by the income method, overseas income and payments will probably have already been included in income-tax returns. However, the usual practice of the National Income and Expenditure Blue Book is to separate the two, in which case care must be taken to ensure that net income from abroad is added to income generated by production at home.

Government calculations of the national income

Figures for the national income are obtained at the income, expenditure and output stages. The results are not identical, because information is not complete, but the proportionate error is small. In practice the expenditure figure is taken as the datum, and the difference between this and the income and output figures is treated as a residual error.

In deciding whether an item should be included in the calculations the student should remember the basic principle: does it represent income earned by expenditure on, or output of goods and services produced by the factors of production of the United Kingdom during the year?

(1) *National income*

National income is the total money value of all incomes received by persons and enterprises in the country during the year. Such incomes may be in the form of wages, salaries, rent, or profit.

In practice, income figures are obtained mostly from income-tax returns but estimates are necessary for small incomes. Two major adjustments have to be made:

(*a*) *Transfer incomes.* Sometimes an income is received although there has been no corresponding contribution to the output of goods and services, e.g. through unemployment-insurance benefit, retirement pensions, students' grants, interest on the national debt, and gifts of money (such as an allowance to a relative) from one person to another. Although most of such incomes would normally be included in income-tax returns, they really represent only a redistribution of income within the nation—chiefly from taxpayers to the recipients. Transfer incomes must therefore be deducted. Otherwise we should have the ridiculous situation where the size of the national income could be increased by raising family allowances, health-insurance benefits, etc.

(*b*) *Income from government activities.* Personal incomes and the profits of companies can be obtained from tax returns. But the government also receives income from its property and may make a profit from such sources as the public corporations. Similarly, local authorities may show a surplus on their trading activities—water supply, housing, transport, harbours and docks, etc. Income earned in these various ways by public authorities must be added in.

(2) National expenditure

National expenditure is the total amount spent on consumer goods and services and on net additions to capital goods and stocks in the course of the year.

Figures for calculating national expenditure are obtained from a variety of sources. The Census of Distribution records the value of shop sales, while the Census of Production gives the value of investment goods produced and the additions to stocks. But these censuses are not taken every year, and so estimates have to be made which are based on data supplied from the National Food Survey, statistics of retail sales collected by the Department of Trade and Industry, the Family Expenditure Survey, etc.

Market prices collected in these various ways, however, are swollen by indirect taxes (e.g. on petrol, cigarettes, cars, etc.) or reduced by subsidies (e.g. on welfare milk, council housing, etc.). What we are trying to measure is the value of the national expenditure which corresponds to the cost of the factors of production (including profits) used in producing the national product. This is known as 'national expenditure at factor cost' and is obtained by deducting indirect taxes from and adding subsidies to national expenditure at market prices.

Adjustments necessary for exports and imports have already been referred to (see p. 342).

(3) National output

National output is the total of consumer goods and services and investment goods (including additions to stocks) produced by the country during the year. It can be measured either by totalling the value of the *final* goods and services produced during the year or by totalling the value added to the goods and services by each firm, that is, the production of every enterprise from the sole proprietor to the government. That the two methods are identical was shown in Fig. 85.

Gross national product and national income

In the course of production, machinery wears out and stocks

(I) INCOME

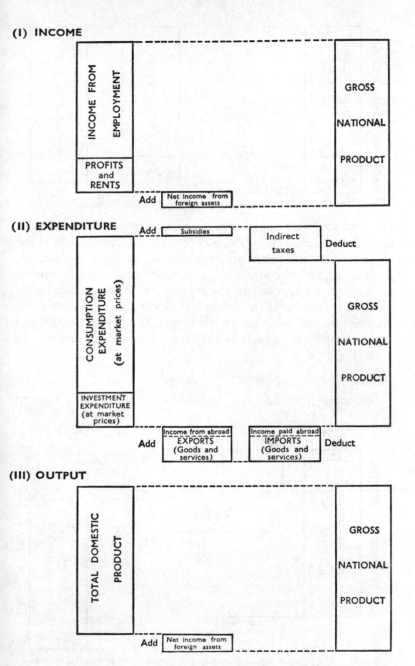

(II) EXPENDITURE

(III) OUTPUT

FIG. 86.—Summary of gross national product calculations.

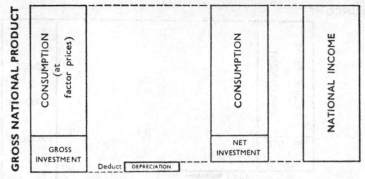

FIG. 87.—Gross national product and national income.

are used up. This represents disinvestment or depreciation of capital. If we make no allowance for this, but simply add in the value of new investment goods produced, we have *gross national product*. But, to be accurate in our calculation of the total output of the year, we should include only net investment, that is, the value of new investment goods and stocks less depreciation on existing capital and stocks used up. This gives us the net national product, which is the true national income for the year (Fig. 87).

Personal disposable income

For some purposes, e.g. an indication of people's current

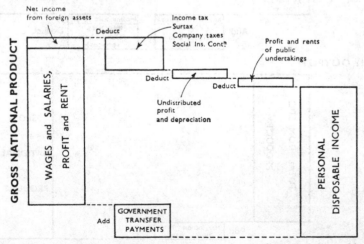

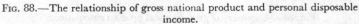

FIG. 88.—The relationship of gross national product and personal disposable income.

living standards, a measurement of personal disposable income, that is, what people have to spend after various adjustments have taken place, is more significant. The necessary adjustments to gross national product to obtain personal disposable income are shown in Fig. 88.

TABLE 6

CALCULATIONS OF THE NATIONAL INCOME OF THE U.K., 1972

A. INCOME

		£mn.
Income from employment		37,138
Income from self-employment		4,764
Profits of private companies and public enterprises		8,374
Rent		4,182
Total domestic income		54,458
less Stock appreciation		−1,319
Residual error		345
Net property income from abroad		456
GROSS NATIONAL PRODUCT		53,940
less capital consumption		−5,824
NATIONAL INCOME		48,116

B. EXPENDITURE

	£mn.
Consumers' expenditure	39,263
Public authorities' current expenditure on goods and services	11,702
Gross capital formation (investment) at home, including increase in stocks	10,774
Total domestic expenditure at market prices	61,739
plus Exports and income from abroad	16,694
less Imports and income paid abroad	−16,347
less taxes on expenditure	−9,279
plus subsidies	1,133
GROSS NATIONAL PRODUCT AT FACTOR COST	53,940
less capital consumption	−5,824
NATIONAL INCOME	48,116

C. OUTPUT

	£ mn.
Agriculture, forestry, and fishing	1,541
Mining and quarrying	827
Manufacturing	16,645
Construction	3,432
Gas, electricity, and water	1,666
Transport	3,428
Communication	1,320
Distributive trades	5,543
Insurance, banking, and finance (including real estate)	4,056
Public administration and defence	3,748
Public health and educational services	3,157
Other services	6,587
Ownership of dwellings	3,125
Total domestic output	55,075
less Stock appreciation	−1,936
Residual error	345
Net property income from abroad	456
GROSS NATIONAL PRODUCT AT FACTOR COST	53,940
less capital consumption	−5,824
NATIONAL INCOME	48,116

III. USES OF NATIONAL INCOME STATISTICS

(1) *To indicate the overall standard of living of the people*

Welfare is not identical with wealth (*see* p. 30), but wealth bears the closest single relationship to it. Income, the flow of wealth, is therefore the nearest indication of welfare.

Nevertheless, the national income figure cannot be accepted solely on its face value. Thus although the national income of the U.K. was £11,000 million in 1950 and £48,000 million in 1972, it does not automatically follow that everybody had quadrupled his standard of living over that period. The following qualifications have to be made:

(*a*) Some allowance must be made for the rise in the general level of prices from one year to another. Even if we apply the Index of Retail Prices to make the adjustment, it does not completely solve the problem, for there are many difficulties connected with index numbers (*see* p. 422).

(*b*) Where the population is increasing, we should expect, as there are more producers, that the national income will rise. Average income per head is a better indication of well-being than the overall figure.

(*c*) The standard of living of a person depends upon the quantity of consumer goods and services he enjoys. But the increase in national income may have come about entirely through an increase in the production of producer goods (as in China today). While these goods may enable a higher standard of living to be enjoyed in the future, they do not increase present welfare. Average personal disposable income might, for this reason, provide a better indication of current living standards, though for the long-run standard of living national income per head is the more satisfactory.

(*d*) The increase in national income may have come about by a surplus of exports over imports. This represents investment overseas, and thus the same remarks as in (*c*) apply.

(*e*) The average income per head figure is merely a statistical average. It does not indicate how the increased national income was distributed; it may have gone entirely to a few rich persons (as in the oil sheikhdoms of the Middle East), leaving the others no better off, or even worse off.

(*f*) An increase in national income may be the result of longer working hours, inferior working conditions, longer journeys to work (with increased discomfort) as towns expand, or more housewives at work (with less comfort in the home).

(*g*) Because government spending is included at cost in national income calculations, no distinction is made between expenditure on defence and expenditure on consumer goods and services. As a result, social services, for instance, could be curtailed to pay for a rearmament programme, but national income would be unchanged.

(*h*) The national income figure is swollen when people pay for services which they previously performed themselves. Thus a married woman who returns to teaching but pays a woman to do her housework adds to the national income twice—although the only net addition is her teaching services.

(*i*) Since national income figures are based on private costs and benefits, social costs or benefits do not enter into the calculations. Thus the erection of electricity pylons would be included at cost, no allowance being made for the social cost of spoiling the landscape.

(2) *To compare the standard of living of different countries*

Fairly accurate comparisons of the national incomes of different countries are often necessary for practical purposes. How much help should be given by the rich countries to the very poor? Which are the very poor countries? What contribution should be made by a country when an international body, such as the United Nations, requires funds? What is the war potential of a country?

But when used to compare the standards of living of different countries, national income figures must be subjected to qualifications additional to those mentioned in (1) above.

(*a*) Because figures are expressed in different currencies, they have to be converted into a common denominator. Using the exchange rate for this purpose is not entirely satisfactory, for the rate may not reflect accurately the respective internal purchasing power of currencies (*see* p. 476).

(*b*) Different people have different tastes. The cheap loincloth may give as much satisfaction to the Indian as the expensive suit to the Englishman. Similarly, the Canadian has to spend more on heating than the Nigerian. Obviously, neither the Englishman nor the Canadian are better off in these respects—though the national income figures, by valuing goods at cost, would seem to indicate that they were.

(*c*) The proportion of national income spent by different countries on defence varies. Countries which spend less can enjoy consumer goods instead, but average national income does not indicate the difference.

(*d*) Countries vary as regards the length of the average working week, the proportion of women who work, the number of jobs which people do for themselves, the degree to which goods are exchanged against money, and the accuracy of tax returns. Some allowance must be made for each of these factors.

(3) *To calculate the rate at which a nation's income is growing*

Is the national income growing? Is it growing as fast as it should? Are the incomes of other countries growing faster? Is there sufficient investment to maintain future living standards? The answers to these and similar questions can be found by comparing national income figures, though for reasons given above, some caution must be observed.

(4) *To assist the government in planning the economy*

Even capitalist countries now regard some central government planning as essential for achieving full employment, a stable currency, and a reasonable rate of growth.

But successful planning requires fairly accurate figures upon which decisions can be based. It is important to know the relative sizes of the various components of the national income and to be able to compare them with past years. Hence the National Income and Expenditure Blue Book shows, for a number of years: private and public expenditure on consumption and investment; the United Kingdom's transactions with the rest of the world; the contribution of each industry to the national product; personal disposable income after tax deductions and transfers; the distribution of personal income before and after tax; the financing of investment; capital formation by sectors of the economy; types of capital formation; expenditure of public authorities. How these figures can be used in planning will be shown in the chapters which follow.

IV. FACTORS DETERMINING A COUNTRY'S MATERIAL STANDARD OF LIVING

We conclude this chapter with a brief survey of the major factors determining a country's material standard of living. Subject to the qualifications mentioned in the preceding section, this can be defined as the national income per head of the population. For a country having economic relationships with the rest of the world, factors can be classified as internal and external.

Internal

(1) *Original natural resources*

It is obvious that 'natural resources' cover such things as mineral deposits, sources of fuel and power (such as coal and hydro-electric supply), climate, fertility of the soil, and fisheries around the coast. It must also be extended, however, to include geographical advantages, such as navigable rivers or lakes and flatness of land, both of which make the development of communications easier.

Variations in national income may take place because natural advantages become exhausted, though on the other hand new techniques may render usable natural resources which were formerly lying idle. Where the economy of a country is predominantly agricultural, variations in weather may produce fluctuations in the national income from year to year.

(2) *The nature of the people, particularly of the labour force*

Factors affecting the quantity and quality of labour have already been discussed. Other things being equal, the standard of living will be higher the greater the proportion of workers to the total population and the longer their working hours.

The nature of the labour force will be affected by the original qualities of the people—their health, energy, adaptability, inventiveness, judgement and ability to organise themselves and to co-operate in production. To these original qualities however must be added the skills that they learn through training and education.

(3) *Capital equipment*

The effectiveness with which natural resources and the labour force are used depends almost entirely on the capital equipment with which they can be combined. Thus coal and mineral resources need machinery to extract them from the soil, while to get any advantage from a waterfall, a turbine generator must be built. Similarly, the output per labourer can be vastly increased by giving him the right capital equipment. Indeed the biggest single cause of material progress is the addition to capital.

(4) The organisation of the factors of production

The available scarce factors of production must be combined in the right proportions, in the right places and in the right way for production. Have we the correct proportion of machinery to each worker? Is the production of the particular good being carried on in the best possible locality? Could the factors be redeployed within the factory itself to better advantage? This is the kind of question which has to be answered by persons organising production.

(5) Knowledge of techniques

Technical knowledge is the result of research and invention. Both involve capital expenditure, though it should be noted that the full use of techniques already learned is often held up for want of the necessary capital. Thus before we can utilise our present knowledge of nuclear energy, much capital development is required. Nevertheless the rapid increase of the standard of living of the United Kingdom over the last hundred years has largely been due to the development of new techniques, such as the steam engine, the internal combustion engine, and power from electricity and oil.

(6) Political organisation

A stable government promotes confidence and thereby encourages saving and investment in long-term capital projects. Production is therefore greater.

External

(1) Foreign loans and investments

A net income from foreign loans and investments means that a creditor country can obtain goods or services from debtor countries without having to give goods and services in return. Similarly, where a country has a net deficit on income from foreign assets, goods and services have to be exported to cover it. Material welfare from this source, however, is only likely to fluctuate over a long period.

(2) The terms of trade

Fluctuations in the terms of trade are likely to be far more important in changing material welfare in a short period, especially if the country, as with the United Kingdom, has a high level of imports and exports.

By the terms of trade we mean the quantity of another country's products which a nation gets in exchange for a given quantity of its own products. Thus, if the terms of trade move in the nation's favour, it means that it gets a larger quantity of imports for a given quantity of its own exports. This has happened because the prices of goods imported have fallen relatively to those exported. Let us suppose, for instance, that a country exports only cars and imports only wheat. If it exports 10,000 cars at a price of £500 per car, the value of its total exports is thus £5 million. If the price of wheat is £5 a quarter it can import 1,000,000 quarters. Assume now that the price of the cars remains unchanged but that the price of wheat falls to £4 a quarter. The result is that it is now possible to import 1,250,000 quarters of wheat in exchange for the same number of cars. Or the same amount of wheat as previously can be imported but only 8,000 cars need be exported. Thus either an extra 250,000 quarters of wheat or 2,000 cars can be enjoyed at home, not, it should be noted, through any increase in productivity, but simply because the terms of trade have moved in favour of the car-manufacturing country.

(3) *Gifts from abroad*

Since the war, the U.S.A. has made grants to various countries for purposes of economic development and defence. Such gifts have had the effect of maintaining or improving the standard of living of the receiving countries.

CHAPTER 25

FULL EMPLOYMENT:
A SURVEY OF THE PROBLEM

I. THE NATURE OF UNEMPLOYMENT

The problem

IN the early 1930s, people's thoughts were dominated not so much by the threat of war as by the spectre of unemployment. Between 1922 and 1939, there were always at least a million workers unemployed in the United Kingdom, and in 1932 the number rose to almost three millions. At its peak in 1932, the national average unemployment rate was 22·1 per cent of the working population, but this conceals the fact that certain areas and industries were hit harder than others. Thus the unemployment rate in Monmouthshire was 36 per cent, and in the ship-building industry generally 62 per cent.

During this period, machines, land and buildings were also standing idle. The national income, and thus the standard of living, were a lot lower than they need have been.

But the real curse of such unemployment is the human misery that results. Many persons, without work for years, lose hope of ever finding a job. Skills deteriorate as the period of unemployment lengthens. Families are forced to live on the minimum of subsistence. Thus the problem of unemployment is usually discussed solely in terms of labour.

It is unlikely that the U.K. will have such a high rate of unemployment again. All governments are committed to maintaining a high and stable level of employment (though what this means in practice is subject to marginal differences of interpretation), and they now know more about eliminating the causes of unemployment. Yet the experience of the 1930s not only showed what can happen if the government does not assume responsibility for full employment, but it has also coloured Britain's economic policy since the war. Especially among the older trade unionists, full employment has become almost an end in itself—and not without good reason. Yet the aim of having more vacancies than there are unemployed workers to fill them has been pressed to the point of overfull employment, and with this has come inflation, balance-of-payments difficulties, a high labour turnover, a shortage of skilled workers, and an unsatisfactory rate of growth of national production—problems which we shall have to return to later.

What do we mean by 'full employment'?

For reasons which will be discussed later, there will always be some persons unemployed. Completely full employment could be achieved only by direction of labour. The question is what percentage of unemployment will conform to 'full employment'? In the last resort, the answer rests with the politicians, for more than economic ends are involved. But the views of economists must carry weight.

Some economists, notably Professor F. W. Paish, have held that unemployment of around 3 per cent is necessary: (1) to allow for people changing their jobs in an economy which responds to new conditions of demand and supply; (2) to secure high productivity per worker; (3) to maintain a stable price level; (4) to achieve a steady rate of growth of the national product. Total production, it is argued, would then be greater than if the unemployment rate were pushed lower, and thus it would be possible to pay higher state benefits to those out of work.

Such a view, however, is open to dispute. In any case, it takes no consideration of the psychological and social effects of condemning more workers than is absolutely necessary to unemployment, even though this may last for only a short period. While, therefore, before the war 3 per cent unemployment was an acceptable level even to so liberal a thinker as Lord Beveridge, any British government today would jeopardise its chances at the next election if it allowed an unemployment rate much above 2 per cent (500,000 workers unemployed) to persist.

British practice, therefore, defines unemployment as occurring where persons capable of and willing to work are unable to find suitable paid employment. In such circumstances the government is expected to take vigorous and effective action.

Important points concerning and arising out of this definition, however, need to be stressed.

(1) Unemployment must be involuntary; persons on strike are not reckoned as being unemployed.

(2) 'Persons capable of work' must exclude the 'unemployables'—those not capable of work through mental or physical disability. On the other hand, unemployables are usually in the pool of unemployed labour seeking jobs and, where labour is scarce, more use will be made of them—provided that minimum wage regulations do not prevent this.

(3) Full employment does not mean that workers will never be required to switch jobs or occupations. Changes in the conditions of demand and supply are bound to occur, and such changes will be more frequent the more dynamic the economy and the more a country is dependent on international trade.

II. THE CAUSES OF UNEMPLOYMENT

Unemployment may occur for many different reasons, and it is important to distinguish between them in order that the appropriate remedies can be applied. We therefore classify unemployment as follows:

(1) *Normal or transitional*

Unless an economy is completely static, there will always be a number of persons changing their jobs. Some merely desire a change of employment or a move to a different part of the country. In certain occupations, e.g. heavy manual labour, workers are not employed regularly by any one employer; when a particular contract comes to an end (e.g. when a motorway is completed) labour is redundant. Occasionally, too, workers are discharged when a factory is being reorganised. In all these instances, unemployment of a week or so occurs before another job is found.

During this period unemployed workers usually register at the local Employment Exchange. There they form a pool or 'stock' of labour from which employers can fill vacancies. And, as in other parts of the economy, a stock enables changes in the conditions of demand and supply to have less violent repercussions.

But how large should this reservoir of labour be? If it is too large, workers remain unemployed for long periods, and what they might have produced is lost. If it is too small, the economy is dislocated. Bottlenecks occur through the inability to fill vacancies; employers hold on to labour which for the present they do not need; labour turnover is excessive because people switch jobs just for the sake of change; demands for wage rises exceed increases in productivity.

(2) *Seasonal*

Employment in some industries, e.g. building, fruit picking, and catering at holiday resorts, is seasonal in character. The difficulty is that the skills required by different seasonal jobs are not substitutable. To what extent, for example, can hotel workers become shop-assistants at Christmas? The price system can sometimes help towards solving the problem. Thus by offering reduced off-season rates, hotels at holiday resorts can be utilised for autumn conferences.

Seasonal unemployment is not completely avoidable. But it can be reduced if a small regular labour force will work over-time during the 'season' and allow such persons as students and housewives (who do not form part of the normal working population) to join them during the busy periods.

(3) *Frictional*

Frictional unemployment occurs where there are unemployed workers of a particular occupation in one part of the country, but a shortage of the same type of worker in other parts. Thus today there is a surplus of unskilled and manual labourers in the north of England, whereas firms in the London area have vacancies unfilled.

Two main reasons can be suggested for this type of unemployment—ignorance of available opportunities and immobility of labour. It has been said that 'of all baggage, human baggage is the most difficult to transport'. Married workers find the cost of moving prohibitive or cannot afford to give up their homes because of the difficulty of obtaining equivalent accommodation in the new area. Where a person is in possession of a rent-controlled or council flat the difficulty is even greater.

Other obstacles prevent workers from moving—an unwill-

ingness to leave friends and connections, a dislike of the new
neighbourhood on social or cultural grounds. Nor must we
forget that unemployment-insurance and supplementary benefits may have the effect of making a worker less willing to try
to overcome his prejudices.

(4) *International*

The United Kingdom, with her dependence on international
trade, is particularly vulnerable to unemployment brought
about by a falling-off in the volume of exports. Such a fall may
occur for two main reasons:

(a) *The prices of British goods are too high to be competitive in world
markets.* Prices of exports have two components, (i) the home
price, (ii) the rate at which the home currency exchanges for
foreign currency. Thus if home prices rise, for example because
of wage increases, the export market is likely to be hit severely.
The demand for exports is usually highly elastic, for substitutes
are generally available from competing countries. The effect on
employment is shown in Fig. 89. The wage increase moves the

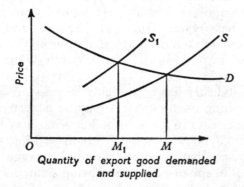

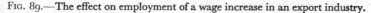

FIG. 89.—The effect on employment of a wage increase in an export industry.

supply curve from S to S_1. Because demand is elastic there is a
considerable fall in the demand for the good, from OM to
OM_1. The industry, and therefore employment, contracts.

Similarly, if at the existing rate of exchange the home
currency is too dear in terms of foreign currencies, exports will
be expensive to countries importing goods from the country
whose currency is overvalued. This was the situation which

faced Britain in 1925, for the pound was too highly valued when she returned to the gold standard.

(*b*) *Incomes of major importing countries may be reduced by a recession or a deterioration in the terms of trade* (see p. 454).

If incomes of importing countries fall, their demand for British goods, especially those having a high income elasticity of demand, will be likely to decrease.

(5) *Structural*

Structural unemployment, like frictional, results largely from the immobility of labour; but in this case it is brought about by long-term changes in the conditions of demand and supply. It is associated, therefore, with major changes in the economy, particularly in the export industries.

On the demand side, there may be a change in any of the factors influencing the conditions of demand. The price of substitutes may fall (Dundee jute products have largely been replaced by plastics), or foreign buyers may switch to competitors' goods (British shipyards have been hit by Japanese production). On the supply side, new techniques or the exhaustion of mineral deposits may make labour redundant. Automation has reduced Imperial Chemical Industries' demand for workers at Stockton; exhaustion of the better coal seams has led to a closure of pits in South Wales and Mid-Scotland.

Where an industry has been highly localised in a particular area, the resulting unemployment may be particularly severe. Thus the depression in the ship-building industry is reflected in the unemployment rate for Scotland in June 1973 being 4·3 per cent, compared with a national average of 2·4 per cent, and this in spite of the region being treated as a Special Development Area by the government.

(6) *Cyclical*

Cyclical unemployment is that associated with the trade cycle—the alternate booms and slumps in the level of industrial activity which were a feature of the hundred years before World War II. It was easily the major cause of the high unemployment of the 1930s.

Since 1939, however, cyclical unemployment has been

largely eliminated. (Depressions nowadays are comparatively mild, and are termed 'recessions'.) For this we are largely indebted to the late Lord Keynes, whose *General Theory of Employment, Interest and Money* (1936) showed governments how income could be maintained at a level sufficient to produce full employment. His views, and the policies which follow from them, are so important in present-day economic thought that they are considered in more detail in Chapter 26.

(7) *Persistent general*

Persistent general unemployment is really a form of unemployment produced by a long trade cycle or a series of cycles, for even at the crest of a boom there still remain many persons out of work. Thus, in 1937, a year of peak activity, the United Kingdom had 1,400,000 unemployed.

The above discussion shows that the causes of unemployment can be reduced to: (a) insufficient total demand to keep the economy fully employed; (b) a lack of demand in particular industries, occupations, or places because total demand is spread unevenly throughout the economy. The first has to be explained by a 'general equilibrium' theory which covers the economy as a whole (Chapter 26). The second is largely a result of frictions—the immobility of labour—which make the price system work imperfectly. Here a 'partial equilibrium' approach, based on demand and supply in a *particular* labour market, can provide an explanation (Chapter 27).

CYCLICAL FLUCTUATIONS IN INCOME AND EMPLOYMENT

I. THE LINK BETWEEN SPENDING AND PRODUCTION

WHEN unemployment is *general* throughout the economy, we have to consider the demand for goods as a whole, just as we did when measuring national income. Consumption, saving, investment, wages, profits, etc., must be considered in aggregate terms.

We will begin by repeating in simplified form the identity which exists between income and expenditure. Take a simple example. A teacher buys a table from a carpenter. With the money he receives, the carpenter pays the timber-merchant for the wood, who in turn pays the man who cut the wood. But where did the teacher obtain the original money to buy the table? Simply from the carpenter, the timber merchant, and the tree-feller, who each use part of their receipts to pay fees to the teacher for instructing their children. So with the other goods the teacher buys. Thus there is a circular flow of income —one person's spending becomes another person's income. Spending is therefore necessary for earnings.

The same applies to the economy as a whole; at any one time spending equals income. Suppose, for instance, that in the economy, all production is in the hands of a Giant Firm which owns all the land and raw materials and employs all the labour. The Firm's income consists of the receipts from the sale of its product. Since it owns all the raw materials and land, these receipts must equal what it pays out in wages and what it has left in profits. This was the principle upon which we measured the national income in Chapter 24.

Since spending on goods, therefore, determines the receipts and thus the profits of firms, it is of vital importance to entrepreneurs. Let us turn back to Fig. 4 which showed a simplified model of an economic system, but let us concentrate, not on the movements of factors and goods, but on the money payments by firms for factors and on the money payments of households for goods. These money payments are shown in Fig. 90.

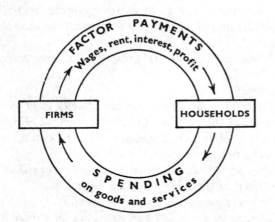

FIG. 90.—The circular flow of income.

If spending on goods and services is maintained, so can factor payments be maintained; in other words, the profitability to firms of production is unchanged and thus there is no need to vary output. If, however, for some reason or another spending should fall, some of the goods produced by firms will not be sold, and stocks will accumulate. Production is not so profitable, and as a result output is curtailed. On the other hand, if spending on goods and services increases, stocks will be run down. Production has become more profitable and, as a result, output is expanded.

Three important points emerge from our discussion so far:

(1) The condition of equilibrium in the economy is a simple one—spending on goods and services equals spending by entrepreneurs (including profits) on factors of production. Equilibrium exists because then there is no impetus towards a contraction or expansion of production.

(2) The level of production, and therefore of employment, is closely related to the level of spending.

(3) There is nothing to guarantee that the level of spending will be sufficient to produce an equilibrium level of production where all factors of production are fully employed.

Definitions and assumptions

Before we show how changes in spending occur, we must tighten up our model by defining terms and making simplifying assumptions.

We define net profit as gross profit less retentions for depreciation.

We assume:

(1) *All retentions for depreciation are actually spent on replacement investment.* Thus, when in future we speak of 'investment', it refers solely to net additions to fixed capital and stocks, that is, net investment.

(2) *All net profit is distributed to the owners of the risk capital.* This means that there is no 'saving' by firms.

(3) *There is no government taxation or spending.*

(4) *There are no economic connections with the outside world; it is a 'closed' economy.* From the above assumptions it follows that: (a) the sum of the factor payments is equal to national income (equals national output) as defined in Chapter 24; (b) income equals disposable income.

(5) *There are no changes in the price level.* Money values of national income are at constant prices; thus any changes in the money value reflect changes in real output.

(6) *The level of employment is directly proportionate to the level of output.* In practice this may not be strictly true; existing machinery, for example, may be able to produce extra output without additional labour. But the simplification does allow the level of employment to be linked directly with the level of national income.

II. REASONS FOR CHANGES IN AGGREGATE DEMAND

Aggregate demand

Our task, therefore, is to discover why changes occur in the national income (hereafter symbolised by Y). Now, as we have just shown, Y depends upon the level of spending, which we shall refer to as aggregate demand (abbreviated to AD). Thus we can find out why Y changes by discovering why AD changes.

Changes in AD

Let us return to our example of the teacher. Suppose he earns £1,000 in a given year. Most of it will be spent on consumer goods and services—but not all. Some will probably be put aside for a 'rainy day'. That part of income which is not spent we can say is 'saved'. What happens to it? The money could be hidden under the mattress; in this case it is 'hoarded', and is obviously lost to the circular flow of income. But the teacher is much more likely to put it in a bank, for there it is not only safer but earns interest. Is it still lost to the circular flow of income?

So far we have looked only at spending on consumer goods. But spending can also be on capital goods and stocks, usually known as *investment*. Entrepreneurs, as we have seen, go to their banks (and other institutions) to borrow money to purchase capital goods. Thus the sum deposited by the teacher stands a good chance of being returned to the circular flow of income by being 'invested', that is, spent on additional capital goods or stocks. And if exactly the same amount of money saved by the public is spent by entrepreneurs on investment, the level of (AD) is maintained (Fig. 91) and the level of Y is unchanged.

But suppose that the amount of income saved does not coincide with what entrepreneurs wish to invest. This can come about by either a change in the amount invested or by a change in the amount spent by consumers.

Let us first assume that consumers' spending remains constant. If now entrepreneurs reduce the amount they borrow for investment, AD is smaller. On the other hand, if entrepreneurs increase their investment, AD will be larger. And, as we shall see, the *ultimate* change in the size of AD will probably be much greater than the initial change in the level of investment (p. 383).

Alternatively, the amount of income spent on consumer goods may alter. Investment, we will now assume, remains unchanged. Here, if more is spent out of a given income, AD will increase; if less, AD decreases.

What it is important to recognise is that in an economy where people are free to dispose of their incomes as they please, and where entrepreneurs are largely left to make their own investment decisions, a difference can easily exist between the amount of income 'saved' (that is, which people do not wish to spend) and the amount which entrepreneurs wish to invest. This is

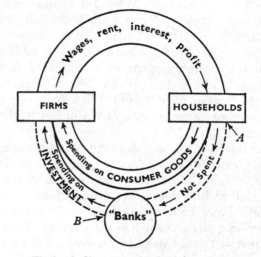

Fig. 91.—The level of income maintained through investment.

because, in their spending, households and firms act for different reasons and mostly independently of each other. Two questions, therefore, have to be asked: (1) What determines spending on consumer goods and therefore 'saving' (at position A)? (2) What determines investment spending (at position B)?

In our analysis, consumption, that is spending on consumer goods and services, will be given the symbol C; saving, that is, income not spent on consumption, S; investment, that is, spending on net additions to capital goods and stocks, I.

III. CONSUMPTION AND SAVING

(1) *Consumption and saving by households: 'personal saving'*

Income is received as wages or salaries, rent, interest and profits. With it, households buy the consumer goods they need. But not all income is spent. That part of income which is not

spent has been defined as 'saving'. Therefore, $Y = C + S$.
Similarly, $C = Y - S$, and $S = Y - C$. It follows that consumption
can be affected by active saving decisions—thrift—while saving
can be affected by active spending decisions.

C and S, therefore, are merely the same coin looked at from
different sides. Thus, whenever we consider C or S, we must
examine the factors which influence both spending and thrift.

Spending decisions are more important in the short run, for a
person's first concern is to maintain his standard of living. They
are influenced by:

(*a*) *Size of income*. A small income leaves no margin for saving.
Only when a man has satisfied what *he* considers are his basic
needs will he save a part of his income. Indeed, if current
income falls below this level, he may spend some of his past
savings or borrow in order to maintain the standard of life he
is accustomed to.

But we can go further. As income increases, the proportion
spent tends to decrease; or, as it is often put, there is a *diminishing marginal propensity to consume*.

The above conclusions are illustrated diagrammatically in
Fig. 92.

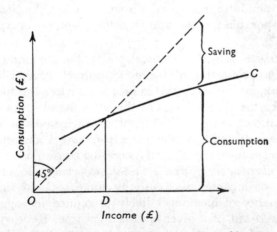

FIG. 92.—The relationship of consumption and income.

Below an income of OD there is dis-saving. At OD all income
is consumed; it is the 'break-even' income. At higher incomes
the proportion spent falls (the proportion saved rises). This

368 THE GOVERNMENT AND THE ECONOMY PART VI

diminishing marginal propensity to consume is shown by the decreasing slope of the consumption curve; for any given increase in income, the extra amount spent grows successively smaller.

(b) *The time-lag in adjusting spending habits.* In addition to the improved possibility and desire to save as income increases, the marginal propensity to consume may diminish, because it takes time for a person to adjust his standard of living as his income increases. In the short period, therefore, saving increases.

The above two factors explain the *shape* of the consumption curve—how spending changes as income changes. But we still have to account for the *position* of the curve—what determines the proportion of any given income which is spent. (We had a similar problem when studying the demand curve; the relationship of demand to price determined, through marginal utility, its shape; the conditions of demand determined its position.)

The amount spent out of a given income can vary (that is, the position of the C curve may change) as a result of:

(c) *Changes in disposable income.* We have assumed that firms have distributed all net profits and that there is no government taxation or transfers. In practice, both profit distribution and government activity will affect the size of disposable income, and thus spending. Increased direct taxation, for instance, reduces disposable income and thus lowers the C curve (Fig. 92).

(d) *Government policy.* By its fiscal policy, the government can influence the proportion of income consumed. A high level of purchase tax, for instance, may induce people to forgo spending on goods for the time being. On the other hand, the replacement of indirect taxes by highly progressive taxes or a high profits tax would tend to take more from savers and less from spenders and so have the effect of increasing consumption.

(e) *The distribution of wealth in the community.* Because the proportion of income saved usually increases with income, greater equality of incomes is likely to reduce the aggregate amount saved out of a given national income. Redistributive taxation, therefore, tends to increase total consumption.

(f) *The invention of new consumer goods.* In recent years family cars, television sets, transistor radios, hi-fi equipment, tape recorders, central heating and dish-washers have all induced spending, especially when backed by intensive advertising.

(*g*) *Hire-purchase and other credit facilities.* A decrease in the initial deposit or an extension of the period of repayment encourages spending. For this reason, hire-purchase terms are often regulated by the government. Easier bank credit also encourages spending.

(*h*) *Anticipated changes in the value of money.* If people consider that the prices of goods are likely to rise, they are more likely to bring forward their spending rather than save for the future.

(*i*) *The age-distribution of the population.* Since most saving is done by people over 35 years of age, an ageing population will tend to reduce the propensity to consume of the community as a whole.

In the long period, people have some concern for their future standard of living, and *thrift* exercises a greater influence in the disposal of income.

The main *factors determining thrift* are:

(*a*) *Size of income.* As already shown, saving increases as income increases *and* at an increasing rate.

(*b*) *The rate of interest.* The classical economists considered that, in order to induce people to forgo present for future enjoyment, compensation in the form of interest had to be paid. The higher the rate of interest, the more people would save.

This view, however, is largely rejected by present-day opinion. While a high rate of interest may tempt people to save, actual saving is influenced to a far greater degree by the ability to save (the size of income) and environmental factors (*see below*). Thus the Radcliffe Committee considered that the rise in both the rate of interest and saving which occurred in the 1950s was purely coincidental; other factors, chiefly less spending on post-war replenishment, played a far greater part. In any case, it must be remembered that much saving is contractual, e.g. by way of insurance and mortgage repayments.

Where people are saving to provide an income for the future and consider that a rise in the rate of interest is likely to be permanent, they may reduce their saving, thereby counter-balancing to some extent any increased saving by persons forgoing present consumption.

(*c*) *Psychological attitudes.* Some communities are by nature more thrifty than others, providing against sickness, unemployment, old age, and for the education of dependants. Certain people even save beyond these needs, either because it gives them a feeling of power, independence or security, or because they wish to leave something to an heir.

On the other hand, ostentation—the desire to 'keep up with the Joneses'—may provide a motive for a high rate of spending.

(d) *Social environment.* Apart from influencing the general attitude to saving, environment can be a major factor in other ways. Such institutions as Savings Movements, the National Savings Bank, Trustee Savings Banks, building societies, insurance companies, unit trusts, etc., encourage regular thrift, so that much saving out of income is contractual.

Political conditions, too, influence saving habits. Countries continually threatened by war or revolution do not provide the stable conditions necessary to encourage thrift.

(e) *Government policy.* The government can influence people's attitude to saving in a variety of ways. While some countries, such as Ghana, may have compulsory saving, others, such as the U.K., try to stimulate personal saving through the rate of interest, propaganda, income-tax concessions (e.g. on the first £21 interest on National and Trustee Savings), and special devices (e.g. National Savings Certificates, British Savings Bonds, Premium Bonds).

On the other hand, it must be remembered that a comprehensive social-insurance scheme or inflation may reduce real personal saving.

Under our simplifying assumptions of all net profits distributed and no government taxation or spending, all saving is done by households. But in real terms, saving represents the release of resources from present consumption for the construction of factories, machinery, etc. In practice, this release of resources can occur at other points in the income flow where some income is retained and not spent. In order to consider these we will temporarily relax the two assumptions above. Saving can now be achieved by businesses and the government.

The distribution of saving in the United Kingdom in 1972 is shown in Fig. 93. It is *personal saving* which has fluctuated the most since the war.

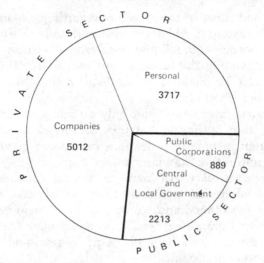

FIG. 93.—Saving in the U.K., 1972 (before providing for depreciation, stock appreciation, and residual error). Figures in £ millions. Source: *National Income and Expenditure Blue Book*, 1973.

(2) *Business saving*

Saving by businesses (which in volume remains fairly stable) is achieved by not distributing to shareholders all the profits made in a year. Some net profits are usually retained, either to be 'ploughed back' for the expansion of the business or to be held as liquid reserves in order to meet tax liabilities or to maintain dividends in the event of reduced trade, a strike or an increase in taxation. In 1973, business saving amounted to about 42 per cent of total saving.

The chief factors affecting this type of saving are:

(*a*) *Profits.* When directors are deciding how much profits should be transferred to reserves, they will be guided almost entirely by the size of profits being currently earned. First, a profit is necessary to effect any saving whatsoever, and the larger the profits, the greater the margin for saving. Secondly, when profits are good, directors are more likely to set aside reserves for expanding the business.

In practice, therefore, company saving is determined principally by the level of AD, for this represents the receipts upon which profits chiefly depend.

(*b*) *Subjective factors.* The financial prudence and the energy, enterprise and ideas of the directors regarding expansion will influence the extent to which retained profits are invested. Thus some directors may retain liquid reserves, not because they have ideas for expanding the business, but as a source from which dividends can be maintained in lean years, thus avoiding criticism from shareholders.

(c) *Estimated future prices.* Not only do rising prices increase profits and thus optimism, but they are an incentive to save out of current income in order that investment goods can be purchased now rather than later on.

(d) *Government policy.* An increased tax on *distributed* profits or a 'dividend freeze' would be likely to increase company saving. On the other hand, control of investment (e.g. by a Capital Issues Committee) would probably have the opposite effect, for there would be little point in retaining profits if investment were impossible.

(3) *Government saving*

Central government saving is achieved chiefly through a 'budget surplus'. This may be secured by increasing revenue (through additional taxation) or by reducing current government expenditure. The surplus may be necessary:

(a) to provide for the government's own investment and loans to local authorities and colonies;

(b) to cover the needs of the nationalised industries, whose capital is now largely provided by the Treasury;

(c) to ensure that, with personal and business saving, total saving will so cover total investment that AD will be sufficient to produce full employment without inflation (*see* p. 400).

Apart from a budget surplus, saving can occur in other forms, e.g. when national insurance and pension contributions exceed current payments.

Public corporations are similar in many ways to ordinary businesses. But as their operations are more directly under government control, and because a large part of their capital requirements is provided by the Treasury, their saving and investment is included under the public sector.

Local authorities, too, may have a budget surplus. In practice, however, they account for only about 4 per cent of total saving, their capital needs being largely met from the Public Works Loan Board and from private saving through loans floated on the open market.

Thus, in the public sector, spending is determined chiefly by government policy, economic and political. Any saving (through a surplus) is primarily to combat inflationary pressure (*see* p. 400).

Conclusion

In the private sector, spending (and therefore saving) depend upon (*a*) the level of income, that is, the size of AD, (*b*) other factors influencing the amount spent out of income. In comparison with changes in AD, these other factors are fairly stable. Hence the main factor affecting short-term changes in consumption spending is the size of AD!

We have, therefore to look elsewhere for the reason why AD changes. It is to be found in the comparative instability of the other form of spending—investment.

IV. INVESTMENT SPENDING

What do we mean by 'investment'?

Investment is spending over a given period on the production of capital goods (houses, factories, machinery, etc.) or on net additions to stocks (raw materials, consumer goods in shops, etc.).

It is important to distinguish between this definition and what is usually referred to as 'investment' by the ordinary man in the street. To the economist, investment takes place only when there is an actual net addition to capital goods or stocks. It cannot be applied to putting money in the bank or to the purchase of securities. This is true even when new securities are bought, though here there is a strong presumption that the money is required to finance real investment in factories, machinery, etc.

It should be noted that the definition above would cover 'gross investment', since it makes no allowance for the depreciation of existing capital assets. But, as already explained, we are analysing in terms of national income (net national product) *not* gross national product. Investment in our model, therefore, must be limited to *net* investment, that is, gross investment less depreciation.

Investment in the private sector of the economy

While, in *the private sector*, some investment in housing is undertaken by owner-occupiers who add garages, rooms, etc., to their property, the amount is insignificant relative to investment by businesses, particularly joint-stock companies.

The level of investment by businesses is governed by the expected yield relative to cost, changes in techniques, changes in the rate of consumption and government policy.

(1) *Expected yield relative to cost*

Entrepreneurs spend on new capital equipment when they think that the cost will be justified by the addition to revenue which will directly result. In short, marginal-revenue productivity must at least equal marginal cost.

Whereas marginal-revenue productivity in the case of labour can be estimated fairly accurately, it is not so with capital. Capital equipment lasts a long time, and the return to it is spread over many years. This involves uncertainty. Is demand for the product likely to change? Are competitors likely to enter the market? Will the present methods of production become obsolete? The return to the capital equipment over its life, therefore, can be no more definite than a series of yearly yields which the entrepreneur reasonably *expects*. It is usual to discount these yields to their present value and to express the return over the initial cost as a rate. This rate will be referred to as the *marginal efficiency of investment* (symbol 'MEI').

We can give more precision to this term by a simple example. Suppose a machine costs £1,000. It has a working life of four years, during which the entrepreneur *expects* that it will add £400 each year to his receipts. We could find a single rate of discount which would make the £400 received during the first year plus the £400 received during the second year plus the £400 received during the third year plus the £400 received during the fourth year just equal to the initial cost of £1,000. This rate of discount is the MEI. (In our example, it is about 22 per cent.) If the MEI is greater than the rate of interest—the cost of borrowing the original £1,000—the entrepreneur will buy the machine; if it is less, he will not.

In the above example, we have shown how the marginal efficiency of a *particular* machine is determined. But what of the marginal efficiency of new capital *in general*? How will this vary as the capital equipment of the community increases or decreases?

For two reasons it can be expected that the MEI will fall as the stock of the community's capital increases. First, as more machines are produced, so will the products made by those machines increase in supply. Thus the price of those products falls, and so the expected yield of the machine will also fall. Secondly, producing more machines will increase the demand for the factors of production making those machines. This will increase the price of those factors, and so the supply price of the machines is likely to rise as more are produced. From the first, we have smaller expected yields to be discounted; from the second, a larger initial supply price as capital increases. Both lead to a smaller discount rate; that is, to a smaller MEI as the supply of capital increases.

In other words, the curve relating MEI to the level of investment slopes downwards from left to right (Fig. 94).

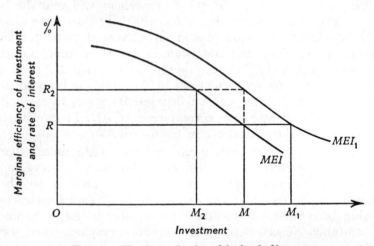

FIG. 94.—The determination of the level of investment.

With an MEI as depicted by the curve *MEI* and a rate of interest of *OR*, the level of investment will be *OM*.

The level of investment may alter through any change in (*a*) the expected yield or (*b*) the rate of interest. Thus if expected yield rises to MEI_1, investment will increase to OM_1. On the other hand, if the rate of interest rises to OR_2, investment will fall to OM_2. What we have to do now, therefore, is to examine the possible extent and frequency of changes in expected yield, and to see whether those changes are likely to overshadow changes in the rate of interest.

Let us look first at (a) *the expected yield*. We have already shown that this is clouded in uncertainty because the entrepreneur will have to look far into the future to estimate changes in the demand for his product and to allow for possible changes in methods of production. Upon what can he base his estimates?

The simple answer is that he has little definite to go on. His estimate of the earning power of an investment over, say, the next five years can be only tentative, and allowance will have to be made according to the confidence he has in its accuracy. The main factors influencing his decisions are: the level of current income; the course of Stock Exchange prices; the future price level; and government policy. Let us consider each in turn.

In making his estimate, the entrepreneur will most likely commence from the position about which he does have some definite knowledge—the present. If current demand for his goods is buoyant, and has been so for some time, future prospects will probably look rosy. On the other hand, if present demand is low, he will think twice before adding to his productive capacity. But the current demand for goods as a whole depends chiefly upon the current level of AD. Investment is likely to be higher, therefore, the higher AD.

Uncertainty in estimating the expected yield means that investment decisions are influenced considerably by prevailing moods of optimism or pessimism. An entrepreneur will be unwilling to extend his factory if current Stock Exchange prices value businesses, particularly those similar to his own, unfavourably. Nevertheless, such a valuation may not reflect the long-term earning capacity of a business, but rather the opinion of speculators seeking to make a profit out of the short-term price movements of the shares. Moods on the Stock Exchange, however, are contagious, and as a result price swings are magnified—with a corresponding influence on the level of investment.

As regards the price level, if the entrepreneur thinks that

prices in future are likely to be higher, he will be more likely
to invest now. Not only will the value of the factory or machine
appreciate, but expected yield will be higher through the rise
in the price of the product.

Political instability and changes in government policy add
to uncertainty. The former discourages investment, particularly by foreign companies operating in the country. The
possibility of the latter has to be allowed for in an entrepreneur's expectations. Is the corporation tax likely to be
increased? Will balance-of-payments difficulties compel the
government to carry out a disinflationary policy to curb future
price rises?

This brings us to (b) *the rate of interest.* Until fairly recently,
economists, following Lord Keynes, stressed the long-term rate
of interest as an important factor in determining the level of
investment. Certainly the rate of interest must be taken into
account. If it rises, investment is more costly. This applies even
if funds come from internal reserves, for the opportunity cost—
the return on the best alternative, e.g. government securities
—has to be considered.

But the Radcliffe Committee doubted whether the rate of
interest was a major factor in determining investment. Their
inquiries revealed that many entrepreneurs were almost
uninfluenced by it, and this view was shared by the Confederation of British Industry. While the prevailing rate of
interest might play an important part in the investment
decisions of small firms—particularly retailers, wholesalers,
and furniture companies—and in projects where the yields
extend far into the future, e.g. housing, these tend to be
exceptions rather than the rule.

For one thing investment decisions, especially for large firms,
are the result of long-term planning. Any alteration of plans
because of a change in the rate of interest might throw the
whole programme out of phase. For another, firms allow a
considerable safety margin when deciding on investment,
probably expecting to recover its cost within five years. This
margin is thus sufficient to absorb a relatively small rise in the
rate of interest. Even the holding of stocks may not be affected
by the rate of interest. Convenience is more likely to decide
the minimum held. In any case the rate of interest may be only

a small part of the cost of holding stocks, warehousing, etc., being relatively far more important.

But probably the main reason why the rate of interest has little effect on investment is that, compared with changes in expectations, it tends to be irrelevant. We can explain this as follows. Uncertainty means that expected yield is subject to frequent reappraisal. In other words, the position of the MEI curve is always liable to change. Hence the cost element—the rate of interest—is of relative insignificance. As we showed earlier (Fig. 94), a rate of interest OR and an MEI curve MEI would give a level of investment OM. A rise in the rate of interest to OR_2 should reduce investment to OM_2. But this assumes that there is no change in the position of the MEI curve. What the more recent view implies is that changes in expectations may cause the MEI curve to change so frequently and by so much that it outweighs the effect which a movement of the rate of interest may have on the level of investment. For example, as the rate of interest rises to OR_2, revised expectations may cause the MEI curve to move to MEI_1. As a result, investment, instead of decreasing, remains the same at OM. Often, therefore, in a slump, a low rate of interest does little to stimulate investment, while in a boom a high rate does not discourage it. It is the fickleness of business expectations which gives investment a central role in the determination of the level of employment.

(2) *Changes in techniques*

New technical developments, such as the railways, the internal-combustion engine, atomic energy and automation, give an added impetus to investment. On the other hand, it has to be recognised that the possibility of new techniques rendering existing capital equipment obsolete must be allowed for by the entrepreneur when estimating the MEI.

(3) *Changes in the rate of consumption: the 'accelerator'*

Our conclusion in (1) above, that the level of investment was tied fairly closely to the size of AD, is capable of further refinement. Changes in the level of investment are closely linked, not to the absolute level of consumption, but to changes in the *rate* of consumption. A simple example will explain.

Suppose that 1,000 machines are fully employed in producing bicycle tyres and that the life of each machine is ten years. This means that 100 machines have to be replaced each year and the industry making this type of capital good must have a yearly capacity of 100.

Now suppose that the demand for bicycles increases by 10 per cent. If there is no excess capacity for producing tyres, it can be seen that 100 new machines, in addition to the replacement requirement, are needed immediately. In this year, therefore, 200 tyre-making machines must be produced. Thus although the increased demand for consumer goods was only 10 per cent, it led to a doubling of the capacity of the industry making the machines.

If consumption of bicycles now remains constant at the new level, production of the machines will have to contract sharply, for until the extra machines wear out in ten years' time, only the annual replacement of 100 machines will be required.

Taking this example as it stands, three conclusions can be drawn. (a) Variations in the rate of consumption will produce changes in investment on a magnified scale. Usually changes in consumption are the result of variations in the level of AD (known today as recession and recoveries). But they may also be brought about by such factors as changes in hire-purchase facilities, the boom in hire-purchase commitments being followed by stagnation for two or three years while repayments are made. (b) Swings in the level of production are much greater in the producer-goods industries than in the consumer-goods industries. The longer a machine lasts before it has to be replaced, the greater will be the swing. Thus in our example, if the machine for making tyres lasts for twenty years, the 10 per cent increase in demand for bicycles would necessitate a trebling of the capacity of the tyre-machine industry. (c) A single change in the level of consumption can produce a built-in mechanism whereby changes in the level of investment will be repeated subsequently at fairly regular intervals.

Nevertheless, when we look at the assumptions which are implicit in our example, it loses some of its precision. In the first place, although we stated that there was no excess capacity in the tyre-producing industry, the opposite was assumed in the tyre-machine-making industry—the 100 per cent increase in demand will be met by the production of 100 extra machines. If extra tyres can be produced by using idle machines or by double-shift working, then there will be no need to increase the number of machines. On the other hand, if there is no surplus capacity in the tyre-machine-making industry, the increased demand for bicycles may simply find its outlet in higher prices, and investment will not increase. Secondly, the model fails to allow for the expectations of entrepreneurs. An increase in the demand for bicycles may have been anticipated by building up stocks or by holding excess capacity in reserve. On the other hand, it may be thought that the increase in demand is unlikely to be permanent, in which case the extra machines would not be bought.

In practice, induced investment may result, not only from an increase in consumption, but from an autonomous increase in investment. Thus it is more accurate to say that the accelerator depends upon changes in AD rather than simply on changes in the level of consumption.

(4) Government policy

To be complete we must again relax our assumption of no government taxation or spending. Government policy may directly influence private investment. After the war, investment expenditure exceeding a certain sum had to be approved by the Capital Issues Committee, and although such control has now ended, banks have been instructed from time to time to restrict credit for certain types of investment. Should it desire to stimulate private investment, the government may give subsidies (e.g. for local authority housing, converting old houses, or improving farm buildings), grant generous investment or depreciation allowances in tax assessments, and revive the optimism of entrepreneurs by increasing its own investment.

Investment in the public sector includes not only the capital expenditure of the central government, but also that of the nationalised industries and local authorities.

Much of the central government investment is fairly stable, depending chiefly on policy commitments—road construction, school and hospital building, etc. To a large extent, too, the same is true of the capital expenditure of the nationalised industries, for in deciding whether or not to expand their capacity, they will be guided as much by their social obligations as by their financial position. Thus in periods of unemployment, they might increase their investment.

Local authority investment, however, may react to changes in the rate of interest. Much of the finance for providing new houses, schools, roads, and bridges has to be raised on the open market. Spending on new houses in particular may vary with the rate of interest. If, after applying government grants, the cost of borrowing is not covered by the rents charged, the difference has to be found from the rates. But because the rates are not a buoyant form of taxation, a rise in interest charges must usually be met from higher rents. Indeed, a high rate of interest can reduce local authority house-building to mere slum-clearance requirements.

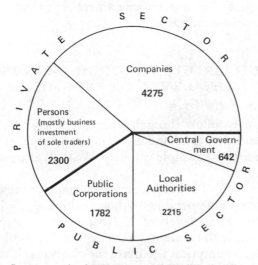

FIG. 95.—Investment in the U.K., 1972 (£ million). (Gross fixed capital formation at home and value of physical increase in stocks and work in progress.)

(Source: *National Income and Expenditure Blue Book*, 1973).

The real importance of public investment is that it is subject to direct government control. Consequently it can be easily adjusted to maintain total investment at the desired level. Should private investment be deficient, the government can increase its spending on its own capital projects. But there is a difficulty when the government would like to curtail its investment because private investment is at a high level. Many projects, such as new road construction, which ought to enjoy high priority, tend to be held back.

Conclusion

By influencing expectations, the current level of income will play a part in determining the level of private investment. Moreover, investment will bear some relationship to the rate of change of income.

But, in order to simplify our analysis, we shall ignore these connections between investment and the level of income and assume that all investment is autonomous. In other words, investment decisions of entrepreneurs are based on a number of considerations, and changes in investment are not automatically induced by income changes.

V. EQUILIBRIUM THROUGH CHANGES IN THE LEVEL OF INCOME

The restoration of equilibrium

We must now follow through what happens when, for some reason, intended saving and investment become unequal. A simple arithmetical example will help. We shall assume:

(1) $Y = 10,000$.

(2) At this level of income there are unemployed resources.

(3) Consumption spending by households is $\frac{6}{10} Y$ (disposable income) at all levels of Y. (In practice consumption is more likely to be about 90 per cent of disposable income, but our assumption will make the diagrams clearer.)

(4) Any increase in Y does not affect the proportion of Y spent by any change in the distribution of Y.

(5) Investment spending by firms is autonomous; that is, it is independent of the level of income. Initially $I = 4,000$.

(6) All figures are in £ million.

Initially, in Period 0, the economy is in equilibrium:

$$AD = C + I = 6,000 + 4,000 = 10,000$$
$$Y = C + S = 6,000 + 4,000 = 10,000$$

Now suppose that, in Period 1, the level of I increases by 2,000 to 6,000. AD is now 12,000. The receipts of entrepreneurs rise to 12,000, and stocks of goods decrease. As a result entrepreneurs expand production—factor payments equal $12,000 = Y$ (Period 1). This expansion of Y has come about solely because I is greater than planned S. Similarly, a contraction of Y will occur if I is less than planned S.

The 'multiplier'

But this is not the end of the expansion. An increase in Y to 12,000 will mean that more workers are employed, and they too will have income to spend. Thus $C = \frac{6}{10}\,(12,000) = 7,200$. Together with $I = 6,000$, this gives a new AD of 13,200. Thus, in Period 2, Y increases to 13,200. And so it continues. We can illustrate how the process works in real life from Nevil Shute's *Ruined City*. After years of idleness, the shipyard obtained an order for three tankers. 'The small, returning ripple of prosperity had not passed unnoticed in the district; a shop, long closed, reopened to sell meat pies, cooked meats, black puddings and small delicacies. It did a good trade over Christmas. Small articles began to be sold at the door for the first time for many years; a man who gleaned a sack of holly in the country lanes disposed of it within an hour, a penny for a spray. A hot roast chestnut barrow came upon the streets, and did good trade.'

In our example the process will only come to an end when Y has expanded to 15,000. At this level of income, $S = 6,000$—sufficient to match $I = 6,000$. Because $S = I$, this is the new equilibrium level of Y.

The sequence outlined above is shown in the Table below and in Fig. 96.

THE EFFECT OF AN INCREASE IN THE RATE OF I ON THE LEVEL OF Y

Period	C	I	S	Y
0	6,000	4,000	4,000	10,000
1	6,000	6,000	4,000	12,000
2	7,200	6,000	4,800	13,200
3	7,920	6,000	5,280	13,920
4	8,352	6,000	5,568	14,352
.				
.				
n	9,000	6,000	6,000	15,000

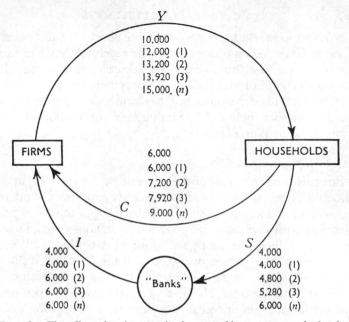

Y
10,000
12,000 (1)
13,200 (2)
13,920 (3)
15,000 (n)

FIRMS   HOUSEHOLDS

6,000
6,000 (1)
7,200 (2)
7,920 (3)
C 9,000 (n)

I S
4,000   4,000
6,000 (1)   4,000 (1)
6,000 (2)   "Banks"   4,800 (2)
6,000 (3)   5,280 (3)
6,000 (n)   6,000 (n)

FIG. 96.—The effect of an increase in the rate of investment on the level of income.

It will be noted that the increase in Y is much larger than the original increase in I. The ratio

$$\frac{\text{increase in } AD}{\text{initial increase in } I}$$

is known as the 'multiplier'.

To see what the size of the multiplier depends upon, we can concentrate on changes in C, S and Y. To signify that we are referring to changes, we shall prefix our symbols with the sign $\triangle$. These changes are shown in Fig. 97.

Fig. 97 is explained as follows. The initial $\triangle I$ leads to an increase in Y. A proportion of these extra factor payments (for example, received by workers previously unemployed) is spent according to the marginal propensity to consume $(\frac{6}{10})$. The proportion not spent $(\frac{4}{10})$ is saved.

This extra spending increases AD and therefore Y still further. And so the process is repeated, extra increments of C going to swell the total increase in AD and therefore of Y.

These totals are shown at the foot of each column. Each is

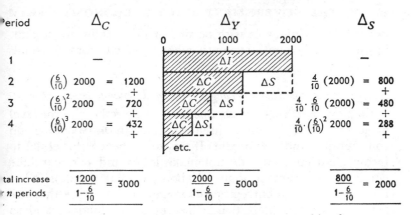

Period	Δ_C		Δ_Y 0 1000 2000	Δ_S	
1	—		ΔI	—	
2	$\left(\frac{6}{10}\right) 2000$ =	1200 +	ΔC ΔS	$\frac{4}{10} (2000)$ =	800 +
3	$\left(\frac{6}{10}\right)^2 2000$ =	720 +	ΔC ΔS	$\frac{4}{10} \cdot \frac{6}{10} (2000)$ =	480 +
4	$\left(\frac{6}{10}\right)^3 2000$ =	432 +	ΔC ΔS	$\frac{4}{10} \cdot \left(\frac{6}{10}\right)^2 2000$ =	288 +
			etc.		
Total increase for n periods	$\dfrac{1200}{1-\frac{6}{10}}$ = 3000		$\dfrac{2000}{1-\frac{6}{10}}$ = 5000	$\dfrac{800}{1-\frac{6}{10}}$ = 2000	

FIG. 97.—Increases in consumption, saving and income resulting from an increase in the rate of investment.

really a geometric progression of the form $a + ar + ar^2$ where r equals the marginal propensity to consume. Now the sum of a geometric progression to infinity where r is less than 1 equals $a/(1-r)$. It follows, therefore, that:

$$\text{total } \Delta Y = \frac{\Delta I}{1 - \text{marginal propensity to consume}}$$

The larger the marginal propensity to consume (c), the greater will be the total increase in Y. Since we defined the multiplier as $\Delta Y/\Delta I$, the value of the multiplier in this example is

$$\frac{1}{1-c} = \frac{1}{1-\frac{6}{10}} = 2\tfrac{1}{2}.$$

This can be verified visually from the diagram, where the shaded area equals the total increase in Y. If the proportion of income spent fell to $\tfrac{1}{2}$, the shaded area would be smaller. Our analysis points to the reason for this. When the fraction of income consumed falls, a higher proportion is saved. Thus income does not have to expand so much in order to bring intended saving into line with investment.

This brings us to the basic difference between saving and investment in the process of income-creation. Whereas an increase in investment will, other things being equal, automatically produce an increase in saving, an addition to saving need not lead to an increase in investment. Instead, when the desire to save increases with no similar increase in investment, income merely contracts until what is saved from it equals investment.

Diagrammatic exposition of changes in the equilibrium level of income

Employment, we have assumed, varies directly with the level of income (AD), which itself depends upon spending on consumption and investment. If this total spending is equal to income, entrepreneurs do not make losses and can continue employing the same amount of labour. If total spending is less than income, then entrepreneurs make a loss because they are getting back less than their expenses of production, and so production is reduced. If total spending increases, then entrepreneurs more than realise their expectations and production is expanded. This is explained in Fig. 98.

The income–expenditure line, at an angle of 45°, traces

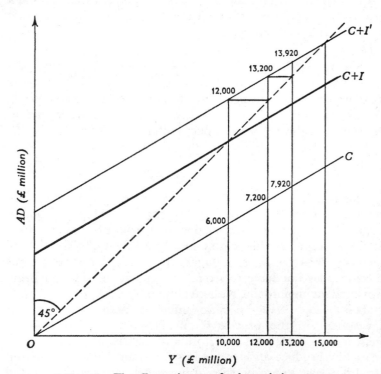

FIG. 98.—The effect on income of a change in investment.

all points where expenditure is equal to income (the same scale being chosen for both the x- and y-axes). Therefore, any point on this line will represent an equilibrium level of income.

The line C shows consumption expenditure at different levels of income. In our example $C = \frac{6}{10}Y$. To this we have to add investment expenditure of 4,000 at all levels of income. Thus the line $C + I$ is vertically distant 4,000 above the C line at all levels of income.

In equilibrium, $Y = AD = C + I$. The only point where this can occur is where the $C + I$ line cuts the 45° line. Here

$$AD = Y = 10,000.$$

When I increases to 6,000, the $C + I$ line moves vertically by 2,000 to $C + I'$. AD immediately increases to 12,000, and so does Y. Of this income, $C = 7,200$, which, with $I = 6,000$, means that AD and Y increase to 13,200. This expansionary process continues until AD and Y are equal to 15,000.

The effect of a diminishing marginal propensity to consume

So far we have assumed that the marginal propensity to consume is constant at all levels of income. But, even if the propensity to consume diminishes as income increases, the principle of the multiplier is the same. The only difference is that the calculations are more complicated because, for each period increment, we have to apply a smaller multiplier, since the marginal propensity to consume diminishes as income increases.

VI. THE EFFECT OF CHANGES IN CONSUMPTION

An autonomous change in consumption

So far we have analysed what happens to AD when there is an increase in autonomous investment. But the result is exactly the same if there is an autonomous increase in consumption, investment remaining unchanged.

Suppose, for instance, that C increases by 2,000 at all levels of Y. That is, $C = 2,000 + \frac{6}{10}Y$. This simply means that the original $C + I$ curve (Fig. 98) would move vertically upwards by 2,000 to the $C+I'$ position (as with an autonomous increase in I equal to 2,000). The increase in C is subject to the same multiplier effect, and thus Y increases as before to 15,000.

The paradox of thrift

But what is the situation when there is a decrease in the propensity to consume, that is, an increase in saving? Here we have what is often called the 'paradox of thrift'.

As we have seen, saving occurs because all income is not spent on consumption; people are limiting their demand for consumer goods. In real terms, they are saying that they will free factors from the production of goods for present consumption so that they can produce capital goods—houses, roads, factories, power stations, machinery, etc. As we saw in Chapter 16, the acquisition of capital involves forgoing present consumption. In this respect, therefore, thrift is a virtue.

But when our peasant farmer reduced present consumption in order to make his plough (*see* p. 260), he automatically carried out investment with the time at his disposal. However, as we have seen, in a modern economy decisions to save and decisions to invest are carried out for different reasons by two different sets of persons—households and firms respectively. When intended saving is greater than investment, not all factors released from producing goods for present consumption are used to produce capital goods. Some are unemployed. From the community's point of view saving can only be in capital goods or additions to stocks. When factors are unemployed there is no real saving—what they could have produced is lost to the community for ever.

What happens as we have seen is that income falls until it has reached that level where intended saving out of income just equals investment. Thus, if additional saving is not matched by additional investment, thrift is a curse, not a virtue, for it leads to a reduced standard of living as factors become unemployed and fewer consumer goods are produced.

Indeed, the fall in consumption is likely to have an adverse effect on entrepreneurs' expectations. Therefore investment itself falls, causing an even greater fall in income. Thus the real paradox of thrift is that, in these circumstances, we can end up with *less* saving than we originally started with.

Summary

Employment depends upon the level of AD—the total amount of money spent on the goods produced. AD fluctuates according to the relationship between intended saving and investment, so that eventually actual saving equals investment.

(1) AD expands if:
   (a) investment increases but saving remains unchanged;
   (b) saving increases but investment remains unchanged.
(2) AD contracts if:
   (a) investment decreases but saving remains unchanged;
   (b) saving increases but investment remains unchanged.

In practice investment is more liable to frequent change than saving. Whereas entrepreneurs' expectations are highly sensitive to new conditions, people's spending habits are fairly stable.

VII. GOVERNMENT SPENDING AND TAXATION

We can now relax our assumption that there is no government activity. The government raises taxes (symbol T). T is a leak out of the circular flow of income, similar to saving.

But government spending (symbol G) is an injection into the flow of AD. Therefore $AD = C + I + G$. This is shown in Fig. 99.

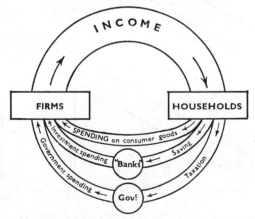

FIG. 99.—The circular flow of income and government spending and taxation.

G performs the same role as other forms of spending. Any increase in G will be subject to the multiplier. This can be illustrated from Fig. 98. If, instead of the increase in I, the increase in AD took the form of $G = 2,000$, the $C + I'$ line would be simply $C + I + G$, and the new level of Y would still be 15,000.

The effect of taxation is a little more difficult to analyse. However, we shall simplify by assuming: (1) taxes are not related to income (that is, they are imposed autonomously by the government as lump sums); (2) households spread the burden of any change in the level of taxation between consumption and saving.

Suppose $AD = C + I + G = 9,000 + 4,000 + 2,000 = 15,000 = Y$; assume also that there is no T. Thus disposable income still equals Y, $C = 9,000$ and $S = 6,000$. The government now decides to raise 2,000 by taxation. Does this mean that Y falls back to

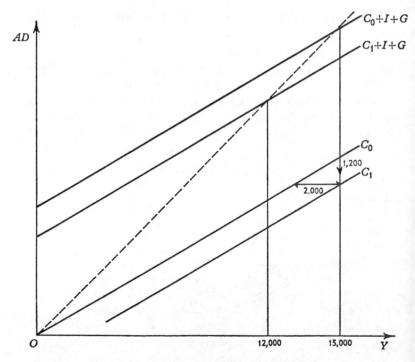

Fig. 100.—The effect of an increase in taxation on disposable income and consumption.

10,000? The answer is 'no'. Disposable income now equals $Y - T$; that is, there is an initial fall to 13,000. As a result there is an initial fall in C ($\frac{6}{10} \times 13,000$) to 7,800. But this fall in C is subject to the multiplier; thus the total fall in Y equals $1,200 \times \frac{10}{4} = 3,000$, giving $Y = 12,000$, with $C = 6,000$, $I = 4,000$ and $G = 2,000$. The reason why Y does not fall to 10,000 is that part of the burden of T falls on S, which is already a leak from the circular flow of income.

Fig. 100 illustrates the above diagrammatically. A tax of 2,000 reduces disposable income. Consumption, therefore, is now only what it would be if disposable income were 2,000 smaller at all levels oɩ income. Thus the C curve moves downward vertically from C_0 to C_1 by 1,200.

It should be noted that in moving from a budget deficit of 2,000 to a balanced budget, the government has reduced Y by 3,000. Similarly a budget deficit of 2,000 from $Y = 12,000$ would increase Y by 3,000. As we shall see, budgetary policy can be an important weapon in securing full employment or in combating inflation.

VIII. THE EFFECT OF FOREIGN TRADE

We can now relax our assumption of a closed economy.

Let us assume that the production of consumer and investment goods is at a given level, and that there is unemployment. Now imagine that British firms obtain orders to supply £2,000 worth of capital equipment to the U.S.A. As a result, in the British economy, AD and Y expand initially by 2,000—paid out in wages, salaries and profits, the cost being covered by entrepreneurs borrowing the money.

But this is not all. Of the initial 2,000 increase, 1,200 will be spent and 800 saved. The 1,200 spent now becomes income of other persons, who in their turn spend 720 and save 480. So we could go on. The position is exactly the same as with investment —additional spending by persons abroad on British exports has a multiplier effect depending upon the marginal propensity to consume. In this case, as a result of the initial additional spending of 2,000 on exports, AD increases by 5,000.

Increased spending on imports, given the conditions of unemployment stipulated above, works in exactly the opposite

THE GOVERNMENT AND THE ECONOMY   PART VI

way. There is now more spending on foreign goods, and less on British. As a result, foreign workers are employed to supply goods for the home market rather than British. Less expenditure on home-produced goods means that income is taken out of the **circular flow**, and AD contracts. As before, the initial loss of income is multiplied according to the marginal propensity to consume.

We can summarise the position as follows. Expenditure on exports is equivalent to an addition to investment—income is generated in producing goods which do not become available on the home market. Expenditure on imports, on the other hand, is a leak from the circular flow of income similar to a reduction of consumption. Hence we can combine the effect on AD of changes in investment, exports and imports as follows:

increase in AD = (increase in I + exports − imports)$[1/(1 - c)]$.

The above explanation, however, does assume that both exports and imports are autonomous, that is, they bear no precise relationship to the level of income. We shall continue this assumption with exports, though it could be that these decline as income expands, since it is now easier to sell on the home market.

But imports are likely to form a proportion of consumer spending, and therefore of income. Thus if we assume that imports form $\frac{1}{6}C$, we can say that the 'propensity to import' is $\frac{1}{10}Y$. We can now treat this import leakage in the same way as saving. Whatever the cause of the initial expansion in Y, leakages occur because some of this increased Y will be saved and some will be spent on imports. Thus, when m represents the *marginal* propensity to import, we have:

change in AD = (change in I + change in exports) $[1/(1 - c + m)]$.

Suppose, for instance, that income is in equilibrium at 10,000. There is no foreign trade, and $C = 6,000$ and $S = 4,000$. At any income above this the marginal propensity to import is $\frac{1}{6}C = \frac{1}{10}Y$. If there are now exports of 2,000, the increase in Y will be 2,000 $1/(\frac{4}{10} + \frac{1}{10}) = 4,000$.

The analysis of this section indicates why, during the 1930s, many countries tried to solve their unemployment problems by pushing exports (which increase income and therefore employment) and by discouraging imports (which decrease income). A little reflection will show, however, that such a restrictionist policy merely 'exports' unemployment to other countries. Nowadays we realise that countries must co-operate with each other in fighting unemployment (*see* pp. 461, 489).

IX. AN EXPLANATION OF THE TRADE CYCLE

So far in this chapter we have been concerned with building up a theoretical model showing how fluctuations in AD (national income) can occur. We must now use this model to explain the phenomenon of the trade cycle and the unemployment connected with it. In particular, the following questions must be answered: (*a*) Why do the upswings and downswings occur? (*b*) Why are they cumulative? (*c*) Why do they eventually come to an end and reverse their direction? (*d*) Why may the boom break before full employment is reached? (*e*) Why are the capital goods industries and export industries more severely hit? (*f*) Why do prices rise in the boom and fall in the depression? (*g*) Why does the cycle last 5 to 9 years? We concentrate our attention on the private sector.

The upswing

Let us start from the bottom of the depression. Until now there has been a cumulative downswing. What causes the upturn? Why does AD begin to increase?

As we have seen, AD can increase because: (*a*) investment, but not saving, increases; (*b*) saving, but not investment, decreases; (*c*) exports increase in value more than imports. All three changes become more likely the lower the level of income falls.

Investment may revive for a variety of reasons. Stocks may have run low. Fixed equipment wears out and replacement cannot be postponed indefinitely. Additional fields of profitable investment arise as, with time, new techniques or even new industries are developed.

Saving decreases because the marginal propensity to consume increases as income falls. People may even spend past savings in order to maintain their standard of living.

Imports tend to fall in value and exports to increase. This occurs because: (a) lower income means a fall in the demand for imports; (b) lower wages and costs, produced eventually by unemployment, lead to lower prices and therefore to increased demand for exports by foreign countries (see p. 484).

But this is not all. When investment increases, the initial effect on AD is magnified by the multiplier. Moreover, a revival in one part of the economy is likely to make entrepreneurs more optimistic elsewhere. They, too, begin to reinvest. The upswing is cumulative.

Added impetus is provided by the accelerator. Until now, entrepreneurs have been reluctant to replace their machinery. Thus the increase in demand for consumer goods finds them short of productive capacity. The acceleration principle shows the marked effect that this has on the capital goods industries. The climb back to greater prosperity gathers momentum as the revival spreads.

The break in the boom

Why should the boom break? The reason is that the increase in AD begins to level off. This happens because both the proportion of income consumed and investment eventually fall.

As income increases, the marginal propensity to consume falls. Not only do people spend a smaller proportion of their income as income rises, but it is likely that more of that income is going to profit-recipients who are likely to spend a smaller proportion of their income than wage-earners. The result is that, unless investment increases to match increased savings as income expands, the expansion in income will come to an end.

But even if there is increasing investment, it is doubtful whether it will be sufficient to maintain the *rate of increase* of AD. If it is not, the accelerator comes into operation. Then the level of investment falls back to where it is just sufficient for replacement purposes only, no additional capacity being required. In addition, new fields of investment, e.g. through the invention of new techniques or the development of new industries, can be expected to become exhausted. There is thus a built-in mechanism which is likely to cause investment to tail off.

But even without this, all types of investment may fall simply because entrepreneurs become less optimistic. Normally this is brought about by the slackening off in demand for the reasons just given. Nevertheless there are other factors at work. When investment is running at a high rate, the confidence of entrepreneurs is vulnerable to even minor setbacks. Capital may prove to be less profitable than expected because it has been invested by different entrepreneurs in competing products so that, in relationship to the total demand, there is over-investment. Or the government, fearing that inflation will develop, raises the rate of interest. While this may have little direct effect on large firms—they can bear the extra cost or expand out of their liquid reserves—they are bound to wonder how it will affect the purchasers of their products. Moreover, when, as in the inter-war period, cyclical fluctuations in the level of activity appear to be inevitable, entrepreneurs' expectations are always more vulnerable to changes in direction than they are today when the government has been fairly successful in maintaining full employment since World War II.

Finally, at some stage in the boom, factors may arise which cause exports to fall or imports to increase. (a) As incomes expand, not only are more imports demanded, but goods which might have been exported are diverted to the home market. (b) The nearer a country approaches full employment, the greater is the tendency for costs and prices to rise (see p. 416). Her exports, therefore, become less competitive. (c) Important buyers of exports may suffer a depression before the home country. As a result, their demand falls. This is particularly serious for a country so dependent on international trade as the United Kingdom. When this happens, AD falls—a slump has been 'imported' (see p. 384). Thus we see that both the depression and the boom contain the seeds of their own destruction.

The downswing

The break in the boom is followed by a downswing which gathers momentum. Falling expenditure in one part of the economy leads to reduced expenditure elsewhere. The multiplier is working in reverse! Pessimistic expectations of entrepreneurs are therefore justified, and the drop to the bottom of the depression is a sharp one. Nor will interest policy prove effective. While a rise in the rate of interest may break a boom, a decrease is unlikely to halt a depression. As expectations of entrepreneurs grow more pessimistic, so the MEI curve falls to the left, and this outweighs any reduction of the rate of interest aimed at restoring investment (see p. 378).

Eventually, however, for the reasons already given, the bottom is reached, and the cycle starts all over again. The cycle varies both in the time taken and its severity.

X. THE CONTROL OF CYCLICAL UNEMPLOYMENT

To eliminate cyclical unemployment, AD must be maintained at an adequate level. For the following reasons, the responsibility for this must rest with the government. First, only the government can exercise the powers, particularly as regards collecting the statistics and information necessary for adequate planning. Secondly, the government's own spending on consumer and investment goods forms such a large proportion (two-fifths) of AD that, to a great extent, it can be used to balance variations in the private sector. Thirdly, the knowledge that the government is committed to a full employment policy will eliminate much of the uncertainty from which cyclical fluctuations begin.

A brief analysis of the task

In order to make our explanation simpler, we shall assume a closed economy.

Employment depends upon the level of national income (Y). If the level of AD is too low, the economy will be in equilibrium where Y is below the full employment level. Thus the government's task is to estimate the level of AD which will produce full employment, and then arrange that AD is increased to this level.

In terms of Fig. 99, this means that the government must increase the size of injections—C, I and G—relative to the size of the leaks—S and T. The multiplier will enlarge any change made to produce a new equilibrium where $AD = Y$. This must be the full employment Y.

The same requirement can also be shown on a 45° diagram

(Fig. 101). Full employment requires Y to equal OE. An AD as shown by $C+I+G'$, however, will produce equilibrium where $Y=OF=OZ$. If we look at the situation from the full employment level of Y there is a deficiency of AD equal to LM—the 'deflationary' gap. The government has to raise the AD curve to $C+I+G$.

Where AD is more than sufficient to produce full employment, $C+I+G''$, there is an inflationary gap, NL. Since output cannot rise above OE, prices rise. The government has to lower the AD curve to $C+I+G$. (The true nature of inflation is examined in Chapter 36.)

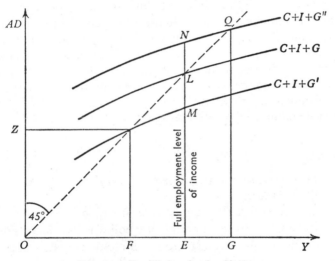

FIG. 101.—Equilibrium levels of income.

The nature of government action

The role of the government in controlling the economy can be likened to that of the driver of a car going to work in a city. At no time can the car run on its own without some direction, and the man at the wheel has to make the necessary adjustments continuously. From time to time, too, he is concerned with more definite alterations, varying his pressure on the accelerator and changing gear. He may even modify his route, making detours to avoid traffic congestion.

But in all these manœuvres, different drivers act differently. Some use the gear lever rather than the accelerator in changing speed. Others estimate that the traffic congestion will not be so bad as to warrant a detour. Nor does the same man do exactly the same things each day. He knows many different routes to work and, being flexible, he makes use of them as he thinks fit.

So it is with the government. Like the driver guessing the traffic congestion along the route, the government has to work from incomplete information in estimating what change in AD is necessary to produce the desired result and the extent to which the measures it adopts will produce that change. It has two main types of control—monetary and fiscal—but it usually has to combine them in different ways. Not only does one reinforce the other, but a different emphasis has to be placed on each at different times in order to meet the needs of the prevailing situation. Where a quick change in the direction or tempo of the economy is required, more weight must be given to those measures which begin to work immediately. Should it be desired, for instance, to increase consumption, it can be achieved much more quickly by reducing taxes than by lowering the rate of interest (to discourage saving).

(1) *Monetary*

Monetary measures are aimed at varying the cost and availability of credit.

The cost of credit is the rate of interest which has to be paid. As we saw in Chapter 23, present-day policy is for the authorities to decide on the overall supply of credit which is appropriate to the economy, and then to allow this supply to be allocated among would-be borrowers by the market rate of interest.

Nevertheless, there are doubts regarding the effectiveness of interest policy in influencing investment, except in so far as it operates on the overall expectations of entrepreneurs or in special circumstances (e.g. long-yielding capital projects). But, apart from being ineffective, interest policy may be undesirable for the following reasons:

(a) raising the rate of interest (especially the short-term rate) puts up the cost of borrowing by Britain abroad, thereby increasing her payments on 'invisibles';

(b) a higher rate of interest increases the cost of internal borrowing, thereby adding to the taxation burden of servicing the National Debt;

(c) the rate of interest does not discriminate in its operation between: (i) firms which export a high proportion of their output and those which do not; (ii) projects of high social value (e.g. slum clearance) and those of less certain merit (e.g. gaming casinos);

(d) in so far as it does have an effect on the level of investment, it may act too slowly, especially when the authorities have failed to check a boom before excess demand has developed.

Even so, interest policy cannot be discarded completely as a weapon for regulating the economy. Although it may be ineffective at the top of the boom or at the bottom of the depression, between these two extremes it can fulfil a useful role both as regards its psychological effects and the increased cost it imposes on certain projects, e.g. long-term investment. Moreover, it can be applied quickly and to a fine degree and, if taken early, can provide advance warning of the authorities' intentions. At times, too, it may be a necessary measure to reverse the outflow of foreign capital.

The availability of credit is concerned with both the overall level of liquidity and selective controls. In the past, controls have been exercised mainly through bank advances and hire purchase.

Banks are 'requested' to discriminate between different types of borrower; for instance, continuing to grant loans to exporting businesses, but refusing credit to firms concerned with property development.

In order to regulate spending on consumer goods, particularly such durables as cars, furniture, refrigerators, and washing-machines, the terms of hire-purchase sales are varied. This policy is quick-acting and normally hits those industries which have expanded most as the result of the inflation. But its value is limited by the following considerations:

(a) It falls almost exclusively on a narrow range of industries. This is unfair, because other forms of spending, e.g. on services, are not penalised in this way.

(b) It dislocates current output of these industries and makes planning for future development difficult. Many of these industries are 'growth' industries, and export a large part of their output. Moreover, inasmuch as they often work under conditions of decreasing cost, restriction of output can lead to higher costs per unit. This may be serious, for the fall in home demand would result in a higher price to export markets.

(c) It may be effective in restricting consumption in the short run, but it does nothing to mop up excess demand, which, in the longer period, is diverted to other goods and services.

(d) In time, sellers invent devices to get round the regulations.

(e) It can lead to a bunching of hire-purchase commitments, repeated at three-year intervals as repayments are completed and new purchases made.

Finally, the government may even restrict capital projects by licensing. This has been applied to the building industry at various times.

The main weakness of selective controls is that they are only really effective when activity is around the full employment level, for they merely vary the ease with which persons can do things they *want* to do. In a depression they do little to revive spending.

(2) *Fiscal*

Indirectly, fiscal policy can influence private consumption and investment by changing the type of taxes levied. Thus a switch from indirect to direct taxation would tend to increase consumption, for it would mean greater spending power for poorer people (those having a high propensity to consume). Similarly, a movement away from taxes on companies would tend to increase investment through improved profitability.

More directly, spending may be influenced by budget policy. Today the budget is regarded, not as the means by which revenue is raised to meet estimated expenditure for the year, but as the weapon to adjust private spending power to the output which can be produced by the resources available. Reducing taxation will increase disposable income. Provided this increase is not all saved, spending will increase (expanding

income according to the multiplier). In terms of Fig. 100, the
C curve will rise. Thus, if government spending remains
unchanged, the curve $C+I+G$ will rise (Fig. 101).

Attention must be paid to the phrase 'if government spending
remains unchanged'. Budgetary policy is essentially one of
adjusting the relationship between government taxation and
expenditure. As we have seen, taxation represents an appro-
priation by the government of a part of private incomes. The
amount so appropriated is retained in the circular flow of
income only in so far as it is spent by the government. Hence
AD will be increased if taxation is less than government
spending, and vice versa. If previously the budget was balanced,
there will now be a budget deficit, and vice versa.

Such a policy is not without its difficulties. The convention
of annual budgets means that major adjustments can be made
only at infrequent intervals, although the 'regulator' does allow
the Chancellor of the Exchequer to vary indirect taxes by 10
per cent at any time. Moreover, reducing taxes may, because
of administrative difficulties, take time to be effective. With
P.A.Y.E., for instance, new tax tables have to be distributed.
Thus reliefs will often have to be concentrated on those items
where extra purchasing power is quickly put into the hands of
consumers, e.g. by reducing national insurance contributions
and indirect taxes. Taxation, too, has objectives other than that
of adjusting AD—redistributing income, for instance. But a rise
in taxation may have to be achieved by increasing indirect
taxes because of possible disincentive effects of high income tax.
Thus policies can conflict. Finally, overall budgetary policy
makes it difficult to direct demand into those districts and
industries where unemployment is highest. Again we see the
necessity of having a variety of measures which can be applied
to the needs of a particular situation.

Nevertheless budgetary policy does allow the national
product to be divided between private and communal uses
according to their relative priorities. There are certain tasks
which can be undertaken better by the state than by private
enterprise, and the government must decide on the proportion
of the national product which shall be devoted to these—defence,
justice, social welfare, roads, health, etc. Thus taxation policy
can be regarded as a means by which private demand is

adjusted to release resources for the needs of the public sector. If there is full employment, excessive private demand will leave insufficient resources to meet the needs of the public sector. Thus taxation must be increased—or public expenditure be reduced. If, on the other hand, private demand is insufficient to employ fully resources which are not required by the public sector, taxation must be reduced. Such a policy means that full employment can be achieved without direction of resources. Once the essential claims of the public sector on the economy have been met, the rest of the national product can be produced through the price system. Thus the main advantages of that system—the efficiency which springs from the profit motive, individual choice, the accurate measurement of consumers' wants, and the provision for those wants—are retained.

CHAPTER 27

REGIONAL AND OCCUPATIONAL UNEMPLOYMENT

I. THE EFFECTS OF THE IMMOBILITY OF LABOUR

The nature of the problem

Even where there is adequate AD, there will still be some unemployment. The reason is that AD is never exactly in line with the resources available. Thus, while in June 1973, the number of persons unemployed was 546,000, there were in existence 419,000 job vacancies.

The reason is that conditions of demand and supply change. Tastes change, incomes rise, foreign competitors produce at a lower price, etc. As a result, demand is buoyant for some goods

TABLE 7

PERCENTAGE RATE OF UNEMPLOYMENT BY REGION, JUNE 1973

United Kingdom	2·4
Region:	
South East	1·3
East Anglia	1·7
South West	2·2
West Midlands	2·0
East Midlands	2·0
Yorks. and Humber	2·6
North West	3·3
North	4·4
Wales	3·3
Scotland	4·3
N. Ireland	5·8

Source: Department of Employment

and slack for others. On the supply side, technological change leads to redundancies. Thus in the United Kingdom since World War II, we have had a buoyant demand for consumer durable goods, services, aircraft, motor vehicles, etc., and a considerably reduced demand for coal, cotton goods, iron and steel, ships, etc. The demand for factors of production is a 'derived' demand; if the demand for a good decreases, the demand for the workers producing that good will also decrease.

Moreover, because of the localisation of industry, these differences in demand relative to resources are carried over into regions, some regions enjoying a high level of economic activity whereas others are depressed. This can be seen from Table 7 where some regions had unemployment rates almost double the national average.

Frictions to the perfect operation of the price system

Theoretically the price system should move those workers who become unemployed to other jobs. The fall in the price of a good through a decrease in demand, and the consequent fall in the demand for the workers producing it, will lead to a relative deterioration in their wages. On the other hand, wages should rise where demand is buoyant (assuming that AD is adequate throughout the economy as a whole). This change in relative wages should have two effects: (*a*) a movement of workers from low-wage to high-wage industries; (*b*) a movement of industries from high-wage to low-wage areas.

While these movements might eventually occur, in practice the time they would take is so long that the free operation of the price system proves to be highly unsatisfactory. Labour cannot move easily from one industry to another because of occupational immobility; it does not move out of the depressed areas because of geographical immobility. Industry does not move into the depressed areas because the unemployed workers do not have the necessary skills, or because the saving in wage costs is not sufficient to offset the higher costs of being separated from main markets or losing other advantages of localisation. Indeed, national wage agreements may mean that there is little difference in the wage rates which have to be paid between one area and another. This elimination of wage differentials undermines the forces which set the price system in motion.

II. GOVERNMENT POLICY

General considerations

In deciding upon specific measures to increase labour mobility, the government must bear in mind the following:

(1) Unemployment arising through immobility is far more difficult to cure when unemployment of a cyclical nature also exists. An unemployed man is much more likely to change his occupation or to move to a new district if he is sure that he will obtain work as a result. But there is no such guarantee when cyclical unemployment is producing a high rate of unemployment, even in the relatively more prosperous areas. Thus in 1932, although the unemployment rate in London was 8·6 per cent below the national average, it was still as high as 13·5 per cent.

(2) On occasions, government interference with the free operation of the price mechanism may add to the problem of immobility. The following are a few examples. High rates of income tax whittle away much of any monetary inducement to move. The higher the rate of unemployment benefit, the less is the incentive to an unemployed worker to seek a job elsewhere. The absence of a free market in rents leads to difficulties in finding accommodation. Uniform, nation-wide wage rates, insisted upon by many trade unions, eliminate the incentive of lower labour costs to firms contemplating building factories in areas of high unemployment. The government must decide the extent to which it is prepared to use the price system as a weapon, since this may clash with some of its social policies.

(3) Usually only a small percentage of the labour force need move out of an area of high unemployment. New industries can be attracted to provide work for the remainder. The younger and more mobile workers are those who should be encouraged to move, but even then only when it is absolutely necessary, for their loss does tend to depress the area still further.

(4) Many changes of both occupation and area occur in a series of 'ripples'. Thus an agricultural labourer may move to road construction to take the place of the Irish labourer who transfers to the building industry.

(5) Government measures take time to become effective. Hence instead of relying on special measures once unemployment has become a problem, there should be a continuous policy of bringing greater diversity to those areas mainly dependent on one or two industries.

Specific measures to improve occupational mobility

The government's first task must be to improve occupational mobility. Entry into certain occupations should be made less difficult. Here the government can give information on opportunities in other industries and occupations and use its influence to persuade trade unions to modify their regulations concerning the length of apprenticeship to be served and the maximum number of apprentices who can be taken on in a year.

But the main objective must be to ensure that people are trained in the new skills required by light engineering as opposed to heavy industry. The government has set up over fifty Government Training Centres to provide courses in skilled trades for the unemployed. Wage-related financial benefits are given, together with travel and lodging allowances. In practice, however, the unemployed have been slow to avail themselves of these courses. The major objective of lump-sum redundancy payments introduced in 1966 is to encourage workers to change jobs when their particular skills are no longer required. In the longer period, the problem can be tackled by seeing that school-leavers are adequately advised on career prospects and by ensuring that recruits to the expanding industries are fully trained. As regards the latter, the Industrial Training Act, 1964, provided for industrial training boards to review training in their respective industries, to pay grants for approved courses, and to impose levies on employers to spread the cost.

Measures for dealing with geographical immobility

Obstacles to geographical mobility are more difficult to overcome. Where a whole area is 'depressed', the government can give first aid by placing its contracts there, e.g. for ships, and awarding it priority for public-works programmes— schools, new roads, hospitals, etc. In the long period, however, it must take measures which will on the one hand encourage the outward movement of workers, and on the other induce firms to move in to employ those workers who find it difficult to move.

The first group of measures—'*taking workers to the work*'—consists of granting financial aid towards moving costs, providing information on prospects in other parts of the country, and removing artificial barriers, such as the shortage of housing accommodation. At present, workers who maintain dependants at home can draw a boarding allowance for twelve months. Free fares to a place of work away from the home town can also be given, and if it is necessary for a worker to buy a house, a part of the solicitors' and agents' fees can be met.

The second policy—'*taking work to the workers*'—is now regarded as the real long-term solution. It avoids forcing workers to move out of areas to which they are attached, relieves the growing congestion in the Midlands and South-East England, and prevents depopulation of districts in the North, with the loss of 'social capital' which this involves. Above all, it must be remembered that the 'multiplier' (which we examined in the previous chapter) operates for regions in much the same way as it does for countries. Thus moving unemployed workers and their families out of depressed areas reduces spending in the area, the incomes of retailers, for instance, falling. We thus have the multiplier working in reverse to make the region still further depressed.

On the other hand, it must be remembered that this may involve firms in higher costs. Their desire to establish plant in the South-East is to secure advantages of localisation, such as a supply of skilled workers or close contact with customers on the Continent.

To move young expanding firms into the depressed areas, the government may use either the carrot or the big stick. So far it has concentrated on the former, though there has been some oblique compulsion through planning requirements.

The carrot must compensate firms for the extra costs incurred by virtue of an inferior location. The Industry Act, 1972, extended the areas where preferential assistance is given by the government to encourage industrial development (Fig. 102).

There are three different categories of Assisted Area: *Special Development Areas*, where the need for jobs is most acute,

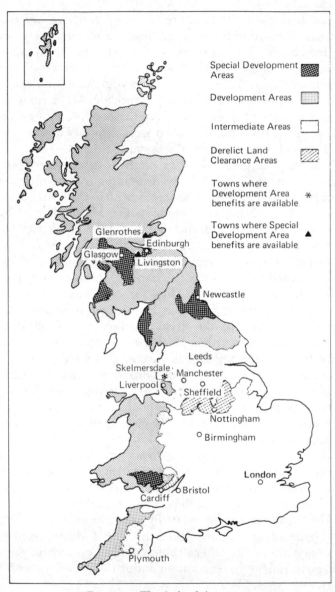

FIG. 102.—The Assisted Areas, 1973.

Development Areas and *Intermediate Areas*. All these areas are suffering from the same sort of problems, though in varying degree. The extent of the financial help available for new industrial projects in the different categories of area varies according to need. In addition, there are the *Derelict Land Clearance Areas* which are receiving some of the help available in the Intermediate Areas for a limited period of two years.

A firm re-locating in one of the Assisted Areas is eligible for a wide range of financial incentives, the most important of which are:

(1) *Regional Development Grants* as follows:

	Plant, machinery, and mining works (%)	Buildings (%)
Special Development Areas	22	22
Development Areas	20	20
Intermediate Areas	—	20
Derelict Land Clearance Areas (for two years only)	—	20

These new grants are not limited to projects creating employment, and so will be available to help with improvements and modernisation. In addition, they are not treated as reducing the capital expenditure which qualifies for capital allowances for tax purposes.

(2) *Removal grants* of up to 80 per cent for certain costs incurred in moving to a Special Development Area or Development Area.

(3) *Loans at favourable rates or interest relief* for projects which reduce unemployment.

(4) *Government factories* for sale or to rent on favourable terms.

(5) A *Regional Employment Premium* of £1·50 per week for adult male employees in a manufacturing establishment in a Special Development Area or Development Area, with lower rates for women and young persons.

(6) *Help for transferring key workers* essential to setting up a new plant.

All the above are in addition to the investment incentives available to manufacturing and service industries throughout the whole country. These include a 100 per cent first-year depreciation allowance for investment in plant and machinery, and a 40 per cent tax allowance on new industrial buildings.

The Department of Trade and Industry also controls three Industrial Estates Corporations which supervise over fifty government-sponsored industrial estates in England, Wales and Scotland. Similare schemes operate in Northern Ireland, where much use is made of advertising the advantages of the region—a plentiful supply of labour, recreational facilities for workers, lower living costs, etc.

Through its planning powers the government can indirectly use some compulsion. Consent of the local planning authority is necessary for any new building or addition to an existing building. Where this involves the creation of industrial floor-space of more than 15,000 square feet (10,000 in South-East England), an industrial development certificate is also required from the Department of Trade and Industry to the effect that the proposal is consistent with the proper distribution of industry, especially as regards the level of employment in the region. These certificates are generally freely available in the Intermediate Areas and are not necessary in the Special Development Areas or Development Areas. Similar controls now operate for office development of over 10,000 square feet in the South-East England region.

In the dispersal of industry the government has set an example whenever possible. Thus the Department of Health and Social Security is centred in Newcastle, and branches of the Department of Inland Revenue have been moved to Wales. The official Location of Offices Bureau provides information about the advantages of areas seeking to attract new office development.

Regional planning

While development area policy deals with special districts needing extra help, the whole country is now divided into ten regions (eight for England and one each for Scotland and Wales), for each of which there is planning on a broad scale as regards the distribution of labour, the diversification of industry and the rate of growth. Primary responsibility, not only for national economic planning but for regional development, lies with the Department of Trade and Industry. In 1972 a Minister for Industrial Development was appointed, responsible for the private sector of industry generally and also for industrial development in the Assisted Areas.

The Department's regional organisation has also been strengthened. *Regional Industrial Development Boards* have been set up in the seven regions requiring most assistance. These Boards advise generally on applications for selective financial assistance for the development of industry in their regions.

Each region still has an Economic Planning Council and an Economic Planning Board. The first consists of people with industrial, commercial and local government experience or who are associated with the universities, etc. Its task is to help in the formulation of regional plans, having regard to the region's resources, and to advise on the regional implications of national economic policies. The second, the Board, consists of civil servants from the main government departments concerned with regional planning. Its task is to help the Council in formulating plans and to co-ordinate the work of the various government departments concerned. As far as possible, the members are brought together in one building.

Present policy seems to be moving away from the idea of help to districts towards planning for larger areas, each with a sound infrastructure of public amenities and a much broader-based industrial structure.

CHAPTER 28

THE LEVEL OF PRICES

THE prices of goods can, as we have seen, rise or fall relatively to each other owing to changes in demand or supply. At times, however, it is observed that the prices of all goods generally are rising or falling, apart from variations in their relative prices. We say then that there is a rise or fall in the general level of prices, or, what is the same thing, a fall or rise respectively in the value of money. It is this problem of the general level of prices which we left when discussing the trade cycle. We must therefore return to the questions: Why do prices tend to rise in the boom and fall in the depression? Why is there an upward movement of prices as full employment is approached? We shall start by looking at the views of the classical economists.

I. THE QUANTITY THEORY OF MONEY

On many occasions in the past, a rise in the general level of prices has been associated with an increase in the supply of money. From this simple relationship the Quantity Theory of Money was derived—an attempt to explain changes in the general level of prices by reference to changes in the quantity of money in circulation.

In its simplest form the theory merely states that the general level of prices will depend upon the amount of money in circulation. An increase will raise prices, a decrease will lower them. Usually, however, it goes further, asserting that the general level of prices varies positively and proportionately with the amount of money in circulation. Thus, if money in circulation is doubled, the general level of prices will double.

The Fisher Equation

But the crude version of the theory fails to see that the volume of goods exchanged against money can alter and that, over a given period, the same amount of money may be used many times to finance different transactions. For example, if each £1 of a total sum of £10 is used on average ten times over a certain period, then in practice that £10 does the work of £100 where each £1 is used only once.

To allow for these refinements, Professor Irving Fisher, at the beginning of the twentieth century, expressed the theory in a more precise form: provided there is a constant volume of goods and that the rate at which money circulates remains constant, an increase or decrease in the quantity of money will result in a proportionate increase or decrease respectively in the general level of prices.

More usually the theory is expressed in the Fisher Equation. If, over a given period of time, M represents the amount of money (coin, notes and bank deposits) available to make payments; V, the velocity of circulation, the average number of times each unit of money changes hands in carrying out transactions; T, the volume of transactions, the total quantity of goods and services exchanges against money; and P, the general level of prices, we have: $P = MV/T$.

Criticisms of the Fisher Equation

If we are just concerned with the Fisher Equation as a statement of fact, there is nothing to quarrel with, for it is merely a tautology. The equation could be written $MV = PT$ but this does not tell us much. The two sides are equal *by definition!* MV, the amount of money in circulation multiplied by the number of times each unit changes hands, is merely the *expenditure* by buyers on goods and services over a given period. Similarly, PT, the average price of goods multiplied by the volume of goods, is simply the *receipts* of sellers. But expenditure on goods bought *must* be the same as receipts from goods sold. Thus MV and PT are simply different ways of expressing the same thing.

Nevertheless, the equation, although tautological, is useful in that it separates and concentrates attention on the three variables which are important in determining the price level.

When, however, the equation goes further and, as shown above, is put in the form of a *theory* to *explain* changes in the price level, it is open to fundamental criticism. It is possible to express it as a theory only if V and T are assumed to be constant. Can we make this assumption? If not, the theory has no validity.

If we are concerned with movements over fairly long periods, 25 years or so, we should find a fairly steady average V and a steady gentle upward rise in T. Given this relative constancy, therefore, changes in M can explain the historical movement in the price level.

But what of the short period and changes in the price level associated with the trade cycle? Here we are up against the difficulty that, in different phases of the trade cycle, V and T may both vary considerably.

Consider an economy which is experiencing a slump. The authorities attempt to encourage spending by buying securities on the open market, reinforcing this by lowering the bank rate. The effect of these moves is to lower interest rates and, by increasing the cash reserves of the banks, make more credit available. But is this increase in M bound to result in increased spending by businessmen? The answer is: only if they are sufficiently optimistic; and, in times of depression, they may be unwilling to borrow at *any* rate of interest. If so, the increase in M has no effect. In terms of the Quantity Theory, what has happened is that V has fallen, for more money is held idle. MV remains unchanged, and so there is no rise in P.

But ignoring this difficulty, let us assume that businessmen do increase their borrowing when, following open market operations, the banks offer more and cheaper credit. M has now increased, and so has MV (total spending). But will P increase? Again, not necessarily. So long as there are considerable unused resources (men and machines) in the economy, the increased spending is more likely to stimulate output than prices. In terms of the Quantity Theory, as MV increases T increases. Thus P remains unchanged. It is only likely to rise as resources become fully employed. Thus, for there to be any close relationship between increases in M and increases in P, it is necessary to assume full employment.

Even then a further complication may arise. Can we now

assume V remains constant as M increases? The answer is 'no'. Once full employment has been reached, any increase in M which produced a rise in P might so increase V (through expectations) that further rises in P result. That is, P rises relatively more than the increase in M. Indeed the situation could develop into hyper-inflation.

Thus we must conclude that the Quantity Theory cannot adequately explain the short-period changes in the price level associated with the trade cycle. Its weakness is that, in seeking to show a direct causal connection between the quantity of money and the level of prices, it oversimplifies. First, by concentrating on the supply of money, it assumes away the demand for it. As a result, it fails to ask: 'Can V be accepted as a constant?' Secondly, by paying insufficient attention to the level of activity, it fails to distinguish between conditions of full employment and those of less than full employment. Finally, from the aspect of policy, it is misleading. In attributing some kind of *direct* influence upon the price level to changes in the quantity of money, the theory suggests that an anti-inflationary policy need consist of little more than mere control of the supply of money. Now there are dangers in the government's increasing the money supply, and the theory draws attention to them. But what is of real significance to the price level is not the quantity of money in existence, but the amount of money offered against goods over a period—in other words, AD.

This means that rising and falling prices are corollaries of changes in the level of activity. Hence any explanation of changes in the price level must be obtained indirectly by looking at what determines changes in the level of output. Only the Keynesian approach can deal adequately with this.

II. THE RELATIONSHIP OF AD, THE LEVEL OF ACTIVITY AND THE PRICE LEVEL

Price rises as full employment is approached

Keynes explains the general level of prices as part of his theory of the determination of the level of activity (outlined in Chapter 26). At different stages in the level of activity, the price level moves differently.

Let us start from the position where AD is at a low level. Here there is a high rate of unemployment, and it is possible that there has been some fall in prices—particularly of primary products (foodstuffs and raw materials) where supply is inelastic. But manufactured goods may also have fallen in price. Production is concentrated on the more efficient workers, raw materials cost less, money wages may have fallen with decreased bargaining power. In addition, manufacturers may be forced to produce where prices do little more than cover variable costs.

As AD expands, these influences will be reversed, and prices may rise to their pre-depression level. But the general picture is one of increased spending being matched by increased output as unemployed resources come into production. The price level, therefore, tends to remain steady.

This situation continues until full employment is approached. When the unemployment rate drops below 5 per cent approximately, output does not increase at the same rate as AD. For one thing, less efficient labour and capital have to be employed; for another, bottlenecks occur through the immobility of factors of production. The last is very important; raw materials and components are not available, skilled labour takes time to train. Bottlenecks mean that the law of diminishing returns comes into operation, and marginal costs rise steeply. The dropping-off in output relative to AD finds its outlet in higher prices, and the rate of the price rise increases as lower levels of unemployment are approached.

Inflation

But when full employment is achieved, a vastly different situation arises. Now any increase in AD can, by definition, no longer bring forth additional output. Yet the increase in AD must have an outlet somewhere, and so it simply bids up prices. At this stage, Keynes says, we have true inflation—*AD is more than sufficient to purchase the full-employment output at current prices.*

To discover the causes of inflation, therefore, we have to ask why AD should increase beyond the full-employment level. Further, since the government is now responsible for the level of AD, why does it find it difficult to prevent the excess? The basic reasons are the unpredictability of spending decisions and the pressure exerted by trade unions.

Spending can be by households on consumption, by firms on

investment, or by the government. Households may increase their spending by drawing on money balances, obtaining credit (largely through hire-purchase), or through tax reductions. Firms may increase their investment spending when their

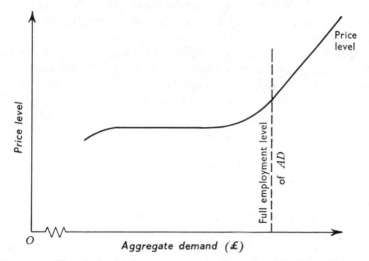

FIG. 103.—The relationship between aggregate demand and the level of prices.

expectations improve or when they can obtain credit. As we have seen, entrepreneurs' decisions are particularly difficult to forecast. The government may increase its own spending by creating money. If full employment has been reached and private spending continues to increase (without any corresponding decrease in government spending), the additional AD simply drives up prices. We have what has been termed 'demand-pull' inflation, prices being 'pulled up' by the extra AD.

In recent years, however, the increase in AD has originated also in the demands for wage increases by organised labour. A high level of employment puts the trade unions in a strong bargaining position. Today, yearly increases in wages have come to be expected, even though there may have been no increase in productivity. Generally speaking, employers do not resist such demands, for they feel that the increases can be passed on in higher prices. In practice their expectations are justified for, unless the government checks the financing of the rise in wages, the higher wages themselves provide the expenditure which is necessary to justify the entrepreneurs' higher costs. We have here what has been termed a 'cost-push' inflation for prices are being 'pushed up' by an initial increase in costs. Alternatively, 'cost-push' inflation may occur through an increase in the price of imported foodstuffs or raw materials, either as a result of changes in demand or supply, or through devaluation.

The nature of such an inflationary situation is shown in Fig. 101. If total expenditure is shown by the $C+I+G''$ curve, AD equals QG. But to maintain full employment, only LE is necessary. There is thus an inflationary gap equal to NL. The government must reduce consumption, investment and its own spending to the $C+I+G$ curve which cuts the 45° line at L.

A note on inflation as a process

The above analysis, while stressing the crucial point in the expansion of AD, that is full employment, oversimplifies the problem of inflation. It tends to suggest that the objectives of full employment and a stable price level can be achieved simultaneously without much difficulty. Policy simply has to aim at finding the full employment level of AD and limiting the expansion to that. In practice, however, prices start to rise when there is still some 5 per cent unemployment; that is, full employment is not a point, but a zone. Cost-push, rather than demand-pull, may be the main initiating force once prices begin to rise. The initial price rises then generate further increases in AD, as higher wages, etc., are paid by entrepreneurs.

And so it continues—the spiral of inflation. Thus, instead of inflation being a condition of excess demand at the full employment level, it is a process. And, as the United Kingdom has discovered since World War II, the remedy is not a simple piece of surgery to remove excess fat, but rather a fight against a cancerous growth (*see* Chapter 36).

III. THE EFFECTS OF CHANGES IN THE LEVEL OF PRICES

We shall concentrate on the effects of rising prices for this is the situation which has prevailed in the United Kingdom since World War II.

Internal effects

The effects of inflation on the internal situation in an economy are mixed. At first sight, some appear to be beneficial; but such a view may disappear upon closer examination.

First, rising prices may make the task of the government in maintaining full employment easier. By improving the climate for investment, AD remains high.

Secondly, rising prices may be conducive to growth. Buoyant demand for labour is likely to increase the labour supply through overtime working and the entry of married women. Moreover, with no fear of the sack, workers may forsake restrictive practices. In addition, investment and innovation by entrepreneurs may be encouraged.

Now while there may have been something in the above two arguments in the 1930s when unemployment was at a high level and remedies for curing it were unknown, the use of rising prices today as a means of encouraging a high level of AD cannot be accepted. Indeed, because of the detrimental effects, chiefly external but also internal, such a policy is largely self-defeating.

For one thing, where inflation arises from increased consumption or government spending, investment may have to be restricted. For another, persistent inflation tends to encourage inefficiency. A buoyant seller's market means that competition loses its edge, for higher prices allow even the inefficient firms to compete and survive. Entrepreneurs are also able to hoard factors and, with plenty of vacant jobs available elsewhere, workers may not work so efficiently or may simply switch jobs for the sake of change.

Furthermore, inflation results in an arbitrary redistribution of income. People on fixed incomes lose—often those people, e.g. pensioners and retired persons, least able to bear it. Those who can adjust incomes reasonably quickly in the face of rising prices, e.g. strong trade unionists and profit-takers, can hold their own or even gain. Similarly, those who have lent on fixed money terms lose; debtors gain. Thus the stability upon which all lending and borrowing depends is undermined. Money rates of interest tend to rise (since lenders require a higher yield to offset the fall in the real value of their capital). For a time the government as the largest debtor gains, for inflation reduces the real burden of servicing the national debt. Suppose, for instance, interest payable is £800 million a year. When the money national income is £24,000 million, one-thirtieth has to be raised by taxation to cover it. If inflation increases the money national income to £32,000, then only one-fortieth is needed. Alternatively, the government could increase its own expenditure without raising tax rates!

It should be noted, too, that the longer rising prices continue, the more difficult is the government's task of bringing the rise under control. Asking for a wage-rise becomes an annual habit of the trade unions, and one which can lead to industrial unrest. Moreover, when people become 'inflation-conscious', they are less willing to buy fixed-interest bearing securities, and may even save less. Indeed, if the price rise gathers momentum, hyper-inflation becomes a possibility.

External effects

Inflation can create serious difficulties for a country dependent on international trade, as Britain has discovered over the past twenty years. Where the level of domestic prices rises relatively to those of foreign competitors in world markets, there are repercussions on the balance of payments. Imports of consumer goods rise, as they become more competitive with home goods and as money incomes rise. Exports are discouraged by being relatively dearer and because manufacturers find it easy to sell on the buoyant home market. This may lead to balance of payments difficulties, and the government is forced to act to check the inflation. The nature of this action in the context of the United Kingdom is discussed in Chapter 36.

IV. A NOTE ON MEASURING CHANGES IN THE GENERAL LEVEL OF PRICES

The difficulty in measuring changes in the general level of prices (that is, in the value of money) is that different kinds of prices—wholesale prices, retail prices, security prices, import prices, etc.—change differently. If we tried to measure changes in all prices, therefore, our task would be stupendous. But more than that, it would lack practical significance. Suppose, for instance, that security prices rose considerably, other prices remaining unchanged. A measurement of the general level of prices would show a rise, but this would be of little interest to the ordinary working man who owned no securities.

When measuring changes in the value of money, therefore, it is usual to concentrate on changes in the prices of those goods which are of most general significance—the goods bought by the majority of people, for it is upon the prices of these that the cost of living really depends.

Method of measuring changes in the value of money

Since we are mainly interested in the extent to which the value of money has altered between one date and another, it can be measured as a relative change by means of an *index number*. The steps are as follows:

(*a*) A base year is selected.

(*b*) In order to ensure that the same goods are valued over the period under consideration, a 'basket' of goods, based on the current spending habits of the 'typical' family (at present where the head has a gross income of up to £66 a week) is chosen.

(*c*) The basket is valued at base-year prices, and expressed as 100.

(*d*) The same basket is revalued at current prices.

(*e*) The cost of the current basket is then expressed as a percentage of the base year. Thus if the cost of living had risen by 5 per cent, the index for the current year would be 105.

In practice, the prices of the selected goods are compared, their percentage changes being 'weighted' according to the relative expenditure on the particular commodity in the base year. Suppose, for instance, that there are only two commodities, bread and meat, upon which income is spent. The index between two years is calculated as follows on page 422. The price in year II is expressed as a percentage of the price in year I. It is then multiplied by the appropriate weight to give a 'weighted price relative'. These weighted price relatives are then totalled and divided by the total of the weights to give the new index number.

		YEAR I				YEAR II	
	Price	Units bought	Expend-iture	Weight	Price	Year II as % of Year I	Weighted price relative
Bread	10p	5	50p	10	15p	150	1500
Meat	50p	11	550p	110	60p	120	13200
				120		120)14700	
							122·5

Index

Year I (base)   100
Year II   122·5

Difficulties in calculating index numbers

The method outlined above of calculating changes in the value of money has obvious snags:

(1) The basket and the weighting are merely an arbitrary average. Different income groups have widely different baskets, and even within the same group the amount spent on each good varies. Thus a change in the Cost of Living Index (officially, the Index of Retail Prices) does not affect all people equally.

(2) The basket becomes more unreal the further we move from the base year. For instance, an increase in income gives a different pattern of expenditure, new goods are produced and the quality of goods changes, and spending is varied according to relative price changes.

The Index of Retail Prices tries to surmount this defect by revising the weights each January on the basis of the Family Expenditure Survey for the previous three years. The index figure for the year is then calculated at current prices (January = 100) and then 'linked' to the main base date (16 January 1962) by multiplying the main index figure by the proportionate change in the year. The result is a continuous index of retail prices from 1962.

(3) Technical difficulties arise both in choosing the base year and in collecting information. Thus the base year may prove to be somewhat abnormal because of a particularly high birth rate, while the establishment of supermarkets may upset standardised methods of collecting prices.

Thus an Index of Retail Prices is merely an indication of changes in the cost of living. But if we bear its limitations in mind, it is the most useful measurement we have of changes in the value of money.

CHAPTER 29

GOVERNMENT FINANCE

I. GOVERNMENT EXPENDITURE

Limits to government spending

TODAY taxation takes about 35 per cent of the gross national product—a remarkable increase over the last sixty years. Even Lloyd George's famous budget of 1910 sought to produce only £200 million, about 10 per cent of the national income. The pressure on the government is always to spend more, not less. Today people demand a full range of government activities.

But this does not mean that the government can curry favour with the electorate by a continuous increase in its spending. Goods and services in the economy as a whole are limited. In practice, therefore, the government is in the same position as everybody else. It can only secure more of the goods and services by allowing the private sector less.

Many items of government expenditure, e.g. retirement pensions, interest on the National Debt, grants to local authorities, are impossible to avoid; by nature they are basically contractual. It may seem, therefore, that the government has merely to estimate its expenditure and then impose taxes to cover it. But this is not the case. Contractual items of government expenditure may be likened to the outgoings of the ordinary individual on necessities—rent, food, fuels, etc. 'Cutting one's coat according to one's cloth' takes place at the margin on such items as a new television set, a longer holiday, or a larger car. So it is with the government. How much can we afford for the Arts Council? How much can we give to sport? Can university education be expanded this year? Can we reduce National Insurance contributions? The economic problem confronts everybody, private persons and the government alike. In the last resort, how the national product is to be divided between the public and private sectors is a political decision.

The distribution of national expenditure

Government spending can be classified under the following headings:

(1) *Defence*. Defence, which must be given priority, is today largely determined by treaty commitments, e.g. NATO, SEATO. Spending on it accounts for one-eighth of all government spending.

(2) *Internal security*. This covers spending on the police, law enforcement and the fire brigades.

(3) *Social responsibilities*. Provision must be made for the adequate education of citizens, and some protection must be afforded against the hazards of sickness, unemployment and old age by means of the health services, unemployment benefits and pensions.

(4) *Economic policy*. The government is now responsible for maintaining a high and stable level of employment, and for securing a steady growth of the national product. It grants subsidies to agriculture and industry, gives help to areas of high unemployment, trains workers, and sets up Employment Exchanges. Most of the capital requirements of the nationalised industries are now provided by the Treasury.

(5) *Miscellaneous*. The largest single item under this heading is interest on the National Debt, but there is also expenditure on colonies and the consular services, and grants to local authorities.

How government expenditure is financed

In the same way that firms have to pay for both variable and fixed factors, so the government has to spend not only on recurrent, one-use goods and services, but on goods whose services are rendered over a long period. Regular yearly expenditure, charged on the Consolidated Fund, should be met out of regular yearly income. But capital spending (charged on the National Loans Fund), on such items as roads, loans to the nationalised industries, colonial development, etc., is more fairly financed by borrowing. These projects render services over a period of years, and it would be unjust if they had to be paid for in the year in which they were completed. Instead, if they are financed by borrowing, interest and capital can be repaid in the future, thereby allowing the burden to be shared by all persons receiving benefits from them.

Current expenditure is met from two main sources:

(1) Miscellaneous receipts, chiefly interest on loans, rents on Crown Lands, and charges on goods and services (such as the charge on prescriptions and for dental treatment).

(2) Taxation, described in more detail later.

Capital expenditure is mostly met by government borrowing, although since the war 'budget surpluses' have provided a larger proportion.

Government borrowing takes the form of:

(1) *Short-term loans.* These loans are mostly obtained by the sale of Treasury Bills. Originally Treasury Bills were used to bridge the time-gap between expenditure and receipts from taxation, but later they became a major means of government borrowing, because it is cheaper to borrow short than long. Nevertheless, inflationary effects resulted, and in recent years the government has had to follow a 'funding' policy, converting short-term into long-term debt (*see* Chapter 23).

(2) *Medium- and long-term loans.* These are represented by stock having a minimum currency of five years. They include undated stocks, such as 3½ per cent War Loan, which since 1951 have fallen in value as the rate of interest has risen.

(3) *'Non-market' borrowing* through National Savings Certificates, Premium Savings Bonds, etc., and the deposits of the National Savings Bank and Trustee Savings Banks.

II. THE MODERN APPROACH TO TAXATION

Taxation and government policy

Until the end of the nineteenth century, the functions of the state were concerned mainly with defence and law and order. Taxation was levied primarily for revenue purposes, those taxes regulating trade having been abolished in the previous century.

To meet the vast increase in government spending over the last fifty years, higher rates of taxation have been imposed and new taxes introduced. These additions have, as we shall see, provided new means for promoting economic and social policies. Briefly, by its fiscal measures, the government can:

(1) *Exercise an overall control of the economy*, mainly with the object of achieving full employment. To secure this, the government:

(a) adjusts individual taxes in order to influence consumption, saving, and investment;

(b) varies the relationship between its own expenditure and revenue through a budget surplus or deficit.

Both were discussed in Chapter 26.

(2) *Promote economic growth*, by such measures as giving generous investment allowances for taxation purposes.

(3) *Modify the influence of the price system*, in order to:

(a) protect an 'infant' industry;

(b) develop a vital industry;

(c) cushion the impact on an industry of fundamental changes in the conditions of demand and supply;

(d) increase trade with the E.E.C.;

(e) improve the terms of trade by levying an import duty on goods whose supply is less elastic than the demand for them;

(f) improve the balance of payments by imposing duties to restrict imports.

These points are discussed in Chapter 30.

(g) compensate for social costs and social benefits, e.g. protecting health by taxing cigarettes.

(4) *Achieve greater equality in the distribution of wealth and income.*

(5) *Secure minor objectives*, such as increasing individual responsibility for government (by ensuring that everybody pays some tax).

The attributes of a good tax system

In his *Wealth of Nations*, Adam Smith was able to confine his principles of taxation to four simple canons. Stated briefly, these were: persons should pay according to their ability; the tax should be certain and clear to everybody concerned; the convenience of the contributor should be studied as regards payment; the cost of collection should be small relative to yield.

While today the main purpose of any tax is usually to raise money, the additional uses of taxation have rendered Adam

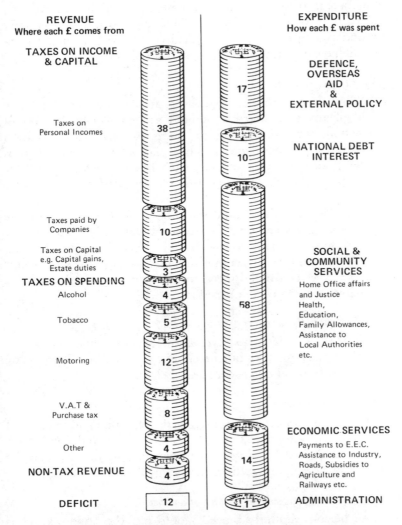

REVENUE
Where each £ comes from

TAXES ON INCOME
& CAPITAL

Taxes on
Personal Incomes — 38

Taxes paid by
Companies — 10

Taxes on Capital
e.g. Capital gains,
Estate duties — 3

TAXES ON SPENDING
Alcohol — 4

Tobacco — 5

Motoring — 12

V.A.T &
Purchase tax — 8

Other — 4

NON-TAX REVENUE — 4

DEFICIT — 12

EXPENDITURE
How each £ was spent

DEFENCE,
OVERSEAS
AID
&
EXTERNAL POLICY — 17

NATIONAL DEBT
INTEREST — 10

SOCIAL &
COMMUNITY
SERVICES
Home Office affairs
and Justice
Health,
Education,
Family Allowances,
Assistance to
Local Authorities
etc. — 58

ECONOMIC SERVICES
Payments to E.E.C.
Assistance to Industry,
Roads, Subsidies to
Agriculture and
Railways etc. — 14

ADMINISTRATION — 1

FIG. 104.—Government revenue and expenditure, 1973–4.

Source: compiled from *National Income and Expenditure Blue Book*, 1974,
and the *Annual Financial Statement*, 1973.

Smith's maxims inadequate. Indeed, objects other than revenue may take priority. Thus when the purchase tax was introduced in 1940 it was primarily to discourage spending and only secondarily to raise revenue. Ideally, therefore, a modern tax would have a variety of attributes. It should be:

(1) *Productive of revenue*

All taxes cost money to collect and are unpopular. The yield of any tax, therefore, should at least cover the cost of collection, with something to spare to offset the vexation caused. In practice, too, a single tax with a high yield is better than a number of taxes each having a small yield, for the latter make the tax structure complicated and not easily understood.

Normally, too, the Chancellor should be able to estimate the yield of a tax with a fair degree of accuracy. This is particularly important if the budget is to be used for the purpose of adjusting overall demand. In this connection it is useful to the Chancellor if some taxes can be adjusted to produce an immediate yield, or, if lowered, afford an immediate relief.

(2) *Certain to the taxpayer*

Not only should a taxpayer know exactly when and where he has to pay his tax, but he should find it difficult to evade payment. Indirect taxes score heavily here.

(3) *Convenient to the contributor*

Bad debts and evasion are reduced if the time and manner of tax payment are related to how people receive and spend their incomes. Thus it is convenient to pay income tax through the P.A.Y.E. system, and indirect taxes when goods are bought.

(4) *Impartial between one person and another*

All persons similarly placed should pay the same tax. Thus while non-smokers do not pay the selective tax on tobacco, all smokers do.

Yet, although there is impartiality in this sense, the old concentration of indirect taxes on a few goods—chiefly tobacco, alcoholic drink and motoring—did penalise severely certain forms of spending. Thus a person who obtained most of his pleasure from cycling and dining-out received many benefits from state expenditure, benefits which are largely paid for by his smoking, drinking and car-driving neighbour! One of the objects of introducing VAT was to broaden the tax base.

(5) *Adjustable*

A tax should be capable of variation, both up and down, according to changes in policy.

(6) *Automatic in stabilising the economy*

Varying the relationship between government expenditure and revenue is one of the major weapons for keeping the economy on an even keel—with full employment but a stable price level. Indeed, today a main object of taxation additional to raising revenue is to vary the amount of purchasing power in the hands of the public. Usually the Chancellor of the Exchequer has to make a deliberate adjustment in his budget, but it would be helpful if taxes could operate automatically in the required direction.

To some extent they do. Thus when money income increases, so does the yield from both income tax and VAT. This has a disinflationary effect. The opposite occurs when money income decreases.

(7) *Unharmful to effort and initiative*

This attribute has become of increasing importance with the growth of direct taxation. High rates of income tax, for instance, may induce the taxpayer to take his income in the form of leisure or reduce his willingness to undergo training or to seek promotion.

However, in practice there is little statistical evidence to support this view. Where a person has fixed money commitments, e.g. hire-purchase instalments, mortgage repayments, school fees, and insurance premiums, he may be compelled to work *harder* in order to meet them when his income is reduced. Furthermore, if we assume that high income tax is a disincentive to effort, we infer that persons always look upon work as distasteful and leisure as a pleasurable alternative. This may be true with the majority, but among the high-income brackets there are many who work because they derive enjoyment from it. Lastly, we have to remember that most people are not free to vary their hours of work except as regards overtime. The normal working week is often an agreement on a national basis between trade unions and employers' associations.

The disincentive effect is more likely to occur when there is a sudden jump in the rate of tax between one income level and another. People reduce their effort at the higher-taxed income level. This is a psychological reaction, for they are not forced to consider whether their standard of living will fall—as happens when there is a general rise in the rate of tax. In other words, the disincentive occurs when the marginal rate of tax exceeds the average rate.

Even with indirect taxes, care must be taken that certain 'incentive goods'—cars, washing-machines, deep-freezers, dish-washers, etc.—are not taxed so heavily that they are priced beyond the reach of persons who would otherwise work overtime in order to secure them.

High direct taxes can also affect enterprise and efficiency. A higher money reward is usually necessary to induce a person to devote time to training and study or to incur the cost of moving a home to secure promotion. It follows, therefore, that where the wage differential between skilled and unskilled labour is eroded by income tax, incentives are proportionately reduced. Similarly, entrepreneurs are only prepared to accept risks if the rewards are commensurate. Direct taxes, therefore, act as a brake on the initiative of workers and on the willingness of entrepreneurs to accept risks.

On the other hand, high taxation of profits and income means that the penalty of inefficiency is not borne entirely by shareholders for a large part falls on the government through loss of revenue.

(8) Consistent with government policy

While the tax structures should not be subject to frequent change, individual taxes must be constantly reviewed to see how they could be used to promote government policy or to prevent their working out of harmony with it. In reaching its decision, the government has to consider the balance of advantage, setting off any loss of revenue against expected gains. It must have in mind such problems as: What tax reliefs should be given to exporters? Should rates be reduced (instead of increased as at present) for people who relieve road congestion by building their own garages? Should the income from work be taxed at a lower rate than investment income to encourage effort? Will an indirect tax, by raising the cost of living, increase wage-push inflation?

Indirect taxes can be made adaptable to specific objectives of policy, e.g. cigarettes bear a selective tax and exports are zero-rated under VAT.

(9) *Minimal in its effect on the optimum allocation of resources*

The imposition of an indirect tax on a *particular* good results in resources not being perfectly allocated according to the real preferences of consumers. In the long period, under perfect competition, no abnormal profits are made—the cost of producing the good is just equal to people's valuation of it. Moreover, consumers have allocated their outlay according to their preferences, so that marginal utility relative to the price of the good is equal in all cases. A tax on one good destroys the equilibrium, for the price of the good rises (unless supply is absolutely inelastic). This results in a redistribution of consumers' expenditure and thus of the factors of production. In addition, there will be some dislocation of the industry concerned, the extent depending upon the elasticity of demand for the product (*see* p. 441).

Finally, selective indirect taxes result in greater loss to the consumer than an income tax which raises an equivalent amount. Unlike an income tax, selective indirect taxes change the relative prices of goods. This means that consumers have to rearrange their pattern of expenditure. This substitution involves a loss of satisfaction in addition to that suffered through the reduction in income.

Direct taxes, too, may affect the supply of factors, particularly capital, to industry. It may be that high taxation discourages saving; it certainly reduces the power to save. This is not serious for large companies, but the major source of capital for the small private company or sole proprietor is the owner's personal savings out of income. Normally firms which are making the largest profits will be the more likely to want to expand. Thus income tax and corporation tax deprive small, risky, but often progressive companies of much-needed capital.

Not only that, but high direct taxes may repel foreign capital. Although the deduction of income tax on dividends may be refunded, the company still has to bear corporation tax on profits (at 50 per cent). The amount available to shareholders is therefore less, and the declared dividend correspondingly smaller. Consequently, people may prefer to invest in companies operating in countries where there is a higher return to capital—a higher return which is the result, not of superior efficiency, but simply of the lower taxes payable.

(10) *Equitable in its distribution of the tax burden*

Taxes can be classified according to the proportion of a person's income which is deducted:

(a) A *regressive* tax takes a higher proportion of the poorer person's income than of the richer. Indirect taxes, for instance, which are a fixed sum irrespective of income (e.g. television licences), are regressive.

(b) A *proportional* tax takes a given proportion of one's income. Income tax is now proportional for the first £4,500 of taxable income, 33 per cent of every pound being taken in tax.

(c) A *progressive* tax takes a higher proportion of income as income increases (Fig. 105). Again, income tax is pro-

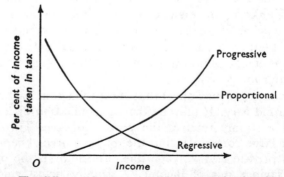

FIG. 105.—The difference between regressive, proportional and progressive taxes.

gressive above £4,500. The next £1,000 is taxed at 43 per cent, and the rate rises in steps until a maximum of 83 per cent is paid on income over £20,000. Estate duty, which has graduated rates of tax, is also progressive.

Justification for taxing the rich man higher than the poor man rests on the assumption that the law of diminishing utility applies to additional income, and that an extra £50 affords less pleasure to the rich man than to the poor man. Thus taking from the rich does not involve such a hardship as taking from the poor. Generally this can be accepted as true, but we can never be sure, simply because there is no absolute measure of personal satisfaction.

III. THE STRUCTURE OF TAXATION

Because certain objectives of taxation conflict with one another, no single tax is completely perfect. Consequently there must be a structure of taxation, combining a number of taxes which the government can vary from time to time according to changes in the emphasis on different objectives.

The following classification of taxes is based on the method of payment:

(1) *Direct Taxes*

With these taxes, the person makes payment direct to the revenue authorities—the Department of Inland Revenue or the Local Authority. Usually each individual's tax liability is assessed separately.

(a) *Income tax.* Income tax was first levied in 1799, but it was repealed soon after Waterloo. Reintroduced in 1842, it has since been continuous.

With the object of simplifying the tax structure, a new unified system of income taxation replaced the old income and surtax in 1973. The basic rates are given above, the main rate being 33 per cent of taxable income. 'Taxable income' is arrived at after allowing deductions depending on marital status, the number of dependent children and other personal circumstances. Investment income above £1,000 per annum is subject to a surcharge of 15 per cent.

(*b*) *Corporation Tax.* In 1965 the profits tax was replaced by a corporation tax.

Under the 'imputation' system adopted in 1973, all profits, whether distributed or not, will be taxed at the same rate (52 per cent). A part ($\frac{33}{67}$ at an income tax rate of 33 per cent) will be imputed to shareholders and be deducted in advance when the dividend is paid. This advance payment will be allowed against the mainstream 50 per cent corporation tax payment (which is always paid in arrears), while for the shareholder it will count as a 'tax credit', refundable if income tax is not payable because of low income.

(*c*) *Capital gains tax.* A tax is now levied on capital gains realised on all assets disposed of at 30 per cent. Owner-occupied houses, cars, National Savings Certificates and goods and chattels worth less than £1,000 are excluded.

Depending on their circumstances, individuals may achieve a lower rate and, where the disposal proceeds of assets do not exceed £500 in any year, no tax is payable.

(*d*) *Estate duty.* The only death duty now payable is that on estates of over £15,000. Rates charged are progressive, varying according to the size of the estate. Thus estates pay 25 per cent in the £15,000–£20,000 band, and this increases to 75 per cent above £500,000. Duty on agricultural property is reduced by 45 per cent.

(*e*) *Other taxes.* These consist of stamp duties (payable on financial contracts), motor-vehicle duties, a land tax and a mineral-rights duty, but only the first two are important. All except motor-vehicle duties are collected by the Department of Inland Revenue.

Local rates, levied by the district authorities are also a direct tax.

Direct taxes yield approximately one-half of total revenue. Their great merit is that, being eventually progressive and assessed according to the individual's particular circumstances, they ensure that the heaviest burdens are placed on the broadest backs. Their progressive character also gives additional weight to their role as a 'built-in stabiliser'.

Their main disadvantage is that, when the rate of tax is high, there may be certain disincentive effects. As a result, indirect taxes also have to be levied.

(2) *Indirect taxes*

Indirect taxes, on goods and services, are so called because the revenue authority (the Department of Customs and Excise) collects them from the seller, who, as far as possible, passes the burden on to the consumer by including the duty in the final selling price of the good (*see* p. 441). They may be *specific* (that is, a fixed sum irrespective of the value of the good) or *ad valorem* (that is, a given percentage of the value of the good).

Indirect taxes may be divided into:

(*a*) Customs duties on imported goods, which will eventually be levied at E.E.C. rates on goods from countries outside the E.E.C.

(*b*) Excise duties on home-produced goods and services, e.g. beer, whisky, petrol, cigarettes and gambling.

(*c*) Value Added Tax (VAT): an *ad valorem* tax introduced in 1973 to replace purchase tax and selective employment tax. It is levied on most goods and services at each stage of production at a basic rate of 10 per cent. Thus, using Fig. 85 as an example, the VAT at 10 per cent paid by the consumer on the table in the shop would be £1·00, making a total purchase price of £11·00. The VAT, however, would have been paid at each stage of production as follows: tree-grower 30p; saw-miller 20p; table manufacturer 30p; retailer 20p. In practice, each producer pays to the Customs and Excise the full 10 per cent tax of the goods as invoiced by him *less* the VAT paid by his suppliers of materials, etc. as shown on their invoices. Thus, for instance, the retailer actually sends to the Customs and Excise £1·00 minus the VAT 80p charged to him, that is 20p.

Some goods, e.g. food, coal, gas, electricity, the construction of buildings, books, newspapers, public transport fares, medicines on prescriptions, etc. are zero-rated. This means that the final seller charges no VAT *and* can re-claim any VAT invoiced by intermediary producers. Other goods, for example rents, loans and medical services, are 'exempt'. Here no VAT is charged by the final seller, but any VAT paid by an intermediary, for example for building repairs, cannot be re-claimed.

Apart from harmonising with the E.E.C. indirect tax system, the main merit of VAT is that it is broader-based than the old purchase tax. Because the latter was applied to a comparatively narrow range of goods, for example cars and consumer durables, the yield did not increase proportionately with consumer spending. More-over, since VAT covers most forms of spending, it does not distort consumer choice to the extent of the old purchase tax (see later). Finally, by zero-rating exports, exporters were given some encouragement by VAT be-cause they paid Selective Employment Tax (the tax it replaced) equally with home-market producers.

On the other hand, it can be argued that a general tax on spending is regressive, for it hits those on lower incomes hardest. This is tempered somewhat, however, by zero-rating goods which can be regarded as necessities.

Through indirect taxes all citizens have to pay something towards government spending, and this tends to promote responsibility. Such taxes give a certain and often an immedi-ate yield and can be adjusted to specific objectives of govern-ment policy. On the other hand, by being regressive, in that they fall more heavily on the poorer sections of the community, they undo some of the redistributive effects of direct taxes.

IV. THE INCIDENCE OF TAXATION

What do we mean by the 'incidence' of a tax?

So far we have considered only the *formal* incidence of a tax. —how the tax is distributed between the various taxpayers. Thus direct taxes, we saw, are progressive, falling heaviest on the higher income groups. Indirect taxes, on the other hand, are regressive as regards consumers, though the direct incidence falls on producers or distributors who actually pay the tax to the Department of Customs and Excise.

But the economist is chiefly concerned with the *effective*, incidence—how the real burden of a tax is distributed after its full effects have worked through the economy.

In the case of *direct taxes*, we have seen that, with some

qualifications, both income tax and corporation tax adversely affect effort, enterprise and risk-bearing, economy in expenditure, and saving (see pp. 429–30).

An increase in income tax can be passed on only by those workers who can secure some addition to their wages by way of compensation. For this to happen, they must be in a strong bargaining position. Certain conditions must be fulfilled (see p. 250), the chief one being that the demand for the good they produce is fairly inelastic. The increase in the price of the good which results from the higher wages will be borne mainly by consumers—which really means workers in other groups who are not in such a strong bargaining position.

Similarly, in the short period, when supply is fairly inelastic, an increase in a tax on profits will be borne chiefly by producers (see p. 268). But in the long period, when some entrepreneurs transfer from the riskier enterprises (which the tax hits hardest), there will be changes in the relative supply of goods, and consumers of those goods whose production involves the most risk will, according to their elasticity of demand, have to bear a part of the tax.

A tax which falls on monopoly profits, however, cannot be passed on. There has been no change in the demand or supply curves, and the monopolist is already producing where his profits are a maximum. Hence if he has to pay, say, a 20 per cent tax, his equilibrium position will be unchanged; four-fifths of maximum profits are still better than four-fifths of anything less.

With indirect taxes, the effective incidence can be analysed more precisely. An indirect tax may be general or selective. A sales tax levied across the board on all goods and services at a standard rate would be a general indirect tax. In the British system, VAT comes closest to such a tax in that it is levied at a standard 10 per cent on most goods and services. The important point is that relative prices remain unchanged and the consumer cannot switch to a substitute which is relatively cheaper because it bears no tax. If the government wishes to reallocate resources, therefore, it must do so by using the proceeds of the tax to subsidise certain industries, or by imposing additional excise duties on goods whose consumption it would like to curtail, for example tobacco.

A *selective* indirect tax is one that is levied at a higher rate on some goods than on others (mostly those bearing 10 per cent VAT), tobacco, alcohol, cars and petrol being examples. Even with VAT, however, there is some selectivity, especially as regards those goods zero-rated, for example, fish-and-chips taken away, meals served in the students' buttery. Here the following questions become important: What is the effect of imposing a selective tax on the size of the particular industry? How will the burden of such a tax be ultimately distributed between the producer and consumer?

We begin by explaining how the imposition of a tax can be shown diagrammatically.

The diagrammatic representation of a tax

Theoretically, the effect of a tax can be analysed on either the demand or the supply side. No matter which is chosen, the same new equilibrium position for price and output will result. Later we shall prefer one method to the other according to the particular problem being analysed.

Suppose a specific tax is imposed on *buyers*. At price OP, without tax, OH was demanded. A tax equal to t is now imposed. If the same amount OH is to be demanded, price must fall by the amount of the tax to Ot. We can carry out a similar procedure at each different price. The effect of the tax, therefore, is to lower the demand curve to D_1, which is vertically equidistant from the demand curve D by the amount of the tax (Fig. 106a).

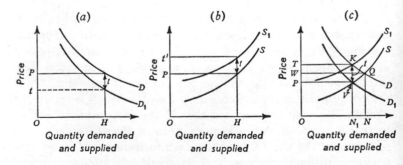

FIG. 106.—The representation of a tax.

Similarly, if the tax is levied on *producers*, the same amount *OH* (Fig. 106*b*) will be supplied only if price rises by the amount of the tax to *Ot*. Thus, as with demand, we have a new supply curve, S_{I}, vertically equidistant from the curve *S*, but to the left of it, by the amount of the tax.

When we combine (*a*) and (*b*), it can be seen that it makes no difference whether the effect of the tax is shown on the demand or supply sides (Fig. 106*c*). The new equilibrium output ON_{I} is the same, both demand and supply having contracted from *ON* as a result of the tax *t*. Total expenditure changes from *ONQW* to $ON_{\mathrm{I}}KT$, but the latter includes tax receipts of *PVKT*.

The effect of an indirect tax on the size of an industry

The greater the elasticities of demand and supply, the greater will be the effect of a tax in reducing production. A complete proof of this proposition is beyond the scope of this book, but by using demand and supply curves, we can show diagrammatically that it is true.

(1) *Elasticity of demand*

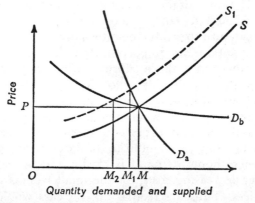

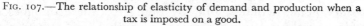

FIG. 107.—The relationship of elasticity of demand and production when a tax is imposed on a good.

Before the tax is imposed, total output is *OM* (Fig. 107). The effect of the tax is to raise the supply curve from *S* to S_{I}. Two demand curves are shown, D_{a} being less elastic than D_{b} at price *OP*. The effect of the tax is to reduce output to OM_{I} where demand is D_a, and to OM_2 where it is D_b. In the latter case consumers switch to buying substitutes.

(2) *Elasticity of supply*

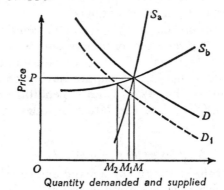

FIG. 108.—The relationship of elasticity of supply and production when a tax is imposed on a good.

Before the tax is imposed, total output is OM (Fig. 108). The effect of the tax is to lower the demand curve from D to D_1. Two supply curves are shown, S_a being less elastic than S_b at price OP. The effect of the tax is to reduce output to OM_1 where supply is S_a, and to OM_2 where it is S_b. In the latter case producers can turn to producing alternative goods.

This proposition has important practical applications. (*a*) The government may use a subsidy (which can be illustrated by moving the supply curve to the right) to increase the production, and thus employment, of an industry. The effect will be more pronounced where demand and supply are elastic. (*b*) Because the effect of a tax is to reduce production, even a temporary tax may be harmful to an industry. This is particularly so where home demand is elastic and production takes place under decreasing costs, for the smaller demand will raise export prices. Thus a selective tax on cars would not only reduce home demand, but, by doing so, lose economies of scale, thereby putting up prices to both home and foreign markets. Even when the tax is subsequently withdrawn, foreign markets may not be regained, for sales organisation, servicing arrangements and goodwill might all have suffered permanent harm.

The distribution of the burden of an indirect tax between consumers and producers

When a good is subject to a selective tax, it does not mean that its price will rise by the full amount of the tax. Consider the following demand and supply schedules for commodity *X*.

Price of X (pence)	Demand ('000 lb.)	Supply ('000 lb.)
12	60	150
11	70	130
10	80	110
9	90	90
8	100	70

The equilibrium price is 9p. Now suppose a tax of 3p per unit of *X* is imposed. The price rises to 11p. (The quantity supplied to the market at 11p is only 70,000 lb., for the producer now really receives only 8p a unit. Alternatively, the quantity demanded at each price is that for which the price is greater by 3p.) Thus we see that the buyer pays 2p more and the supplier receives 1p less per unit. This is shown diagrammatically in Fig. 109.

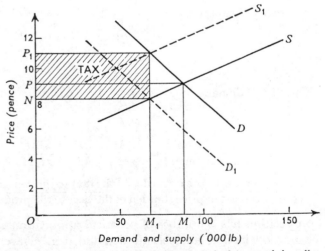

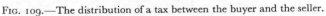

FIG. 109.—The distribution of a tax between the buyer and the seller.

The amount of the tax falling on consumers as compared with that falling on producers is directly proportional to the elasticity of supply to the elasticity of demand. That is:

$$\frac{\text{consumers' share of tax}}{\text{producers' share of tax}} = \frac{\text{elasticity of supply}}{\text{elasticity of demand}}$$

That this proposition is likely to be true can be seen from the following argument. When a tax is imposed, the reaction of the producer is to try to push the burden of the tax on to the consumer, while similarly the consumer tries to push it on to the producer. Who wins? Simply the one whose bargaining position is stronger. This will depend upon the ability to switch to producing substitutes if the price falls as compared with the ability to switch to buying substitutes if the price rises. Now the possibility of substituting largely determines elasticities of supply and demand. Thus the relative burden of the tax paid by producers and consumers depends upon relative elasticities of supply and demand.

The proposition can be proved geometrically as follows. As a result of the tax, price rises from OP to $OP_{\scriptscriptstyle 1}$, and the quantity demanded and supplied falls from OM to $OM_{\scriptscriptstyle 1}$.

$$\text{Elasticity of supply at } OP = \frac{\dfrac{M_{\scriptscriptstyle 1}M}{OM}}{\dfrac{NP}{OP}}$$

$$\text{Elasticity of demand at } OP = \frac{\dfrac{M_{\scriptscriptstyle 1}M}{OM}}{\dfrac{PP_{\scriptscriptstyle 1}}{OP}}$$

$$\frac{\text{elasticity of supply}}{\text{elasticity of demand}} = \frac{M_{\scriptscriptstyle 1}M}{OM} \times \frac{OP}{NP} \times \frac{OM}{M_{\scriptscriptstyle 1}M} \times \frac{PP_{\scriptscriptstyle 1}}{OP}$$

$$= \frac{PP_{\scriptscriptstyle 1}}{NP} = \frac{\text{increase in price (burden of the tax) to the consumer}}{\text{decrease in price (burden of the tax) to the producer}}$$

This proposition has a number of practical applications: (a) A tax on a good having an inelastic demand, e.g. cigarettes, falls mainly on the consumer. (b) Where supply is inelastic compared with demand, the tax falls mainly on the producer. Thus an increase in oil royalties imposed by a Middle East government has to be borne mainly by the particular company concerned. (c) Because in the long period supply tends to be more elastic than in the short period, so, as time passes, the price will tend to rise as consumers are required to bear a greater share of the tax. (*d*) Where supply is inelastic even in the long period, a tax will take longer to pass on to the consumer. Thus if there are any unoccupied houses, an increase in rates will have to be borne mainly by owners of property. (*e*) An increase in price as a result of a tax will vary according to the relationship of elasticity of supply to elasticity of demand. The greater the elasticity of supply relative to the elasticity of demand, the greater will be the price rise.

PART VII

INTERNATIONAL TRADE

CHAPTER 30

THE NATURE OF INTERNATIONAL TRADE

I. INTRODUCTION

How international trade arises

INTERNATIONAL trade arises simply because countries differ in their demand for goods and in their ability to produce them.

On the demand side, a country may be able to produce a particular good, but not in the quantities it requires. The U.S.A., for instance, is a net importer of oil. On the other hand, neither Zambia nor Kuwait require all the copper and oil respectively which they can produce. Without international trade, most of their deposits would lie untapped.

On the supply side, as we have already shown, both men and localities are better at producing some goods than others. Nor can the advantages that they possess be easily transferred. What happens, therefore, is that they specialise in producing those goods in which they have the greatest relative advantage and exchange the goods they make for all the other things they want.

The same applies to countries. Factors of production are not evenly distributed throughout the world. One country may have an abundance of land; another may have a skilled labour force. Capital, oil, mineral deposits, cheap, unskilled labour and a tropical climate are other factors possessed by different countries to different degrees.

Nor can these factors be transferred easily from one country to another. Climate, land and mineral deposits are obviously specific. Labour is far more immobile internationally than within its own national boundaries, for additional obstacles are encountered—differences in language, immigration quotas and regulations, ignorance of opportunities, trade-union prejudice against foreign workers, unfamiliar customs and living conditions. Capital, too, moves less easily; political instability in some countries or simply ignorance of possibilities may prevent investors from moving funds abroad. In addition, many governments have restricted the movement of capital because it imposes a strain on the balance of payments.

Because factors are difficult to shift, the alternative—moving the goods made by those factors—is adopted. What happens, therefore, is that countries, if the terms of trade are appropriate, specialise in producing those goods in which they have the greatest comparative advantage, exchanging them for the goods of other countries. Thus international trade arises.

Why make a separate study of international trade?

So far we have said nothing which is different in principle from trade between persons or between localities within a country. A carpenter who makes a chair exchanges it through the price mechanism for the food and other goods he needs. Similarly, cars made in Oxford are exchanged for washing-machines made in South Wales. Why then, apart from the fact that longer distances are involved, do we treat separately the exchange of cars made in Britain for the wool produced in Australia?

The answer is that although the same theoretical principles apply, international trade gives rise to different problems. Exporters lack knowledge of foreign markets, find demand more difficult to predict, and have to cope with differences of language, weights and measures, government regulations, and changes of currency. Such factors tend to reduce the volume of international trade. Above all, since goods have to cross frontiers and be paid for in the currency of the country selling them, international trade may be regulated by governments for both economic and political reasons (*see* p. 457). What we have to do, therefore, is to show the theoretical gains which result from international trade and then indicate why our theoretical argument has to be modified in practice.

II. THE ADVANTAGES OF INTERNATIONAL TRADE

(1) *It enables countries to obtain the benefits of specialisation*

Specialisation by countries improves the standard of living for all, enabling a greater variety and a larger number of goods to be consumed.

(a) It is obvious that, without international trade, many countries would have to go without certain products. Iceland, for instance, has no coal, Britain no gold or aluminium, and Sweden no oil.

(b) More important, many goods can be enjoyed which, if produced at home, would be within the reach of only the very wealthy. In Britain this would apply to bananas, spices, oranges, peaches and indeed to most of the goods imported. How international trade can benefit people in this way is explained by economists in what is usually known as the 'law of comparative costs'. This shows that countries can gain by specialisation and trade in certain commodities providing that there is some difference in the relative costs of producing those commodities. The following imaginary examples will explain.

Suppose that there are two countries, A and B, producing just two commodities, wheat and cars. Each has the same amount of capital and the same number of labourers, but A has a good climate and fertile soil compared with B. B's workers, on the other hand, are far more skilful. All factors are fully employed.

When both countries divide their factors equally between the production of wheat and cars, they can produce as follows:

Country	Wheat (units)	Cars (units)
A	500	100
B	100	500
Total production	600	600

But if A specialises in producing wheat and B cars, total production would be 1,000 wheat and 1,000 cars. There is thus a net gain of 400 wheat and 400 cars to be shared between them (*see* p. 451).

Here the gains are obvious, because A is better at producing wheat whereas B is better at producing cars. But suppose A has skilled labour and capital also, and is better at producing both wheat and cars, as follows:

Country	Wheat (units)	Cars (units)
A	500	300
B	400	100
Total production (no specialisation)	900	400

Are there still gains to be achieved by specialisation?

Provided the rate at which cars can be exchanged for wheat lies within certain limits (see p. 451), the answer is 'yes'. The reason for this is that A's superiority in producing cars is far more marked than her superiority in producing wheat. In the production of the former she is three times as efficient, but with the latter only one-and-a-quarter times. Relative, rather than absolute, advantages are what are really important. The result is that if A specialises in producing cars, leaving B to produce wheat, total production will be 800 wheat and 600 cars.

Suppose now that world conditions of demand and supply are such that 2 wheat exchange for 1 car; that is, the price of cars is exactly twice that of wheat. A now exchanges 200 cars for 400 wheat, giving her a total of 400 wheat and 400 cars, and B 400 wheat and 200 cars.

It can be seen, therefore, that through specialisation B is 100 cars better off. But has specialisation improved A's position? She now has 400 cars but only 400 wheat, a gain of 100 cars but a loss of 100 wheat. To produce the cars she has gained would have taken $\frac{1}{6}$ of her factors of production, but the loss of wheat represents only $\frac{1}{10}$ of her factors. In effect, therefore, specialisation has increased B's productive capacity. Alternatively, we can say that if B gave up 100 wheat, by her own efforts she would obtain only 60 cars, whereas through exchange she gets 100.

The above argument can be put in terms of opportunity costs. If there is no specialisation, A has to give up 3 cars in order to produce 5 units of wheat. On the international market, however, the terms of exchange are such that 3 cars can obtain 6 units of wheat. It will obviously pay A, therefore, to specialise in producing cars and to obtain her wheat by exchange.

Similarly with B. For 4 units of wheat she can, by her own efforts, obtain only 1 car. On the world market she gets 2 cars. It will thus pay her to specialise in producing wheat and to obtain her cars by exchange.

It must be emphasised that the law of comparative costs merely shows possibilities on the supply side—how two countries can specialise to advantage when their opportunity costs differ. But until we know the terms upon which goods can be exchanged, we cannot say definitely whether specialisation will take place or, if it does, to what extent (*see* p. 451).

It is the difference in relative prices which moves goods between countries. Hence, although a country may be favourably placed to produce certain goods, a large home demand and thus a relatively high price may mean that it is a net importer of that good (as the U.S.A. is of oil). It must also be remembered that few advantages in production are permanent. Climate and, to a large extent, mineral deposits persist, but new techniques can make factors more productive. Thus India now exports cotton goods to Britain! In any case, the above explanation must be amplified to allow for:

(i) *Transport costs*, which reduce the gains postulated by the law of comparative costs and therefore make for less specialisation. Indeed, it is conceivable that transport costs could more than offset A's superiority in producing cars so that B found it better to produce her own requirements.

(ii) *The more realistic conditions where many countries and many products enter international trade.*

(iii) *Interference by nations with the free movement of goods* by customs duties, quotas, exchange control, physical controls, etc. (*see* p. 455).

(iv) *The possibility of diminishing returns setting in as the production of a good increases.* The theory as stated assumes that, at all stages of production, wheat can always be produced instead of cars by both A and B at a constant ratio. Thus at any output, A can have 5 wheat instead of 3 cars and B 4 wheat instead of 1 car. But it is likely that as B increases her output of wheat, diminishing returns set in, for inferior land and labour have to be used. Thus instead of getting 4 additional wheat for 1 car, she receives only 3, and later only 2, and so on. The same applies, too, as the production of cars is increased by A.

Eventually, therefore, it pays to specialise no longer. A can obtain her wheat cheaper by producing herself than by buying it on the world market, and the same applies to B as regards cars. Diminishing returns, and thus increasing costs, usually mean in practice that there is only partial specialisation—up to the point where opportunity costs are less than those offered by the terms of trade. Thereafter it is better for a country to produce the good itself. Most countries, in fact, both produce and import the same goods (e.g. the United Kingdom and agricultural produce).

(2) *By expanding the market, international trade enables the benefits of large-scale production to be obtained*

In contrast to those goods where diminishing returns soon set in as output increases (*see above*), there are many products (e.g. aircraft, cars) which are produced under conditions of decreasing cost. Here the home market is too small to exploit fully the advantages of large-scale production. This applies particularly to small countries such as Switzerland. In such cases, international trade lowers costs per unit of output.

(3) *International trade increases competition and thereby promotes efficiency in production, particularly where otherwise a monopolist might gain control of the home market*

As we have seen, any limitation in the size of a market makes it easier for one seller to gain control. In contrast, international trade increases competition. A government must always consider the risk of a monopoly developing when it gives protection to the home industry by tariffs, etc.

(4) *International trade promotes beneficial political links with countries*

Examples of this occur in Western Europe with the Common Market, and within the Commonwealth, of which trade is still an important link.

III. THE TERMS OF TRADE

The limits of the exchange rate

In our example, A specialises in producing cars and B in producing wheat. By her own efforts, A could have 5 wheat for 3 cars. Obviously, therefore, she will not specialise in cars if, by exchange, she receives less wheat than this. Similarly, B will not specialise in producing wheat if she has to give up more than 4 wheat for 1 car.

Thus for specialisation to be beneficial to both A and B, the rate at which wheat exchanges for cars must lie somewhere between the upper limit of $\frac{5}{3}$ and the lower limit of 4.

Determination of the exchange rate

But how is the actual rate of exchange (which we assumed to be 2 wheat for 1 car) determined?

The answer is quite simple. When we say that 2 wheat exchange for 1 car, we are really comparing relative values. Hence the price of cars will be twice that of wheat. Their relative prices will be fixed in the market, like all other prices, by demand and supply. We can explain by developing our simplified example still further.

Suppose A and B are the only two countries engaged in trade and that only two commodities, wheat and cars, are produced. Through specialisation, but before exchange, A has 600 cars and B 800 wheat. As the relative prices of wheat and cars change, so we have the following imaginary demand and supply schedules:

Price (exchange ratio) Wheat : Cars	A Wheat demanded	Cars offered	B Cars demanded	Wheat offered
3 : 1	1,500	500	100	300
$2\frac{1}{4}$: 1	900	400	240	540
2 : 1	650	325	325	650
$1\frac{3}{4}$: 1	350	200	400	700

It can be seen that, given the conditions of demand and supply as shown in the above schedules, only at a price of 2 wheat to 1 car is there market equilibrium. The example could be extended to cover more than two countries and more than two commodities.

For both A and B, the rate at which wheat exchanges for cars represents the *terms of trade*. If there are changes in demand or supply, so that more wheat has to be given for a car, then the terms of trade have improved so far as A is concerned, but have worsened for B. On the other hand, if less wheat has to be given for a car, the terms of trade have improved for B but worsened for A.

Changes in the terms of trade

The terms of trade, therefore, are the rate at which a country exchanges its exports for imports. Where goods are traded internationally, this rate is fixed by the world conditions of demand and supply. It follows that any change in the terms of trade must come about through a change in the conditions of either demand or supply. Thus, in our example, if there is a large increase in A's demand for wheat, the price of wheat will move nearer to the higher limit of $\frac{5}{3}$: 1. Likewise, if there is a decrease in A's demand for wheat, the price will move nearer to the lower limit of 4 : 1. Or, if the conditions of supply change so that A can produce 1,000 cars instead of 600, she would probably be willing to supply more cars in exchange for a given quantity of wheat, and so the price of wheat rises, the terms of trade moving in favour of B. On the other hand, if A's skilled labour emigrates and tends to be replaced by unskilled labour, she may be able to produce only 500 cars instead of 600, and the price of cars rises. The terms of trade move in favour of A.

Examples of how changes in the terms of trade can originate in the real world are:

(1) *Changes in the conditions of demand*

    (a) Demand may increase through technological development. Thus the increased demand for oil has improved the terms of trade for all exporting countries.

    (b) A large increase in world demand for foodstuffs, without any corresponding increase in production, would worsen the United Kingdom's terms of trade.

    (c) A decrease in the demand for raw materials resulting from a fall in the production of manufactured goods may, when supply of these materials is inelastic, bring about a large fall in the price. This happened during the depression of the 1930s, when the United Kingdom's terms of trade improved considerably.

(2) *Changes in the conditions of supply*

    (a) Technical improvements may increase supply, e.g. in

agriculture during the 1920s and 1950s. Where demand is inelastic, the price of a good may, as a result, fall considerably.

(b) Political or labour unrest or war in a country which is the main producer of a good, e.g. Chile (copper), may raise world prices and so improve the terms of trade for other major producing countries, e.g. Zambia.

(c) Where primary-producing countries begin to produce their own manufactured goods, e.g. Argentina (cotton goods), Australia (cars), the increased supply tends to lower world prices, and the terms of trade of manufacturing countries worsen compared with producers of primary products.

Measurement of the terms of trade

The terms of trade express the relationship between the price of imports and the price of exports. In practice, however, our interest is centred on this relationship not so much at any one time but rather as it changes over a period of time. We therefore measure relative changes in the terms of trade from one period to another.

Because countries import and export many goods, and the prices of different goods move in different ways and by varying amounts, we have to measure changes in the price of imports and exports as a whole by index numbers. And, it must be remembered, these are subject to certain defects (*see* p. 422).

In practice, therefore, the terms of trade are measured as follows:

$$\frac{\text{Index showing average price of exports}}{\text{Index showing average price of imports}} \times \frac{100}{1}$$

Actual figures for the last thirteen years are given in Table 8.

When a country's exports become cheaper relative to her imports, she will have to give more goods in exchange for a given quantity of imports. It is then said that the terms of trade have 'deteriorated', 'moved against her', or 'become less favourable'. If the opposite occurs, the terms of trade are said to have 'improved', 'moved in her favour', or 'become more favourable'. Table 8 shows that the terms of trade have, despite fluctuations, tended to move in the United Kingdom's favour until 1972, with a deterioration in 1973.

TABLE 8

THE TERMS OF TRADE OF THE UNITED KINGDOM, 1961–73
(Base year 1961)

Year	Export unit-value index (1)	Import unit-value index (2)	Terms of Trade (1) ÷ (2)
1961	100	100	100
1962	101	99	102
1963	104	103	101
1964	106	107	99
1965	108	107	102
1966	112	109	103
1967	114	109	105
1968	123	121	102
1969	127	126	101
1970	136	132	104
1971	147	136	109
1972	157	143	110
1973	170	185	92

Results of changes in the terms of trade

The direct effects of an improvement in a country's terms of trade are beneficial. First, she obtains more imports for a given quantity of exports (*see* p. 354). Secondly, her balance of payments may be improved. Suppose, for instance, that Britain's imports and exports are equal in value. The price of imports in sterling falls, but the price of Britain's exports in sterling remains unchanged. If Britain's demand for imports is inelastic, the direct effect will be to improve her balance of trade for less will be spent in sterling on imports.

But the indirect results may make an improvement in the terms of trade, especially for a developed country, seem less desirable.

First, countries whose terms of trade have worsened may not be able to afford to buy the exports of the countries whose terms of trade have improved. For example, suppose that the price of wheat falls from £5 to £4 a quarter, but that an exporting country finds that demand increases only from 900,000 quarters to 950,000 quarters. Total expenditure on wheat drops, therefore, from £4,500,000 to £3,800,000. But this expenditure equals approximately the income of farmers who are exporting the bulk of their crop. As a result of the fall in income, their demand for imports from a country such as the United Kingdom would drop.

Secondly, the fall in income will also mean that less is spent on home-produced goods. This means lower profits in home industries and thus lower invisible earnings through lower dividends on capital invested in the country by foreigners, say by the United Kingdom.

Thirdly, a fall in the incomes of underdeveloped countries may mean that the loss must be made good by an increase in the amount of aid given.

Fourthly, the economies of countries which are dependent on foreign trade may be subjected to frequent adjustments if there are swings in the terms of trade. If, for instance, the demand for raw wool is inelastic and its price fluctuates, incomes will be greater in Australia when the price of wool is high, and smaller when the price of wool is low. This has far-reaching effects on a policy aimed at a stable level of income and employment.

IV. FREE TRADE AND PROTECTION

The advantages of free trade

The theory of comparative costs shows how every country can enjoy a higher standard of living when each applies the principle of the division of labour to the production of goods. Theoretically, it seems to follow that trade should be as free as possible, for only then can the maximum specialisation according to the law of comparative advantage take place. In practice, however, we find that all countries follow policies which, to varying degrees, prevent goods moving freely according to differences in relative prices.

Methods of controlling international trade

(1) *Customs duties*

Customs duties, for example the common external tariffs of the Common Market, are both revenue-raising and protective. They become protective when the imported good bears a higher rate of tax than the similar home-produced good.

(2) Subsidies

While countries which subscribe to the General Agreement on Tariffs and Trade cannot follow a policy of 'dumping' by giving direct subsidies to exports, the volume and pattern of international trade may be influenced indirectly by other means, e.g. government assistance to the ship-building industry. Less obviously, high welfare benefits, such as family allowances, by keeping down labour costs, may give one country a price advantage over another which would not be justified by the real cost of producing.

(3) Quotas

If demand is inelastic, the increase in price resulting from a customs duty will have little effect on the quantity imported. Hence when the government wishes to restrict the importation of a good to a definite quantity, quotas can be imposed. Thus foreign films can be exhibited only in a fixed proportion to British films.

Compared with duties, quotas have two main disadvantages: (a) As a result of the artificial shortage of supply, the price may be increased by the foreign supplier or by the importer. Hence unless the government also introduces price control, it is they who gain the advantage and not the public. (b) Quotas make for rigidity in the economy, for they are calculated on a formula, usually based on volume of imports over a given period, which grows increasingly out of date with time. This penalises the efficient firm wishing to expand.

(4) Exchange control

A tighter check on the amount spent on imported goods can be achieved if quotas are fixed in terms of foreign currency. This necessitates some form of exchange control (see p. 327). All earnings of foreign currency or claims to foreign currency have to be handed over to the government or its agent (in the case of the United Kingdom, the Bank of England), who alone can authorise withdrawals from this fund for the purpose of paying for imports, foreign travel, and capital movements. Goods can be imported only under licence. Thus the government, not the free market, decides the priorities for imports.

(5) *Physical controls*

A complete ban—an embargo—may be placed on the import or export of certain goods. Thus narcotics cannot be imported, while the export of strategic goods to Iron Curtain countries is forbidden. Similarly, strict regulations regarding the importation of live animals (e.g. cattle, dogs and parrots) make trade more difficult.

Reasons for government control of international trade

In general, trade is controlled because governments think and act nationally rather than internationally. Although people as a whole lose when trade is restricted, those of a particular country may gain.

Many reasons are put forward to justify control. Occasionally they have some logical justification; more usually they stem from a narrow interest seeking to gain an advantage. We can examine the arguments, therefore, under three main headings: (1) those based on strategic, political, social and moral grounds; (2) those having some economic basis; (3) those depending on shallow economic thinking.

(1) *Non-economic arguments*

(a) *To encourage the production of a good of strategic importance.* Where a nation is dependent on another for a good of strategic importance, there is a danger of its supply being cut off in the event of war. Thus one argument for subsidising aircraft production in the United Kingdom is to ensure the survival of plant and skilled labour.

(b) *To foster closer political ties.* In 1932 the United Kingdom imposed tariffs on many imports in order to give preferential rates to the Commonwealth.

Now, as a member of the E.E.C., Britain must impose a common external tariff as part of a movement towards political as well as economic unity.

(c) *To prosecute political objectives.* Trade can be a weapon of foreign policy, e.g. sanctions against Rhodesia.

(d) *To promote social policies.* Although in the past, Britain has subsidised her agriculture mainly for strategic reasons,

458 INTERNATIONAL TRADE PART VII

today the purposes are basically social—to avoid depression in rural districts and a further movement to already congested towns.

(2) *Economic arguments having some justification*

(*a*) *To improve the terms of trade.* The incidence of a selective tax is shared between producer and consumer according to the relative elasticities of supply and demand (*see* p. 441). A government, therefore, can levy a tax on an imported good to improve the terms of trade if demand for the good is more elastic than the supply, for the increase in price is borne mainly by the producer, while the government has the proceeds of the tax. In practice this requires that: (i) the producing country has no alternative markets to which supplies can be easily diverted; (ii) her factors of production have few alternative uses; (iii) the demand for the exports of the country imposing the tariff must be unaffected by the loss of income suffered by countries who now find their sales abroad reduced.

(*b*) *To protect an 'infant industry'.* It may be possible to establish an industry in a country if, during its infancy, it is given protection from well-established competitors which are already producing on a large scale. It is argued that the guaranteed home market will enable it to get over its teething troubles and in time it will be so strong that it can compete on equal terms with the rest of the world. Britain's car industry, for instance, benefited from such protection.

The difficulty is that most industries come to rely on such protection, so that tariffs are never withdrawn, e.g. American duties on manufactured goods imposed in the eighteenth century are still in existence today. Moreover, often industries are encouraged which, without protection, would have no chance of survival. This leads to a maldistribution of the resources of a country.

(*c*) *To enable an industry to decline gradually.* Fundamental changes in demand for a good may severely hit an industry. Such, for instance, was the fate of the British cotton industry in the 1950s. Restrictions on imports can cushion the shock, giving the industry more time to contract.

(*d*) *To correct a temporary balance-of-payments disequilibrium.* A temporary drain on gold and foreign currency reserves may be halted by controlling imports. But if the depletion of the reserves is due to fundamental and lasting causes, other measures should be used (*see* Chapter 33).

(*e*) *To prevent 'dumping'.* Goods may be sold abroad at a lower price than on the home market. This may be possible because: (*a*) producers are given export subsidies; (*b*) discriminating monopoly is possible (*see* p. 214); or (*c*) it enables the producer to obtain the advantages of decreasing costs. People in the importing country benefit directly from the lower prices. If, however, the exporter is trying to obtain a monopoly position which he can exploit once he has driven out home producers, then there is a case for giving the home market some protection.

(3) *Economic arguments having little validity*

(*a*) *To retaliate against tariffs of another country.* The threat of a retaliatory tariff may be used as a bluff to influence another country to change its restrictive policy. Thus in 1963 the U.S.A. threatened to impose higher import duties on a number of Common Market goods to force a reduction of duties on imported American poultry. Here some concession was obtained, but such measures are usually ineffective, for countries often retaliate by imposing still higher duties, with everybody losing.

(*b*) *To maintain home employment in a period of depression.* When there is a general depression in world trade, countries have tended to place restrictions on imports in order to ensure that income is spent on home-produced goods, thus providing employment at home. The difficulty is that other countries retaliate, thereby leading to an all-round contraction in world trade. The General Agreement on Tariffs and Trade endeavours to prevent this from happening (*see* p. 461).

(*c*) *To protect home industries from 'unfair' foreign competition.* The demand that British workers must be protected from competition by cheap, 'sweated' foreign labour is frequently heard. Occasionally it comes from emotionalists with little knowledge of economics, but more usually from narrow interests—the industry and its workers facing competition. When economic analysis is applied, however, the argument can be seen to have little justification, and any protection given to an industry must be on other grounds, e.g. home workers cannot move to other occupations or industries.

(i) It is the antithesis of the whole principle of comparative costs, which says that a country should specialise where it has the greatest relative advantage. That advantage may be an abundance of land, capital, tropical climate, minerals—or of cheap labour.

(ii) Carried to its logical conclusion, the U.S.A. should refuse to import British cars because wages in Britain are much lower than in the U.S.A.

(iii) Low wages do not necessarily denote low labour costs. Wages may be low because labour is inefficient, that is, because productivity is low. What we have to look at is the wage cost per unit of output. Thus the U.S.A. can export manufactured goods to the United Kingdom even though her labour is the most highly paid in the world. The threatened industry can compete by improving productivity and thereby lowering wage-cost per unit.

(iv) A tax against a poor country with cheap labour merely makes the country poorer and its labour cheaper. The way to raise wages (and the price of the good produced) is to increase demand in foreign markets.

(v) If imports from poor countries are restricted, other help has to be given. They prefer 'trade to aid'. Thus by importing cheap manufactured goods from Hong Kong, Britain reduces the amount of relief which is necessary.

(vi) Protection, by reducing the income of the poorer countries, means that they have less to spend on Britain's exports.

(vii) The policy breeds retaliation.

(viii) The country whose goods are excluded may as a result be forced to compete more aggressively elsewhere, making it more difficult for the protecting country to sell abroad. It is probable that for this reason Japan captured many of Britain's foreign markets for cotton goods when the British market was restricted to her.

In conclusion, we must emphasise that any restriction of trade has a social cost—a lower standard of living. But there may be other benefits—economic, political and social. Usually the economic gains are doubtful. Others cannot be measured, and it has to be left to the politicians to decide where the balance of advantage lies. But it must always be remembered that protection creates a vested interest, which opposes any subsequent removal.

The General Agreement on Tariffs and Trade (GATT)

At Geneva in 1947 twenty-three nations drew up the General Agreement on Tariffs and Trade. The objectives were: (a) to reduce existing trade barriers; (b) to eliminate discrimination in international trade; (c) to prevent the establishment of further trade barriers by getting nations to agree to consult together rather than take unilateral action. It operates as follows.

Member nations meet together periodically to try to agree on a round of tariff reductions. Here the 'most-favoured-nation' principle applies. This means that if one country grants a tariff concession to another it must apply automatically to all the other participating countries. Thus if the E.E.C. agrees to reduce her tariff on American automatic vending machines by 5 per cent in exchange for a 5 per cent reduction in the American tariff on E.E.C. man-made fibres, then both concessions must be extended to every other member of GATT.

Today (1974) there are some one hundred member nations, representing almost the whole of the international trade of the free world. Through the organisation, a progressive reduction in existing tariffs has been achieved, and the principle has been established that problems of international trade should be settled by co-operative discussion rather than by independent unilateral action. But difficulties have arisen. (a) The principle of reciprocity means that low-tariff countries have to begin from an inferior bargaining position, and the concessions they can make are thus limited. Such countries may, therefore, prefer a low-tariff regional arrangement, such as the Common Market. (b) In certain circumstances, the 'most-favoured-nation' principle may deter a country from making a tariff reduction to another country for the simple reason that it has to be applied to all. (c) The Articles of the Agreement have had to be waived to allow for special circumstances—balance-of-payments difficulties, American protection of her agriculture, the United Kingdom's imports from the Commonwealth, the establishment of 'infant' industries in the underdeveloped countries, and the discriminatory character of the European Economic Community.

CHAPTER 31

THE BALANCE OF PAYMENTS

I. PAYING FOR IMPORTS

Differences in currencies

OCCASIONALLY, international trade may take the form of a barter arrangement, one country agreeing to take so much of another country's produce in exchange for so much of its own. Normally, however, exchanges are arranged by private traders who, according to relative prices, decide whether it is profitable to export and import goods.

But each country has its own currency—Spain (pesetas), France (francs), the U.S.A. (dollars), the United Kingdom (pounds sterling) and so on. Even though currencies may have the same name, they are still different. Thus the pounds of the Egypt, Syria, and the United Kingdom are quite different from one another. This difference is important in international economics for two reasons: (*a*) sufficient foreign currency has to be obtained to pay for imports; (*b*) a rate has to be established at which one currency will exchange for another. The first will be considered forthwith, the second in the chapter which follows; but neither is independent of the other.

How are imports paid for?

We can best answer this question by first considering the purchases made by an individual, say a housewife, Mrs Jones. Each week she buys a variety of goods. No shopkeeper will *give* her these goods. They have to be paid for. What is important for our purposes, however, is that there are at least seven sources from which she can obtain the money to make payment.

The first and most usual source is the week's earnings. Her husband probably makes her an allowance from his wages each week, and Mrs Jones pays the shopkeeper on the spot with this money. It must be noted, however, that what in fact Mrs Jones is really doing is exchanging the goods which Mr Jones has specialised in producing for all the other goods needed. Thus, if Mr Jones is a tailor, the suits he makes are sold, and it is from the money thus obtained that Mrs Jones buys the goods she needs. Furthermore, money is often earned, not by making goods, but by performing a service. Thus Mrs Jones herself may earn wages by working a day each week for the shopkeeper, sending out his accounts and answering his correspondence. Lastly, interest on savings may provide some current income. Provided that all the weekly expenses are met out of this combined weekly income, we should say that the Jones family was 'paying its way'.

It might happen, however, that Mrs Jones's expenditure was not covered by the current weekly income. This might occur, for instance, because she bought a costly good, such as a washing-machine, which was not a regular item of weekly expenditure. In such circumstances, Mrs Jones would have to raise the money from other sources. First, she could draw money from her National Savings Account or from any other 'nest-egg' which she had by her. Secondly, she could sell some goods from her household stock, such as the piano or the television set, for which she had a less urgent need. Thirdly, she might be able to borrow the money from a friend or, what amounts to the same thing, ask the shopkeeper to forgo payment for the time being. Finally, if she were extremely fortunate, she might be able to obtain a gift of money, say from a doting father. Such methods of payment would be fairly satisfactory for a good which is in use over a long period, provided that her savings were gradually replenished, or the assets sold were replaced by assets of equal value, or that the loan was repaid during the lifetime of the good. Where, however, such replenishment of savings and assets or repayment of the loan is not made, either because insufficient savings are put by out of weekly income or because the over-expenditure is a frequent occurrence, then we would say that Mrs Jones is 'not paying her way'. In time her savings would run out, her home would be sold up, and she would be unable to obtain any more loans or credit from the shopkeeper.

Broadly speaking, a nation trading with other nations is in exactly the same position as Mrs Jones. The same alternatives are open to it in paying for goods it imports. The main source is money received from the sale of current exports. Fig. 110 shows how an export earns foreign currency. In normal times, importing and exporting are done by firms, and payments are arranged through banks, who exchange the currency of one country for the currency of another *provided that they have the necessary reserves of that currency*. Such reserves are earned by customers who export to foreign countries.

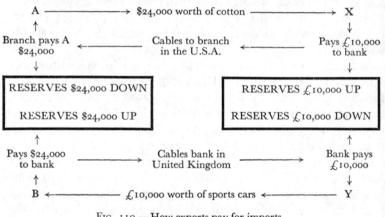

FIG. 110.—How exports pay for imports.

Let us assume that £1 sterling exchanges for $2.40 and that there are no currency restrictions. Suppose a British merchant X wishes to import cotton from A in the U.S.A. to the value of £10,000. The American exporter requires payment in dollars, for all his payments, e.g. his workers' wages, have to be made in dollars. Hence the importer goes to his bank, pays in £10,000 and arranges a 'documentary credit'. The bank cables its branch in New York, authorising it to make the equivalent dollar payment to A on production of the necessary documents, e.g. the bill of lading. (Most banks have branches in foreign capitals; if not, they engage local banks to act for them.) But how is it that the branch has dollars available to honour the draft?

We can see this if we imagine that another British firm Y has sold £10,000 worth of sports cars to an importer B in the U.S.A. This firm wants payment in pounds sterling. Hence the

American importer of the cars pays $24,000 into his bank in the U.S.A., and the same procedure follows. It is obvious that the two transactions—buying cotton from the U.S.A. and selling sports cars from Britain—balance one another. The British bank's branch has had to pay out dollars, the American sterling. The British bank has received sterling, the American bank dollars. If the two get together, their requirements match. (In practice it is more likely that they would meet their needs through the foreign-exchange market.) Thus the dollars needed for paying for the cotton are obtained by selling the sports cars and vice versa. In short, exports pay for imports.

'Exports' in its wider sense

In this connection the term 'exports' needs qualification. In the same way that Mrs Jones received payment for the service of sending out the shopkeeper's accounts, so a nation may receive payment, not only for the goods it exports, but also for services rendered to other countries. Goods exported are termed 'visible exports', because they can be seen and recorded as they cross the political boundaries between countries. Services performed for people of other countries, however, are called 'invisible exports', because they cannot be seen and recorded as they cross frontiers. Nevertheless, since both goods and services involve payment by persons of the importing or receiving countries to persons in the exporting country, they are both 'exports' in this wider sense.

The main sources of invisible earnings and payments are:

(1) *Government expenditure abroad*, e.g. overseas garrisons, diplomatic services;

(2) *Shipping services*, e.g. an American travelling in the *Queen Elizabeth II* or shipping exports in a British merchantman;

(3) *Civil aviation;*

(4) *Travel*, e.g. sterling required by an American tourist for spending on a visit to London;

(5) *Other services*, e.g. royalties earned on books and records, income from the transactions of overseas oil companies which ship direct from wells and refineries abroad to other countries;

(6) *Interest, profits and dividends from overseas investments;*

(7) *Private transfers*, e.g. remittances to relatives abroad.

Payments for any of the above transactions involve changing into another country's currency. Thus they represent 'imports' to the paying country and 'exports' to the receiving country.

II. THE BALANCE OF PAYMENTS

Most countries give an account each year of their monetary transactions with the rest of the world. The accounts presented are known as 'the balance of payments'. The balance of payments for the United Kingdom for the year ended 31 December 1972 is given in Table 9. The description which follows deals with the form of presentation introduced in 1969.

The current account

The current account shows, on the one hand, the foreign currency which has been *spent* on *imported goods* and *invisibles* in the course of the year, and, on the other, the foreign currency which has been *earned* by *exporting goods* and *invisibles*.

That part of the current account which shows the payments for just the *goods* exported and imported is known as the *visible balance* (formerly the *balance of trade*). Where the value of goods exported exceeds the value of goods imported, we say that there is a favourable visible balance. If the opposite occurs, the visible balance is unfavourable. Too much, however, must not be read into the terms 'favourable' and 'unfavourable'. They are derived from the Mercantilists of the sixteenth century who thought that a country's wealth depended upon its having a favourable balance of trade. In the first place, we have to know the reasons for the unfavourable balance. It may be brought about, for instance, by an increased demand for raw materials—which will later be exported in the form of manufactured goods. Secondly, a favourable or unfavourable visible balance can be reversed when the invisibles are taken into account.

When we add to the visible balance, payments and income on the invisible items, we have what is known as the current balance. These items are shown in Table 9.

There is no special reason why earnings from goods and invisibles exported between 1 January and 31 December in any one year should equal expenditure on the goods and

invisibles imported during that period. In fact, it would be
an extraordinary coincidence if they did so. How often does
what you earn during the week tally *exactly* with what you
spend?

The current account, therefore, is likely to show a difference
between earnings and expenditure. When the *value* of goods
and invisibles exported exceeds the *value* of goods and invisibles
imported, we say that there is a surplus current balance;
when the reverse occurs, we say that there is a deficit current
balance. But once again too much should not be made of
these terms 'surplus' and 'deficit'. The current account is
only part of the statement covering a nation's overseas financial
transactions. Capital flows must also be scrutinised. As we
shall see, a current deficit need cause no alarm if it is covered
by borrowing which will be put to a productive use. On the
other hand, a current surplus may be insufficient to offset a
heavy drain on the reserves through the outward movement of
short- and long-term capital. The balance of payments statement must be examined as a whole.

Investment and other capital flows

If the current account transactions were a country's only
dealings with the world, the balance of payments accounts
would be quite simple. A surplus of £100 million, for example,
would add that amount to the reserves or allow the country to
invest that amount overseas or to pay off short-term borrowings from the International Monetary Fund (I.M.F.) or other
foreign creditors. A deficit of £100 million would reduce the
reserves by that amount or have to be financed by disinvestment or short-term borrowing abroad.

However, there are other flows of money into or out of a
country which affect its ability to build up reserves or to pay
off government debts. These are flows of capital—leaving
Britain for investment or loans abroad, and coming into
Britain for similar purposes. Thus investment by private
persons resident in the United Kingdom in factories or plant
overseas (whether directly or by the purchase of shares),
or a loan by the British government to an underdeveloped
country, lead to an outflow of capital and the spending of
foreign currency. Similarly, investment in the United Kingdom

by persons overseas or borrowing from abroad by the British government, local authorities, nationalised industries or companies lead to an inflow of foreign capital and the receipt of foreign currency. Whereas the current account covers *income* earning and spending in the course of the year, 'investment and other capital flows' deals with the movement of *capital* in and out of the country.

Until 1969, the United Kingdom distinguished between short- and long-term investment in calculating the overall Balance of Payments, adding the balance of long-term investment to the current balance to obtain what was known as the 'basic balance'. While this 'basic balance' was a good indication of the United Kingdom's position over the longer term, it did, when in deficit, tend to overstate the pressure on the reserves, and this could have serious repercussions on foreign confidence in sterling.

The fact is that much of Britain's overseas investment is financed by short-term capital borrowed from foreigners, e.g. from the growing pool of Euro-dollars deposited in London. To the extent that this occurs, there is no net outflow of foreign currency. Britain's overseas investment which is undertaken in order to make a profit is, in fact, like private business ventures. And, just as the shopkeeper borrows from his bank to cover the holding of stocks before Christmas, so the United Kingdom borrows to finance investment overseas in factories, plantations, oil-wells, nickel-mines, etc.

The new form of the United Kingdom's balance of payments accounts allows for this short-term borrowing. It concentrates attention on what is really significant to Britain—the extent to which currency flows as a whole influence her reserves of gold and foreign currencies. This is shown in the *total currency flow*.

The total currency flow

The total currency flow shows how much foreign currency is earned or is required to cover: (*a*) the current balance; (*b*) investment and other capital flows; (*c*) the 'balancing item'.

The *balancing item* arises as follows. When the total effect of recorded capital transactions is added to the current balance, the total never adds up exactly to the amount of foreign currency the country has in fact gained or lost, which is known precisely to the Bank of England. Government spending overseas, for instance, is easier to record exactly than the foreign spending of people taking holidays abroad. Exports, too, may go abroad in December, but payments for them come in the following February.

A 'balancing item' is therefore added to make up the difference between the total value of the transactions recorded and the precise accounts kept by the Bank of England. If the balancing item is ' – ', as in 1972, it means that more foreign currency has actually come in than the estimates of transactions have indicated. When there is a ' + ' balancing item, the opposite is the case.

Official financing

If there is a net currency *outflow*, the necessary payments must have been covered. For instance, imports must have been paid for even though receipts may not have been currently earned. *Official financing* shows how this has been achieved.

Similarly, if there is a net currency *inflow*, the official financing account shows how the balance has been disposed of.

It is in this sense that we can say that the Balance of Payments always balances.

Suppose that there is a net currency outflow. This can be covered by the monetary authorities by:

    (*a*) official borrowing from the I.M.F. or from the monetary authorities of other countries;

    (*b*) drawing on the United Kingdom's reserves of gold and foreign currency.

As we shall see in Chapter 33, a net currency outflow cannot go on indefinitely. Measures to correct the outflow, especially when the main cause is a persistent deficit on the current balance, will have to be taken.

Similarly, a net currency inflow enables the authorities to:

    (*a*) repay official borrowing;

    (*b*) add to the United Kingdom's reserves of gold and foreign currency.

Here any corrective measures which may be necessary are less painful, for an embarrassing inflow can to a large extent be taken care of by more lending abroad—which will increase investment and capital flows outwards.

An examination of the United Kingdom's Balance of Payments, 1972
    The above explanation can be illustrated by examining the United Kingdom's Balance of Payments for 1972.

TABLE 9
THE BALANCE OF PAYMENTS OF THE UNITED KINGDOM,
1972 (£ mn.)

CURRENT ACCOUNT		
Visible trade		
Exports (f.o.b.)	+9,134	
Imports (f.o.b.)	−9,819	
Visible balance		− 685
Invisibles (net)		
Government	− 548	
Shipping	− 54	
Civil aviation	+ 64	
Travel	+ 22	
Other services	+ 903	
Interest, profits and dividends	+ 456	
Private transfers	− 75	
Invisible balance		+ 768
CURRENT BALANCE		+ 83
TOTAL CURRENCY FLOW		
Current balance		+ 83
Investment and other capital flows (net)		− 756
Balancing item		− 592
Total currency flow		− 1,265
Allocation of Special Drawing Rights		+ 124
Total		− 1,141
OFFICIAL FINANCING—drawings on (+), repayments or additions to (−)		
IMF		− 415
Other monetary authorities		+ 864
Official reserves of gold and foreign currency		+ 692
		+ 1,141

Source: *United Kingdom Balance of Payments, 1973* (HMSO)

Imports exceeded exports; there was a visible balance deficit of £685 million. On invisibles, the United Kingdom had a favourable balance of £768 million. The overall surplus on the Current Balance was then £83 million.

But apart from this surplus on her current trading, the United Kingdom also had a net outflow of currency of £756 million from her lending and borrowing. This, together with a

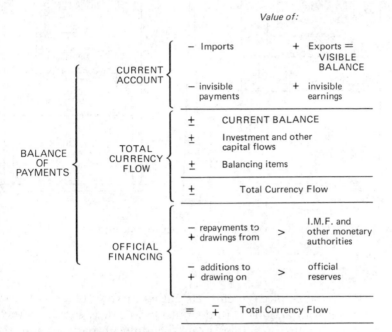

Value of:

FIG. 111.—The balance of payments in outline.

balancing item of − £592 million, meant that her net currency outflow was £1,265 million. Even though the United Kingdom was allocated £124 million of newly-created Special Drawing Rights, it still meant that £1,141 million had to be covered by official financing.

Because the United Kingdom repaid £415 million of previous borrowings to the International Monetary Fund, she had £1,556 million to find. This was obtained by borrowing £864 million from monetary authorities of other countries (the Group of Ten) and by withdrawing £692 million from the reserves.

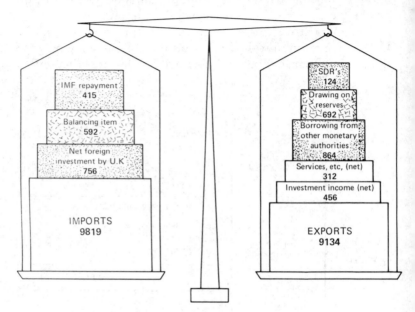

FIG. 112.—The balance of payments 1972.

Summary

The balance of payments sets out an analysis of a country's financial transactions with the outside world. It shows, in the current account, whether, in its spending abroad, a country is living within its total overseas income; in the investment and other capital flows, how any deficit or surplus has been aggravated by capital movements and, in the 'official financing', how the necessary foreign currency to meet an overseas payments deficit has been obtained or how any surplus has been disposed of.

CHAPTER 32

FOREIGN EXCHANGE RATES

How are exchange rates determined?

TRADE between countries involves, as we have seen, an exchange of their currencies. But how is the rate at which one currency exchanges for another determined? Why is it that we have to give a pound note to obtain about 2.40 American dollars, 7·25 Swiss francs, 10·25 French francs, and so on?

The simple answer is that the price of the pound sterling, like all other prices, is determined by the forces of demand and supply. In this case the market is known as the 'foreign-exchange market'. It meets in no one place, but consists of all the institutions and persons—banks of all kinds, dealers, and brokers—who are buying and selling foreign currencies. The foreign-exchange market is a world market, dealers throughout the world being in constant contact with one another by telephone.

Let us assume that we have 'freely fluctuating exchange rates'; that is, rates are not fixed by governments, but are free to move from day to day according to changes in the conditions of demand and supply. To discover how a change in the exchange rate can come about, we can glance once again at the mechanism of foreign payments.

When the British merchant wished to import cotton from the U.S.A. (*see* p. 464), he went to his bank to obtain the necessary dollars for payment. These dollars, we saw, were obtained from its branch in the U.S.A., and this branch in its turn had received them from an American importer of sports cars who had deposited them in exchange for the pounds sterling he needed to pay the British motor firm. Let us assume that the existing exchange rate is $2.40 to the pound sterling and that trade is such that the same quantity of dollars is both demanded and supplied.

The situation, we will imagine, now changes. Imports of cotton from the U.S.A. increase in value, but exports of sports cars remain the same. The bank now finds that because more dollars are being demanded than are being deposited, its reserves of dollars are depleted. In short, the demand for dollars exceeds the supply. It is possible that the bank will be able to find on the foreign-exchange market another bank or dealer who is receiving more dollars than pounds sterling. But if its experience is typical of the rest of the market, that is, there has been a general increase in the demand for dollars relative to pounds, it will be able to replenish its reserves of dollars only by offering more pounds sterling in exchange. The dollar thus appreciates in value, say, to $2.38 to the pound. (As we shall see later, this will, to a large extent, bring a self-correcting mechanism into operation as regards the lack of balance between the value of imports and the value of exports.)

Arbitrage

We have concentrated our attention on the rate of exchange between the dollar and the pound. But there is also an exchange rate between the pound and the German mark, the French franc, and so on; and all these rates are linked with one another. If, for instance, £1 = $3 and $1 = 2 marks, then £1 must equal 6 marks. Otherwise, what are known as arbitrage operations by foreign-exchange dealers would bring the rates into line. Thus suppose in London 7 marks can be obtained for the pound. A dealer would buy marks for pounds in London, sell them for dollars in New York, and exchange the dollars for pounds, making 16p profit on the deal. This would not last for long, because the world market in foreign exchange is so perfect that the increased demand for marks in London would soon bring the price there into line with the world price.

What are the factors upon which the demand for or supply of foreign currency depend?

It can be seen that an increased demand for dollars by people in Britain is one and the same thing as an increase in the supply of sterling being offered for dollars. An increased demand for dollars may be counteracted by an increased demand for sterling (that is, an increased supply of dollars) by Americans. For the sake of simplicity, we will concentrate our attention on the factors leading to a demand for sterling by Americans. These factors are:

(1) To pay for the import of goods from Britain.

(2) To pay for 'invisibles', e.g. a tour of Britain, government spending on troops in Britain, etc.

(3) To meet capital movements into Britain. *Long-term capital* movements may take the form of: (*a*) purchasing securities held by people in Britain; (*b*) taking over a British-owned company, e.g. the Ford Motor Company of Dagenham; (*c*) loans to the British government. Demanding sterling for any of these purposes would have the effect of appreciating the value of sterling. *Short-term capital* is usually moved to cover: (*a*) short-term lending, where persons having funds to lend for a short period move them from New York to London to take advantage of the higher rate of interest being offered there, e.g. on Treasury Bills (*see* p. 483); (*b*) *speculation*, where dealers who expect the value of the pound sterling to rise will wish to hold sterling or securities with a fixed nominal sterling value; (*c*) an excess value of American exports over British imports, whereby an American exporter adds to his 'sterling balances' by giving credit to the British importer. In the latter instance, an exact supply of dollars is made available to meet the increased demand, and so there need be no alteration in the exchange rate.

What are the underlying economic forces influencing how much foreign currency is demanded and supplied?

So far we have merely indicated the items for which foreign currency will be demanded or supplied. Now we examine the economic forces which determine how large each of these items will be. They are:

(1) *Relative prices*

The chief factor affecting trade, both visible and invisible, is the price of home-produced goods as compared with the price of similar goods abroad. If, for example, American prices are high, Americans will wish to import cheaper British goods, whereas the British will prefer home-produced goods to

American. The increased demand for sterling will, in a free exchange market, so raise the value of the pound sterling that eventually the prices of British goods are in line with those of the 'high-cost' American producer.

Some economists, notably Professor Gustav Cassel in 1922, carried this argument a stage further. They said quite categorically, in what became known as the *Purchasing Power Parity Theory*, that the value of a foreign currency in terms of another depends mainly on the relative purchasing power of the two currencies in their respective countries. In other words, the exchange rate settles at the level which makes the purchasing power of a given unit of currency the same in whatever country it is spent.

For example, suppose that there is only one commodity, a type of machine, and this machine sells for £20 in Britain and for $48 in the U.S.A.; then the rate of exchange would be 2.40 dollars to the pound. If now the price in Britain rises to £24, the rate of exchange will be 2 dollars to the pound. Thus a fall in the internal purchasing power of a currency through a rise in the general level of prices leads to a corresponding fall in its foreign-exchange value. Or, mathematically, the Purchasing Power Parity Theory says that:

$$\text{Foreign exchange price of £ (e.g. in dollars)} = \frac{\text{U.S. price level}}{\text{British price level}}.$$

When we are considering the long period, there is considerable truth in this theory. If, for instance, there is an inflation of prices in Britain relative to the U.S.A., there will be less demand for British exports, but an increased demand for American imports. As a result, the price of the pound sterling falls in terms of the dollar. But, particularly in the short run, to say that overall purchasing power is the sole factor governing exchange rates is a gross over-simplification. The theory fails to allow for the following:

(a) Not all goods enter into international trade. Quite a number, for instance the Indian's loin-cloth, satisfy local and particular wants. Others, like houses, railway travel, gas and electricity, haircuts and personal and professional services, cannot be transported easily from one country to another. The prices of such goods may rise considerably, whereas those of exports remain the same. Eventually, export industries will be forced by competition to pay higher wages, etc., but owing to immobility and imperfections of the market, this may take a very long time to come about. In the meantime, exchange rates will not be affected—in spite of the statistical rise in the general level of prices.

(b) Such factors as indirect taxes, subsidies and transport costs may change the prices of goods within a country but not affect exchange rates in the way the theory predicts. Suppose a 100 per cent tariff is placed on an important import, the demand for which is not absolutely inelastic. The price in the home market would rise, but since less foreign currency would be spent on it, the exchange rate would tend to improve!

(c) A change in the exchange rate may originate in factors quite independent of the internal price level. When national income rises, for instance, imports are likely to increase in value relative to exports. As a result, the external value of the currency will depreciate. Similarly, a change in the terms of trade may affect the exchange rate. Suppose, for instance, improved techniques increased the supply of oil, thereby leading to a fall in its world price. If the demand for oil were inelastic, a country such as Kuwait would earn less foreign currency, and her own currency would fall in value on the foreign-exchange market.

(d) The theory ignores the effect of movements of capital upon the exchange rates, an influence which is particularly important in the short period (see p. 478).

The Purchasing Power Parity Theory, therefore, is not a complete explanation of what determines exchange rates. But this does not mean that the theory has no value. Since imports and exports are the major items in a country's balance of payments, it draws attention to what, in the long run, is the dominant influence on exchange rates—how the internal price level moves relative to that of other countries. Indeed, there is a close link between this and the movement of capital for speculative purposes, for the latter is likely to reinforce changes in the exchange rates originating in the current account of the balance of payments.

The fundamental link between internal price levels and the external value of currencies is only too vividly illustrated by Britain's experience since World War II. During this period, the basic cause of the pressure on her gold and dollar reserves has been her inability to maintain the internal value of the pound sterling.

(2) *Relative money incomes*

When a country's money income expands, its demand for imports increases. Potential exports also tend to be diverted to the home market.

(3) *Long-term investment prospects*

People can invest capital in foreign countries either by buying the bonds of foreign governments or the equities of companies there, or directly by building factories abroad as offshoots of parent companies in the United Kingdom. The chief factor influencing such investment decisions is how the prospective yield compares with that which could be obtained elsewhere, although an allowance has to be made for political and other risks, such as the monetary policies of the countries concerned.

(4) *The rate of interest*

Short-term capital moves from one country to another as changes take place in the rate of interest being offered by each. The government can, therefore, vary interest rates to attract or repel foreign capital as it sees fit.

(5) *Expected future movements of the exchange rate*

Inflation in a country will be interpreted by foreign holders of its currency as being likely to lead also to a fall in the external value of the currency. Selling of the currency follows, thereby helping to bring about the fulfilment of those expectations!

(6) *Government expenditure*

Military expenditure and economic aid abroad now provide large sources of supply of certain currencies, e.g. the American dollar and the pound sterling, to foreigners.

(7) *Political factors and government policy*

Both of these may exert a significant influence on movements of capital.

It can be seen, therefore, that exchange rates are not dependent on any single factor. The only safe generalisation which can be made is that the value of a currency depends upon all the forces which give rise to the purchase or sale of that currency in the foreign-exchange market.

CHAPTER 33

THE CORRECTION OF A BALANCE-OF-PAYMENTS DISEQUILIBRIUM

I. ALTERNATIVE APPROACHES

When do corrective measures become necessary?

TAKEN as a whole, the balance of payments must always balance. Foreign currency necessary for making payments abroad must have come from somewhere. If earnings from exports and invisibles are insufficient, the balance must be achieved by drawing on the gold and convertible currency reserves or by borrowing.

In the short period, a withdrawal from the reserves may not be serious. It could easily happen that, just prior to 31 December, the date usually chosen for drawing up the accounts, imports of raw materials were running at a high rate. Later, when the goods manufactured from these raw materials are sold abroad, the reserves will be replenished. Reserves of gold and foreign currencies are held for this very purpose—to provide a 'cushion' when current earnings are temporarily insufficient to cover payments abroad. Even individuals usually carry spare cash to bridge the gap between income and spending.

Alternatively, an underdeveloped country may run an adverse balance of payments for a number of years. The deficit is covered, not by drawing on reserves, but by borrowing. Loans are used to buy capital equipment. Eventually, this equipment will allow her to export goods which will cover the interest due on the loan and then the repayment of the loan itself. Once again, the balance-of-payment deficit need not be frowned upon; it is just good business—like a firm obtaining a loan from the bank.

But the situation is different when year after year a country is running a balance-of-payments deficit and there is little likelihood of its being able to reverse the trend. This disequilibrium between credits and debits is then said to be of a 'fundamental nature'. If not corrected, reserves will run out (see p. 463). Other countries will refuse to lend to the country in difficulties—they doubt whether the spendthrift will ever be in a position to repay.

A broad analysis of the problem

In such circumstances, therefore, there must be some mechanism whereby the persistent balance-of-payments deficit can be corrected, bringing about an increase in earnings from exports and a decrease in payments for imports. The main way is to make exports cheaper to the foreigner and imports dearer to the home buyer. We shall now examine how this can be achieved.

Partly for the sake of simplicity and partly to be as real as possible, we conduct our analysis in terms of the specific problem of increasing Britain's exports to the U.S.A. In other words, we assume that the most effective attack on the balance-of-payments deficit can be mounted by increasing our dollar earnings and decreasing our dollar spending. It is a simplified approach because it concentrates on a deficit to the exclusion of a surplus. But it can be assumed that if the opposite measures to those discussed are put into operation, then the problem of a surplus can be removed. It is realistic on two counts. First, while a fundamental deficit must be dealt with, there is less urgency about a surplus. Provided a country is willing to accumulate gold, or better, to lend abroad, it can run a surplus for a number of years, although the International Monetary Fund would probably hint that some revaluation of its currency might be helpful. Secondly, a balance-of-payments deficit is the problem which has persistently faced the United Kingdom for the last quarter of a century.

The price of exports has two components: (*a*) the home price in sterling; (*b*) the rate at which the pound sterling exchanges against the dollar. It is possible, therefore, to reduce export prices by an attack on either, or both, of these fronts.

In theory, if the balance-of-payments deficit is to be corrected by reducing home prices, the *gold standard* provides an automatic mechanism. On the other hand, if the correction is to be achieved by an adjustment of the exchange rate, the *freely operating foreign-exchange market* fulfils a similar role. In practice, however, both methods have serious drawbacks, so serious indeed that today most countries recognise that a compromise system, backed by international agreement, is essential. In what follows, therefore, we discuss the ways by which automatic corrections can take place first by deflation, and secondly by depreciation. We then proceed to describe how 'managed flexibility' has worked under the Bretton Woods agreement. This section is retained in the present tense for, although recent developments have undermined the specific provisions of Bretton Woods, most countries still adhere to it in principle. We conclude, therefore, with a brief survey of the current international monetary scene.

II. DEFLATION: THE GOLD STANDARD

Meaning of the 'gold standard'

A country is said to be 'on the gold standard' when its standard monetary unit can be exchanged for gold at a fixed rate and without restriction. Thus, in 1914, the pound sterling was exchangeable for 113·0016 grains of fine gold, and the American dollar for 23·22 grains. As a result: (a) a country's currency was virtually equivalent to gold; (b) the rate at which each country's currency could be exchanged for another's was fixed through their common link with gold; (c) gold was a world currency; (d) there was an automatic mechanism for correcting a balance-of-payments disequilibrium.

Mechanism of the gold standard

Suppose that the value of Britain's imports from the U.S.A. exceeds the value of her exports. Dollars would be required to pay for these imports and the price of the dollar would rise relative to the pound on the foreign-exchange market.

Now £1 sterling would buy 113 grains of fine gold; and this quantity of gold could also be exchanged for $4.86. Therefore, £1 = $4.86. If, on the exchange market, a British importer could obtain only $4.70 for a pound, it would be cheaper for him to change his sterling into gold at the fixed price, and then ship this gold to the American exporter in order to pay for the goods. In practice, therefore, £1 could never exchange for less than $4.86 minus the cost of buying gold and shipping it to America (about ½ per cent). Similarly, if exports were greater in value than imports, £1 could never exchange for more than $4.86 plus the cost of buying and shipping gold from America. Thus the rate of exchange between the pound and the dollar could only fluctuate within very narrow limits—the gold points. Fixed exchange rates had a favourable effect on the volume of international trade. But what results followed from the export of gold to meet the balance-of-payments deficit?

Purchases of gold were paid for by cheques drawn on the commercial banks. The commercial banks drew the gold from the Bank of England, thereby lowering the cash balances they held there. This reduced their reserve ratio, and so unless the Bank of England restored the position by buying securities on the open market, the commercial banks had to reduce their lending activities.

Furthermore, the Bank of England's power to issue notes was limited by its gold reserve and the Fiduciary Issue. With gold leaving the country, it would be forced to reduce its note issue. Any application to increase the Fiduciary Issue would have been regarded as a panic measure. Hence in order to protect the gold reserves, it raised the bank rate, supporting this policy with open-market operations. Other interest rates, particularly the discount rate, moved in sympathy.

This had two effects. First, the higher rate of interest charged reduced the flow of bills sent to London for discounting. Thus the export of short-term capital was reduced. Secondly, the relatively higher rates of interest which could now be earned not only made the short-term balances held in London for settling trading accounts more profitable, but attracted short-term foreign loans looking for the highest possible yield. The two taken together had an immediate, first-aid effect of halting, and even reversing, the outflow of gold. But to remove the real cause of the outflow of gold—the decrease in the earnings from exports compared with expenditure on imports—fundamental changes in the economy were necessary. These came about as follows.

Higher interest rates led to a reduction both in the holding of stocks and in capital investment at home. This brought about a fall in the demand for imported raw materials—another fairly immediate benefit. But the fall in investment also led, through the multiplier, to an all-round contraction of incomes at home. This, it was assumed, would bring a proportionate fall in costs and thus lower home prices, making it easier to export. In practice events did not work out like this. Costs, particularly wages, proved sticky. Restoration of a balance-of-payments equilibrium was achieved, not so much by increasing exports, as by reduced imports as incomes fell. Eventually, however, the unemployment which resulted from the deflation had its effect. Wages were forced down, costs reduced, prices of home-produced goods fell, exports became cheaper relative to foreign goods, and the flow of trade was reversed. The full mechanism is shown in Fig. 113.

U.K.—BALANCE OF PAYMENTS (–)	U.S.A.—BALANCE OF PAYMENTS (+)
(1) Demand for dollars, therefore price rises,	(1) Supply of pounds, therefore price falls,
therefore gold loss	therefore gold gain
(2) Bank rate raised	(2) Bank rate lowered
Higher interest rates	Lower interest rates
(A) INFLOW OF FOREIGN CAPITAL	(A) OUTFLOW OF FOREIGN CAPITAL
(3) Deflation of home income	(3) Inflation of home income
(B) DECREASED DEMAND FOR IMPORTS	(B) INCREASED DEMAND FOR IMPORTS
(4) Fall in wage rates and prices, therefore exports cheaper	(4) Rise in wage rates and prices, therefore exports dearer
(C) INCREASED DEMAND FOR U.K. EXPORTS BY U.S.A.	(C) DECREASED DEMAND FOR U.S.A. EXPORTS BY U.K.

(5) Balance of payments brought into equilibrium
(*see* p. 495 *re* elasticity of demand for imports and exports)

FIG. 113.—The mechanism of the gold standard.

The failure of the gold-standard mechanism

The great merit of the gold standard was that, in maintaining stable exchange rates, it facilitated international trade. Its main

drawback was that, while in theory its mechanism was automatic, in practice its operation was clumsy, so clumsy in fact
that countries could not afford to continue working it.

First, an outflow (or inflow) of gold was not always the result
of rises (or falls) in costs and prices at home. Gold movements
could be produced by speculative capital movements, susceptible to frequent waves of optimism and pessimism. To use the
gold-standard mechanism, with its dislocative effect on the
whole of the economy, to offset such changes in the flow of
capital was like taking a sledge-hammer to crack a nut.

Secondly, if the mechanism were to operate successfully, it
was necessary that countries should obey what are known as
the 'rules of the gold standard'. Put briefly, these are: (a) gold
should be allowed to move freely according to the dictates of
trade; (b) an inflow of gold should be followed by an expansionary policy through lower interest rates, and vice versa; (c)
the movement of trade should depend upon relative prices and
not be artificially restricted by tariffs, quotas, exchange control,
etc. During the twentieth century these rules were applied only
imperfectly. Countries receiving gold were afraid to follow an
inflationary policy, knowing that it would probably produce
unemployment in their export industries. Instead of the inflow
of gold being reversed, reserves of gold were accumulated and
frozen. Nations losing gold were therefore forced to restrict
imports by tariffs, etc. The volume of international trade was
thus reduced.

Thirdly, the complete mechanism was dependent upon
making exports relatively cheaper by lowering prices at home.
But this proved difficult. Costs are not easy to lower—rent and
interest payments are usually contractual, and monopolies and
cartels combined to resist a fall in prices. Above all, it involved
workers accepting lower money wages. This they have always,
through their trade unions, resisted, preferring to remain
unemployed instead. In short, the gold-standard mechanism
was at variance with trade-union policy. The amount spent on
imports dropped, not because home-produced goods fell in
price and became more competitive, but because the demand
for imported goods decreased as unemployment at home
brought about a fall in money national income (see p. 392).
After prolonged heavy unemployment, workers were eventually

forced to accept lower wages, and only then did exports revive. In the meantime, the deflation caused severe suffering. Rather than continue with this, the United Kingdom and most other countries finally abandoned the gold standard in 1931.

III. DEPRECIATION: FREELY FLUCTUATING EXCHANGE RATES

How exchange depreciation works

The big disadvantage of the gold-standard mechanism is that a country cannot follow an independent internal monetary policy in order to promote full employment. Even short-term capital movements may affect policy through their influence on the flow of gold. More important, if there is unemployment abroad, the reduced demand for the home country's exports brings about an outward movement of gold through the balance-of-payments deficit which ensues. Thus deflation is forced upon the home country—it too suffers unemployment. Only if full employment is maintained abroad can a major exporter like the United Kingdom hope to preserve full employment at home.

Exchange depreciation, on the other hand, leaves home prices and incomes as they are, but makes exports cheaper and imports dearer by lowering the external value of the home currency. (*Depreciation* usually refers to a reduction of the value of a currency in terms of other currencies through the operations of the foreign-exchange market. *Devaluation* is a reduction in the value of a currency, usually by adjusting the rate at which it is pegged to gold, by a deliberate decision of the government. In practice, the results of the two can be analysed in the same way.)

Let us suppose once more that Britain has a deficit on her balance of payments with the U.S.A. There is thus a demand for dollars relative to the pound, and the exchange rate moves in favour of the U.S.A. British importers have to give more pounds to obtain the dollars needed to buy American goods; prices of American goods have risen to the British buyer. Similarly, prices of British goods have fallen to the American buyer. Provided that, taken together, the demand for both exports and imports is sufficiently elastic (*see* p. 495), there will be a correction of Britain's balance-of-payments disequilibrium.

Advantages and disadvantages of exchange depreciation as a means of correcting a balance-of-payments disequilibrium

Exchange depreciation has the advantage that this correction is effected without the tribulations of deflation. Instead a country can follow its own internal monetary policy—even inflating if it thinks that unemployment is around the corner (though this would not be easy if the balance of payments were in deficit, as Britain has discovered since the war).

Moreover, with freely fluctuating exchange rates (when the value of the currency 'floats'), the correction is secured without the many controls which are often necessary when the exchange rate is 'pegged' (*see* p. 493).

Unfortunately, fluctuating exchange rates are themselves not without disadvantages. First, the demand for exports and imports may be so inelastic that the balance-of-payments disequilibrium is made worse by depreciation rather than better (*see* p. 495). Supply, too, may be so inelastic that a country cannot take advantage of the expanded demand for its exports which follows a fall in the exchange value of its currency (*see* p. 496). It should be emphasised, however, that, particularly in the long-run, such conditions are possible rather than likely in the real world.

Secondly, and more important, when exchange rates are allowed to fluctuate freely, not only is speculation encouraged, but movements are more frequent and pronounced. Foreign importers of British goods, who expect the price of sterling to depreciate, delay paying for the goods as long as possible; British importers of foreign goods make their payments in foreign currency as soon as possible—'lags' and 'leads'.

Above all, not only trade, but the shifting of capital between countries influences the exchange rates, and this applies particularly to that capital which is moved according to the holder's estimate of the future value of currencies. And, as we have seen, this movement can bring about the very rise or fall in the exchange rate which was expected.

By the time an exporter receives payment for his goods, the exchange rate may so have moved against him that his expected profit has been turned into a loss. In such circumstances he may prefer not to take the risk of trading with somebody in another country. Although arrangements can usually be made with a dealer to supply 'forward exchange' (that is, the foreign currency can be obtained at a given future date at an agreed price), trade may still not be worthwhile through the additional cost involved.

IV. MANAGED FLEXIBILITY

Flexible exchange rates and the Exchange Equalisation Account

When Britain left the gold standard in 1931, she followed a policy of flexible exchange rates. The external value of the pound was determined by the free operation of the forces of demand and supply on the foreign-exchange market. As a result, by 1932 the dollar rate for the pound had fallen from the old par value of 4.86 to 3.17, but the pound subsequently recovered.

Nevertheless, to cancel out fluctuations in the exchange rate brought about by movements of short-term capital, particularly that transferred for speculative purposes, the government set up an *Exchange Equalisation Account.*

Basically, this Account operated by the simple application of the laws of price. It had a stock of gold and foreign currencies (mostly borrowed against Treasury Bills), and this stock was either replenished or offered on the market according to whether short-term capital was moving into or out of London. A movement of capital into London would increase the demand for the pound and drive up its price; the Account could therefore prevent this rise by offering pounds in exchange for dollars. The value of the pound would not change, but the Account would add to its stock of dollars. On the other hand, if there was a movement of capital out of London, there would be a fall in the demand for the pound, and its price would fall. In this case, therefore, the Account would offer dollars in exchange for pounds—in other words, it would increase its demand for pounds relative to dollars. The value of the pound would again remain stable, but here the Account would reduce its stock of dollars, increasing its holding of pounds. These pounds were usually held in the form of Treasury Bills so that a small rate of interest could be earned on them.

The knowledge that such an Account existed to even out

exchange fluctuations did much to prevent speculation in the value of the pound. The Account could, however, let that value appreciate or depreciate within its discretion.

After Bretton Woods, 1944, the main purpose of the Exchange Equalisation Account was to maintain the value of the pound within the limits declared with the International Monetary Fund.

'Managed flexibility'

The major defect of freely fluctuating exchange rates is that they discourage international trade. Countries recognised that the system was one of the reasons why trade failed to revive in the early 1930s. Yet they had turned their backs once and for all on the gold standard, with its corollary of domestic income adjustment.

The solution was a compromise—'managed flexibility'. Instead of exchange rates being allowed to fluctuate freely according to the prevailing conditions of demand and supply, countries agreed to stabilise the exchange value of their currencies over a long period. This was achieved by setting up Exchange Equalisation Accounts on the British pattern. Reserves of gold and foreign exchange (and sometimes direct controls) were used to offset short-term variations in demand for their currencies. By such official intervention the exchange rate was 'pegged' within narrow limits.

The Bretton Woods Agreement, 1944

It can be seen that the difference between freely fluctuating exchange rates and managed flexibility is that with the former the rate varies from day to day, but with the latter it remains stable over a long period and is changed only by a deliberate decision of a country's monetary authority. Such a change would be necessary when there was an excessive accumulation or depletion of the reserves.

But inter-war management of exchange rates was imperfect. Since it was easier to maintain home employment if exports were cheap, governments were often tempted to reduce the exchange value of their currency, and competitive devaluation resulted. Moreover, the reserves of many countries were inadequate to maintain the rate in periods of prolonged strain.

Hence a conference was held at Bretton Woods, U.S.A., in 1944 to discuss how countries could best promote world recovery after the war. It drew up an international code of monetary behaviour and established the International Monetary Fund (I.M.F.) and the International Bank for Reconstruction and Development (the World Bank). Managed flexibility now works under the International Monetary Fund as follows:

(1) Each member country declares a par value for its currency in terms of gold, thereby fixing the exchange rates between all currencies. Thus the exchange rate between the pound and dollar was originally $4.03, but this was altered in 1949 to $2·80, in 1967 to $2·40, and in 1971 to $2·60.

(2) Countries agree to maintain free convertibility of their currency for current transactions at its declared value, within fairly narrow limits (agreed in 1971 as $2\frac{1}{4}$ per cent above or below).

(3) To see a country through a period when it is running a short-term deficit, the I.M.F. will make gold and foreign currencies available. The reserves which are held for this purpose were originally subscribed on a 'quota' basis by each member. In exchange for its own currency, a country can purchase from the Fund the currency of another member up to 25 per cent of its 'quota' per annum, provided that the Fund's holding of the country's currency is not more than double its quota.

(4) When downward adjustment of the exchange value of a currency is necessary, certain rules apply to prevent devaluation from becoming competitive. A country may devalue up to 10 per cent by merely notifying the Fund, but a greater or subsequent change requires the consent of the governing body.

(5) In order to prevent the limitation of international trade, the Fund may make recommendations to members. A currency may be declared 'scarce', in which case it may be rationed out and the country concerned may even be asked to revalue. Or a country may be requested to follow an employment policy which will maintain its volume of imports (*see* p. 392).

In past years Britain borrowed from the Fund when her reserves were under stress. And, although today much of Bretton Woods has, largely through the weakness of the American dollar and pound sterling, been left high and dry, the I.M.F. still provides the inspiration and the means for member countries to co-operate in international monetary affairs.

The International Bank for Reconstruction and Development (the World Bank)

Whereas the I.M.F. makes short-term funds available to meet a temporary balance-of-payments deficit, the World Bank provides long-term finance for reconstruction and development —roads, irrigation projects, power stations, etc., especially in the underdeveloped countries.

Funds are obtained by: (1) a 'quota' subscribed by member nations roughly in proportion to their national incomes; (2) borrowing on the international market by the issue of bonds backed by the quotas of members. In addition, in order to encourage private lending, the Bank will, in return for a small premium of $\frac{1}{2}$ to 1 per cent, guarantee repayment of the loan.

Countries which have economically sound projects but cannot obtain loans from private sources at a reasonably low rate of interest may borrow from the Bank for a period of five to twenty-five years at about 4 per cent.

V. THE CORRECTION OF A BALANCE-OF-PAYMENTS DEFICIT UNDER 'MANAGED FLEXIBILITY'

Objectives of management

The post-war system of managed flexibility retains stable exchange rates—the advantage of the gold-standard mechanism —but does not require that the rate shall be maintained by an automatic mechanism of inflation and deflation. Instead, it allows a country to adopt a variety of measures to maintain its foreign-exchange rate and, where necessary, to alter the rate. But it recognises that any such action has international repercussions and that co-operation between countries is therefore essential. Consequently, in correcting a balance-of-payments disequilibrium, countries should honour their obligations under the Bretton Woods and subsequent agreements and GATT— though this may not always happen!

Suppose a country has a recurrent deficit on the current account of her balance of payments. Because payments exceed earnings, the demand for foreign currency exceeds the supply. Hence in order to maintain the existing rate of exchange, the Exchange Equalisation Account is forced to run down its reserves. Measures must therefore be taken to defend the reserves. While initially such action may aim at attracting loans, eventually it must secure an increase in the value of exports or a decrease in the value of imports, or both.

Measures are of two kinds: (a) those supporting the existing rate; (b) devaluation.

Measures which may be taken to maintain the existing rate of exchange
(1) *First-aid remedies*

Two first-aid remedies could be followed by the United Kingdom: (a) the minimum lending rate is raised; (b) reserves are strengthened by borrowing from the I.M.F. and other central banks. The former attracts funds to London much as it did under the gold-standard mechanism (*see* p. 483), while the latter helps to restore confidence in sterling.

(2) *Import duties and quotas*

Tariffs may be levied to increase the price of imports. But if demand is inelastic, as it may well be for foodstuffs and raw materials, imports will not be greatly discouraged or the expenditure on them decrease. Sometimes, therefore, an import quota in terms of volume is fixed beyond which further imports are not allowed. As a result, however, the advantages of free trade are reduced, while the efficiency of the home industry may be impaired by its protection from foreign competition. Moreover, tariffs displease other countries.

(3) *Exchange control*

Exchange control (*see* p. 456) may be introduced for the following purposes:
  (a) to limit the amount of foreign currency spent on imports;
  (b) to discriminate against those countries whose currencies are 'hard' (that is, cannot easily be earned by exporting to them), and to favour those countries whose currencies

are 'soft' (because they buy exports from the country concerned);

(c) to distinguish between essential and non-essential goods;

(d) to control the export of capital.

Exchange control is essential when a country's currency is overvalued—that is, its declared exchange rate is higher than it would be if it were determined by demand and supply in the foreign-exchange market. What this really means is that foreign currencies are valued below the market price—and so they have to be rationed.

Pegging the rate at a high level, however, may be advantageous to the country concerned, particularly if her demand for imports and supply of exports is inelastic. In such circumstances, the balance of payments would not be improved by reducing the external value of the currency (*see* p. 495).

This was the position facing the United Kingdom after the war. Imports of foodstuffs and raw materials were essential, but her productive capacity was such that she could not deliver all the exports on order. Because foreign currency was scarce, the purposes for which it was required had to be carefully scrutinised. Imports from hard-currency areas, such as the U.S.A. and Switzerland, were severely curtailed. Spending on non-essentials, such as foreign travel, was strictly limited. Even today exchange control still operates for certain capital movements.

Nevertheless, exchange control suffers from many of the disadvantages associated with rationing. Inefficient home firms are protected from foreign competition. Regulations are evaded, and 'black markets' in the currencies occur. Many administrators are needed who could be more productively employed elsewhere. Moreover, it can lead to uncertainty in international trade. Countries may find their regular markets closed, and firms cannot plan ahead because of uncertainty as to whether they will be allowed to purchase their raw materials from a hard-currency area. Furthermore, the confidence of foreigners is impaired if any attempt is made to prohibit the movement of their funds out of a country. Finally, when people are prevented from buying in hard-currency countries, it often means that they are forced to purchase dearer or inferior goods elsewhere.

(4) *Mild deflation*

From our study of the gold-standard mechanism, we saw that deflation means abandoning full employment as an essential of policy. Therefore governments are loath to follow it. On the other hand, one of the major causes of balance-of-payment difficulties since the war has been the inability of countries, including Britain, to prevent costs and prices rising at home.

For this reason, disinflationary measures may be forced upon a country dependent upon exports in a balance-of-payments crisis. A reduction in incomes reduces the demand for imports and releases goods for the export market. Costs and prices may be stabilised, thereby making exports more competitive in world markets.

(5) *Measures to promote exports*

Governments may pursue a vigorous policy to promote exports. Thus the British government guarantees payment through the Export Credits Guarantee Department and gives information on the possibility of developing markets abroad. Moreover, in the granting of loans, banks are asked to discriminate in favour of exporters. Although under the terms of GATT it is impossible to grant direct tax reliefs, incentives can be incorporated in indirect taxes, for example zero-rating VAT on exports. Help to exports can also be given by exempting earnings from them from controls on dividends during a price-freeze.

Devaluation

Where a country is faced with a persistent deficit in her balance of payments, it may have to devalue. Devaluation, unlike depreciation, is a once-for-all reduction in the declared gold value of a country's currency by deliberate government decision. This means that the exchange value of the currency in terms of other currencies falls. Hence devaluation works in the same way as depreciation—not by bringing down the internal price level, but by reducing the rate at which it exchanges for other currencies.

Let us suppose that the United Kingdom trades only with the U.S.A. and that she has a persistent balance-of-payments deficit. She therefore decides to devalue from $2.40 to $2 to the

pound sterling. Whether such devaluation is successful or not
will depend upon the answers to the following questions.

(1) *What is the elasticity of demand for exports and imports?*

The effect of the devaluation will be to make British exports
cheaper in terms of dollars to the American buyer and imports
from America dearer in terms of pounds to the British buyer.

A British good formerly selling in the U.S.A. for $2.40 need
now cost only $2. This fall in price should lead to more British
goods being demanded, and, if elasticity of demand is greater
than unity, more dollars will be earned.

Similarly, an American good worth $2.40 formerly cost the
British buyer £1. After the devaluation, the price will rise to
£1·20. But will this mean that we have to spend more *dollars* on
our imports? The answer is 'no'. (Suppose that you are on a
camping holiday in France and that the pound is devalued.
Will your bread, camp site, etc., change in price?) The worst
possible situation is when demand for imports is absolutely
inelastic; then the same quantity of imports will be demanded
and the same amount of dollars spent on them. Otherwise there
will be some contraction of demand (because the price in terms
of pounds has risen) and then expenditure in dollars will fall.

The two elasticities of demand for exports and imports must
be considered together. Even if the demand for imports is
absolutely inelastic (so that the same amount of foreign
currency is spent on them), the balance of payments will not
deteriorate provided that there is a gain of foreign currency
from an increased demand for exports.

What is the probable situation in the real world for the
United Kingdom as regards the elasticities of demand for
imports and exports? Demand for imports is likely to be fairly
inelastic. Most of Britain's imports are necessities—foodstuffs
and raw materials. Indeed, if her exports expand, her demand
for raw materials will increase. Offsetting this is a likely fall in
British demand for luxuries and foreign travel on account of
the greater cost, home-produced goods and holidays now being
more competitive.

On the other hand, the demand for British exports as a whole
is probably elastic. Not only could she undersell her competitors,
e.g. in cars, electrical equipment, etc., but the lower export

price resulting from devaluation would convert what were formerly 'potential exports' into real exports. Moreover, such items as tourism are likely to have a highly elastic demand. But it must be remembered that the price of exported goods will not fall by the entire amount of the devaluation. Their home price will rise when they are made from imported raw materials.

(2) *Will the U.S.A. retaliate by itself devaluing?*

If the U.S.A. retaliates it will wipe out Britain's advantage. As we have seen, the rules of the I.M.F. are designed to prevent such competitive devaluation. Devaluation by Britain would only be allowed if she had a chronic balance-of-payments deficit. If, while still in equilibrium, she devalued merely to increase her exports further, then other countries would be forced to follow suit. Such a breach of the 1944 rules would mark the end of international monetary co-operation, at least for the time being.

(3) *What is the elasticity of supply of exports?*

It is on the supply side that the greatest obstacles to a successful devaluation are likely to be encountered. The fall in the price of exports will probably lead to an expansion of demand, but this will be of no advantage if the supply of exports cannot be increased.

Two important questions have to be asked. (*a*) Has devaluation become necessary because prices at home have risen through full employment? If so, unless productivity increases, it is possible to increase exports only by diverting goods from the home market. This could be achieved by physical controls, an increase in price at home through taxation, or by a reduction of incomes through a deflationary policy. In full employment, therefore, devaluation should be accompanied by one or all of these measures. (*b*) What will be the reaction of the trade unions following devaluation? An increase in the cost of imports, together with any addition to indirect taxes, raises the cost of living. There is thus a strong temptation to demand wage increases. Moreover, labour is in a strong position, because demand for exports is running at a high level following the devaluation. If the trade unions exploit their position, the resultant rise in wages could soon wipe out the cost advantage which Britain had gained through devaluation. In this way, devaluation could be self-defeating, for a country would be back to the position from which she started—exports insufficient to pay for imports

It should be noted, however, that where demand for British exports is inelastic, then inelasticity of supply may not be detrimental. The higher price at which exports will be supplied will be paid by foreign importers, and British earnings of foreign currency may not fall.

(4) *What is the elasticity of supply of imports?*

If foreigners are dependent on the British market, and supply is inelastic, then they may be willing to reduce their prices. This may reduce Britain's expenditure of foreign currency, although in volume imports are almost as great.

(5) *What is the nature of British and American investments with each other?*

Suppose British investments in the U.S.A. are mostly in the form of shares in companies there. Profits will be earned in dollars, and so there will be no loss of foreign currency after devaluation.

On the other hand, if American investments in the United Kingdom are in stock with interest fixed in sterling, the U.S.A. will lose by British devaluation, for she gets fewer dollars than formerly in invisible earnings.

(6) *Will countries regard devaluation as a once-for-all measure, or will they fear further devaluation?*

Devaluation by Britain reduces the value of sterling securities held by foreigners, including the sterling balances held in London. In the first place, this may destroy confidence in sterling, undermining London's position as a banking centre. Business is transferred elsewhere, and invisible earnings are lost. Secondly, unless devaluation is accompanied by positive measures (including a wages policy) to correct the underlying inflation, foreigners will fear a further devaluation and so hasten to remove their capital from London. This will give rise to a further depletion of the reserves, and make a new devaluation even more likely.

The above argument suggests that a country like Britain will turn to devaluation only as a last resort. Not only does it involve loss of face, but it may entail a serious deterioration in the terms of trade, a large amount of additional exports having to be given to achieve a small gain in the balance of payments. Indeed, the possibility exists that devaluation may cause the balance of payments to deteriorate still further. In this case, a country has to resort to exchange control.

It should be noted, too, that much of the above analysis applies to a depreciation of the pound sterling even though this happens through the mechanism of the foreign exchange market (as it did in 1972–3).

VI. RECENT INTERNATIONAL MONETARY DEVELOPMENTS

The weaknesses of Bretton Woods

The Bretton Woods agreement worked tolerably well for 25 years. Moreover, the principles which it embodied are still heeded today, even if they are not always followed, by the major trading countries. Thus what remains of Bretton Woods is still of value until a new arrangement for co-operation between countries engaged in international trade can be hammered out.

The Bretton Woods system suffered from two main weaknesses:

(1) the pressure of exchange adjustment fell almost entirely on debtor nations (who were forced to devalue) rather than on creditor nations (who could have eased part of the burden by re-valuing);

(2) in spite of Keynes' arguments at Bretton Woods, little provision was made for the expansion of international liquidity necessary to service an increasing world trade.

We can consider each in turn.

Exchange adjustment

While the United Kingdom and, later, the U.S.A. were frequent 'persistent debtor' nations, Germany and Japan were 'persistent creditor' countries. Both the latter countries, however, proved reluctant to revalue their currencies, fearing that the rise in the price of their exports which this would entail would make them uncompetitive in world markets.

The result was that, in order to maintain the existing exchange rate, the United Kingdom in particular had to deflate her economy whenever balance of payments difficulties arose. To some extent this could be regarded as the just penalty which she had to pay for her inability to prevent prices rising as her economy expanded. Even so, if the major creditor countries had been willing to revalue, the process of 'stop' in the United Kingdom need not have been so drastic. And, as we see below, any weakness in the pound gathered momentum because sterling was held as a reserve currency.

The decisive step was taken in June 1972, when once again sterling came under pressure as the British economy expanded. Now the 'pegged' pound was abandoned; instead the pound was allowed to 'float', its value being arrived at according to the day-to-day demand for and supply of sterling on the foreign exchange market. Originally it was probably intended that the 'float' should be temporary in order to indicate a realistic rate at which it could be re-pegged when Britain entered the Common Market in January 1973. But the pound, together with the Italian lira, continued to float indefinitely. In Britain, the Heath government made it quite clear that expansion of the economy was to have first priority and that the obstacle of maintaining a fixed exchange rate should not stand in its way. Thus a major trading nation threw overboard the Bretton Woods system of international co-operation which had been so laboriously built up over the previous 28 years. Even though other countries continued with declared rates, the Bretton Woods system could never be the same again, for Britain had made it quite clear that a nation could opt out whenever it considered the price of defending an exchange rate through deflation was too high (*see also* Chapter 36).

International liquidity

Just as money in our pockets or at the bank is necessary to finance our everyday purchases, so people dealing in international markets require reserves of an acceptable form to finance international trade.

The one form that is always acceptable is gold. Unfortunately, the supply of gold is not increasing fast enough to keep pace with the expansion of world trade and the corresponding need for larger reserves. In the past, the difficulty has been overcome by holding reserves in other currencies—dollars and sterling. These were convertible into gold, and were known as 'reserve currencies'. Holding reserve currencies instead of gold had the additional advantage that a rate of interest was earned, whereas there is no return on holding gold.

The willingness to hold a reserve currency, however, only lasts as long as there is little possibility of the reserve currency being devalued. Persistent balance of payments deficits undermine confidence in the currency concerned, and there will then be a tendency to move out of the reserve currency. This is what happened in 1972 and 1973 first to the pound sterling, and then to the dollar.

To some extent the shortage of international liquidity has been made good by economising in the reserves through pooling arrangements, e.g. in the I.M.F. and by the central banks of the Group of Ten. But even these arrangements proved inadequate in the speculation against the pound in June, 1972. A new form of reserve is essential.

In 1967 it looked as though this new form would be gradually forthcoming. Then the member countries of the I.M.F. at long last agreed that Special Drawing Rights (SDR's) should be created. At first these SDR's were to be created on a limited scale—approximately 3·5 billion dollars worth in 1970 and 3 billion dollars worth in each of the two years, 1971 and 1972. They would be credited to members of the I.M.F. on a quota basis and could be used to cover deficits with creditor countries. Since they were convertible into gold, they were known as 'paper gold'.

Although the value of the SDR's was quite inadequate to provide sufficient international liquidity, an important principle had been established. This was that internationally-created credit could be used to finance world trade. It was hoped that the value of SDR's would be raised, perhaps by crediting underdeveloped countries with them as a means of giving overseas aid. But talk of de-monetising gold proved premature. Loss of confidence in the dollar and in the pound sterling in 1973 led to a further movement into gold, the price of which more than doubled on the free market. Moreover, no SDR's were created in 1973. The problem of international liquidity therefore still remains to be solved.

The future of the Sterling Area

The Sterling Area consisted of those countries, mostly Commonwealth, who continued to link their currencies with sterling at a stable rate of exchange. Within the Sterling Area, therefore, there was a stable rate of exchange. This had certain advantages:

(1) The stability of exchange rates within the Area promoted trade between members.

(2) Sterling was freely convertible between members. Thus exchange control, which Britain imposed upon outsiders in 1939, did not apply to the Sterling Area. This facilitated trade and the movement of capital.

(3) All gold and foreign currency earnings went into a central pool—the Exchange Equalisation Account. This pooling of reserves increased trade with non-sterling countries, the balances of the net earners of foreign currencies being available to the net spenders of foreign currencies.

(4) For Britain it brought loans at a comparatively low rate of interest (since most of the balances were invested in Treasury Bills) and banking, insurance and commodity-market business.

The Sterling Area did not work perfectly largely because the gold and convertible currency reserves were too small relative to the trade with non-member countries. When countries over-spent on imports from these non-members, Britain had to bear the brunt of deflationary policies to protect the reserves—the 'stop' policy. Nor did the net earners of foreign currency obtain as much capital as they would have liked, largely because Britain was not running a sufficiently large balance of payments surplus.

There was always some doubt, therefore, as to whether the Sterling Area was worthwhile. Moreover, many members (e.g. Australia) discovered that their trade was growing much faster with non-members (particularly Japan and the United States) than with Sterling Area members.

But it is the comparatively recent developments which have, to all intents and purposes, spelled the end of the Sterling Area. The first upset was the weakness of sterling, even after the 1967 devaluation. Hence in the Basle agreement of 1968 a minimum price (in terms of dollars) at which sterling balances could be exchanged was guaranteed. But this guarantee was not given to maintain the Sterling Area as an entity but rather to prevent the too-rapid withdrawal of the sterling reserves from Britain. The guarantee proved somewhat empty in practice for later depreciation of the pound sterling was accompanied by a parallel depreciation of the dollar! Nevertheless, the guarantee was rolled over for a further two years in 1971 and again for six months in 1973.

While few countries would want to tie their currencies to an ever-depreciating pound, it was Britain's joining the Common Market which was the final death-blow. Not only would Britain's trading future lie with the E.E.C., but an undertaking was given to France that sterling's role as a reserve currency would be phased out. As a step towards this the Treasury, when the pound was floated in 1972, took the opportunity to impose on the Sterling Area some of the exchange controls which already applied to the rest of the world. By April, 1973 the decline in the importance of sterling as a reserve currency had gone so far that the Bundesbank reported that, against its own wish, the Deutschemark had become the world's second most important reserve currency.

CHAPTER 34

THE EUROPEAN ECONOMIC COMMUNITY

I. BACKGROUND TO THE E.E.C.

The legacy of wars

The devastation produced by the two World Wars of the first half of the twentieth century convinced statesmen in Western Europe that the cult of nationalism had to be ended in favour of political unity. The original idea was that some form of federation of states should emerge. Thus in 1949 the Council of Europe, based in Strasbourg, was created. This, it was hoped, might form the basis of a European Parliament.

In terms of actual achievement, however, organisations of countries for definite functions proved more fruitful than the Council of Europe with its broad aims. In the economic field, the organisation for European Economic Co-operation was set up in 1948 to administer American aid. It was reconstituted in 1961 as the Organisation for Economic Co-operation and Development (O.E.C.D.) with the aims of liberalising trade, developing nuclear energy for peaceful purposes, stimulating industrial efficiency and co-ordinating aid to developing countries. Co-operation in defence was also achieved through The North Atlantic Treaty Organisation (1949) and the Western European Union (1954).

Supra-national organisations

While all the above organisations involved co-operation, and thus experience in 'give and take' between the nations concerned, they were merely voluntary associations which member nations could join or withdraw from as they chose. Federation implies the handing over of sovereign powers to a supra-national organisation so that policies can be integrated in the interests of the Federal body.

Western European statesmen who supported federation began to see that it could only proceed piecemeal on a functional basis. The first step in this direction was the formation of the European Coal and Steel Community in 1951. This was a supra-national organisation, controlling the whole of the iron, steel and coal resources of the six member countries—France, West Germany, Italy, Holland, Belgium and Luxembourg. The old divisions created by inward-looking national interests were thus broken down.

The success of the E.C.S.C. led to the setting up in 1957 of the Atomic Energy Community (EURATOM, a similar organisation for the peaceful use of atomic energy) and the European Economic Community (E.E.C., an organisation to develop a 'Common Market' between the six member countries). All three communities have now been brought within the E.E.C.

Britain's attitude to the E.E.C.

In spite of the fact that Sir Winston Churchill had been the original advocate of European confederation, Britain, when she was offered membership of E.C.S.C., Euratom and E.E.C., refused to join. She still thought she could go it alone through her links with the Commonwealth and her 'special relationship' with the U.S.A. Not only would joining the E.E.C. have meant a weakening of Commonwealth ties, but Britain was unwilling to forgo the right to follow independent policies in economics and defence. A looser, free-trade area aimed at liberalising trade was more to her liking. Thus, with six other countries, she formed the European Free Trade Area (EFTA). This, it was also envisaged, could be used as a bargaining counter to enable her to be accepted eventually into membership of E.E.C. on terms modified to her own particular interests and attitudes.

Britain applies to join the E.E.C.

Contrary to Britain's expectation, the E.E.C. grew in strength, for the overriding desire of its leaders to make it a success allowed difficulties to be resolved as they arose. Moreover, although trade between the EFTA countries increased as tariffs were reduced, Britain's trade with the E.E.C. increased at a faster rate. In other words, British goods tended to be more complementary to the economy of the E.E.C. countries than they were to those of the EFTA countries.

Above all, President De Gaulle began to direct the six members of the E.E.C. towards political union. In this France would play the dominant role—and with a foreign policy which was cool towards the U.S.A. and which sought a *rapprochement* with Russia! Britain, on the other hand, could see that she would have little influence in such developments. Accordingly, in 1961, she opened negotiations for terms upon which she could join the E.E.C.

Negotiations were protracted, largely through the opposition of President De Gaulle, and were even broken off on two occasions. But Britain's application was never withdrawn. President De Gaulle retired from politics, negotiations were resumed and terms were arranged which were acceptable to Edward Heath, the British Prime Minister. On 1 January 1973, therefore, the United Kingdom entered the E.E.C.

II. THE INSTITUTIONS OF THE E.E.C.

The Rome Treaty of 1957 created the E.E.C., which includes the E.C.S.C. and Euratom. As already indicated it has political aims—formally stated in the Treaty as 'to establish the foundations of an ever closer union among the European peoples'.

However, while this makes the broad political aim explicit, it has been realised that the objective will only be achieved over a long period as experience is gained through co-operation in specific economic fields.

The essential point to grasp, however, is that the Treaty of Rome set up a 'Community', a Community which, to some extent, is bigger than any one of the other member nations. Moreover, it has a government and institutions, and these have been developed from the old E.C.S.C. When the United Kingdom joined the E.E.C., the general principle was agreed that she should have a position in the institutions equal to those enjoyed by France, Germany and Italy.

There are four main institutions:

(1) The Commission

This is the most important organ of the E.E.C. Its thirteen members (two from the U.K.) serve for four years. Once chosen, however, the members of the Commission act as an independent body in the interests of the Community as a whole, and not as representatives of the individual governments that have nominated them.

The Commission is responsible for formulating policy proposals for submission to the Council of Ministers, for promoting the Community interest, for trying to reconcile national viewpoints, and for implementing Community decisions.

(2) The Council of Ministers

Each member country sends a cabinet minister (usually the Foreign Secretary) to the Council of Ministers. This is the supreme decision-making body. Its task is to harmonise the policy of the Commission with the wishes of the member governments. Thus while the Commission drafts community policies, they have to be approved by the Council before they can be implemented. Originally it was intended that Council decisions should be on a majority basis, members being given weighted voting strengths. Today, on matters of major importance which affect vital national interests, the rule in practice is that decisions shall be unanimous. Thus one member can veto a proposal affecting what it considers to be a vital interest.

So far, Community decision-making can be said to have been harmonious and successful. This achievement has been possible because of the system by which proposals and compromise plans are exchanged between the Council and the Commission. If the Council becomes deadlocked, the Commission reconsiders the proposal in order to meet some or all of the demands of the opposing countries.

(3) The Court of Justice

This consists of ten judges appointed for a six-year term by agreement among member governments. Its task is to interpret the Treaty and adjudicate on complaints, whether from

member states, private enterprises or the institutions themselves. Its rulings are binding on member countries, community institutions and individuals.

(4) *The Assembly or European Parliament*

This is a body of 198 members (36 from the U.K.) drawn
from the nine national Parliaments. These nominated members sit according to party affiliation and not nationality.
The Assembly is consulted on and debates all the major
policy issues of the Community, and also examines and approves the Community's budget. It can dismiss the Commission by a two-thirds majority.

(5) *Special Institutions*

Apart from the four main institutions above, there are also
special institutions to deal with particular policies, e.g. the
Economic and Social Committee, the European Investment
Bank, The European Social Fund, The European Monetary
Co-operation Fund, etc.

III. ECONOMIC OBJECTIVES OF THE E.E.C.

As we have seen, integration of policies of member countries
is the overriding aim of the E.C.S.C., Euratom, and the E.E.C.
We shall concentrate on the latter, usually referred to as The
Common Market. Integration of overall economic policy is
based on two main principles; (1) a Customs Union, (2)
harmonisation of particular aspects of policy to produce a
Common Market.

(1) *A customs union*

We have to distinguish between a free-trade area and a
customs union. The former simply removes tariff barriers
between member countries, but at the same time allowing
individual members to impose their own rates of duty against
outsiders. A customs union goes further. While it has internal
free trade, it also decides upon the common external tariffs
to be levied by all member countries.

The latter is the position regarding the E.E.C. Indeed, a
customs union is essential for an integrated Common Market

as otherwise goods would enter the Market through low-tariff countries and be resold in the markets of those members who impose higher rates of tariff.

(2) *A Common Market*

In essence the Common Market of the E.E.C. means that goods and factors of production shall move completely freely within the community through the operation of the price system. Only in this way can the full benefits of the larger market (see later) be realised. The overall aim, therefore, is that trade within the whole of the Community shall be just as free as trade within an individual country.

However, while this is the broad aim there are particular difficulties to be overcome for it to be completely successful. Member countries had developed their own individual taxes, welfare benefits, policies for dealing with monopoly, methods of removing balance of payments imbalances, full employment policies, and so on. If such differences were allowed to persist, they would tend to disrupt the working of the price system because they would give some members of the Community an advantage over others.

We can illustrate by two simple examples. Suppose, on joining the E.E.C., Britain had retained purchase tax on refrigerators compared with no purchase tax on binoculars. This would weight the possibilities of trade against Italy (which has a comparative advantage in producing refrigerators) in favour of Germany (which has a comparative advantage in producing high-grade binoculars). Alternatively, the comparative advantage of some countries may lie in the expertise of the professional services they can provide. Usually this means that such services have to be taken to where the customer is (e.g. know-how regarding property development). There must therefore be mobility of labour within the Market, e.g. for property-developers.

Emphasis has thus been placed on 'harmonisation' policies in order to merge a number of separate economies into one. Thus, when Britain joined, arrangements had to be made for her to bring certain aspects of her economic policy into line with the position already achieved by the original members of the E.E.C.

We shall now outline the most important details of the 'Common Market' policy.

IV. THE AIMS OF COMMON MARKET POLICY

(1) *Common external tariffs (C.E.T.)*

All members will impose tariffs on imports from non-member countries at the same rates. For Britain, adjustment will take place over a four-year period beginning on 1 January 1974.

(2) *Free trade between member countries*

This involves the removal of all duties, quotas and other barriers to free trade between members. Britain will achieve this gradually. Thus tariffs on industrial products will be eliminated over a $4\frac{1}{4}$-year transitional period, the first 20 per cent reduction being made on 1 April 1973.

(3) *A common agricultural policy (CAP)*

Because the demand for agricultural products tends to be inelastic, changes in the conditions of supply can have far-reaching effects on the incomes of farmers. Thus a bumper harvest which lowers the price of foodstuffs generally will result in less total revenue (which is largely farmers' incomes). All countries, therefore, give support to their own farmers. But the means of doing so have differed. Britain has, in the past, followed a 'cheap food' policy, allowing foodstuffs to enter the country free of duty and subsidising farmers by 'deficiency payments' which covered the difference between the market price and the agreed 'guaranteed' price.

CAP works on the basis of maintaining farmers' incomes by high prices on the home market. These are achieved through import levies on imported foods. Three prices are fixed for each product:

(a) a *target price*, which it is estimated will give farmers an adequate return in a normal year;

(b) a *threshold price*, which is used as the basis for assessing levies on imports which will ensure that they do not enter the E.E.C. below this price;

(c) the *intervention price*, at which surplus supplies (e.g. owing to a good harvest or simply over-production through the setting of too high a threshold price) are bought up by various agencies to be disposed of outside the Market. The butter sold to the U.S.S.R. in 1973 is an example.

Obviously CAP confers greater benefits on countries in which agriculture is important (e.g. France) compared with countries which are more dependent on manufacturing (e.g. Germany and the U.K.). We shall return to this problem later.

(4) *Harmonisation of tax systems*

As already shown, some standardisation of methods of taxation is necessary in order to remove any 'hidden' barriers to trade. This applies particularly to indirect taxes. In the E.E.C., VAT is to be the basic form of indirect tax, and it is proposed that eventually it will be imposed by all member countries at the same rates.

No proposals exist for harmonising income taxes, but most countries have adopted the 'imputation' system of corporation tax.

(5) *Free movements of persons and capital*

It is necessary that people and capital should be able to move from one part of the Community to another, just as today they can move from one part of their own country to another.

(6) *Complete monetary integration*

As we saw in Chapter 33, countries can adjust the prices of goods which are traded internationally by varying the exchange rates of their currencies. If this were allowed within the E.E.C. it could enable a member-country to obtain a competitive advantage by depreciating its currency in terms of those of other member countries. It is agreed, therefore, that currencies of member countries are to be kept to a fixed exchange rate with only narrow adjustments. The eventual aim is a common currency system, with one currency in London, Paris, Bonn and Rome, just as there is one currency in London, Cardiff and Edinburgh.

A European Monetary Co-operation Fund, administered by the governors of the central banks, has been set up to intervene in the monetary flows between member countries in order to narrow the margin of fluctuations in currency values and to promote long-run integration.

The United Kingdom was expected to declare the exchange rate for the pound which it would maintain when it entered the E.E.C. At the time the pound sterling was 'floating', and care had to be taken that it was not fixed at an over-valued rate, thereby putting British goods at a price disadvantage compared with those of other member countries. However, the pound continued to float after Britain's entry, though this must be regarded as merely a temporary arrangement.

(7) *A common regional policy*

Just as one nation cannot allow depressed areas to persist, so the E.E.C. is expected to help regions of high unemployment. Northern Ireland and Southern Italy are two such regions. Apart from the establishment of a Regional Development Fund, however, little has so far been done to integrate the various methods of encouraging industry to the problem areas.

(8) *A common transport policy*

By regulating such items as freight rates, licences, taxation and working conditions, the E.E.C. can seek to ensure that transport undertakings compete on an equal footing. Again, any hidden advantages through special freight rates would tend to distort the free movement of goods within the Market.

(9) *Common rules on competition*

With the object of preventing the distortion of competition in trade between member countries, uniform regulations have been introduced to cover price fixing, sharing of markets and patent rights.

(10) *A Community budget*

A Community budget is necessary to meet the costs of administration and to provide funds for operating the main areas of policy which require collective expenditure, for example CAP and Regional policy. Contributions are collected nationally from two main sources—import duties and a 1 per cent VAT. Britain has agreed to contribute 8·64 per cent of the total budget in 1973, rising to 18·92 per cent over a five-year period.

V. ADVANTAGES OF BELONGING TO THE E.E.C.

The possible advantages which can accrue to countries by forming a Common Market can be summarised as follows:

(1) *Increased possibilities of specialisation*

The extent of the division of labour is, as was shown in Chapter 7, limited by the size of the market. The E.E.C. provides a market of 260 million people, larger than that of the United States. This allows economies of scale to be achieved, especially as regards sophisticated products requiring high initial research expenditure, for example computers, nuclear reactors, supersonic aircraft, and modern defence weapons. Even before she joined the E.E.C., Britain had been forced to combine with other European countries to cover research costs, e.g. with France on the development of the Concorde.

(2) *Increased efficiency through competition in the larger market*

Within the Common Market there are no trade barriers which, in effect, protect inefficient firms. Free trade means that goods and services can compete freely in all parts of the market and that factors of production can move to their most efficient use, not merely within a country, but between countries. Thus our basic economic principle—the maximisation of satisfaction by using scarce resources in their most efficient manner—operates within an economy of 260 million people rather than within one of only 56 million.

(3) *A faster rate of growth*

Over the last fifteen years, the G.N.P.s of the six original members of the E.E.C. have grown twice as fast as that of the United Kingdom. Indeed, apart from Italy, each of these countries now has a higher G.N.P. per head of the population than the United Kingdom.

It is likely that, to a large extent, this faster rate of growth was the result of the increased economies of scale and competition enjoyed by the Common Market. But it is also possible that the Market generates growth by the mood it engenders.

(4) *Political advantages*

As already explained, the ultimate objective of the original advocates of European co-operation was some form of political union. A Western Europe which could speak with one voice would carry weight when dealing with other major powers, particularly the U.S.A. and the U.S.S.R. Moreover, the integration of defence forces and strategy would give them far greater security. It is not possible, therefore, to separate the political from the economic advantages, for the two are interlinked.

VI. PROBLEMS FACING THE UNITED
KINGDOM AS A MEMBER OF THE E.E.C.

By remaining outside the E.E.C., Britain would have denied herself the possible advantages of being within the larger market. Nor could she have influenced the way in which the Common Market might develop. As a member, however, her views would at least have to be considered.

In defence, Britain is inextricably tied to Western Europe. And, in recent years, although she was outside the E.E.C., her foreign trade was being pulled in that direction. Why then was there so much opposition to Britain's entry? We can pinpoint six major difficulties.

(1) *The C.E.T. could lead to the diversion of trade toward less-efficient E.E.C. suppliers*

The duties imposed by the customs union may allow firms within the Common Market to compete in price with more efficient firms outside.

Suppose, for instance, that the same machine can be produced by both the U.S.A. and Germany but, because the American firm is more efficient, its machine is 10 per cent cheaper than the German. In these circumstances, Britain would, other things being equal, import from the United States. As a member of E.E.C., however, Britain would have to discriminate against the American machine by the appropriate C.E.T., say, 20 per cent. This would make the German machine cheaper, and so trade would be diverted to the less efficient producer.

The main problem this poses for the British concerns foodstuffs, for these have entered Britain duty free. As a result, for instance, dairy produce (particularly butter) from New Zealand has been able to compete with European producers. The imposition of a tariff against New Zealand would alter the pattern of trade in dairy produce.

(2) *The CAP has particular disadvantages for the United Kingdom*

There are four main criticisms of the CAP:

(*a*) The import duties levied on foodstuffs in order to maintain prices for farmers within the Community hits Britain particularly hard. Since she is dependent on imports for one-half of her food supplies, it is obviously to her advantage to obtain them from the most efficient producer.

The CAP, on the other hand, could mean that Britain has to switch her imports of foodstuffs to dearer producers within the Market. In doing so she is subsidising, as it were, inefficient methods of farming in other countries.

(*b*) High prices encourage supply by Common Market countries but not demand, so that over-production (as in the case of butter) can occur.

(*c*) High food prices hit low-income groups hardest; that is, compared with the old U.K. system of deficiency payments, CAP is regressive.

(*d*) The distortion of the normal pattern of international trade in foodstuffs may penalise the under-developed nations since these are often food-producers. Thus it could widen the income-gap between the developed and under-developed countries.

(3) *The U.K.'s trade with the Commonwealth has been sacrificed*

Both Britain's former EFTA partners and the under-developed nations of the Commonwealth have been offered the benefits of special association with the E.E.C. Moreover, the import levy against New Zealand dairy products is to be imposed only gradually over a period of five years. But exporters of manufactured goods, among whom are Australia, Canada and Hong Kong, will lose the favoured treatment which they formerly enjoyed. Indeed, the C.E.T. will work against them.

In the past, trade has been an important link between the Commonwealth countries, although it must be recognised that the importance of Britain's trade with the Commonwealth has been diminishing over the past twenty years.

(4) *Certain producers will be particularly hit by concessions to Common Market regulations*

In the past, some branches of horticulture (e.g. tomatoes and fruits) have enjoyed a quota protection from Continental producers. This will end with Britain's entry to the E.E.C. Moreover, it is also proposed that by 1984 territorial waters will be open to the fishing fleets of all member countries. Few concessions have been made to these particular producers.

(5) *Britain's contribution to the Community budget will place a severe strain on her balance of payments*

Originally it was estimated that when Britain bears her full share of the budget it will amount to £300 million a year, with £100 million being returned as aid for the 'assisted areas'.

But even in 1973, Britain's contribution proved to be greater than that estimated at the beginning of the year. One major cause of this was the fall in the values of the dollar and pound sterling. CAP prices were fixed in terms of the dollar and, when this fell in value, farmers incomes had to be maintained from an increased Community budget.

Britain's loss of foreign currency in this way will be justified only if she can increase the value of her exports as a result of Common Market membership.

(6) *Harmonisation of taxation and the adoption of a common monetary system involves a serious loss of economic sovereignty*

As regards taxation, two examples can be given. (*a*) Protection of agriculture by import duties rather than by deficiency payments means that the consumer pays to maintain Community farmers' incomes rather than the taxpayer. In effect, therefore, the change from subsidies to protective duties is regressive in nature. (*b*) The substitution of VAT for purchase tax also tends to be more regressive inasmuch as the old purchase tax imposed a higher rate on luxury goods.

But it is through the adoption of the common monetary policy that Britain really stands to lose freedom of action over major economic policy. A country which is trading internationally has the option when exports fall in value of either lowering internal costs (the old gold standard mechanism) or lowering the exchange rate (exchange devaluation or depreciation) in order to make its exports more competitive. The latter policy will be denied to Britain under a common monetary policy. The exchange rate will have to be maintained within limits (at present termed 'the snake') which are narrower than the current I.M.F. limits ('the tunnel'). Exports will have to be revived by lowering home prices and this may lead to unemployment. Thus Britain could be a permanent depressed area of the E.E.C. if her goods are not competitive.

Against this, however, some economists might argue that this will present no problem for Britain provided she can hold her inflation in check. And here, the Common currency requirement will impose the necessary discipline.

Conclusion

Britain's membership of the Common Market provides the opportunity for an all-round improvement in her standard of living. But the benefits will only be secured if she braces herself to compete in the larger market. Two major problems face her: (*a*) an increase in the rate of capital investment in industry; (*b*) controlling the rate of inflation at home. Both are essential if Britain is to be cost-competitive within the E.E.C. and world markets.

PART VIII

SOME CURRENT ECONOMIC PROBLEMS OF THE UNITED KINGDOM

CHAPTER 35

THE POPULATION OF GREAT BRITAIN

In many ways it would have been more satisfactory to have examined in an early chapter the population of the United Kingdom—the people who comprise 'households', the consumers of finished products and the suppliers of the factors of production. But in order to proceed beyond a mere description it is essential to apply certain principles of economics, and so it was first necessary to examine these.

We shall look at the problems of composition, size and industrial and geographical distribution of the population. But first we must describe briefly how it has grown over the last 200 years.

I. THE GROWTH OF POPULATION

Changes in the rate of growth

Table 10 shows how Great Britain's population has grown since 1801. It can be seen that in the nineteenth century it roughly doubled every fifty years; but over the first half of the twentieth century it increased by less than one-third. In fact the rate of growth averaged just over 13 per cent per decade during the nineteenth century, and only 5 per cent during the twentieth century.

There are thus three main questions which have to be answered: (a) Why was there such a rapid growth of population during the nineteenth century? (b) Why did the rate of growth fall off so markedly during the first half of the twentieth

TABLE 10

POPULATION (IN 000'S) 1801–1971

Date	Great Britain (England, Wales and Scotland)	Northern Ireland
1801	10,501	—
1851	20,816	1,443
1901	37,000	1,237
1951	48,854	1,371
1971	53,832	1,528

century? (c) What is likely to happen to the population during the remainder of the twentieth century?

Causes of changes in the rate of growth

The factors affecting population changes are shown in Fig. 114. On the one hand, we have the natural increase—the excess of births over deaths; on the other, migration—the

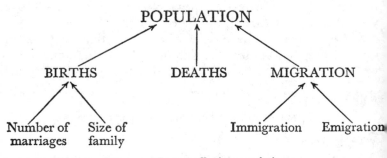

FIG. 114.—Factors affecting population.

balance between immigration (inwards) and emigration (outwards). In fact, apart from the years 1931–41 and 1951–71, Great Britain has lost by migration on average about half a million people each decade. The changes in the rate of growth, therefore, are chiefly the result of changes in the natural increase.

The reason for the rapid rate of increase during the nineteenth century was that, while the birth rate remained high, there was a considerable fall in the death rate. The latter was the result of improved medical knowledge, sanitation and water supply, and chiefly of general advances in the standard of living following the agricultural and industrial revolutions.

But the situation changed in the twentieth century. The death rate did not fall so rapidly. More important the birth rate fell considerably. The reason for this was a fall in the average size of family—from between five and six children to just over two. A variety of factors contributed to this:

(i) improved methods and social acceptance of birth control;
(ii) the increased economic burden of parenthood due, for instance, to the gradual raising of the school-leaving age;
(iii) the higher standards which parents generally set themselves for their children's welfare;
(iv) the growth of competing alternatives to children, such as holidays, foreign travel, the cinema and motor car;
(v) the emancipation of women, politically, economically and socially, with the consequent desire to be free from home ties;
(vi) the momentum which social example, smaller houses and advertisement provided when once the movement towards smaller families had started.

What of the future? The Royal Commission on Population, reporting in 1949, estimated that unless there were a change in people's attitude to the size of family, or immigration on a considerable scale took place, Britain's population would be declining absolutely in numbers by the end of the century!

Already, however, it seems that such a decline will not occur. While the high birth rate immediately after World War II was due to unusual circumstances and was therefore not maintained, it has not fallen to its pre-war level. People, it appears, are building larger families. Various reasons can be suggested for this: younger marriages, greater economic prosperity, increased government help to the family man and more facilities for young mothers to resume work.

While any projections of population are dependent upon the reliability of assumptions, especially as regards births and migration, it now seems likely that the population of the United Kingdom will be in the region of 65 million at the end of the century.

II. THE AGE-DISTRIBUTION OF THE
POPULATION

The decline in the rate of increase in the population during the twentieth century has brought about a change in the age-composition of Great Britain's population compared with a hundred years ago. This is shown in Fig. 115.

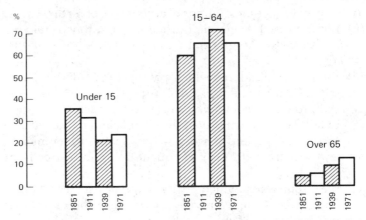

FIG. 115.—Changes in the age-distribution of the population of Great Britain, 1851–1971.

The two factors which have brought about this ageing population are:

(a) the lengthening of life due to the various factors which have led to a fall in the death rate;

(b) the fall in the birth rate at the end of the nineteenth century and the consequent fall in the number of births each year between 1911 and 1941.

The trend is likely to continue until 1982, when the 15–64 age-group will form about 61 per cent of the population, and those under 15 years and those over 65 years, 23 per cent and 14 per cent respectively. Thereafter the working age-group should form an increasing percentage of the total population.

The economic effects of an ageing population

It should be noted that a part of this trend is due to the fall in mortality and is a normal development. To some extent, therefore, we are forced to adjust ourselves to these changing circumstances, and, if we try to prevent them by a rapid increase in the birth rate, we shall increase the size of the population—which may give rise to further problems, as we shall see later.

(1) *An increased dependence of retired persons on the working population*

Current wants can only be provided for by current production. An ageing population means that the proportion of workers to consumers is falling. Whereas in 1851 there were over 12 workers to every person over 65 years of age, in 1951 there were only 6, and by 1981 the number will have fallen to just over 4! One particular result will be the increased burden of retirement pensions, more pensioners having to be supported by proportionately fewer contributors.

(2) *A changing pattern of consumption*

An ageing population means, to take extreme examples, that bath-chairs will be wanted in place of prams, walking-sticks in place of hockey-sticks, tea in place of milk. For many of these new 'wants', consideration has to be given well in advance. We must, for instance, make more provision for aged couples without families when planning a housing programme.

(3) *Lower mobility of labour*

In the past it has hardly been necessary for the older persons to uproot themselves and to learn new techniques. The expanding industries have been supplied by new trainees who are leaving the university, college or school, and just starting their working lives, while the decaying industries have declined fairly quietly by failing to recruit new entrants to replace the workers who retire on account of old age. Now, with a working population static in size, expanding industries have to draw on older workers from the declining industries to meet their labour requirements, teaching them new skills and moving them to new areas.

(4) *The possibility that the community will become less progressive*

While older people are more patient, more experienced and more broadminded than younger people, the latter excel in energy, enterprise, enthusiasm and the ability to adapt themselves to learn new things.

III. THE SIZE OF THE POPULATION

By the end of the twentieth century, the United Kingdom's population is likely, as we have seen, to have increased by nearly 20 per cent to 65 millions. Is this a good or a bad thing? To lay bare the issues, it is helpful if we glance briefly at certain important theories of population.

The Malthusian theory of overpopulation

Until the middle of the eighteenth century, the population of Britain grew slowly. But from then on it became more rapid, and in 1798 the Rev. Thomas Malthus's first essay on *The Principle of Population as it affects the future improvement of Society* made it a major subject of discussion.

Originally, Malthus merely wished to reply to certain philosophers of the period who he considered were taking a far too optimistic view of the future of civilisation. But this led him to examine the likely results if the rapid population increase of the previous fifty years were to continue. The interest his views evoked induced Malthus to develop his arguments and to carry out research. As a result a more refined essay on the problem was published in 1803, and it is his arguments in this that we shall consider.

Malthus begins from two postulates: (*a*) that the passion between the sexes is necessary and will remain nearly in its present state; (*b*) that food is necessary to the existence of man. Given these two postulates, his arguments force him to conclude that: (*a*) the population will, if unchecked, double itself every twenty-five years; (*b*) the means of subsistence can, at a maximum, increase by only the same amount every twenty-five years. In other words, while population multiplies in a geometric progression, food supplies increase in an arithmetic progression.

The first conclusion was based on information collected by Malthus of the populations of various countries. But the second conclusion was based on no evidence whatsoever. In order to substantiate it, Malthus appealed to the 'known properties of land'. Here he was virtually stating the law of diminishing returns—although it was not until 1845 that this law was given precise formulation by John Stuart Mill.

From these two conclusions the important result followed that the power of population to increase was 'indefinitely greater than the power of the earth to produce subsistence for man'. In short, there would always be a tendency for the population to outrun the means of subsistence, though it is important to note that Malthus stressed that this was a tendency which was always with us rather than the tragedy bound to occur at some future date.

If man cannot live without food, what, Malthus asks, keeps population within its means of subsistence? The answer he finds in certain 'checks', which are of two kinds. First, there are 'positive checks'. These involve misery—famine, war, disease, epidemics. Secondly, there are 'preventive checks' which, with one exception, all involve 'vice'—'promiscuous intercourse, unnatural passions, violations of the marriage bed, and improper arts to conceal the consequences of irregular connections'. (Contraception would thus be considered by Malthus as vice.) The one preventive check that did not involve vice was 'moral restraint', by which was meant that people deliberately refrained from marrying at an early age. It was only by adopting this solution that civilisation could escape from the alternatives of misery and vice. Since such a possibility was remote, the growth of population, Malthus concluded, was the big stumbling-block in the way of mankind's progress towards happiness.

Malthus's 'blind spots'

Although at the beginning of the nineteenth century Malthus's views were widely accepted, the final tragedy of starvation, the logical outcome of his two conclusions, has not yet materialised in the United Kingdom. Where, therefore, did Malthus go wrong?

First, we must note that to some extent his argument was illogical, for he did not answer the fact, well known at the time, that in spite of the rapid increase in the population over the previous fifty years, people on the average were no worse off. This showed that the means of subsistence must at least have increased in proportion. Had Malthus possessed a precisely formulated law of diminishing returns, he could have based his argument on a fixed total supply of land which would sooner or later make itself felt. Secondly, Malthus was preoccupied with people as consumers. He failed to see that, by and large, a consumer is also a producer, for 'with every mouth God sends a pair of hands'. Here again the law of diminishing returns, with its reference to a fixed factor, could have overcome this objection. Thirdly, Malthus failed to foresee change. On the one hand, the geometrical increase in Britain's population did not come about because of the increasing stream of emigration and, above all, by the reduction in the size of family. On the other, improved agricultural techniques and the vast increase in imports meant that Britain's food supplies were not limited to increasing in an arithmetic progression. In short, the conditions necessary for the operation of the law of diminishing returns were not fulfilled.

Thus Malthus's arguments possess validity only if it is accepted that in the very long period land is a fixed factor. It is, for instance, this limited supply of land which brings about a Malthusian situation in the Far East today and, as we shall see, increases Britain's difficulties as she tries to produce a larger proportion of her foodstuffs at home.

The concept of an 'optimum population'

To Malthus, increasing numbers were a bad thing, as they pressed on the means of subsistence and lowered the standard of living. But his views lost ground towards the middle of the nineteenth century, for as the capital investment of the Industrial Revolution began to yield benefits, it was seen that the standard of living was keeping pace with the increase in population.

Indeed, it began to be asked whether improvements in the standard of living were not directly linked to an increasing population. But J. S. Mill considered that increased production was solely the result of the use of more capital equipment. Such investment would have taken place even if the population had been smaller, when the average standard of living would have been still higher.

At the turn of the century, however, Professor Edwin Cannan showed that population could be too small. Where this happened, full advantage could not be taken of available technical knowledge, with the result that resources could not be used to the full. For example, a larger population might justify large-scale production, more use being made of division of labour, specialised machines and technical discoveries. In short, a doubling of the population could lead to more than doubling production.

Since, therefore, population could either be too large or too small, there must be an intermediate point where it is just right. The *optimum population* is that population at which, given existing technical knowledge, capital equipment, and exchange possibilities with other countries, average output per head is at a maximum. Thus if we refer to Table 2 on p. 156, the optimum population for the example given would be 4 labourers. It follows that any country is over- or under-populated if its population is respectively more or less than the optimum.

But the concept of an optimum population is not without difficulties. In the first place, it is unjustifiable to apply the conditions of 'given existing technical knowledge, capital equipment, and exchange possibilities' and then to speculate as to what production would be if the population were larger or smaller. Had the population increased differently, these variables themselves would have been different. The same mistake is apparent in J. S. Mill's argument that the world would have been better off if, with the improvements that had taken place, population had been more restrained. The truth is that such improvements would not have taken place, for a large or rapidly growing population accumulates knowledge and equipment differently from a smaller or slowly growing one. Even more important is that, from the practical point of view, the concept is of little help. Any optimum population at which a country was aiming would only remain the optimum so long as technical knowledge, etc., did not change. It is obvious that long before an optimum was achieved, some new figure would have taken its place. All that can be done, therefore, is to consider the present composition of the population, forecast the population which will result from it, and then relate this population to likely changes in the above variables.

We now apply these principles to a study of Britain's population.

The advantage to Great Britain of an increasing population

An increasing population has certain advantages which stimulate growth:

(1) *It increases the size of the home market*

The additional output needed for a larger population should benefit industries working under conditions of decreasing costs, for example aircraft, computer, nuclear reactor. It should be noted, however, that this applies only if the extra output is provided by existing firms and not by additional firms entering the industry.

(2) *It facilitates market mobility*

With an increasing population, unemployment resulting from the immobility of labour is a less intractable problem. This is because expanding industries can obtain most of their additional workers from new entrants to the labour force rather than by retraining the older workers of the declining industries.

(3) *It stimulates investment*

An increasing population makes it easier to maintain the level of replacement investment. More than that, the extra consumer demand necessitates additional investment in machinery, factories, schools, houses, transport, etc. Consequently, it stimulates improved techniques, thereby accelerating the replacement of existing equipment.

(4) *It promotes vitality*

By weighting the age-distribution in favour of youth, an increasing population provides more workers to a given number of retired persons and makes for energy, mobility, inventiveness, and the willingness to accept new ideas.

It should be noted that the disadvantages of a decreasing population could be stated as the opposite of the four above.

The disadvantages of an increasing population

Against the advantages given above, it is necessary to set certain disadvantages which may make it difficult for an increasing population to raise present living standards. Resources have to be used in adding to capital equipment instead of producing consumer goods or improving existing buildings. The growing population in Britain since the war, for example, has delayed slum-clearance and rehousing schemes, for new houses for the extra people have had to be built. Old schools and large classes, too, have persisted largely for the same reason.

Above all, an increasing population adds to the pressure on the fixed supply of land available in Britain. The saying that 'with every mouth God sends a pair of hands' ignores two important facts. The first is that not every person is a producer; for a time the additional mouths have to be provided with food, education, etc., by the working group. The second is more important—the increase in the number of labourers on a fixed amount of land may well bring the law of diminishing returns into operation, with a consequent fall in living standards.

As we have seen, it was the law of diminishing returns which was at the root of the problem of increasing numbers which Malthus viewed so gravely. With the Far Eastern countries it simply results in a lower output per head, as extra people have to obtain their subsistence from a fixed amount of land. But for Britain the problem is presented in a slightly different form. Some of her additional food supplies can be produced at home by improving techniques. But in the main, Britain 'produces her food in her workshops', exporting machinery, cars, electrical equipment, etc., for the meat, cereals, fruit, etc. that she requires. What Britain has to ask, therefore is, can exports be increased sufficiently to pay for the extra imports necessitated by the larger population? In short, can she maintain a healthy balance-of-payments position so that she suffers no reduction in her standard of living if population grows?

Throughout the nineteenth century Britain proved that this was possible. Indeed, a balance-of-payments surplus allowed her to invest heavily abroad. But since then the problem of finding and holding foreign markets has become more acute.

Competitors have made inroads into markets formerly supplied almost entirely by Britain; substitutes have been developed for such goods as cotton and coal, which formed a major proportion of her exports; agricultural countries have industrialised; trade barriers have been erected. In addition, as a result of two wars, she has lost much of her income from abroad.

Moreover, it must be remembered that a given increase in the population necessitates a much larger proportional increase in exports if the standard of living is to be maintained. Any expansion of present food production in Britain could encounter rapidly diminishing returns. Most of the extra foodstuffs required, therefore, would have to be imported (not just one-half, which is the present proportion). In addition, imports are required for other goods the extra population would use. Finally, if exports are to be increased, more raw materials, too, would have to be imported.

Nor does this take into consideration any possible deterioration in Britain's terms of trade. Will there be as much raw materials and foodstuffs available from the underdeveloped countries as they industrialise and improve their own incomes? Or will the latter lead to a vastly increased demand for British exports?

Finally, with population growth, environmental problems intensify. As city congestion increases and more open space is required for housing, roads and industry, arguments for conservation and control of pollution gain momentum.

Conclusion

The answer to most of the questions posed above depends upon the turn of events. At present, Britain is managing to support increasing numbers while improving the standard of living.

In the Far East, however, the situation is critical. The birth rate remains high, but the death rate is falling as a result of modern medical discoveries. There are four possible solutions to the problem: (*a*) improved agricultural techniques; (*b*) limitation of the size of family by birth control; (*c*) the development of export industries; (*d*) economic aid from outside.

IV. THE INDUSTRIAL DISTRIBUTION OF THE WORKING POPULATION

The working population

Great Britian's population in 1971 was estimated to be 53,882,000 persons. Of these, 28,827,00 persons (16,260,000 males and 8,935,000 females), are described by the Department of Employment as 'the working population'.

The working population is defined as persons, over school-leaving age, 'who work for pay or gain or register themselves as available for such work'. It therefore includes all persons who are: (*a*) in civil employment, even if they are over retirement age or are working only part-time; or (*b*) in the Armed Forces or on release leave; or (*c*) registered as unemployed. Excluded by the definition are: (*a*) children under 16 years of age and students above 16 years of age who are receiving full-time education; (*b*) persons, such as housewives, who do not work for pay or gain; (*c*) persons who, having private means, e.g. from investments or gifts, do not need to work; (*d*) retired persons.

Changes in the industrial distribution of the working population

Table 11 shows that the chief changes in the distribution of the working population between 1901 and 1971 were:

(*a*) A large decrease in the percentage of the population employed in the primary (extractive) industries—agriculture and mining;

(*b*) An increase in the percentage employed in secondary (manufacturing) industries;

(*c*) A relatively large increase in the tertiary (service) industries, with the notable exception of domestic servants.

The basic explanation of these broad changes can be found in the increase in real income (which more than doubled) over the period. In this respect, the changes are merely a continuation of the trend of the previous century. As income increases, people tend to spend a smaller proportion of it on food, and more on comforts and luxuries. In 1901, for example, the average labourer spent 60 per cent of his income on food; by 1973 it had fallen to 25 per cent. Now the distribution of labour

TABLE II

INDUSTRIAL DISTRIBUTION OF THE WORKING POPULATION 1841–1971

| | Percentage Distribution | | | Numbers (000's) |
| | England and Wales | Great Britain | | G.B. |
	(1) 1841	(2) 1901	(3) 1971	(4) 1971
Agriculture, forestry and fishing -	22·8	9·0	1·4	345
Mining and quarrying - -	3·0	5·8	1·6	401
Manufacture (including gas, electricity and water supply) -	35·4	32·6	35·4	8,801
Construction - - - -	6·1	8·1	5·0	1,249
Transport and communication -	2·9	9·3	6·3	1,564
Distributive trades ⎫			10·4	2,583
Financial, professional and ⎬ scientific services ⎭	8·5	15·4	15·6	3,875
Public administration - -	0·6	1·4	5·7	1,416
Catering and domestic services -	18·7	15·3	2·3	559
Miscellaneous services - -	1·2	2·0	5·0	1,235
Armed Forces - - -	0·8	1·1	1·5	368
Registered unemployed - -	—	—	2·8	687
Employers and self-employed -	—	—	7·0	1,744
TOTALS - - -	100·0	100·0	100·0	24,827

Sources: Cols (1) and (2) compiled from Colin Clark, *Conditions of Economic Progress* (quoting Booth, *Journal of Royal Statistical Society*, 1856). Cols (3) and (4) compiled from *Britain, 1973* (H.M.S.O.).

between industries is largely a reflection of the way in which people spend their incomes. Thus, as agriculture declined in relative importance, workers moved into the new luxury industries, particularly those providing services.

But there have been other influences at work, especially important in explaining changes within these broad groups. Briefly these influences are:

(1) changes in exports (e.g. manufacturing, mining), or in imports (e.g. agriculture);

(2) improved techniques and increased use of machines (e.g. agriculture, construction, transport, mining);

(3) the increase in exchange (e.g. insurance, banking and other services);

(4) the increase in state activities (public administration);

(5) the acceptance of women workers in industry and commerce, where high wages attracted them from domestic service.

V. THE GEOGRAPHICAL DISTRIBUTION OF THE POPULATION

Geographically, the population of the United Kingdom is dominated by two features: it is concentrated, and it is urban.

The concentrated nature of the population

As a result of the Industrial Revolution, industry migrated to the coalfields which were located in the Midlands and north of England. And today, even though electricity frees industry from being located on the coalfields and the basic industries of these areas have declined, they still remain important centres of industry and population (*see* Fig. 116). There are two main reasons for this. First, many industries remain on account of acquired advantages, particularly the availability of labour. Second, new industries have been attracted by the government's development area policy.

Nevertheless, since World War II, the main areas of natural expansion have been the Midlands and South-East England (particularly London and the Home Counties). In comparison the coalfield and rural areas have declined. This is what one might expect with the expansion in the demand for light engineering and electrical products, aircraft, motor vehicles, consumer durable goods, luxury goods and services of various kinds, and the relative decrease in demand for the products of agriculture and heavy industry. The result is that today 55 per cent of the population live in a strip area, with south Lancashire and west Yorkshire at the northern end, the London area at the southern end, and the Midland region forming a broader centre.

The urban nature of the population

This concentration of population is in towns (unlike the concentration in the Nile and Ganges deltas which consists

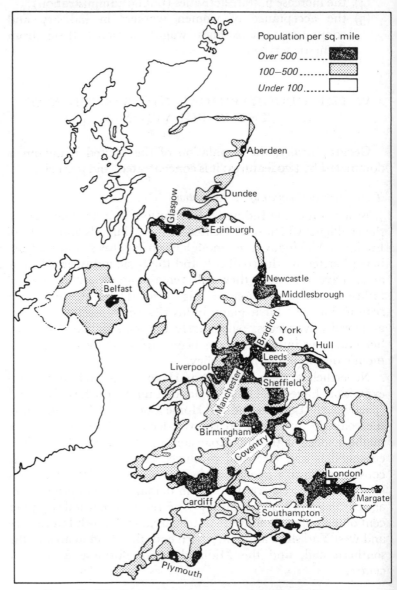

Fig. 116.—Distribution of the population of the United Kingdom.

mainly of rural communities). 80 per cent of the population of England and Wales is urban. More than this, 35 per cent of Great Britain's population lives in the seven conurbations (where there is a continuous built-up area) of Greater London, south-east Lancashire (Manchester), west Midlands (Birmingham), central Clydeside (Glasgow), west Yorkshire (Leeds and Bradford), Merseyside (Liverpool) and Tyneside (Newcastle).

Changes in population take place, however, within the main centres. As towns become too crowded, or as the standard of living improves, or as offices take over residential areas, so people tend to move from the centre to the suburbs or even further, commuting to work by car and public transport.

CHAPTER 36

THE BALANCE OF PAYMENTS, GROWTH AND INFLATION

SINCE World War II, the main economic aims of government policy have been: (1) full employment; (2) a healthy balance of payments; (3) a satisfactory rate of growth; (4) a steady price level. What successive governments have discovered is that it has been impossible to achieve all four aims simultaneously.

The theoretical analysis set out in this book indicates that to some extent these aims are mutually incompatible, for success in one of them creates difficulties in achieving others. Full employment, for instance, is dependent on an adequate level of aggregate demand. As aggregate demand is increased, so spending on imports rises and home-produced goods are diverted from exports to the home market. Thus the balance of payments position becomes less favourable. Full employment also means that eventually less efficient labour has to be employed, bottlenecks occur in the supply of certain factors of production, and trade unions are in a stronger position to bargain for wage increases. Thus on the cost side alone, there are forces which make for a rise in the price level as full employment is approached.

In essence, therefore, the government is somewhat like a juggler who is endeavouring to keep four balls in the air simultaneously. At any given moment, one is going up, a second has reached its peak, a third is on the way down and the fourth is being passed from one hand to the other to be given a new upward thrust.

Nevertheless, other developed economies are in the same position, and it has to be admitted that most of them, particularly West Germany, Japan and the U.S.A., have been more successful than Britain in achieving these objectives, except perhaps as regards the level of employment attained. Even here, however, while unemployment in Britain has been reduced to 2 per cent of the working population and even less, this figure has had to be raised from time to time, and particularly in the period 1969–72, because it has been necessary to deflate the economy in order to protect the gold and convertible currency reserves. This can be the starting-point of our examination of Britain's current prospects.

I. BRITAIN'S POST-WAR BALANCE OF PAYMENTS

A fundamental weakness has been Britain's balance-of-payments position, a weakness that has stemmed from a variety of causes.

From the turn of the century Britain has found it more difficult to maintain export markets as other countries industrialised and competed with her. During World War I markets were lost which were not fully regained, and overseas assets had to be realised to pay for the war. Moreover, the depression in world trade during the inter-war period was particularly harmful to the heavy industries upon which British exports had been heavily dependent.

World War II increased her difficulties. £1,000 million worth of overseas investments had been sold; an extra £3,000 million external debts had been accumulated. There was thus a considerable fall in net income from abroad. On the other hand, defence commitments involved heavy government spending abroad. In addition, for the first ten years after the war, the terms of trade were adverse to Britain. Some people would argue, too, that British industry was ill-equipped to meet competition in world markets because of lack of investment and small-scale organisation.

Such long-term changes weakened Britain's position in international trade. But, because her reserves of gold and convertible currencies were small relative to the size of her trade, she was vulnerable to short-term shocks whenever confidence in sterling faltered. A continuing balance of payments deficit could initiate a run on sterling for the holders of sterling balances could see that such deficits could not be covered for long by the slender gold and convertible currency reserves. Fearing devaluation, they began moving funds out of London. This short-term capital movement increased the pressure on the reserves. Confidence in sterling had to be restored either by deflation or by actual devaluation of sterling

Thus, after World War II, Britain's immediate need was to maintain a balance-of-payments surplus on current account. This would have enabled her to build up reserves of gold and convertible currencies and to have invested abroad and given aid to underdeveloped countries within her means. Instead she had periodic deficit problems, largely because exports did not expand sufficiently. Britain's inability to control rising prices at home meant that exports were uncompetitive in world markets. Indeed internal inflation soon eroded the price advantages secured by the devaluations in 1949 and 1967. We shall return to this problem of inflation later in this chapter.

II. ECONOMIC GROWTH

Economic growth can be measured roughly by increases in the Gross National Product per head of the population. While it can start from a position of less than full employment, economic growth usually refers to the rate at which output continues to expand in the long-term once full employment has been achieved. It is in the latter sense that we discuss it here.

Even when resources are fully employed, the national product can be expected to grow in real terms at approximately 3 per cent per annum through the increase in capital goods (net investment) and the application of new techniques. Such growth presents the government with four main problems.

(1) *Adequate aggregate demand*

Growth means that there is an ever-increasing potential output of the nation's resources. The government has to ensure that aggregate demand is expanded sufficiently to purchase the growing output at constant prices. If aggregate demand is too little, unemployment will result; if it is too much, prices rise.

(2) *The level of investment*

If a faster rate of growth is desired, a higher level of investment is essential. To achieve this it is necessary to reduce consumption. In a private enterprise economy where there is freedom of personal choice, it is unlikely that cuts in living standards will be acceptable. Nevertheless, a government may be able to increase saving marginally through its monetary and fiscal policies in order to free resources for investment.

(3) *'Indicative' planning*

It has to be admitted that the private enterprise system works to some extent by trial and error. Production in advance may be based on incomplete information. The result is that the plans of different industries do not harmonise. If, for instance, production of cars is to be increased, more sheet steel and power will be required. But will these industries have the right capacity? If they have too little, there will be bottlenecks; if too much, there will be a waste of resources. In the long-term, the price system makes the necessary adjustment, but it would be more satisfactory if the plans of all industries could be indicated in advance so that they could be dovetailed.

This was the object of 'indicative' planning introduced by the government in the 1960s, first through the National Economic Development Council, later through a Department of Economic Affairs. Both had planning functions, which could be broken down into three parts:

(1) to decide on the rate of growth that the economy as a whole could achieve;
(2) to examine plans for the future in both the private and public sectors of the economy in order to see how well these dovetail with each other and with the overall rate of growth;
(3) to suggest, and seek agreement upon, ways to increase the rate of sound growth.

In contrast to central planning where the state decides output targets, estimates of production were based on discussions with industrialists themselves. The differences between the two forms of planning can be illustrated by likening it to a road system. Under authoritarian planning, road users are permitted to travel only when, where and how they are directed by the state planning authority. With free enterprise 'indicative planning', the state prescribes driving rules and regulations, traffic signs, etc., but leaves everyone to travel where he likes so long as he obeys the rules under the 'planning' system.

The National Plan of 1965 aimed at a 4 per cent per annum rate of growth. But in July 1966 restrictive measures had to be introduced because of the balance-of-payments deficit. These invalidated many of the assumptions of the plan, which was therefore shelved.

(4) *The balance of payments*

The failure of the National Plan of 1965 highlights the basic weakness for Britain of forward planning—it is dependent upon achieving the assumptions made with regard to the balance of payments. But when the economy is working at full employment, it becomes more difficult to prevent prices rising.

Once more, therefore, we are up against the difficulties created by inflation. This is the problem to which priority must be given.

III. INFLATION

Policy difficulties

An inflationary process begins, as we have seen, before Keynes's position of full employment is reached. This suggests that a government can only reduce the level of unemployment at the expense of increasing the rate at which prices rise. Indeed, until recently, the empirical evidence seemed to indicate a fairly stable inverse relationship between the rate of unemployment and the rate of inflation.

From the point of view of government policy, this created difficulties: there had to be a 'trade-off' between unemployment and the price level.

Government policy prior to 1970

When it came to policy decisions, economists were broadly divided into two main schools. The first considered that a high level of employment must be the goal. Apart from ethical considerations, it held that the fewer factors that are unemployed, the greater will be the national output.

The second emphasised the inflationary troubles which result from running the economy at too high a level of employment. Excess demand develops in certain sectors through the inelasticity of supply of certain factors. As a result, higher wages are paid, and these are diffused throughout the economy by national wage agreements. Moreover, wage demands look for larger increases and occur more frequently. These economists argued that a higher rate of unemployment will not necessarily result in a lower national product. First, a pool of unemployed resources allows expanding industries to satisfy their demands more quickly and encourages employers to release supplies of labour which are surplus to their immediate requirements. Second, the efficient working of the price system is not hampered by physical controls, e.g. a prices and incomes policy which otherwise has to be imposed by the government. Third, the elimination of windfall gains through rising prices forces inefficient firms out of business, thereby concentrating production on the more efficient. Fourth, a steady price level would improve the balance of payments position and thus allow the economy to work without the disrupting effects of 'stop–go'.

Politically, however, there could not be a straight choice between the two, for no government in Britain could survive if it tried to work the economy at the level of unemployment required to eliminate price rises. In practice all governments stressed the importance of a low level of unemployment. To combat the rise in prices which followed, policy consisted of a mixture of the following measures.

(1) *Exhortation*

Publicity campaigns and appeals by ministers sought to moderate demand on the nation's resources and to increase output. Thus we had the National Savings Campaign, the

'I'm backing Britain' movement, and exhortations to business-men and workers to increase productivity and export more.

No harm is done by such exhortation (except when a government uses it as a substitute for positive action), but the effect can be only marginal. In a private enterprise economy where the mainspring is the profit motive, it is unreasonable to expect persons to act continuously in the 'national interest', especially when there is no certainty that others will act similarly. Thus measures must be taken to control demand and to provide the necessary incentives for productivity and exports.

(2) *Deflation (or disinflation)*

By monetary and fiscal measures aggregate demand was reduced in order to limit the pressure on prices. Such measures were discussed in Chapters 26–29. They represent the 'stop' of the 'stop–go' policy which was followed over this period.

(3) *Direct Controls*

Direct controls were used to curb both demand-pull and cost-push inflation.

As regards the former we had price control and rationing of consumer goods, hire-purchase restrictions, building controls over investment by the Capital Issues Committee, and over local authorities and the nationalised industries by the government. Such a policy is often referred to as 'suppressed inflation'. It may either postpone demand or divert demand to under-used industries (e.g. the railways, cinemas) or to non-controlled industries (the most likely result unless controls are applied vigorously to the whole economy, an administratively impossible task). When demand is postponed, difficulties arise because consumers accumulate liquid funds which enable them to go on future spending sprees (e.g. after World War II). If demand is diverted to non-controlled goods, their prices rise and so resources move into the production of non-essential goods. Yet, while suppressed inflation does not remove the cause, it might provide a breathing-space in which this can be achieved.

Controls were also placed on prices and incomes in order

to check the price–cost spiral. If the price rise can be checked, the justification for inflationary wage increases is eliminated. If income increases can be prevented, then prices need not rise (except in so far as import prices have risen). One objective of an incomes policy has always been to keep wage increases in line with productivity increases, the idea being that higher spending power handed over for real increases in output is not inflationary. However, problems arise on the practical front when attempting to measure productivity (e.g. for policemen, teachers and nurses).

In practice, wage-freezes, 'periods of severe restraint', controls on price rises, etc. secure only a temporary respite. They may, nevertheless, reduce 'inflationary expectations' by tackling the psychological aspect of inflation—that once prices are rising, trade unions, firms and consumers *expect* prices to rise and act in ways which will *make* them rise. The difficulty, however, is that when a freeze is imposed, some workers will just have received an increase in wages, whereas others will have their claims in the pipe-line. The longer the freeze continues, the greater will be the grievance of this latter group. Militant trade unions, too, soon begin to oppose the policy. As a result, in 1966 the Labour government took legal powers to prevent rises in prices and incomes.

Government policy after 1970

Even if control of wages and dividends proves successful, the problem of allocating labour and capital between industries arises, for it removes the basis—changes in relative prices —upon which the allocating functions of the price system works. How, for instance, can labour be channelled into the industries where it is most needed if a relative rise of wages in these industries is not permitted? Similarly, how shall capital be allocated if the returns on it (as with rent control) are frozen? Logically, if wage and profit controls are to work satisfactorily over the long-term, there must be some central direction of labour and production!

Such considerations helped to formulate the policy of the Conservative government when it took office in June 1970. Market forces, it argued, could be relied upon to keep price rises in check. As regards wage increases, the government would set an example by limiting the size of any rises in the public sector of the economy.

Moreover, with a strong balance of payments position, there was room for expansion in the economy. As far as possible this should come about by investment-spending by firms. Such extra investment would improve the growth rate.

Above all, Britain was experiencing simultaneously a high level of unemployment (over 3 per cent) and a rise in prices of 7 to 8 per cent. To explain this marked departure from previous experience of the relationship between the level of unemployment and price rises, economists suggested different reasons. One possibility put forward was that inflation had become 'imported' to a greater degree, increases in import prices raising the prices of food and raw materials in particular. Another view was that a 'restructuring' process had been taking place whereby industrial change (partly brought about by the relative rise in wage-rates) had resulted in more men being laid off. A third reason emphasised the narrow viewpoint of trade unions who persisted in their demand for wage rises in spite of the fact that the overall level of unemployment was increasing. Curing unemployment, the trade unions argued, was the task of the government. As such it lay outside the field of wage negotiations, which were simply a matter confined to trade unions and employers.

In spite of the comparatively high rate of inflation, therefore, the Heath government decided to reflate the economy. Its first budget was expansionary in that it made considerable cuts in taxation. In addition, the rate of interest charged by the banks was brought down.

But the economy was slow to respond in the way the government had hoped for—increased investment expenditure. Instead the extra spending power found its way largely into the consumer durable goods' markets, and later into houses. Since in the short-term houses can be regarded solely as a stock, the result was almost a doubling in the price of houses during 1971–2. Not until 1973 did increased spending on capital equipment really get under way.

Before then, however, Britain was again facing balance-of-payments difficulties. Not only was a part of the increased aggregate demand spent on imports but, as output and investment increased, more was spent on imported basic materials and machinery. On previous occasions when this had happened, the declared exchange value of the pound and the reserves of gold and convertible currencies had been protected by the 'stop' policy of deflation. For a long time many economists had advocated that the external restraint on expansion, the fixed exchange rate, should be abandoned, and this view was shared by the government. Accordingly, in June 1972, the pound sterling was 'floated'; that is, its value would be determined by the day-to-day conditions of demand and supply on the foreign exchange market.

Moreover, by now it had become obvious that free market forces could not deal with rising prices. The coal-miners and railway locomotive-drivers had shown that a single-minded trade union in a key industry could, by strike action, hold the economy to ransom. Both managed to secure wage increases in excess of the 'norm' laid down by the government, and these successes established the level of other wage demands.

The government had hoped that, in exchange for the promise of continued expansion, it could obtain a voluntary agreement to limit price and wage rises. Such an agreement on prices had been given earlier by the Confederation of British Industry, but the firms participating were unwilling to renew it unless the trade unions were prepared to reciprocate. The unions, however, were smarting under the Industrial Relations Act, 1971, and they therefore rejected proposals put forward by the government.

Consequently, in November 1972, a statutory freeze was imposed on most increases in prices, rents, pay and dividends which would end after a period of 90 days from enactment, with the possibility of an extension of up to 60 days. The bill was subsequently enacted on 30 November 1972. The government also announced that a more detailed 'Stage 2' programme would be introduced later.

Stage 2 of the government's counter-inflation proposals were outlined in a White Paper, and were brought into effect in March 1973 when a Price Commission and a Pay Board were established to administer it. Under Stage 2, annual pay increases were limited to £1 per week plus 4 per cent, and prices, dividends, rents and profits were subjected to the most stringent controls ever imposed in peace-time.

During Stage 2 it was hoped that voluntary agreement

could be reached for Stage 3, which was intended to introduce some flexibility into the controls. By now, however, not only the unions but also the Confederation of British Industry were smarting under the rigid controls of Stage 2. Moreover, the unions complained that, while wages had been restricted, prices had risen disproportionately.

This was true. Simply floating the pound was no solution to internal inflation. Not only was there a worldwide rise in the prices of foodstuffs and raw materials, but an 18 per cent drop in the external value of the pound against most currencies apart from the U.S.A. dollar represented a serious worsening of Britain's terms of trade. In part the pound was weak because, while the price of imports increases immediately when the exchange rate falls, it takes time to recover the cost of imported raw materials since they have to be manufactured before they are exported.

Agreement on Stage 3 was therefore impossible. Indeed at the T.U.C. conference in September 1973, some trade unions let it be known that substantial wage-increases would be sought later in the year. Even so the government announced that it was still giving growth the priority in its objectives, the only concession to deflation being a comparatively small cut in proposed government expenditure.

It is important to note, too, that floating the pound did not succeed in checking the drain on Britain's reserves of gold and convertible currencies. Holders of sterling balances, fearing that the militancy of trade unions and the government's 'gamble on growth' would result in a further fall in the rate of exchange, started to move funds out of London. Without the support of the Bank of England and the attraction of an abnormally high rate of interest, the value of the pound would have dropped below that at which compensation had to be given to the holders of sterling. Such support came from the reserves, which consequently fell.

Moreover, the high rate of interest clashed with government policy internally. Depositors could obtain higher rates of interest outside the building societies, and the latter responded by raising their mortgage rates to 11 per cent, with a possibility that they would go even higher. This, together with the previous rise in the price of houses, put house-purchase beyond the reach of many prospective owner-occupiers.

At present (September 1973) it is difficult to see how Stage 3 of the government's counter-inflation policy can be anything but tough. There must be room in the economy to produce the increased exports which depreciation of the pound has made possible. Since it is doubtful whether all this production can come from increased productivity, it means that some cut-back in consumption and government spending is essential.

INDEX